WOMEN WRITERS
IN THE UNITED STATES

A Timeline of Literary, Cultural, and Social History

CYNTHIA J. DAVIS

AND

KATHRYN WEST

New York   Oxford

OXFORD UNIVERSITY PRESS

1996

Oxford University Press

Oxford   New York
Athens   Auckland   Bangkok   Bombay
Calcutta   Cape Town   Dar es Salaam   Delhi
Florence   Hong Kong   Istanbul   Karachi
Kuala Lumpur   Madras   Madrid   Melbourne
Mexico City   Nairobi   Paris   Singapore
Taipei   Tokyo   Toronto

and associated companies in
Berlin   Ibadan

Published by Oxford University Press, Inc.,
198 Madison Avenue, New York, New York 10016

Oxford is a registered trademark of Oxford University Press

Library of Congress Cataloging-in-Publication Data
Davis, Cynthia J., 1964–
Women writers in the United States: a timeline of literary, cultural,
and social history / Cynthia J. Davis and Kathryn West.
p. cm.   Includes bibliographical references (p.) and index.
ISBN 0-19-509053-5
1. American literature—Women authors—Chronology.   2. Women and
literature—United States—Chronology.   3. Women authors, American—
Biography—Chronology.   4. Women—United States—Biography—
Chronology.   I. West, Kathryn, 1962–   . II. Title.
PS147.DF38   1996
810.9'9287—dc20   95–31815

1 3 5 7 9 8 6 4 2

Printed in the United States of America
on acid-free paper

for all the women,

for all they've done,

and especially for three,

Cathy N. Davidson,

Sally A. West,

and

Kathryn Ann Davis

ACKNOWLEDGMENTS

First and foremost we thank Cathy Davidson and Linda Wagner-Martin for giving us the opportunity to contribute to their *The Oxford Companion to Women's Writing in the United States* and to put together a timeline for it. They provide invaluable models of scholarship and friendship. This book would not exist without Cathy's advice, guidance, and support.

At Oxford University Press, we thank Liz Maguire for taking an interest in this project and guiding us through the first stages of production. Although she left Oxford before it was completed, a piece of it certainly belongs to her. We also thank Elda Rotor for her assistance. Most of all, Joellyn Ausanka has provided hours of essential advice and assistance and has been unfailingly wise, astute, and cheerful over the course of a project that just grew and grew. We couldn't have done it without her.

Thanks to Frances Frame for indispensable computer assistance with the index.

Finally, to all the friends and family who have borne with us through long hours of work and worry, excitement and despair, thank you for being there.

FOREWORD

If a student came to me wanting to know what everyday life was like for women living in the United States a century ago, this is the book I would lend her. From this book she would learn, virtually at a glance, that life in 1895 was as complicated as it is in 1995, with women of different economic, regional, religious, and racial backgrounds living lives that were sometimes parallel and sometimes radically divergent. She would learn how women, then as now, were encouraged by advertisers to emulate unrealistic beauty standards: in 1895, the model was the "Gibson Girl," an upper-class white woman with a corseted hour-glass figure, upswept hair, and a pure ivory complexion. Since Sears, Roebuck distributed its first catalogue in 1895, women all across the nation could purchase (or just dream about) dresses and undergarments that promised to transform them into mail-order Gibson Girls. Many African American women, influenced by this ideal of white womanhood, bought creams that purported to lighten the skin, as well as pomades and hair straighteners. Recognizing a trend, Sarah Breedlove, an African American entrepreneur, went on to found the Madame C. J. Walker laboratories for black hair-care products, eventually becoming the richest business woman in America.

On a more serious note, my inquisitive student would learn from this book that a hundred years ago suffragists celebrated every time another state (typically out West) granted women of all races the right to vote (in 1895, it was Utah and Idaho). Yet these were also ominous times politically, particularly for recent immigrants and women of color. In 1895, the newly formed Immigration Restriction League sounded the alarm against the social and economic "costs" of immigration, leading to increased restrictions on immigration and on the civil rights of people deemed to be immigrants, an anti-immigration movement that foreshadowed our own era and California's recently passed Proposition 187. Similarly, in the South, Jim Crow laws existed and would be legally sanctioned by the *Plessy v. Ferguson* ruling of 1896. A high-sounding phrase, "separate but equal," was used to justify segregation, but it did not obscure the horror of racist violence, meticulously documented by black journalist and activist Ida B. Wells in *A Red Record: Tabulated Statistics and Alleged Cases of Lynchings in the United States, 1892–1893–1894.*

Looking across the pages, my student could learn not only how women lived but what they wrote and read. She would learn that women were writing other controversial books a hundred years ago, including suffragist Elizabeth Cady Stanton's critique of the masculine bias in the Judeo-Christian tradition, *The Woman's Bible.* She would also learn that 1895 was a rich year for women's literature: Alice Ruth Moore Dunbar-Nelson published a volume of stories, Mary E. Wilkins Freeman a mystery novella, Sarah Orne Jewett a short-story collection, Constance Fenimore Woolson a novel, Josephine Lazarus a religious treatise *(The Spirit of Judaism)*; Elizabeth Stoddard and Emily Pauline Johnson (Tehakionwake) each published a volume of poems. On the other hand, elite writers were feeling themselves threatened, both by the emergence of increasingly popular pulp novels and magazines and by a new cultural form, the cinema. In 1896, New Yorkers flocked to the first public exhibition of motion pictures. The same year, shocked viewers began calling for stricter movie censorship after seeing actors May Irwin and John C. Rice kiss on the silver screen.

As much as any reference book I know, this one gives a feel for the texture of life for women of other eras. It does so through a principle of determined inclusiveness. That is, most books bracket off knowledge into disciplines (literature, sociology, history, art, political science, economics, etc.) or group interdisciplinary studies around core interests (women's studies, ethnic studies, cultural studies, etc.), whereas *Women Writers in the United States* conjoins all of these fields and interests in one efficient timeline. I learn something new every time I leaf through these pages. With knowledge, wisdom, vigor, rigor, and wit, Cynthia J. Davis and Kathryn West have assembled the fullest, most extensive, and most thoughtful timeline of women's writing and women's lives compiled to date. They have been able to do so precisely because we have now had over two decades of feminist research on topics that once were not even considered legitimate. The wealth of research produced, collectively, by women's studies scholars over the last decades is mind-boggling, and this book manages to bring much of that work together, in a form both condensed and original.

As Davis and West mention in their introduction, they began their project as an "addendum" to *The Oxford Companion to Women's Writing in the United States.* However, the more they researched, the longer their timeline grew, until it evolved into a book in its own right. A labor of love, this fact-filled and fascinating book is the best labor-saving device I know for anyone who teaches or studies the history of literature of the United States. But this is more than a handy reference guide. Through its visual arrangement of literary history against social and cultural history (of text against context), one gains a new appreciation for women's lives and women's writing. This book helps us understand the complex forces that inspired women to express their ideas, opinions, and imaginings in print and helps make visible the lens through which women understood the books they read.

Women Writers in the United States both nourishes and whets the appetite. It reveals new connections, new juxtapositions, and new contradictions. Even glancing through it, one expands one's definition of "women's history" or "women's literature." I can easily imagine how this book will generate important new courses and even new books in women's cultural studies. Cynthia J. Davis and Kathryn West are to be congratulated and thanked. *Women Writers in the United States* is a stunning achievement.

October, 1995   Cathy N. Davidson

INTRODUCTION

In June of 1993, after a lengthy search in which numerous eminent male candidates' names were raised and appraised, President Clinton appointed D.C. Court of Appeals Judge Ruth Bader Ginsburg to the Supreme Court. After a speedy confirmation process, Ginsburg joined Sandra Day O'Connor on the bench and became the second woman (after O'Connor) to so serve in U.S. history. In her acceptance speech the day of Clinton's nomination, Ginsburg cannily addressed the promises and possibilities of being a "second," arguing that "it contributes to the end of the days when women, at least half the talent pool in our society, appear in high places only as one-at-a-time performers."[1]

Whether or not those days are at an end, we envision this project as yet further evidence that women are not nor have they ever been "one-at-a-time performers," that their accomplishments are by no means exceptions that prove the rule. Although we have spent a lot of time unearthing and acknowledging "firsts" in this project, *Women Writers in the United States* also attempts to acknowledge "seconds," "thirds," "fourths," and so on—as well as to trace the links or passages between the sequences.

The twelve years that separate O'Connor's appointment in 1981 and Ginsburg's in 1992 may strike some as remarkably speedy when compared with the temporal gaps that separate other firsts and seconds (and thirds): for example, in 1656 an all-woman jury heard and acquitted a woman of murdering her infant; in 1701, the first sexually integrated jury met in Albany, New York. It was not, however, until nearly 200 years later, in 1898—when Utah women began to

---

1. Ruth Bader Ginsburg, "On Being Nominated to the Supreme Court," in *Feminism in Our Time: The Essential Writings, World War II to the Present*, Miriam Schneir, ed. (New York: Vintage Books, 1994), 483.

serve as jury members—that women were (re)admitted to the jury box, and it was not until 1975 that the Supreme Court outlawed automatic exclusion of women from jury duty.

On the other hand, some readers may be surprised by how early and how consistently women have played an active, incisive role in the shaping of this nation. Given that even present-day revisionist history texts often overlook women's contributions, this surprise is not all that surprising. Indeed, it is not so unusual to encounter the assumption—in some academic works, as well as in the popular media—that around 1970, women changed. That they suddenly became beings concerned about and often dissatisfied with their place in the world. That they began to take actions that had historical significance. Only some twenty years ago, the story goes, women suddenly developed a whole new way of thinking, a whole new set of aspirations and goals and even talents. While this lumping of all women into one amorphous and homogeneous group is obviously troubling, equally disturbing is the lack of a sense of history behind such a premise, the lack of awareness of the hundreds of thousands of women who, long before 1970—decades, even centuries before—said and wrote and did important, significant, and interesting things in both their private and public lives. This is true of women all over the world; here, we hope to give a sense of the richness of this history in the United States.

Women Writers in the United States weaves this rich and multi-hued historical fabric out of political and world events, everyday occurrences, medical advances, founding moments, lifestyle changes, demographics, conferences, crusades, statistics, inventions, survey results, crazes, and more. These in turn encompass the broad spectrum of women's writing that serves as the core of this timeline, providing them and you, the reader, with what we hope will prove an illuminating and thought-provoking context. It is a truism of literary studies that no work emerges out of nowhere; what we hope to provide is the rich tapestry of the "somewhere" in which these authors lived and wrote.

"No work emerges out of nowhere" is eminently true of this volume, too. *Women Writers in the United States* grew out of our work as research assistants for Cathy N. Davidson and Linda Wagner-Martin on their *The Oxford Companion to Women's Writing in the United States*. It began as a brief chronology to be included with *The*

Oxford Companion. Indeed, a much-abridged version of *Women Writers in the United States* appears there, but what was intended to be only some ten to twenty pages in length grew and grew as we unearthed books and phenomena that added essential dimension and depth to our sketch of women's writings and women's lives.

Like its foremothers, *The Oxford Companion* and *The Oxford Book of Women's Writing in the United States*, *Women Writers in the United States* operates with a broad definition of "writing" that has led us to locate in "Texts—U.S. Women Writing" not only authors of fiction and nonfiction but magazine and newspaper editors, readers and their habits, songwriters, and certain events important to the fact of women writing in America. Indeed, the writing represented spans a wide range of genres, traditional and nontraditional, including fiction, poetry, short stories, political manifestos, cookbooks, advice columns, songs, essays, social history and analysis, biography, autobiography, medical treatises, books for children, journalism, and travel writing. As our first entry on Native American storytelling illustrates, we also record creative contributions that involve processes similar to those of writing but that are less tied to the published or written word. To take another example of this, one early entry describes how, in 1645, then Governor of Hartford Edward Hopkins took his wife Anne to Boston for medical help, where John Winthrop declared she had lost her wits "by occasion of her giving herself wholly to reading and writing and hath written many books." Or, taking a later example, in 1891 Martha Morton established the Society of Dramatic Authors when women were barred from membership in the American Dramatists' Club. "Texts" illustrates that writing by women can be literary, poetic, social, political, informative, humorous, and entertaining. It encompasses all forms involving words that women have employed to express themselves.

Reading down as well as across the timeline, the reader can gain a sense of the trajectory of many careers and reputations. Many names will appear several times as one reads through and down. For instance, on April 15, 1862, Emily Dickinson sent four poems to Thomas Wentworth Higginson. In 1890, 115 of her poems were published by Roberts Brothers of Boston, but it was not until 1955 that the first reliable edition of her poetry became available—thus suggesting concrete ways in which the availability of Dickinson's poems may intersect with issues of reputation and scholarly focus. In addition to trajectory, variety is highlighted here: Zora Neale Hurston figures not only as the noted novelist of *Their Eyes Were Watching God* (1937), but also as an important anthropologist and collector of folk stories.

To experience the pleasures and surprises of reading across the page, take an example from approximately 100 years ago. In 1886, popular author Louisa May Alcott published *Jo's Boys*, one of the sequels to *Little Women;* children's author Frances Hodgson Burnett published *Little Lord Fauntleroy;* African American evangelist Julia A. J. Foote published her autobiographical *A Brand Plucked from the Fire;* temperance reformer and advocate of women's rights Frances E. Willard published *How to Win: A Book for Girls;* and New England chronicler Sarah Orne Jewett produced one of her most successful collections, *A White Heron and Other Stories*, the title story of which is widely anthologized today. That same year, Coca-Cola was invented, as was an early form of dishwashing machine. Divorce was on the rise, and the Haymarket bombings led to the hanging of four protesters. Electric railways were introduced, the American Federation of Labor was formed, and the Statue of Liberty was dedicated with a poem by Emma Lazarus on the base. We might not think of Louisa May Alcott, Coca-Cola, divorce, and electric railways in the same breath, but to do so expands and adds nuance to our understanding of the world in which these authors lived and wrote.

Thus, "Texts" is paralleled by "Contexts," a chronology of social, political, cultural, medical, and legal issues and events important to women's lives and texts. This section depicts not only the particularities of daily existence but also the major and minor events that create the full portrait of any cultural moment—events that include, for example, the 1649 trial of Goodwife Norman and Mary Hammon for lesbianism; the 1848 beginning of the spiritualism movement in the U.S. when the Fox sisters heard astonishing rapping sounds in their house; the 1939 introduction by Leona Lax, an employee of Warner Bros., of cup-sizing for brassieres; and the 1993 appointment of the first woman U.S. Attorney General, Janet Reno.

In "Contexts" as with "Texts," we have been expansive in our sense of what matters, balancing events traditionally seen as historically relevant—such as wars, strikes, and court decisions—with often overlooked but still significant moments. These latter include the fact that a squaw-sachem, known to the colonists as the "Massachusetts Queen," governed the Massachusetts Confederacy for nearly fifty years beginning some time before 1620; that Ann Lee, leader of the Shaker religious sect (which she established in 1774), became, through her dissent and imprisonment in 1780 during the Revolutionary War, the nation's first conscientious objector; that the first known strike involving women occurred in 1824, when male and female weavers in Pawtucket, Rhode Island, protested increasing hours and decreasing wages (four years later in New Hampshire women needleworkers would strike alone citing the same complaints); that the first known native-born U.S. woman public speaker was an African American, Maria Stewart, who began her career in the 1830s; that a woman, Maria Mitchell, was the first person to identify a comet with a telescope (1847) and thus became the first woman elected to the American Academy of Arts and Sciences (1850); that we may have already had a woman president given that Edith Bolling Wilson took on many of her spouse's presidential responsibilities after her husband, Woodrow, suffered a stroke in 1919; and that among those taken hostage in Teheran, Iran, in 1979 were two women, Kathryn Koob and Elizabeth Ann Swift.

While our primary focus throughout this section is on events clearly related to women's writing and lives, we have also chosen to include items that are, perhaps, more tangentially or covertly connected but nonetheless integral to the cultural moment(s) chronicled—for example, events of national and international importance such as wars, assassinations, uprisings, demographic trends, and immigration policies. And while we have attempted to document as amply as possible instances where women have acted as historical agents, we also include social and political policies not necessarily enacted by women but that affect their ability to function in the world—such as the passage of the Fugitive Slave Laws of 1793 and 1850, or of the Comstock Law in 1873, which outlawed birth control information being passed or advertised through the mails.

In addition, it should be noted that in some sense all our recorded "firsts" are provisional, since women's history remains in a process of rediscovery. *Women Writers in the United States* aims to be comprehensive but is clearly not exhaustive. We are keenly aware that the history we present here is still being written and rewritten. The important archival work scholars continue to perform convinces us that despite the wealth of detail we have attempted to provide here we will still have overlooked much.

That this is so is proven by such instances as when, in 1993, Frances Smith Foster, who was compiling and editing an anthology of writings by Frances E. W. Harper, author of *Iola Leroy* (1892), found three previously undiscovered short novels by Harper: *Min-*

nie's Sacrifice, Sowing and Reaping, and *Trial and Triumph.* Serialized between 1867 and 1888 in the *Christian Recorder*—the official publication of the African Methodist Episcopal Church—these novels significantly enlarge the body of Harper's work available to us (they can now be found in one volume published in 1994 by Beacon). As Foster notes, "these three texts offer an unprecedented opportunity to witness the development of a nineteenth-century African American writer's concerns and style over a forty-year period. . . . but probably most important, these three novels are interesting, provocative works that should enlarge and diversify the current readership of African American literature."[2]

Foster's discovery of the three Harper novels is in many ways paradigmatic for us. It reminds us that many writings by women, perhaps particularly by women of color, remain to be unearthed. It also reminds us of the many and varied understandings such rediscoveries can provide—insights into aesthetic tastes, social concerns, political causes, domestic life, and religious beliefs. And it reminds us that the project we present here is, in many respects, woefully incomplete. If the known number of nineteenth-century novels written by African American women can increase by thirty percent with Foster's find, what other treasures may be lurking in attics, old magazines, and little-explored archives? Today's "first" could tomorrow be a "second" or a "third." While this fact makes our task impossible to complete, it also makes it that much more exciting.

Our goal has been to present as wide an array of writings and events relevant to women's writing in the U.S. as possible. The process has, inevitably, required establishing some parameters. We present here primarily writers born in the geographical United States, or who, through their citizenship, publishing choices, or living arrangements have identified themselves as "American." This choice meant that we were unable to include entries for the rich writings of Canadian and Latin American authors who have been both popular and critically acclaimed in the United States, such as Canadians Margaret Atwood, Joy Kogawa, and Lucy Maud Montgomery (author of the Anne of Green Gables series), or Latin American authors such as Laura Esquivel, Elena Poniatowska, and Isabel Allende. In a few cases, we have decided to include in "Contexts" influential works by

---

2. Frances Smith Foster, ed., *"Minnie's Sacrifice," "Sowing and Reaping," "Trial and Triumph": Three Rediscovered Novels by Frances E. W. Harper* (Boston: Beacon Press, 1994), xii.

women of other nations that have been extremely important to U.S. women and women authors, such as Mary Wollstonecraft's *A Vindication of the Rights of Woman* (1792), Virginia Woolf's *A Room of One's Own* (1929), and Simone de Beauvoir's *The Second Sex* (1953).

In addition, the wealth of data post-first and especially post-second waves of feminist movement tilts this timeline toward the twentieth century. In part, this is a structural problem; by arranging our data according to years, it proved much more difficult to excavate information in eras that were less oriented toward number-crunching and statistics than is our own period. When combined with the fact that in the early days of this country women were much more apt to be left out of records—at times included under their husband's or father's name or simply considered not worth counting or accounting for—our efforts to do justice to the women of this period met with some difficult challenges. We look to the comments of readers to help us in our editing process for future editions.

The two sections that constitute *Women Writers in the United States* are meant to be read together, and, demonstrating that the division between women's writing and its context is often blurry, arbitrary, even vexed, many women appear on both sides of the page. Margaret Sanger, for example, is well known for her work in making birth control available and in educating the public about it; some of this important social work she did through published writing. Zitkala-Ša (also known as Gertrude Bonnin), president of the National Council of American Indians, published stories in the *Atlantic Monthly* and a collection entitled *American Indian Stories* (1921). This collection educates readers about the displacement she and other Native Americans experienced as children when they were taken from their natural parents and sent to schools where they were not allowed to maintain their cultural customs. Zitkala-Ša's work, recorded here in both "Texts" and "Contexts," testifies to her lifelong struggle to fight such wrongs.

One of our hardest tasks has been to decide within which "category" certain data best fit: Do we consider the meeting of Alice B. Toklas and Gertrude Stein, for example, a literary event or a social event? A meeting between two people would appear to be a social event, but it is also decidedly literary in that *The Autobiography of Alice B. Toklas* (1932) would not have been written without it. To take another example: Was the 1901 bestowal of a Doctorate of Letters by Bowdoin College on Sarah Orne Jewett a literary milestone or a social milestone? How about the founding of *Peterson's Maga-*

zine? It was certainly an event important to women who would subsequently publish their writing in the journal, but does it constitute an event that can be classified under the rubric women's writing? Wrestling with such determinations has challenged our own thinking about what counts as "literature" and what as "context" or "history"; we would like to think that it will do the same for our readers.

Although due to demands of form we have imposed what is without doubt an artificial binary structure on our data, the juxtaposition of the two chronologies demonstrates that works—be they literary, social, professional, private, charitable, activist, profit-oriented, or artistic—do not occur in a vacuum. Taken as a whole, *Women Writers in the United States* should demonstrate that women's work and works inform each other in specific and illuminating ways.

In 1776, Abigail Adams's plea to her husband to "remember the ladies" when framing this country's constitution fell on deaf ears. Responding to Adams's plea some 200 years after it was made, we hope this account of the multiple ways in which women's works and words have made a difference in this country will insure that not simply the "ladies" but all the actors—across races, genders, age groups, creeds, and religions—who have played a role in advancing U.S. women's social position will not only be remembered but cited and celebrated.

WOMEN WRITERS

IN THE UNITED STATES

AUTHORS' NOTE

Author entries are arranged alphabetically within years. Authors are identified in their first entry by their birth and death dates as well as by the types of writing they do. When we felt it added clarity, we have added racial and ethnic heritage or regional affiliation. Subsequent entries generally focus only on the work(s) published in that particular year. Diaries and journals are typically listed according to the date of the writing, rather than the date of publication. Unless otherwise noted, dates are first known U.S. publication. We have included birth and death dates for authors and artists only, when available. We have not provided dates for the living.

TEXTS	CONTEXTS
U.S. Women Writing	*Social, Political, and Arts History*

Native American women of many tribes participated in storytelling, creating and continuing oral traditions that explained the creation and nature of the world; recorded their tribal and personal histories; taught skills, values, and beliefs; and provided humor and entertainment.

More than 11,600 years ago, a woman lived and died in what is now Midland, Texas. Her bones were unearthed in 1992.

---

1 A. D.–1300

1 A. D.–1300 The Anasazi inhabit the Four Corners region (Colorado, Utah, Arizona, and New Mexico's conjoining borders) of what is now the United States. As it was an advanced civilization, anthropologists are still uncertain as to the reasons behind its virtual disappearance from the face of the earth.

1492

1492 Isabella and Ferdinand of Spain finance the first voyage of Christopher Columbus to search for the Indies.

An estimated 900,000 to 1,000,000 Native Americans live on what is now known as the North American continent.

* * *

3

TEXTS	CONTEXTS	
1492–1770	1492–1770	More Africans arrive in America than Europeans.
1493	1493	Papal bull divides the "New World" between Portugal and Spain.
1526	1526	Spanish explorers land in South Carolina, bringing black slaves who flee for the interior. Many marry Native Americans.
1539	1539	The first printing press in the Americas is set up in Mexico City.
1565	1565	The first permanent European settlement in North America, St. Augustine, is founded by Spain in Florida.
1587	1587	Virginia Dare becomes the first child of English parents to be born on American soil; her parents are members of the Roanoke colony on Roanoke Island off North Carolina. By 1591, these colonists have mysteriously disappeared.
1600	1600	200 contraceptive and abortion methods, both medicinal and mechanical in nature, are in common use.

* * *

TEXTS	CONTEXTS	
1606	1606	The Virginia Company of London, granted a royal charter, sends 120 colonists to Virginia.
1607	1607	Jamestown is founded, the first English settlement on the American mainland; its first women—Mistress Forrest and her maid, Anne Burras—arrive in 1608. As an act of mercy or as part of a tribal adoption ritual, Pocahontas saves Captain John Smith from death; she mediates between the colonists and her people for several years.
1609	1609	The first known wedding between colonists is held in Virginia when Anne Burras marries John Laydon.
1613	1613	English colonists in Virginia destroy the French settlement at Port Royal, Nova Scotia, and prevent French colonization of Maryland.
1614	1614	Pocahontas marries John Rolfe, a European immigrant; they have a son. She assumes the name Rebecca and dies in England a few years later.

TEXTS	CONTEXTS

TEXTS		CONTEXTS
1619	1619	The first African women—three of twenty captives—arrive in Jamestown, Virginia, as indentured servants.
		The first representative colonial assembly in America is held at Jamestown, Virginia.
		The House of Burgesses petitions the London company to grant equal lots of land to wives as to husbands in the colonies, claiming that in the new territories they could not be sure as yet whether women or men would be more necessary; the petition is granted.
1620	1620	Pilgrims land in Provincetown on Cape Cod and a month later locate Plymouth Harbor; Mary Chilton is the first European to step onto Plymouth Rock. While more than half the Pilgrims die from winter and illness by the following year, the survivors celebrate the help they received from Native Americans with the first "thanksgiving" feast.
		The first library opens in Virginia.
		In Jamestown, a planter must pay 150 pounds of

TEXTS	CONTEXTS	
1620	1620	tobacco to marry one of 140 unmarried women sent by the London Company.
1624	1624	The first known African American child is born in the colonies: William, son of Anthony and Isabel Tucker, a free black couple in Virginia.
1626	1626	Peter Minuit, of the Dutch West Indies Company, purchases the entire island of Manhattan from a Native American chief, for trinkets valued at 60 guilders ($24).
1630	1630	Boston is founded by approximately 1000 settlers led by John Winthrop; this year marks the beginning of the decade-long "Great Migration" of some 10,000 to 24,500 English Puritans fleeing religious persecution.
1636	1636	The country's first college, Harvard, is established.
1637	1637	The Pequot War is fought between Native Americans and colonists in Massachusetts.
		Anne Hutchinson, leader of the opposition in the anti-authority crisis, is tried and found guilty for

TEXTS	CONTEXTS
1637	1637 behavior "not fitting for her sex" in challenging clergymen; she is banished from Massachusetts.
1639	1639 Mary Mandame is convicted of a "dallyance" with a Native American in Plymouth, Massachusetts; after being whipped, she is sentenced to wear a badge of shame on her sleeve, the first woman so sentenced in the colonies.
1640	1640 Ann Hibbens is tried by the church as a "contentious woman" for disputing the quality and price of work done by town carpenters.
	The first press in the colonies (Cambridge, Massachusetts) prints its first book, the Bay Psalm Book.
1641	1641 Massachusetts becomes the first colony to recognize slavery as legal.
1642	1642 English Civil War begins.
	The first tavern opens in Manhattan.
1643	1643 Antinomian Anne Hutchinson and all but one of her children are murdered by Indians in New Netherlands, where she had

TEXTS	CONTEXTS
1643	1643 · settled after her banishment from *Massachusetts* in 1637.
1645 Anne Hopkins, wife of the Governor of Hartford, is taken to Boston for medical help for having "written many books" and lost her wits "by occasion of her giving herself wholly to reading and writing."	1645
1647	1647 The first known colonial book-seller, Hezekiah Usher of Boston, adds books to his general merchandise.
1648	1648 The first "witch"—a woman—to be executed in the Massachusetts Bay Colony is midwife and lay healer Margaret Jones.
1649	1649 King Charles I is beheaded; England is declared a Commonwealth under the leadership of Oliver Cromwell. Goodwife Norman and Mary Hammon of the Massachusetts Bay Colony are the first women tried for lesbianism; Norman is found guilty and Hammon acquitted.
1650 Anne Dudley Bradstreet (1612?–1672): *The Tenth Muse Lately Sprung Up in*	1650

TEXTS	CONTEXTS
1650 *America*, the first collection of verse produced in the "New World" and one of the most salable volumes in 17th-century London. She produced this and her other two volumes while, in the words of Adrienne Rich, "rearing eight children, lying frequently sick, keeping house at the edge of the wilderness."	1650
1655	1655 Illiteracy among women is about 50 percent. Deborah Moody, the first woman to receive a land grant and to run a colonial settlement, is also the first woman to cast a vote, a right she earns as a landowner.
1656	1656 The first all-woman jury in the colonies (Patuxent, Maryland) assembles to hear evidence against Judith Catchpole, accused of murdering her child. Judith claims she has never even been pregnant. The jury acquits her. When the first Quaker women, Mary Fisher and Ann Austin, arrive in the Massachusetts colony, authorities imprison, then banish them.

TEXTS	CONTEXTS
1656	1656 Ann Hibbens is accused of witchcraft and executed.
1660s	1660s Early colonial statutes impose stricter penalties on fornication between blacks and whites than between whites.
1660	1660 Charles II returns to England; his coronation occurs the following year. Mary Dyer, a Quaker, is hanged in Boston for her "unorthodox" beliefs.
1662	1662 Virginia passes a law declaring that the status of the child follows the condition of the mother, slave or free.
1664 Anne Dudley Bradstreet: *Meditations Divine and Moral.*	1664 Maryland bans marriages between English women and African American men.
1667	1667 The "Massachusetts Queen," a squaw-sachem who governed the Massachusetts Confederacy from before 1620, dies, ending her long reign.
1675–1676	1675–1676 King Philip's War is fought between Indian tribes and Plymouth colonists.

*   *   *

TEXTS		CONTEXTS	
1676		1676	Mary Rowlandson becomes the first woman captive released by Native Americans.
1681	Sarah Goodhue (1641–1681): *Valedictory and Monitory Writing*.	1681	
1682	Mary Rowlandson (1636–1678): *Narrative of the Captivity and Restoration of Mrs. Mary Rowlandson*. After having been held captive by members of the Algonquin tribe, Rowlandson documented her surprise at her own ability to endure and adapt, as well as her shifting attitude toward her captors, writing that "not one of them ever offered me the least abuse of unchastity to me, in word or action."	1682	
1683		1683	The first German immigrants arrive in America.
1685		1685	Philadelphia gets its first press. Boston constructs its first almshouse.
1688		1688	Quakers in Pennsylvania pass the first antislavery resolution in the colonies. *Advice to a Daughter*, by George Savile, Marquis of Halifax, one of the first

TEXTS	CONTEXTS	
1688	1688	etiquette texts, is published: it greatly influences American women writers of that genre.
1690	1690	Estimated colonial population: 213,500.
		Publick Occurrences is the first newspaper to appear in the colonies; it is stopped by the government of Massachusetts after four days.
1691	1691	The Virginia legislature outlaws interracial union and banishes from the colony any white man or woman who marries or fornicates with a "Negro, mulatto, or Indian."
1692	1692	Bridget Bishop is the first person hanged in Salem for alleged witchcraft.
1692–1693	1692–1693	The Salem Witch Trials: 19 Salem residents, almost all women, are found guilty of witchcraft and executed. A West Indian slave named Tituba is said to have influenced the other accused witches. Hundreds of "witches" await trial or execution by the time the new English governor dismisses the court and frees the prisoners.

* * *

TEXTS		CONTEXTS
1693	1693	The College of William and Mary is founded in Williamsburg, Virginia.
1695	1695	New York gets its first press.
1697	1697	Hannah Duston of Massachusetts kills and scalps ten Native Americans and is publicly rewarded £25 for doing so. Her week-old baby had been killed previously by a band of Native Americans.
1700	1700	The total slave population numbers around 28,000, with 23,000 living in the South.
1701 Sarah Fiske (1652–1692), American spiritual autobiographer: *A Confession of Faith; or, A Summary of Divinity* (published posthumously, originally written 1677).	1701	The first sexually integrated jury, made up of six men and women, hears a case in Albany, New York; it is not until well into the 20th century that this becomes a common practice.
1704	1704	The first underground sewer is used in Boston.
1704–1706	1704–1706	The *Boston News-Letter* is the first official newspaper.
1705	1705	Colonial Virginia passes a law classifying slaves as real estate; similar laws are enacted in Kentucky (1798) and the Louisiana Territory (1806).

TEXTS		CONTEXTS	
1707	Elizabeth Bradford (1663?–1731), poet, along with husband William, writes prefatory poems for an edition of Benjamin Keach's *War with the Devil*.	1707	
1709	Bathsheba Bowers (1672?–1718): *An alarm sounded to prepare the inhabitants of the world to meet the Lord in the way of his judgments*, a detailed autobiographical account of Bowers's painful search for understanding and peace with God.	1709	
1710		1710	Henrietta Johnson, who emigrated from Ireland with her husband a few years previously, is providing much of the support for her extended family with proceeds from her efforts at pastel portraiture. Her small, single-figured portraits are greatly valued today, both for their historical significance and their aesthetic charm.
1711		1711	The hoop for hoop skirts is invented.
1712		1712	Slaves revolt in New York; on account of the death of nine whites, 21 blacks are executed and six others kill themselves.

* * *

TEXTS	CONTEXTS
1714	1714 Tea is introduced to the colonies, but chocolate continues to be the favorite non-alcoholic drink.
1715	1715 Sybilla Masters, the first female inventor born in the newly settled colonies, invents a machine to prepare Indian corn.
1716	1716 The first colonial theater opens in Williamsburg, Virginia.
1718	1718 New Orleans is established by the Mississippi Company. The General Assembly of Pennsylvania gives wives of mariners or deserted wives the right to operate businesses in their own names. Massachusetts resident Mary Butterworth successfully counterfeits paper money through a clever cloth-copying process.
1721	1721 The first independent American newspaper is the *New England Courant*. Rifles are introduced into America.
1725	1725 The first New York newspaper is the *New York Gazette*.

	TEXTS		CONTEXTS
1727		1727	Quakers in the United States call for the abolition of slavery.
			George II succeeds his father George I on the throne of England.
1730s		1730s	The first drawings of the female skeleton appear in Europe.
1730		1730	Estimated colonial population numbers 654,900, about 90,000 of whom are slaves.
1731		1731	The first subscription library is founded, in Philadelphia.
1732		1732	Benjamin Franklin begins annual publication of *Poor Richard's Almanac*; it stops in 1757.
1733	Mercy Wheeler (1706–1796): *An Address to Young People; Or, . . . Warning from the Death*.	1733	A group of "she merchants" in New York City place a public notice in a newspaper arguing that since they too pay taxes and hence support the government, they should be entitled to some of its "sweets."
1734		1734	The religious revival known as the Great Awakening begins in New England; it lasts at least until the early 1740s.

TEXTS		CONTEXTS
1734	1734	The first horse race is run in America.
1735	Jane Colman Turell (1708–1735): *Reliquiae Turellae et Lachrymae Paternal*, includes correspondence, diary extracts, short religious essays, and verse; reprinted in 1741 as *Memoirs of the Life and Death of the Pious and Ingenious Mrs. Jane Turell.*	1735	The first opera produced in the colonies premieres in Charleston, South Carolina.
1738	1738	Elizabeth Timothy becomes the first woman to publish a newspaper, the *South Carolina Gazette.*
1739	1739	Bloody slave revolts break out in South Carolina.
1740	1740	Benjamin Franklin invents his stove.
1741	Elizabeth White (1637?–1699): *The Experiences of God's Gracious Dealing with Mrs. Elizabeth White.*	1741	Eliza Lucas Pinckney, who successfully serves as business manager for several of her family's plantations and conducts a series of agricultural experiments, introduces her most successful discovery—indigo—to South Carolina, thereby creating a dyestuffs industry. The first magazine in the colonies is Andrew Bradford's *American Magazine*; its appearance is followed three days later by

TEXTS	CONTEXTS
1741	**1741** Benjamin Franklin's *General Magazine*, both Philadelphia journals.
1742 Sarah Parson Moorhead, religious polemicist and poet: "To the Reverend James Davenport on His Departure from Boston by Way of a Dream."	**1742**
1743 Sarah Prince Gill (1728–1771), a Puritan, begins keeping a diary at age 15, which she continues through most of her life, writing on such subjects as her love of books and the recurring need she feels to recommit herself to God. Parts of the diary, a verse, and a letter are published in 1773 as *Devotional Papers*.	**1743**
1745	**1745** Pennsylvanian Christine Zeller uses an ax against attacking Native Americans, killing three.
1746 Lucy Terry (1730–1821), author of "Bars Fight, August 28, 1746," is the first known African American poet in the United States. Handed down orally for a century, the ballad is first printed in 1855. Enslaved at age five, Terry married in 1756 a free black man who purchased her freedom.	**1746**

	TEXTS		CONTEXTS
1748	Sophia Hume (1702–1774), Quaker religious writer: *An Exhortation to the Inhabitants of the Province of South Carolina.*	1748	
1750		1750	Slave population numbers 236,400; 206,000 live south of Pennsylvania; slaves now represent about 20 percent of the colonial population. The first playhouse opens in New York.
1754		1754	Margaret Green Draper (1727–1807), one of the most successful 18th-century female printers and a staunch loyalist, publishes the *Massachusetts Gazette and Boston News-Letter* from 1754 to 1776, when she evacuates with the British army.
1754–1757	As do many colonial women, Esther Edwards Burr (1732–1758) keeps a diary; it is published in 1984.	1754–1757	
1754–1760		1754–1760	French and Indian War.
1755	Sarah Osborn (1714–1796): *The Nature, Certainty, and Evidence of True Christianity*, spiritual autobiography.	1755	"Yankee Doodle" is a popular song, originating as a British satire of the colonists but later taken up by the Yankees as a favorite marching song during the Revolutionary War.

TEXTS	CONTEXTS
1756	**1756** Mrs. Josiah Taft becomes the first known woman to have her vote recorded when she votes in favor of a town tax.
1757 Martha Wadsworth Brewster: *Poems on Divers Subjects*, includes acrostics, eulogies, epithalamiums, verse letters, scriptural paraphrases, a love poem, a quaternion, verse prayer, and occasional pieces.	**1757**
1758 Elizabeth Sandwich Drinker (1734–1807) keeps a continuous journal from 1758 to 1787, giving an intimate view of a prosperous Quaker family in colonial Philadelphia. In 1937, selections from the 36 volumes are edited and published by her great-grandson as *Not So Long Ago*. Annis Boudinot Stockton (1736–1801), poet and sponsor of literary salons: Her first known publication, "To the Honorable Colonel Peter Schuyler," appears in *New-York Mercury* and in *New American Magazine*; at least 21 of her poems would appear in notable periodicals during her lifetime.	**1758**

*   *   *

TEXTS	CONTEXTS
1760 Jean Lowry: *A Journal of the Captivity of Jean Lowry and Her Children, Giving an Account of Her Being Taken by Indians, the 1st of April 1756, from William McCords in Rocky Spring Settlement in Pennsylvania.* Anna Steele (1717–1778?), poet: *Poems on Subjects Chiefly Devotional*, two volumes published under the pseudonym "Theodosia." She donates the proceeds to charity.	**1760** Barbara Heck establishes Methodism in the colonies and applies her efforts to having the first Methodist church built.
1762	**1762** The first woman newspaper editor, Ann Franklin (sister of Benjamin), begins work at the *Mercury* in Newport, Rhode Island.
1763	**1763** By this date, all 13 colonies have printing presses.
1764	**1764** In *Davey v. Turner*, the Supreme Court in colonial Pennsylvania rules on the status of married women's property rights and requires the *feme covert*'s (married woman's) consent before her property can be sold or transferred.
1765	**1765** In Massachusetts, Jenny Slew, an African American, sues for and wins her freedom.

TEXTS	CONTEXTS
1768 Elizabeth Graeme Fergusson (1737–1801), poet and hostess of literary salons, known for her *vers de societé* and her letters and accounts of travels, usually signed "Laura": "The Dream of the Patriotic Philosophical Farmer," a political verse arguing for an American embargo on British goods. Milcah Martha Moore (1740–1829), poet, anthologist, and teacher: "The Female Patriots. Address'd to the Daughters of Liberty in America, 1768," verse.	**1768** Encyclopedia Britannica is founded.
1769	**1769** American printers stop relying on England for their presses and begin producing and purchasing them domestically. The first known interior "water closet" is built.
1770s Abigail Adams (1744–1818) authors hundreds of letters to family and friends which provide a multidimensional and warmly human picture of life in her times.	**1770s**
1770	**1770** Boston Massacre.

TEXTS	CONTEXTS
1770	**1770** A hairstyle once popular in 1710 is adopted by wealthy colonial women: "the Tower," for which hair is piled high on the head, greased, and decked with all kinds of paraphernalia.
1771 Jane Dunlap, American poet from Boston: *Poems upon Several Sermons Preached by the Rev'd George Whitefield.* Anna Green Winslow (1759–1780) keeps a diary of her experiences at school in Boston; it is published as the *Diary of Anna Green Winslow: A Boston School Girl of 1771* in 1895.	**1771** The umbrella as protection against the sun is first introduced to the colonies in Philadelphia and is ridiculed as effeminate.
1772 *The Adulateur*, the first propaganda play by America's first female playwright, Mercy Otis Warren (1728–1814), is first performed.	**1772** A British judge orders slavery abolished in England and the freeing of all the nation's slaves; in 1807 the slave trade is outlawed in Britain, and in 1834 slavery is abolished in the British Empire, including the West Indies. Patience Lovell Wright (1725–1786), the first known U.S. woman sculptor, travels to London and exhibits some of her life-size portraits in wax. During the Revolutionary War, Wright reportedly provides to the Americans

TEXTS		CONTEXTS	
1772		1772	information she gained while sculpting well-known Englishmen.
1773	Bridget Richardson Fletcher (1726–1770), American hymn writer: *Hymns and Spiritual Songs.* Phillis Wheatley (1753?–1784): *Poems on Various Subjects, Religious and Moral,* first book of poems published by a black American.	1773	Boston Tea Party. The Philadelphia Museum opens.
1774	Elizabeth Sampson Ashbridge (1713–1755), Quaker preacher and autobiographer: *Some Account of the Fore-Part of the Life of Elizabeth Ashbridge,* written in 1746 as an account of her spiritual development.	1774	
1774–1776	Janet Schaw, travel writer: *Journal of a Lady of Quality.*	1774–1776	
1775	Anna Young Smith (1756–1780?), poet and protégée of Elizabeth Graeme Fergusson: "An Elegy to the Memory of the American Volunteers," the first of her poems to be published, appears in the *Pennsylvania Magazine.* She uses the pseudonym "Sylvia."	1775	Nancy Ward is the first known white woman to sit on a Native American Council. She is given this honor by the Cherokee for her bravery during a battle against the Creek.

	TEXTS		CONTEXTS
1775	Mercy Otis Warren, play-wright, poet, historian: *The Group: A Farce.*	1775	
1775–1783		1775–1783	The American Revolution: perhaps the most famous woman associated with the battlefield is known by the sobriquet "Molly Pitcher," a nickname given Mary Ludwig after she carries water to American troops; other possible candidates for this legendary nickname include Margaret Corbin, wounded and disabled for life in a battle against the British in 1776, and Mary Hays, who fought in an artillery battle in 1778. Corbin is the first American woman to receive a war pension for her disability.
1776		1776	The Declaration of Independence is signed. Mary Goddard, who, in addition to serving as postmaster of Baltimore, had turned her husband's failed printing business into a success, becomes the first publisher to print the Declaration of Independence. Abigail Adams advises her husband, John, to "Remember the Ladies" when

TEXTS	CONTEXTS
1776	1776 drafting the new government's laws or women might "foment a Rebellion."
	New Jersey grants suffrage to women, making it the first colony to do so, although it repeals the right in 1807.
	A New York barmaid, Betsy Flanagan, invents the first cocktail.
1777 Phillis Wheatley: "On the Death of General Wooster."	1777 Betsy Ross is commissioned to sew a stars-and-stripes flag after a congressional resolution declares it the national emblem.
	A group of anonymous slaves petition the Massachusetts Bay Colony's House for their freedom.
1779 Susannah Johnson Hastings (1730–1810), autobiographer: *The Captive American*.	1779 Dr. William Alexander writes a history of women which suggests that women's arts have been devalued for the simple reason that it is men who write history.
1780s	1780s Many married couples practice some form of contraception, including *coitus interruptus* and prolonged breastfeeding.
1780 Esther de Berdt Reed (1747–1780): *The Sentiments of an American Woman*.	1780 Pennsylvania enacts a law aiming for the gradual abolition of slavery, the first state to do so.

TEXTS		CONTEXTS
1780	1780	Ann Lee, leader of the Shaker religious sect (which she established in 1774), becomes the first conscientious objector; she is imprisoned for her public opposition to the war.
1781	1781	The Articles of Confederation go into effect. Elizabeth Freeman (Mumbet), a slave woman who would go on to be largely responsible for rearing author Catharine Maria Sedgwick, successfully sues in county court for her freedom with the legal help of Theodore Sedgwick, father of Catharine. Her challenge establishes a precedent for the abolition of slavery throughout Massachusetts. Sedgwick would later write of Freeman's example in "Slavery in New England," published in *Bentley's Miscellany* in 1853.
1782	1782	Deborah (Gannett) Sampson, who some historians believe was African American, enlists in the Fourth Massachusetts Regiment in the American Revolutionary War under the alias Robert Shutleff (or Shirtliff). She fights in

TEXTS		CONTEXTS	
1782		1782	several battles before her sex is discovered during treatment for fever in a Philadelphia hospital.
			New England discontinues its use of the scarlet letter for adulterers.
1783		1783	Statutes are passed outlawing "crimes against nature" (including sodomy and fellatio).
			The first daily newspaper is the *Pennsylvania Evening Post*.
			The Federalist papers first appear in a New York newspaper, the *Independent Journal* (1783–1840).
1783–1784	Elizabeth House Trist keeps a journal of her travels from Philadelphia to Natchez; in it she records her sense of awe at the vastness of the wilderness.	1783–1784	
1784	Hannah Adams (1755–1831), probably the first professional woman writer in the U.S., researcher and historian: *Alphabetical Compendium of the Various Sects Which Have Appeared from the Beginning of the Christian Era to the Present Day*.	1784	

TEXTS	CONTEXTS
1784 Judith Sargent Murray (1751–1820), poet, essayist, playwright, and feminist: "Desultory Thoughts upon the utility of encouraging a degree of Self-Complacency, especially in FEMALE BOSOMS."	**1784**
1785	**1785** Alexander Hamilton and John Jay start a New York-based "Society for the Promotion of the Manumission of Slaves and Protecting such of them that have been or may be limited."
1786–1787	**1786–1787** Shays's Rebellion: some 1200 Massachusetts farmers led by Daniel Shays protest strict foreclosure laws and heavy taxes before they are put down by federal troops.
1787 Frances Hornby Barkley begins keeping diaries of her travels with her husband, a captain exploring the Northwest coast; it is the only pre-Lewis and Clark expedition narrative by a woman that has been found.	**1787** Dollar currency is introduced in the U.S. In New York, the first African Free School is founded. Congress bans slavery from the Northwest Territory. In the first issue of his *American Magazine*, Noah Webster proclaims, "The expectation of failure is

TEXTS	CONTEXTS
1787	**1787** connected with the very name of a Magazine," and he is right: of the 71 magazines begun in the last 15 years of the 18th century, 15 lasted for more than two years and only seven for more than five. Webster's magazine was not among these latter, as it folded in 1788.
1787–1792	**1787–1792** One of the few successful magazines of the 18th century, *American Museum*, begins publication.
1788 Susanna Rowson (1762–1824), novelist, playwright, poet, lyricist, and educator: *Poems on Various Subjects.* Mercy Otis Warren: *Observations on the New Constitution, and on the Federal and State Conventions.*	**1788** The U.S. Constitution goes into effect but grants such basic rights as suffrage to white propertied males only. New York is declared the U.S. capital.
1789	**1789** George Washington becomes the first President of the United States of America. The French Revolution begins. The first juvenile magazine, *Children's Magazine*, appears in Hartford, Connecticut; only three issues are printed.

TEXTS	CONTEXTS
1789	1789 Pennsylvania repeals its law prohibiting the performance of plays.
1790s	1790s The average age of marriage for white women is 27; 100 years later it is 22.
1790 Sarah Wentworth Morton (1759–1846), poet: *Ouabi; or, The Virtues of Nature: An Indian Tale in Four Cantos,* poetry published under the name "Philenia, a Lady of Boston." Morton was called the American Sappho in her time. Judith Sargent Murray: "On the Equality of the Sexes." Mercy Otis Warren: *Poems, Dramatic and Miscellaneous.*	1790 Philadelphia becomes the U.S. capital. Washington, D.C., is founded. The first U.S. census: U.S. Africans are the second largest segment of the total U.S. population of 3,929,000. African American population equals 757,181; 91 percent are slaves. The first Naturalization Law excludes all but free white immigrants from citizenship; the "white" qualification is not officially stricken from the statute books until the McCarran Act of 1952. The first U.S. patent law enables printers and authors to protect their copyright. The first musical competition in America is held.

TEXTS		CONTEXTS
1790	1790	High heels go out of fashion and sandal-like footwear comes into style.
1791	Margaretta V. Faugeres (1771–1801), playwright, poet, essayist, and editor of the works of her mother, Ann Eliza Bleecker: "A Salute to the Fourteenth Anniversary of American Independence."	1791	Toussaint L'Ouverture leads a slave insurrection in Haiti. The Bill of Rights is signed.
	Jenny Fenno (1765?–?), poet and religious writer: *Occasional Compositions in Prose and Verse.*		
	Sarah Porter (?–1831), poet: *The Royal Penitent, in Three Parts, to Which Is Added David's Lamentation over Saul and Jonathan.*		
	Susanna Rowson: *Charlotte Temple: A Tale of Truth* first appears in London. By 1794, when published in the U.S., its sales will make Rowson the country's first best-selling novelist.		
	Eunice Smith, religious writer: *Some Arguments Against Worldly-Mindedness.*		
1792	Anna Beeman (1739?–?), American hymn writer and religious polemicist:	1792	Catherine Littlefield Greene hosts Eli Whitney in her home for six

TEXTS	CONTEXTS
1792 *Hymns on Various Subjects* deals with God's boundless love and man's responsibility to prepare himself for grace. Eunice Smith: *Practical Language Interpreted.*	**1792** months, supporting him while he designs the idea she is said to have suggested to him: the cotton gin. Two political parties are formed in the U.S.: the Whig under Thomas Jefferson and the Federalist under Alexander Hamilton and John Adams. In England, Mary Wollstonecraft (1759–1797) publishes *A Vindication of the Rights of Woman.*
1793 Ann Eliza Bleecker (1752–1783), poet, short-story writer, and correspondent: *The Posthumous Works of Ann Eliza Bleecker*, which traces the heavy personal toll of the American Revolution.	**1793** The "Reign of Terror" in France begins. U.S. proclaims its neutrality in world affairs. The first fugitive slave law is enacted. Mrs. Samuel Slater becomes the first U.S. woman to be granted a patent: she receives it for cotton sewing thread.
1794 Susanna Rowson: *Slaves in Algiers; or, A Struggle for Freedom*, a play; and "America, Commerce and Freedom," a drinking song.	**1794** Elizabeth Hog Bennett's husband operates on her and she thus becomes the first woman to undergo the first successful Cesarean section in the U.S.

* * *

TEXTS		CONTEXTS	
1795	Lucy Allen publishes 26 hymns. The author is described as a devout Baptist who could neither read nor write but was moved to compose verse by "accidents, and other occurrences" of her life in the mid-1780s, including the death of her daughter. Margaretta V. Faugeres: *Belisarius: A Tragedy*.	1795	Sarah Waldrake and Rachael Summers become the first female federal government employees when they begin work at the Philadelphia mint.
1796	Judith Sargent Murray: *The Traveller Returned*, a play. Amelie Simmons: *American Cookery*.	1796	John Adams is elected President. Statute laws first introduce the concept of "Indian country," the idea that Native Americans could have land legally belong to them.
1797	Ann Eliza Bleecker: *The History of Maria Kittle*, an epistolary novel, possibly the first fictional captivity narrative (published posthumously). Hannah Webster Foster (1758–1840), novelist and conduct book author: *The Coquette; or, the History of Eliza Wharton*, highly successful and influential anonymously published epistolary novel. Sarah Wentworth Morton: *Beacon Hill*, poetry	1797	Escaped slaves petition Congress for "our relief as a people"; Congress rejects the petition. Author and playwright Susannah Rowson leaves the theater and opens an academy for young ladies, which she operates until her retirement in 1822. Nathaniel Briggs's design for the washing machine is patented.

	TEXTS		CONTEXTS
1797	published under the name "Philenia."	1797	
1798	Hannah Webster Foster: *The Boarding School; or, Lessons of a Preceptress to Her Pupils.* Judith Sargent Murray: *The Gleaner*, a 3-volume collection of her writings. Susanna Rowson: *Reuben and Rachel*, a novel.	1798	
1799	*Memoirs of the Life of Mrs. Sarah Osborn, who Died At Newport, Rhode Island, on the Second Day of August, 1796. In the Eighty Third Year of Her Age*, Samuel Hopkins, ed. Tabitha Tenney (1762–1820), novelist and advice writer: *The Pleasing Instructor*, an advice manual and anthology of classical literature.	1799	
1800	Sally Barrell Keating Wood (1759–1855), among the first to publish more than one novel in the U.S.: *Julia, and the Illuminated Baron.*	1800	An average of 7.04 children are born to each American woman. Abortion is legal in every state. The Library of Congress is established.
1801	Tabitha Tenney: *Female Quixotism: Exhibited in*	1801	Thomas Jefferson becomes President.

TEXTS	CONTEXTS
1801 *the Romantic Opinions and Extravagant Adventures of Dorcasina Sheldon*, a satirical novel. Sally Wood: *Dorval; or, The Spectacular*, a novel.	1801 One of the most successful and popular magazines of the nation's early years, the weekly *Port Folio*, begins publication and stays in print until 1827; its founder and editor, Joseph Dennie, uses the periodical as a forum for his Federalist views. Alexander Hamilton founds the New York *Evening Post*; it is edited from 1829 to 1878 by poet William Cullen Bryant.
1802 Sally Wood: *Amelia; or The Influence of Virtue*, a novel.	1802 The first official hotel opens in America in Saratoga, New York. The American Company of Booksellers is organized.
1803 Sukey Vickery (1799–1821), novelist and poet: *Emily Hamilton*, an epistolary novel.	1803 The Louisiana Purchase, land acquired at approximately four cents an acre, doubles the size of the nation. The first ice box used in an individual home appears. Writer Charles Brockden Brown begins publishing his *Literary Magazine and American Register*; it folds in 1807.

* * *

	TEXTS		CONTEXTS
1804	Susanna Rowson: *Miscellaneous Poems.* Sally Wood: *Ferdinand and Elmira, a Russian Story*, a novel.	1804	The first regular book trade catalog, *The Catalogue of All the Books Printed in the United States,* is issued in Boston.
1804–1806		1804–1806	Shoshone woman Sacajawea acts as guide and interpreter for the Lewis and Clark expedition.
1805	Mercy Otis Warren: *History of the Rise, Progress, and Termination of the American Revolution, Interspersed with Biographical and Moral Observations.*	1805	
1806		1806	Georgia and Louisiana pass laws sentencing to death slaves who rape white women (as do Kentucky in 1811, Mississippi in 1814, Tennessee in 1833, Texas in 1837, and South Carolina in 1843).
1807	Hannah Adams: *The Abridgement of the History of New England for the Use of Young People.* Sara Pogson: *The Female Enthusiast*, a play.	1807	
1808		1808	The external slave trade is abolished in the U.S.; however, the number of U.S. slaves triples between 1790 and 1860.

TEXTS		CONTEXTS
1808	1808	James Madison becomes President.
1809	1809	The first religious order founded in the U.S., Sisters of St. Joseph, is established by Elizabeth Bayley Seton.
		Mary Kies becomes one of the earliest U.S. women to earn a patent, for her method of weaving straw into silk and thread for bonnets.
		Without the benefit of anesthesia, Jane Todd Crawford survives the very first operation to remove an ovarian tumor.
1812 Hannah Adams: *History of the Jews from the Destruction of Jerusalem to the Nineteenth Century.* Rebecca Rush (1779–?): *Kelroy, A Novel.*	1812	The War of 1812 begins; Lucy Brewer, disguised as "George Baker," enlists as the first woman marine.
1813	1813	The stereotype is introduced; it enables printers to produce multiple copies of a text simultaneously and helps to make possible the mass marketing of books as well as the "best-seller."
1814	1814	Emma Hart Willard opens the Middlebury Female Seminary, a girls' boarding school.

TEXTS	CONTEXTS
1814	**1814** The first steam-driven "double-press" is introduced at the *Times* in London.
	The publishing house of John Wiley & Sons opens; it focuses almost exclusively on English and European works for its first five years.
1815 Mary Carr Clarke: *The Fair Americans*, a play.	**1815** Napoleon is defeated at the Battle of Waterloo.
Hannah Mather Crocker (1752–1829), memoirist, poet, and polemicist: *A Series of Letters on Free Masonry by a Woman of Boston.*	Pennsylvania expands its grounds for divorce to include impotence; Michigan does so in 1832.
Lydia Sigourney (1791–1865), poet, novelist, advocate of higher education for women, known as the "Sweet Singer of Hartford": *Moral Pieces in Prose and Verse.*	*North American Review* is founded; it remains a leading review periodical until it folds in 1840.
1816 Hannah Mather Crocker: *The School of Reform or the Seaman's Safe Pilot to the Cape of Good Hope.*	**1816** James Monroe becomes President.
Nancy Maria Hyde: *The Writings of Nancy Maria Hyde, of Norwich, Conn., Connected with a Sketch of Her Life.*	The African Methodist Episcopal (AME) Church is established.

* * *

TEXTS	CONTEXTS
1817 Isabella Marshall Graham (1742–1814), religious writer: *The Power of Faith, Exemplified in the Life and Writings of the Late Mrs. Isabella Graham of New York*, published posthumously by her daughter Joanna Graham Bethune, with an accompanying biography.	**1817** The American Colonization Society is founded, with the aim of sending all African Americans living in the U.S. to colonies in Africa and elsewhere. The publishing company Harper & Bros. is first established as J & J Harper, a small printing firm that soon becomes one of the major publishing houses in U.S. history, famous especially in the 19th century for its series of books known as "libraries": Harper's Family Library, Library of Select Novels, Boys' and Girls' Library, and Classical Library. Miniaturist Ann Hall's (1792–1863) works are exhibited in New York City; Hall later becomes the first woman to be a full member of the National Academy of Design.
1818 Hannah Mather Crocker: *Observations on the Real Rights of Women with their appropriate duties, agreeable to Scripture, reason, and common sense.*	**1818** The barrier between Canada and the U.S. (the 49th parallel) is agreed upon. Thin, low-cut, and close-fitting muslin dresses are the fashion. The Seminole War begins in Florida.

	TEXTS		CONTEXTS
1819	Emma Hart Willard (1787–1870), poet, author of textbooks, advice books, and histories, educator: *Plan for Improving Female Education*, published at her own expense. Frances Wright (1795–1852), feminist essayist and playwright: *Altorf,* a play.	1819	Economic Depression.
1820	Maria Brooks (1794–1845), poet: *Judith, Esther, and Other Poems, by a Lover of the Fine Arts.*	1820	In accordance with the Missouri Compromise, Maine enters as a free state and Missouri enters as a slave state in 1821. U.S. population totals approximately 9.6 million. African American women number 870,860, 750,010 of whom are slaves; total African American population is 1,771,656. 512 newspapers are currently published in the colonies; 42 of these are dailies, which begin as a means of advertising the arrival of ships and the sale of imported goods but soon expand their function and format to approximate the dailies we read in the 1990s. Writing in the *Edinburgh Review*, Sydney Smith, ex-

TEXTS	CONTEXTS
1820	**1820** pressing a general belief in the paucity of American literature, asks, "In the four quarters of the globe, who reads an American book?"
1821	**1821** The American Colonization Society founds Liberia in order to provide a home for emancipated slaves other than in the U.S.
	The first issue of the *Saturday Evening Post* appears; it remains in print until 1969 and is revived in 1971.
	Emma Hart Willard founds the Troy Female Seminary, which is renamed for its founder in 1895.
1822 Sarah Wentworth Morton: *My Mind and Its Thoughts.*	**1822** Denmark Vesey's conspiracy to kill all of Charleston, South Carolina's, whites is foiled, and Vesey and his aides are hanged.
Catharine Maria Sedgwick (1789–1867), novelist, short-story writer, biographer: *A New England Tale; or, Sketches of New-England Character and Manners*, a novel.	Samuel Thomson publishes the *New Guide to American Health* and founds a movement to democratize medicine, making every person his/her own healer.
	Zilpah Grant founds the Adams Academy for Girls

TEXTS	CONTEXTS
1822	**1822** (Derry, New Hampshire), the first school to award diplomas to females.
1823	**1823** The Monroe Doctrine establishes the U.S. sense of Manifest Destiny over the Americas. Catharine Beecher opens the Hartford Seminary.
1824 Lydia Maria Child (1802–1880), novelist, short-story writer, editor, biographer, advocate of Native American and African American rights: *Hobomok, a Tale of Early Times*, a historical novel. Catharine Maria Sedgwick: *Redwood*, a novel. Margaret Bayard Smith (1778–1844), novelist, Washington socialite: *A Winter in Washington*, published anonymously.	**1824** The first strike involving women takes place in Pawtucket, Rhode Island, when male and female weavers protest increasing hours and decreasing wages. The first public high school for girls opens in Worcester, Massachusetts.
1824–1825	**1824–1825** In a series for *Blackwood's Magazine*, John Neal makes the first known detailed attempt to describe and define "American literature."
1825 Lydia Maria Child: *The Rebels; or, Boston before the Revolution*, a novel. Sarah Kemble Knight (1666–1727), diarist, poet,	**1825** John Quincy Adams becomes President. Fanny Wright founds Nashoba, a utopian community in western

TEXTS	CONTEXTS
1825 and businesswoman: *The Private Journal of a Journey from Boston to New York in the Year 1704 Kept by Madam Knight*, a vivid picture of colonial life written during a horseback journey.	1825 Tennessee. Five years later she frees the Nashoba slaves after pronouncing the community a failure.

Sarah Peale (1800–1885), considered one of the first American women painters, begins to advertise herself as having "painting rooms in Peale's Baltimore Museum." She is known for her portraits of many of the important figures in the young United States, and for still lifes, such as *A Slice of Watermelon*.

Hannah Lord Montagu of New York invents a detachable shirt collar for men; her inspiration comes after growing tired of washing her husband's shirts when only the collar was dirty.

The United Tailoresses Society of New York, the first women's labor organization, is formed; six years later it has over 600 members.

The American Tract Society is founded as an avenue for evangelical comment.

The first patent is taken out for tin cans.

TEXTS	CONTEXTS
1825	1825 Married couples have an average of five to six children.
1826 Lydia Maria Child founds the nation's first periodical for children, *Juvenile Miscellany*. Anne Newport Royall (1769–1854), novelist, editor, travel writer: *Sketches of History: Life and Manners in the United States by a Traveller*. Jane Johnston Schoolcraft (1800–1841), an Ojibwa woman born Bame-wa-was-ge-zhik-a-quay, with her husband Henry Schoolcraft begins a reading society at a frontier outpost; a magazine, "The Literary Voyager or Muzzenyegun," grows out of the effort. Jane Schoolcraft writes essays, poems, and sketches for the publication, which is grounded in Ojibwa culture.	1826 The lyceum program of adult education is first introduced in Massachusetts.
1827 Sarah Josepha Buell Hale (1788–1879), novelist, biographer, and editor: *Northwood: A Tale of New England*, a novel. Eliza Leslie (1787–1858), short-story writer and author of children's literature, cookbooks, poetry, and etiquette manuals:	1827 Illinois passes a law setting the age of consent for marriage at 14 for women, 17 for men. At a convention of the General Council of the Cherokee Nation, the delegates draft a constitution; however, an 1830 law passed by the Georgia

TEXTS	CONTEXTS
1827 *Seventy-five Receipts for Pastry, Cakes, and Sweetmeats.* Elizabeth Ruffin, of Evergreen plantation in Virginia, keeps an ironic journal that records her view of plantation life. Catharine Maria Sedgwick: *Hope Leslie; or, Early Times in Massachusetts*, a novel. Lydia Sigourney: *Poems.*	1827 Legislature (and upheld by the courts in 1831) abolishes Cherokee governmental authority, stripping the Nation of many of its rights and appropriating its land. Mardi Gras is first celebrated in New Orleans. The first African American newspaper, *Freedom's Journal*, is printed in New York. The children's magazine *Youth's Companion* appears, intending to encourage "virtue and piety" in its young readers; it remains in print for 102 years. *McClure's Magazine* begins 100 years of publication.
1827–1828 Eliza Lee Follen (1787–1867), abolitionist, editor of first American edition of Grimms' fairy tales and from 1843 to 1850 of the *Child's Friend*, a juvenile periodical, as well as prolific author of fiction for children: *The Well-Spent Hour.*	1827–1828
1828 Virginia Randolph Cary, southern author: *Letters on Female Character*, an advice book.	1828 The first labor strike by women only takes place when needleworkers in Dover, New Hampshire,

TEXTS	CONTEXTS
1828 Lydia Maria Child: *The First Settlers of New-England; or, Conquest of the Pequods, Narragansets and Pokanokets: as Related by a Mother to Her Children, and Designed for the Instruction of Youth.* Eliza Leslie: *The Mirror*, a work for children. Margaret Bayard Smith: *What Is Gentility? A Moral Tale*, an anonymously published novel. Catharine Read Arnold Williams (1790–1872), novelist, poet, biographer, and historian: *Original Poems on Various Subjects.*	**1828** protest a wage cut as well as their ten-hour work day. Side-laced boots first become fashionable as women's footwear. Frances Wright is the first known woman to speak in public before both women and men.
1829 Catharine Beecher (1800–1878), writer and advocate of female educational reform: *Suggestions Respecting Improvements in Education.* Lydia Maria Child: *The Frugal Housewife*, an advice book. Lucretia Maria Davidson (1808–1825), poet: *Amir Khan, and Other Poems*, published posthumously, edited by her mother. Sarah Josepha Hale:	**1829** Andrew Jackson becomes the seventh President. The first anthology of American literature appears: Samuel Kettell's 3-volume *Specimens of American Poetry, with Critical and Biographical Notes.* The first carnival "Fat Ladies" in America are two sisters, Deborah and Susan Tripp; when Deborah was three and Susan was five, they weighed 124 and 205 pounds, respectively.

	TEXTS		CONTEXTS
1829	*Sketches of American Character*.	1829	The first omnibus premieres in New York City.
	Frances Wright begins publication of *The Free Enquirer*, a newspaper dedicated to examining social, political, and religious issues. She publishes *Course of Popular Lectures* this same year.		
1830s		1830s	Cookstoves, as distinct from heating stoves, come into their own in America.
1830	Frances Manwaring Caulkins (1795–1869) begins 30 years of writing for the American Tract Society, including religious and educational books for children.	1830	The average work week is 79 hours.
			Women's skirts become shorter, sleeves are enormous, hats are large and sport flowers and ribbons.
	Sarah Josepha Hale: *Poems for Our Children*.		Philadelphia becomes the first city to have a fully operative municipal water system, supplying running water to its citizens; New York develops one in 1842 and Boston in 1848.
	Catharine Maria Sedgwick: *Clarence; or, A Tale of Our Own Times*.		
			The Mormon Church is founded.
			Because of gradual emancipation in the North, the region is home to only 2,780 out of the 2,009,043 African American slaves.

TEXTS	CONTEXTS
1830	**1830** The Indian Removal Act enables President Andrew Jackson to forcibly remove Native American tribes from their homelands to designated (distant and dusty) "Indian Territory," now known as Oklahoma.
	Godey's Lady's Book is founded; it folds in 1898.
1830–1835 Catharine Read Williams: *Tales, National and Revolutionary*, 2 vols.	**1830–1835**
1831 Lydia Maria Child: *The Coronal*, a book of poetry.	**1831** William Lloyd Garrison establishes *The Liberator*.
The History of Mary Prince, a West Indian Slave, a dictated slave narrative.	The first series of paperback editions appear.
	The first horse-drawn buses are in use in New York.
	The first Convention of People of Color/National Negro Convention is held in Philadelphia.
	Nat Turner leads a slave rebellion in Virginia; he and his followers kill at least 55 whites; Turner and other rebels are later hanged after a trial.
	Two African American women's literary societies—the Female Literary

TEXTS	CONTEXTS
1831	**1831** Association of Philadelphia and the Afric-American Female Intelligence Society of Boston—are formed.
	The publishing house of Appleton brings out its first book; in 1838 the firm becomes known as D. Appleton & Co.
1832 *Memoir of Mrs. Chloe Spear, a Native of Africa, Who Was Enslaved in Childhood, and Died in Boston, January 3, 1815,* by a "Lady of Boston."	**1832** The New England Anti-Slavery Society is founded in Boston.
Fanny Newell: *Memoirs of Fanny Newell, Written by Herself.*	Maria Stewart, an African American, becomes the first native-born U.S. woman to make public speaking her career.
	The word "socialism" comes into use in English and French.
	Cholera epidemic.
	The first commuter steam rail service is introduced in New York.
	In *Worcester v. Georgia,* Chief Justice Marshall upholds the supremacy of U.S. treaties and thus denies Georgia any control over Cherokee territory; in 1838 President Jackson and the state of Georgia ignore the ruling as they begin the Indian

TEXTS		CONTEXTS
1832	1832	"removal" dubbed the "Trail of Tears."
		The Black Hawk War ends the last Native American resistance in the territory north of the Ohio River and east of the Mississippi River.
		The Houghton Mifflin publishing company is founded.
1832–1865	1832–1865	The publishing firm Allen & Ticknor (later William D. Ticknor & Co.) occupies the Old Corner Book Store in Boston, a virtual mecca for novelists, poets, actors, historians, and other eminent figures of the day; in 1849 the imprint Ticknor & Fields first appears in its books. Harriet Beecher Stowe and Julia Ward Howe are among the authors on its list.
1833	Maria Brooks, writing as "Maria del Occidente": *Zophiel,* an epic poem.	1833	The American Anti-Slavery Society is formed.
	Lydia Maria Child: *An Appeal in Favor of That Class of Americans Called Africans.* One of the first anti-slavery works, this piece creates so much controversy and causes the loss		Lucretia Mott, abolitionist and a leader of the 19th-century woman suffrage movement, forms the Philadelphia Female Anti-Slavery Society (PFAS), one of the first political organizations for women.

TEXTS	CONTEXTS
1833 of so many subscribers that Child is forced to close down her children's magazine, *Juvenile Miscellany*.	**1833** On June 27, Prudence Crandall, teacher and abolitionist, is arrested for violating Connecticut's infamous "Black Law," which made it illegal to set up a school for blacks not from Connecticut; the school is closed and is put up for sale the following year.
Eliza Leslie: *Pencil Sketches*.	
Penina Moise (1797–1880), poet, hymnologist, teacher: *Fancy's Sketch Book*, probably the first published book to which a Jewish woman appends her full name.	George Palmer Putnam becomes an associate at the firm of Wiley & Long; after Long's departure in 1840, the firm becomes Wiley & Putnam and soon is publishing works by Poe, Hawthorne, and Melville in its Library of American Books series.
Abigail Goodrich Whittesley becomes the first editor of the nation's first magazine for mothers: *Mother's Magazine*.	
Catharine Read Williams: *Fall River, an Authentic Narrative*, an early example of investigative journalistic writing, tells of the murder of Sarah Maria Cornell, a young textile worker, and the subsequent trial of the Reverend Ephraim Kingsbury Avery.	The first "penny press" is the *New York Sun*; whereas paper had previously cost between eight and ten dollars a year, the invention of power presses and machine-made paper allowed smaller newspapers to begin selling for a penny a copy.
	The Knickerbocker Magazine begins its 32 years in print.
	Oberlin College, the first coeducational, multiracial

TEXTS		CONTEXTS
1833	1833	college in the States, is founded in Ohio.
		The first tax-supported public library opens in New Hampshire.
		Alexis de Tocqueville visits America.
1834 Sarah Flower Adams (1805–1848) composes the hymn "Nearer, My God, to Thee." She also writes poetry and magazine articles. Caroline Howard Gilman (1794–1888), poet, memoirist, editor of a children's magazine, *The Rose Bud;* known as a humorous chronicler of middle-class domesticity: *Recollections of a Housekeeper*, published under the pseudonym "Mrs. Clarissa Packard." Lydia Sigourney: *Sketches* and *Poems.* Harriet Beecher Stowe (1811–1896), novelist, short-story writer, abolitionist, author of domestic manuals: "A New England Sketch" in *Western Monthly Magazine.*	1834	Mary Ayers sends the first petition for a change in married women's property laws to the New York State legislature; when unrolled, it measures approximately 15 feet. The National Trade Union is founded. William Whewell coins the term "scientist" and declares "there is a sex in minds." Elizabeth Palmer Peabody becomes Bronson Alcott's assistant at his Temple School, staying for two years even though Alcott was notoriously difficult to work for and frequently did not pay her for her labors. The *Southern Literary Messenger* begins its 30-year run.

*   *   *

	TEXTS		CONTEXTS
1835	Lydia Maria Child: *The History of the Condition of Women, in Various Ages and Nations*, 2 vols.	1835	The nation's first women's prison, New York's Mount Pleasant Female Prison, opens.
	Sarah Josepha Hale: *Traits of American Life*.		Pimps make their first appearance in New York City.
	Catharine Maria Sedgwick: *Home: Scenes and Characters Illustrating Christian Truth, Tales and Sketches*, and *The Linwoods*, a novel.		The *New York Herald* is founded, the first newspaper to proclaim and maintain its political independence.
	Lydia Sigourney: *Zinzendorff, and Other Poems*.		Baby bottle nipples are first introduced.
	Maria Stewart (1803–1879), African American religious author: *Productions of Mrs. Maria W. Stewart*, a spiritual autobiography.		
	Women of the American Female Moral Reform Society begin publication of *The Advocate*.		
1835–1842		1835–1842	Second Seminole War.
1836	Catharine Beecher: *Letters on the Difficulties of Religion*.	1836	Battle of the Alamo.
	Elizabeth Margaret Chandler (1807–1834), Quaker poet and essayist, the first American woman author to make slavery the principal theme of her writing:		Congress institutes a "gag rule" whereby no antislavery petitions could be introduced before it after this date; since for many women petition-signing is the only acceptable (because relatively private)

TEXTS	CONTEXTS
1836 *Essays, Philanthropic and Moral* and *The Poetical Works of Elizabeth Margaret Chandler*, published posthumously.	1836 mode of protest, this action effectively stifles their voices in the public debate over slavery. The gag rule is not repealed until 1844.
Lydia Maria Child: *Philothea*, a novel.	The first McGuffey's Reader is introduced: the series of readers is widely used in public schools and is still in use today in some schools.
Eliza Farrar (1791–1870): *The Young Lady's Friend*, an extremely popular advice book.	
Angelina Emily Grimké (1805–1879), abolitionist and woman's rights pioneer: *Appeal to Christian Women of the Southern States*. It is widely banned in the South for its persuasive argument that women should use their influence on the men in their lives to abolish slavery and its evils.	The Philadelphia newspaper the *Public Ledger* appears.
	In Boston, a group of African American women storm a courtroom and help two fugitive slave women escape to freedom before the two can be returned to their masters under the Fugitive Slave Law.
Jarena Lee (1783–1849?), unordained but licensed minister of the African Methodist Episcopal Church, begins writing and selling autobiographical pamphlets, culminating in a book, *Religious Experiences and Journal of Jarena Lee, Giving an Account of Her Call to Preach the Gospel*, published 1849.	Having reached the Continental Divide while migrating west with their husbands, Eliza Hart Spalding and Narcissa Whitman become the first white women to cross it and the Rocky Mountains.
Margaret Morris: *Private Journal Kept During a Portion of the Revolutionary*	Georgia Female College in Macon, Georgia (later Wesleyan College) becomes the first chartered women's college to confer on women honors, de-

TEXTS	CONTEXTS
1836 *War, for the Amusement of a Sister* by Margaret Morris of Burlington, New Jersey.	**1836** grees, and licenses "usually conferred in colleges and universities."
Almira Hart Phelps (1793–1884), pioneer for female education, writer of stories and textbooks, especially for girls: *The Female Student; or, Lectures to Young Ladies on Female Education* (republished as *The Fireside Friend*, 1840).	Martin Van Buren is elected President. The New Orleans *Picayune* begins circulation.
1837 Catharine Beecher: *An Essay on Slavery and Abolitionism.*	**1837** Victoria becomes Queen of Great Britain, the beginning of a 64-year reign; her coronation is held in 1838.
Caroline Howard Gilman: *Recollections of a Southern Matron*, a novel, and "Mary Anna Gibbes, the Young Heroine of Stono, S.C.," a dramatic poem about a young girl's adventures in the Revolutionary War.	The U.S. experiences economic depression; 600 banks close. The first Anti-Slavery Convention of American Women is held in New York City.
Sarah Josepha Hale: *The Ladies' Wreath.*	
Hannah Lee (1780–1865): *Elinor Fulton*, a novel, and *Three Experiments of Living*, both published anonymously.	Mary Lyon founds the Mount Holyoke Seminary for women, believing that to educate young women "to a new direction" it was necessary to remove them from their homes and their private concerns. To save money and demonstrate that the seminary was not subversive in intent, Lyon requires students to perform all the housekeeping. The semi-
Catharine Maria Sedgwick: *Live and Let Live.*	
Lydia Sigourney: *History of the Condition of Women.*	

TEXTS	CONTEXTS
1837	1837 nary is swamped with applicants; the school becomes Mount Holyoke College in 1893. By this year there are 77 all-female antislavery societies. *The Democratic Review* begins publication; it folds in 1859. The Baltimore newspaper the *Sun* appears; it still circulates today. P. T. Barnum pulls his first successful hoax by convincing credulous audiences that a 46-pound African American woman, Joyce Heth, was actually 161 years old and had once been George Washington's nurse. Mary Ann Lee (1826–1899) becomes the country's first ballerina.
1837–1877 Sarah Josepha Hale starts her long reign as author and editor for the influential *Godey's Lady's Book and American Ladies' Magazine*.	1837–1877
1838 Maria Brooks: *Idomen: or the Vale of Yumuri*, a fictionalized autobiography serialized in the *Saturday Evening Gazette*.	1838 The Anti-Slavery Convention of American Women is held in Pennsylvania; Angelina Grimké, who only the day before had

TEXTS

CONTEXTS

1838   Elleanor Eldridge (1785–
1865), African American
author: *Memoirs of El-
leanor Eldridge.*

Emma Catherine Em-
bury: *Constance Latimer;
or, The Blind Girl*, a novel
written to help support
an institution for the
blind.

Eliza Lee Follen: *Sketches
of Married Life*, a moral
tale.

Caroline Howard Gilman:
*The Poetry of Traveling in
the United States*, a novel.

Sarah Moore Grimké
(1792–1873): *Letters on
the Equality of the Sexes
and the Condition of
Women.*

Louisa Medina: *Ernest
Maltravers*, a play.

Catharine Maria Sedg-
wick: *A Love-token for
Children.*

Ann Sophia Stephens
(1810?–1886), novelist,
short-story writer, humorist, poet, and journalist:
"Mary Derwent," a short
story, which wins a *La-
dies Companion's* prize.
Twenty years later Ste-
phens expands it into a
novel.

1838   married fellow abolitionist
Theodore Weld, is a fea-
tured speaker; three days
later, the site of the convention, Pennsylvania
Hall, is burned to the
ground by a mob angered
by the convention's inter-
mingling of African
Americans and whites.

English phrenologist
George Combe popular-
izes phrenology, the study
of the shape of the head,
in the U.S. during his
two-year lecture tour.

Vegetarianism has its be-
ginnings in the U.S. when
the American Health Con-
vention endorses vegeta-
ble diets.

Cherokee Indians expelled
from the East Coast begin
the infamous "Trail of
Tears" toward reserva-
tions in the Midwest: one
out of four of the 15,000
Cherokees who are "re-
moved" in the 1830s die
on the journey to what is
now known as Oklahoma.

When Angelina Grimké
speaks before the Massa-
chusetts state legislature,
she becomes the first
woman ever to speak be-
fore a legislative body.

John Quincy Adams, in a

TEXTS		CONTEXTS
1838	1838	series of speeches published this year, defends the right of women to collect signatures and sign petitions.
1839	Sarah Josepha Hale: *The Lecturess; or, Woman's Sphere*, published anonymously.	1839	Margaret Fuller begins her "conversations" or discussion series for women in her home in Boston.
	Caroline Stansbury Kirkland (1801–1864): *A New Home—Who'll Follow? or, Glimpses of Western Life*, a novel published under the pseudonym, "Mrs. Mary Claver, an Actual Settler."		The American Female Moral Reform Society includes several hundred local and state associations.
	Frances Sargent Osgood (1811–1850), poet: *The Casket of Fate*.		Educator Elizabeth Palmer Peabody opens a bookstore in Boston that soon becomes the meeting place for the Transcendentalists. The Transcendental journal *The Dial*, to which Peabody contributes several pieces, will be published in the back room of the store from 1842 to 1843; the store burns to the ground in 1844.
	Eliza Wilkerson, a Charleston author: *Letters*.		
	Catharine Read Williams: *Biography of Revolutionary Heroes*.		
			Josephine Amelia Perkins becomes notorious as the first woman horse-thief of record in the U.S.
			The first married women's property act, allowing women to retain property that had automatically gone to their hus-

TEXTS	CONTEXTS
1839	1839 bands upon marriage, passes in Mississippi; Maryland, Arkansas, and Pennsylvania soon follow with their own acts—the fact that the first three states to pass such laws were southern is in large part a sign of these states' interest in preserving slaves as property.

The Anti-Rent War is fought in New York's Hudson Valley.

George Rex Graham purchases a monthly magazine, *The Casket* (1826–1840), and merges it with *Burton's Gentleman's Magazine* (1837–1840) to create *Graham's Magazine*, a leading literary journal, with its heyday in the 1840s.

With the publication of two weekly periodicals, *Brother Jonathan* and, in 1840, the *New World*, the novels in newspaper format eventually known as the "story papers" get their start, priced at between 6¼ and 12½ cents; they serve as the prototypes for paperback novels.

*   *   *

TEXTS		CONTEXTS	
1840s		1840s	Some 800 works of fiction by American authors are published in this decade alone.
1840	Margaret Fuller (1810–1850), journalist, essayist, and feminist, begins a two-year tenure as editor of the Transcendentalist magazine *The Dial*.	1840	Lucretia Mott and Elizabeth Cady Stanton go to London as delegates to the World Anti-Slavery Convention but are not admitted to the floor on account of their sex.
	Caroline Howard Gilman: *Love's Progress*, a novel published anonymously.		The Liberty Party—the first antislavery political party—is established.
	Eliza Leslie: *The Housebook; or, A Manual of Domestic Economy*.		William Henry Harrison is elected President; a year later, he becomes the first President to die in office and is succeeded by John Tyler.
	The first issue of *The Lowell Offering*, a periodical featuring the articles and poetry of women employed by the Lowell Textile Mills, is published.		Eleven percent of the population is urban.
1841	Catharine Beecher: *A Treatise on Domestic Economy*.	1841	Oberlin College graduates its first female student.
	Margaret Miller Davidson (1823–1838): *Biographical and Poetical Remains of the Late Margaret Miller Davidson*, Washington Irving, ed., published posthumously.		Horace Greeley founds the New York *Tribune*.
			Elizabeth Adams invents and patents a pregnancy corset.
	Mrs. A. J. Graves: *Women in America: Being an Examination into the Moral and*		

TEXTS	CONTEXTS
1841 *Intellectual Condition of American Female Society.* Eliza Leslie: *Mr. and Mrs. Woodbridge, with Other Tales.* Ann Plato (1820?–?): *Essays; Including Biographies and Miscellaneous Pieces in Prose and Poetry*, the first known collection of essays by an African American. Lydia Sigourney: *Pocahontas, and Other Poems* and *Poems, Religious and Elegaic.*	**1841**
1841–1846	**1841–1846** Transcendentalists and literary figures, including at certain moments Margaret Fuller and Nathaniel Hawthorne, gather at Brook Farm in Massachusetts in an attempt to found a Utopian community under the leadership of George Ripley.
1842 Harriet Farley Donlevy (1813–1907) becomes co-editor of *The Lowell Offering.* Elleanor Eldridge: *Elleanor's Second Book.* Caroline Kirkland: *Forest Life*, a novel.	**1842** The Supreme Court upholds a 1793 act allowing slaveowners to retrieve fugitive slaves. *Southern Quarterly Review* begins its 15-year run. The New York Philharmonic Society Orchestra gives its first performance.

TEXTS	CONTEXTS
1842 Elizabeth Oakes Smith (1806–1893), poet, novelist, essayist, reformer: *The Western Captive*, a novel.	**1842**
1842–1898	**1842–1898** *Peterson's Magazine* begins publishing under its original name, *Ladies' National Magazine;* it is co-edited by Charles Jacobs Peterson and author Ann S. Stephens.
1843 Margaret Fuller: "The Great Lawsuit: Man *versus* Men. Woman *versus* Women." Caroline Lee Hentz (1800–1856), southern author of ten novels, short-story writer, and playwright: *De Lara; or, the Moorish Bride; a Tragedy*, a prize-winning play. Rebecca Cox Jackson (1795–1871), a free black woman who, in 1830, leaves her husband, home, and family for a life of spiritual commitment, becoming a Shaker visionary and preacher. She begins to write her memoirs, which include a series of dreams and visions. Eliza Leslie: *Mrs. Washington Potts, and Mr. Smith: Tales.*	**1843** The typewriter is invented. The word "millionaire" is first coined in obituaries of banker, landlord, and tobacconist Pierre Lorillard. The Alcott family is among those gathered at Fruitlands in Harvard, Massachusetts, a short-lived utopian community.

TEXTS	CONTEXTS
1843 Maria Jane McIntosh (1803–1878), novelist and children's author: *Woman an Enigma; or, Life and Its Revealings*, published anonymously. Phoebe W. Palmer (1807–1874): *The Way of Holiness*. Ann Sophia Stephens: *High Life in New York*, a humorous novel. Harriet Beecher Stowe: *The Mayflower; or, Sketches of Scenes and Characters among the Descendants of the Puritans*.	**1843**
1844 Charlotte Barnes Conner: *The Forest Princess*, a play. Fanny Crosby (1820–1915), blind poet and hymnwriter: *The Blind Girl, and Other Poems*. Margaret Fuller: *Summer on the Lakes*, a travel narrative. Mrs. A. J. Graves: *Girlhood and Womanhood; or, Sketches of My Schoolmates*. Estelle Lewis (1824–1880), poet and playwright: *Records of the Heart*, collection of poetry.	**1844** For the first time documented, women are allowed to study in an American art school. The first female manikin ever exhibited in America is used by Pauline Wright in her lectures on the physiology of women to women audiences. James K. Polk is elected President.

TEXTS		CONTEXTS	
1844	Cornelia Mee: *A Manual of Knitting, Netting and Crochet.*	1844	
	Catharine Maria Sedgwick: *Tales and Sketches, Second Series,* including the novella *Wilton Harvey.*		
	Ann Sophia Stephens: *Alice Copley,* a novel.		
	Louisa Caroline Tuthill (1799–1879), author of household manuals, advice books, children's tales, and novels: *The Belle, the Blue, and the Bigot; or, Three Fields for Woman's Influence,* a moral tale.		
1845	Frances Manwaring Caulkins, after a long career as a tract writer, begins a second career writing local histories: *The History of Norwich, Connecticut, from Its Settlement in 1660 to January, 1845.*	1845	Sarah Bagley, the first notable woman trade unionist, founds and serves as president of the Lowell Female Labor Reform Association, making her the first known woman union leader. She helps organize a petition to the Massachusetts legislature for restriction of the workday to ten hours.
	Margaret Fuller: *Woman in the Nineteenth Century,* salutes the "triumphs of Female Authorship" as a "sign of the times."		
	Sarah Josepha Hale: *Keeping House and Housekeeping: A Story of Domestic Life.*		Theophilus B. Peterson, perhaps the leading publisher of sensational fiction and cheap reprints, begins his publishing career; among the authors on his list is E.D.E.N. Southworth.
	Caroline Kirkland: *Western Clearings,* a highly		

TEXTS		CONTEXTS
1845	praised collection of sketches. Anna Cora Mowatt Ritchie (1819–1870), novelist, actress: *Fashion,* witty satire of 19th-century New York society.	1845 *American Whig Review* begins its seven-year run.
1846	Catharine Beecher: *The Domestic Receipt Book.* Emily Chubbuck: *Alderbook: A Collection of Fanny Forrester's Village Sketches, Poems, Etc.* Susan Fenimore Cooper (1813–1894), writing as "Amabel Penfeather": *Elinor Wyllys; or, The Young Folk at Longbridge,* a novel. Zilpha Elaw, African American antebellum minister, writes of her life's religious work in *Memoirs of the Life, Religious Experience, Ministerial Travels and Labours of Mrs. Zilpha Elaw, an American Female of Color; Together with Some Account of the Great Religious Revivals in America* (published in England). Eliza Woodson Farnham (1815–1864), novelist, essayist, suffragist, abolition-	1846 The influential southern journal *Debow's Review* appears in print. The Donner Party is lost in the Sierra Nevada Mountains on their way to California; the 47 survivors out of the original 87 are said to have practiced cannibalism in order to survive. The sewing machine is patented by Elias Howe. Mount Union College in Ohio grants absolutely equal rights to its women students, the first coeducational U.S. college known to do so. The National Medical Convention, which in the following year takes the name the American Medical Association, is formally established; at their annual convention, doctors would often toast "Woman—God's best gift to man and the chief

<table>
<tr><th>TEXTS</th><th>CONTEXTS</th></tr>
</table>

1846	ist, and prison reformer: *Life in Prairie Land.*
	Sarah Josepha Hale: *"Boarding Out": A Tale of Domestic Life*, published anonymously.
	Caroline Lee Hentz: *Aunt Patty's Scrap Bag*, a story collection.
	Maria Jane McIntosh: *Two Lives; or, To Seem and To Be*, a novel.
	Catharine Maria Sedgwick: *The Morals of Manners.*
	Louisa Caroline Tuthill: *My Wife*, a moral tale.
	Frances Whitcher (1811?-1852), writing as "Frank" for *Neal's Saturday Gazette*, becomes the first woman to publish serial satirical writing.

1846	support of the Doctors."
	The state of Maine passes the first statute prohibiting the sale, manufacture, or transportation of alcohol; by 1855, twelve additional states have passed such laws (known as "Maine Laws"), although by the end of the Civil War, nine of these states have repealed or declared unconstitutional their earlier statutes.
	Charles Scribner begins his publishing career.

1846–1848	

1846–1848	The Mexican War results in the U.S. appropriating territories that will become California, Texas, Arizona, and New Mexico.

1847	Mary Andrews Denison (1826–1911), prolific author of short stories, sketches, nonfiction, and novels, including many dime novels: *Edna Etheril, a Boston Seamstress.*

1847	Frederick Douglass starts his abolitionist paper *The North Star.*
	The *Massachusetts Quarterly Review* begins publication; it is colloquially

TEXTS		CONTEXTS	
1847	Asenath Hatch Nicholson: *Ireland's Welcome to a Stranger; or an Excursion through Ireland, in 1844 and 1845, for the Purpose of Personally Investigating the Condition of the Poor.*	1847	known as "the *Dial* with a beard," presumably because of its male editorship—Ralph Waldo Emerson, Theodore Parker, and J. Elliot Cabot—and its focus on politics and literary criticism.
	Mrs. Henry Owen: *The Illuminated Book of Needlework.*		The Chicago *Tribune* begins publication.
	E.D.E.N. Southworth (1819–1899), *Retribution*, the first of more than 60 novels by one of the most prolific and widely read novelists of her day; it is first serialized in the Washington, D.C., newspaper *National Era.*		The imprint of Little, Brown & Co. is first used.
			The American Association for the Advancement of Science is founded.
1847–1903		1847–1903	The *New York Ledger* appears as a weekly story-paper; it features such writers as "Fanny Fern" (Sara Payson Willis Parton), E.D.E.N. Southworth, and Harriet Beecher Stowe.
1848	*Cherokee Rose Bud*, a school newsletter, is published by the Cherokee Female Seminary in Tahlequah, Oklahoma. Nancy E. Hicks, a member of the Cherokee people, serves as editor for a time.	1848	Gold is discovered in California.
	Elizabeth Ellet (1812?–1877), first historian of		The first Chinese woman immigrant, Marie Seise, disembarks in San Francisco. She arrives on the *Eagle* with the Charles V. Gillespie household, for whom she works as a servant.

TEXTS	CONTEXTS
1848 American women: *The Women of the American Revolution*, 2 vols., supplemented by *Domestic History of the American Revolution* in 1850.	1848 New York State passes its Married Women Property Act.

American women: *The Women of the American Revolution*, 2 vols., supplemented by *Domestic History of the American Revolution* in 1850.

Eliza Leslie: *Amelia; or, A Young Lady's Vicissitudes*, a novel.

Maria Jane McIntosh: *Charms and Counter-Charms*, a novel depicting the need for women's emotional independence; it sells over 100,000 copies.

Almira Hart Phelps: *Ida Norman; or, Trials and Their Uses*, a moral novel.

Catharine Maria Sedgwick: *The Boy of Mount Rhigi*.

Elizabeth Oakes Smith: *The Salamander*.

Louisa Caroline Tuthill: *History of Architecture from the Earliest Times*.

New York State passes its Married Women Property Act.

The "Declaration of Sentiments and Resolutions" is delivered at the Seneca Falls Convention, becoming the first major document to define the issues and goals of the 19th-century's woman's rights movement. Because of censures on women speaking in public, a man chairs the meeting, although the "Declaration" itself is written by Elizabeth Cady Stanton, Lucrettia Mott, and other women. The first formal woman's rights convention in the country draws about 300 people and receives much negative press.

The first school integration suit is filed in Boston by African American Benjamin Roberts, whose daughter, Sarah, is forced to pass five white schools every day on her way to her segregated school. In 1849, in *Sarah C. Roberts v. City of Boston*, the state supreme court is the first to use the "separate but equal" doctrine in upholding the legality of segregation.

TEXTS	CONTEXTS
1848	1848 The utopian Oneida Community, noted for its liberated sexual arrangements and practice of birth control, is established; it disbands in 1881.
	The Fox sisters, Margaret and Kate, launch the spiritualist craze when they claim to be mediums for a spirit named Charles B. Rosma. The spirits "communicate" with them through rappings; these sounds are later revealed to have been produced by the sisters' double-jointed toes.
	The Working Women's Protective Union is formed.
	The Free Soil Party is founded.
	Zachary Taylor is elected President.
	Chewing gum is first sold commercially in the U.S.
1849 Representative of many women of her era, Catherine Haun keeps a diary of her trip across the plains with her family. Caroline Kirkland: *Holidays Abroad*.	1849 Harriet "Moses" Tubman escapes from slavery and spends the next decade helping other slaves to escape through "The Underground Railroad." Elizabeth Blackwell becomes the first woman to earn her medical degree

TEXTS	CONTEXTS
1849 Lucretia Mott (1793– 1880), abolitionist, femi- nist, author: *Discourse on Woman*.	1849 (from Geneva Medical School in New York, where the all-male stu- dent body had agreed to admit her as a sort of prac- tical joke).
Mary Sargeant Nichols (1810–1884): *Agnes Morris; or, The Heroine of Domestic Life* and *The Two Loves; or, Eros and Anteros*, both published anony- mously.	Cholera epidemic. Amelia Jenks Bloomer, ad- vocate for women's dress reform, begins editing and publishing *Lily*, a feminist temperance paper.
Catharine Seeley: *Memoir of Catharine Seeley, Late of Darien, Connecticut*.	Lilly Martin Spencer (1822–1902), renowned artist and painter of still lifes and family life,
Lydia Sigourney: *The Young Ladies' Offering; or, Gems of Prose and Poetry*.	moves with her family to New York, where she studies and exhibits at the National Academy of De- sign. She supports her family through her paint- ing while her husband takes care of domestic re- sponsibilities; their mar- riage lasts 46 years and produces 13 children. One of the most popular of the genre painters, she specializes in humorous domestic scenes such as *Domestic Happiness, The Jolly Washerwoman, Peel- ing Onions*, and *The Young Husband: First Marketing*. Throughout the century, many of her works are re- produced as lithographs and engravings.

TEXTS	CONTEXTS
1849	1849 The safety pin is invented. Agdalena Goodman patents a broom-duster.
1850s	1850s Women begin suing for custody of children in divorce cases, and winning. Spiritualism's popularity soars in the U.S.; many seances are held and at least six periodicals devoted to the subject appear. Women begin working as waitresses in restaurants. Approximately 6000 prostitutes are working in New York City, or one for every 64 men.
1850 Catharine Beecher: *Truth Stranger than Fiction.* Emily Edson Briggs: *Ellen Parry; or, Trials of the Heart.* Susan Fenimore Cooper: *Rural Hours*, a nature diary. Eliza Ann Dupuy (1814–1880): *The Conspirator*, a gothic fiction. Ann Lewis Hardeman, living near Jackson, Mississippi, with her extended	1850 U.S. population totals 23 million; this includes 3.2 million blacks, approximately 1,827,550 of whom are female, and 1,601,779 of these are slaves. As part of the Compromise of 1850, territories won in the Mexican War are allowed to enter the union as either free or slave states according to their respective constitutions upon admission. The slave trade is abolished in Washington,

TEXTS		CONTEXTS
1850	family, begins keeping a journal of her life and religious thought; she continues it through 1867. Caroline Lee Hentz: *Linda; or, The Young Pilot of the Belle Creole*, a novel. Charlotte A. Jerauld (1820–1845): *Chronicles and Sketches of Hazlehurst: Poetry and Prose by Mrs. Charlotte A. Jerauld, with a Memoir by Henry Bacon,* published posthumously. Jerauld is believed to have been writing some of the works in this volume as early as 1843. Sara Jane Lippincott (1823–1904), writing under the pseudonym "Grace Greenwood," journalist, travel writer: *Greenwood Leaves,* best-seller combining tales, sketches, letters, and parodies. Alice Emilly Bradley Neal (1827–1863): *The Gossips of Rivertown: With Sketches in Prose and Verse.* Nancy Prince (1799–?): *A Narrative of the Life and Travels of Mrs. Nancy Prince,* travel narration of an African American woman who went abroad with her husband, em-	1850	D.C., as a concession to the North, but the Fugitive Slave Law, requiring escaped slaves to be returned to their masters, is also incorporated into the Compromise as a concession to the South. A California statute nullifies all marriages between whites and "Negroes [or] mulattoes." Seventeen states now grant a married woman the legal right to own and manage her own property. Author E.D.E.N. Southworth makes inquiries in Washington, D.C., about a divorce from her husband; her editor, Robert Bonner, gets a bill submitted to Congress on Southworth's behalf which would give D.C. courts the power to grant divorces. *Harper's New Monthly Magazine* begins publication; its circulation soon tops 200,000 largely due to its handsome illustrations and its serializing of popular English novels. Alabama passes the first adoption law; Massachusetts follows the next year.

TEXTS	CONTEXTS

1850

ployed by the czar of Russia.

Lydia Sigourney: *Poems for the Sea.*

Sojourner Truth (1797?–1883): *Narrative of Sojourner Truth, Northern Slave, Emancipated from Bodily Servitude by the State of New York, in 1828* (ghostwritten). Born into slavery with the name Isabella, she takes the name Sojourner Truth from mystical visions she had in 1843 and becomes one of the most forceful female orators of her time.

Susan Warner, writing as "Elizabeth Wetherell" (1819–1885): *The Wide, Wide World.* After numerous rejections, including a dismissive "fudge" from the house of Harper, Warner submits her manuscript to the house of Putnam; when Putnam brings it home to his mother, thinking she would find it amusing, she begs him to publish it at once. Putnam does so, and it goes on to become a huge bestseller. With this novel, Warner becomes the first U.S. woman author to sell one million copies. Many other women writers turn

1850

Married couples have an average of 5.42 children.

Infant mortality among slaves is twice that for whites.

The Female (later Woman's) Medical College of Pennsylvania, one of the first medical colleges for women, is established.

When Lucy Sessions graduates with a degree in literature from Oberlin College, she becomes the first known African American woman in the U.S. to earn a college degree.

Abby Alcott, mother of author Louisa May and wife of educator Bronson, opens an employment agency in Boston and advocates fair and equal wages for immigrant women.

Maria Mitchell becomes the first woman elected to the American Academy of Arts and Sciences; in 1847 she identifies the comet known as Comet Mitchell, becoming the first person to identify a comet with a telescope. She is considered one of the greatest women scientists

TEXTS	CONTEXTS
1850 to Putnam, hoping to du-plicate her success.	**1850** of her generation and en-courages many women to enter scientific fields.
	P. T. Barnum announces that he will be bringing the world-renowned "Swedish Nightingale," Jenny Lind, to the U.S. for a tour of 150 concerts. Lind is to be paid $1000 plus half of all receipts for each concert. The tour is a great success. The fol-lowing year Lind, now the "Sweetheart of All America," weds her pian-ist in Boston.
	Antoinette Brown (Black-well) completes theologi-cal courses at Oberlin but is not allowed to graduate because of her sex. Al-though Oberlin is coedu-cational, it will not grant a woman a degree in the-ology.
1850–60	**1850–60** In every year of this ten-year period except 1857, a National Woman's Rights Convention is held.
1850–1885	**1850–1885** At least 26 different types of pessaries—a diaphragm-like contracep-tive—are patented.

* * *

TEXTS		CONTEXTS	
1851	Catharine Beecher: *The True Remedy for the Wrongs of Woman.*	1851	Black activist Sojourner Truth, after listening to descriptions of "woman's" frailty and dependency, gives her famous speech, asking "Ain't I a Woman?"
	Alice Cary (1820–1871), regionalist fiction writer: *Clovernook, or Recollections of Our Neighborhood in the West*, sketches of frontier life from a woman's perspective.		The Cherokee Female Seminary opens in Park Hill, Oklahoma. Destroyed by fire in 1887, it is rebuilt in Tahlequah, Oklahoma, eventually to become Northeastern Oklahoma State University.
	Caroline Chesebro' (1825–1873), author of 20 volumes of fiction: *Dream-land by Daylight: A Panorama of Romance*, a collection of stories.		The *New York Times* is established.
	Muriel Goaman: *Judy's Book of Sewing and Knitting.*		Isaac M. Singer devises the continuous stitch sewing machine.
	Caroline Lee Hentz: *Rena; or, the Snow Bird*, a novel.		An ice-making machine is invented.
	Jane Caroline North, a society belle in South Carolina, keeps a two-year journal of her experiences.		Elizabeth Smith Miller invents the trouser-like undergarments that would later come to be known as "bloomers" after they are worn by feminist Amelia Bloomer.
	Elizabeth Stuart Phelps (1815–1852), author of five children's books, two novels, and several volumes of stories, sometimes written under "H. Trusta" and sometimes anonymously: *Kitty Brown and Her Bible Verses*, for children, and *The Sunny*		Elizabeth Taylor-Greenfield (1809–1876), widely acclaimed vocalist with a range embracing 27 notes, first appears before audiences in New

TEXTS		CONTEXTS
1851	*Side; or, The Country Minister's Wife*, a novel.	1851	York City. She will later tour across Europe.

	Lydia Sigourney: *Letters to My Pupils: with Narrative and Biographical Sketches.*	The first school to train African American girls to be teachers opens in Washington, D.C. It closes in 1859.
	E.D.E.N. Southworth: *The Mother-in-Law; or, The Isle of Rays* and *The Discarded Daughter.*	

1852	Alice Cary: *Hagar: A Story for Today* and *Lyra and Other Poems.*	1852	Catharine Beecher founds the American Women's Education Association.
	Caroline Chesebro': *Isa: A Pilgrimage*, a novel.	Rebecca Mann Pennell of Antioch College in Ohio becomes the first woman college professor at a coed institution granted the same privileges as male professors; at other such schools women professors are, among other things, typically not allowed to attend faculty meetings.
	Sarah Josepha Hale compiles the 903-page *Woman's Record; or Sketches of All Distinguished Women, from "the Beginning" till A.D. 1850. Arranged in Four Eras with Selections from Female Writers of Every Age.*	
	Caroline Lee Hentz: *Marcus Warland* and *Eoline; or, Magnolia Vale.*	Women represent the majority of public school teachers.
	Elizabeth Stuart Phelps: *The Angel over the Right Shoulder*, a collection of stories; *Kitty Brown and Her Little School*, for children; and *A Peep at "Number Five"; or, A Chapter in the Life of a City Pastor*, a novel.	The *Lady's Home Magazine* is first published. The first "day nursery" opens in New York City. *Godey's Lady's Book* begins featuring paragraphs headed "Employment of

TEXTS	CONTEXTS
1852 Lydia Allen Rudd keeps a diary of her experiences journeying across the frontier to settle in Oregon. E.D.E.N. Southworth: *The Curse of Clifton*, one of this prolific author's most popular books. Later editions were entitled *Fallen Pride* and *The Mountain-Girl's Love*. Harriet Beecher Stowe: *Uncle Tom's Cabin; or, Life Among the Lowly*. It had appeared serially in *National Era* in 1851. During its first year 350,000 copies are sold, garnering the author $10,000 in the first three months. Anna Warner, writing as "Amy Lothrop": *Dollars and Cents*. Susan Warner, writing as "Elizabeth Wetherell": *Queechy*.	**1852** Women," which focus on women in business and industry. The first paper bags are manufactured. The word "lingerie" comes into general circulation. Matrimonial agencies arranging marriages for couples become popular. Antioch College becomes the first nonsectarian college to grant women and men absolutely equal rights. Franklin Pierce is elected President. E. P. Dutton begins his publishing career as a partner in the firm of Ide & Dutton; in 1858, he buys his partner out and renames the firm E. P. Dutton & Co.
1852–1898	**1852–1898** *Arthur's Home Magazine* is in circulation.
1853 Alice Cary: *Clovernook; or, Recollections of Our Neighborhood in the West*, second series. Caroline Chesebro': *The Children of Light*, a novel.	**1853** Antoinette Brown Blackwell, woman's rights reformer, theologian, and social scientist, becomes the first ordained woman minister of a mainstream U.S. denomination.

TEXTS	CONTEXTS
1853 Paulina Davis begins publishing *Una*, the first woman's rights newspaper in the U.S.	1853 A group of women, concerned over the deterioration of Washington's estate, form the Mount Vernon Ladies' Association, raise some $200,000, and succeed in buying the estate in 1859 for preservation.
Sarah Josepha Hale: *The New Household Receipt Book.*	
Caroline Lee Hentz: *Helen and Arthur; or, Miss Thusa's Spinning-Wheel.*	A fire burns the plant of the famous publishing house of Harper & Bros. to the ground, causing a loss of more than one million dollars; a huge crowd gathers to watch the fire, and when the new fire-proof buildings are built two years later, they become instant tourist attractions.
Caroline Kirkland: *The Helping Hand*, about her experiences as an officer of the Female Department of the New York Prison Association, and *A Book for the Home Circle.*	
Maria Jane McIntosh: *The Lofty and the Lowly; or, Good in All and None All-Good.*	American surgeon Walter Burnham is credited with performing the first successful hysterectomy by the abdominal route.
Sara Payson Willis Parton, writing as "Fanny Fern" (1811–1872): *Fern Leaves from Fanny's Portfolio.*	
Elizabeth Stuart Phelps: *The Tell-Tale; or, Home Secrets Told by Old Travellers*, a collection of stories, published posthumously.	
Therese Albertine Louisa Robinson, writing as "Talvi": *The Exiles.*	

TEXTS		CONTEXTS
1853	Metta Victoria Fuller Victor (1831–1885), poet, dime novelist, humorist, publishing under several pseudonyms: *The Senator's Son*, a temperance novel. Sarah Helen Whitman (1803–1878), poet and Poe biographer, advocate of educational reforms, divorce, the prevention of cruelty to animals, woman's rights, and universal suffrage: *Hours of Life, and Other Poems.*	1853
1853–1857		1853–1857	*Putnam's Monthly Magazine* is published.
1854	Mary Ann Shadd Cary, born in Wilmington, Delaware, and educated in Pennsylvania by Quakers, becomes the first black woman editor when she begins publishing an anti-slavery newspaper, the *Provincial Freeman*, in Canada. Caroline Chesebro': *The Little Cross-Bearers.* Maria Susanna Cummins (1827–1866): *The Lamplighter*, best-selling novel, published anonymously. Julia Caroline Ripley Dorr (1825–1913), novelist, poet, and travel	1854	The first observation of the fusion of sperm and egg proves children inherit equally from mothers and fathers. Kansas-Nebraska Act. The Republican Party is established. Dr. Elizabeth Blackwell founds the New York Infirmary for Women and Children, staffed entirely by women. In 1868 Blackwell opens the Women's Medical College at the Infirmary. Lincoln University, originally called the Ashmum

TEXTS		CONTEXTS	
1854	writer, writing as "Caroline Thomas": *Farmingdale*, a novel.	1854	Institute, becomes the first African American college in the U.S.
	Charlotte L. Forten (Grimké, 1837–1914), abolitionist, poet, and educator, an African American woman born free into a prosperous Philadelphia family, begins keeping a diary which she continues through 1864, then again from 1885 through 1892. Portions of the diary are collected and published as *The Journal of Charlotte L. Forten* in 1953.		In the first substantial Chinese immigration to the U.S., some 13,000 Chinese people arrive in San Francisco.
	Frances Ellen Watkins Harper (1825–1911), African American poet, novelist, abolitionist, and advocate of woman's rights: *Forest Leaves and Poems on Miscellaneous Subjects*.		
	Sarah Marshall Hayden, writing as "Mary Frazaer": *Early Engagements, and Florence (A Sequel)*.		
	Caroline Lee Hentz: *The Planter's Northern Bride*, a novel.		
	Mary Jane Holmes (1825–1907): *Tempest and Sunshine; or, Life in Kentucky*, one of the best-selling novels of the decade.		

TEXTS	CONTEXTS
1854	1854

1854   Jane Elizabeth Roscoe Hornblower: *Vara; or, The Child of Adoption*, a novel, published anonymously.

Caroline Kirkland: *Autumn Hours, and Fireside Reading*.

Sara Willis Parton, writing as "Fanny Fern": *Fern Leaves from Fanny's Portfolio*, second series, and *Little Ferns for Fanny's Little Friends*.

Mary Hayden Green Pike (1824–1908), writing as "Mary Langdon": *Ida May: A Story of Things Actual and Possible*, a novel.

Lydia Sigourney: *The Western Home, and Other Poems* and *Past Meridian*, a nonfiction exploration of old age.

Elizabeth Oakes Smith: *Bertha and Lily; or, The Parsonage of Beech Glen* and *The Newsboy*, a reform novel.

Ann Sophia Stephens: *Fashion and Famine* and *Ladies' Complete Guide to Crochet, Fancy Knitting, and Needlework*.

TEXTS		CONTEXTS	
1854	Harriet Beecher Stowe: "An Appeal to the Women of the Free States."	1854	
	Mary Virginia Terhune (1830–1922), writing as "Marion Harland," novelist, author of influential domestic advice books and cookbooks: *Alone*, a novel.		
	Metta Victoria Fuller Victor: *Fashionable Dissipations*, a temperance novel.		
1855	Harriette Newell Woods Baker (1815–1893): *Cora and the Doctor; or, Revelations of a Physician's Wife*, an evangelical novel, published anonymously.	1855	Peru abolishes slavery; all countries in the Western Hemisphere are now free except Brazil, Cuba, and the U.S.
	Catharine Beecher: *Letters to the People on Health and Happiness*, advocates physical education for women.		In a letter to his publisher, author Nathaniel Hawthorne decries the "scribbling women" whom he claims are saturating the market and stealing his potential readers.
	Caroline Chesebro': *Getting Along: A Book of Illustrations*, an examination of women's commitment to marriage, and *The Beautiful Gate, and Other Stories*.		*Frank Leslie's Illustrated Newspaper*, one of the first illustrated magazines, appears; later known as *Leslie's Weekly*, it stays in print until 1922.
	Lydia Maria Child: *Progress of Religious Ideas through Successive Ages*, 3 vols.		*Cyclopaedia of American Literature* (2 vols.) appears; a supplement is issued in 1866.
	Augusta Jane Evans (Wilson, 1835–1909), prolific		

TEXTS	CONTEXTS
1855 — southern novelist and journalist: *Inez: A Tale of the Alamo*, published anonymously.	1855 — Mary Ann Shadd Cary becomes the first female corresponding member of the National Negro Convention.
Caroline A. Hayden: *Carrie Emerson; or, Life at Cliftonville*, a novel.	Horseback-riding for American ladies becomes fashionable.
Caroline Lee Hentz: *Robert Graham*, a novel.	Abolitionist Lucy Stone is the first U.S. woman to keep her maiden name after marriage.
Mary Jane Holmes: *The English Orphans; or, A Home in the New World*, a novel.	William Alcott publishes *The Young Woman's Book of Health*.
Elizabeth Latimer (1822–1904): *Our Cousin Veronica*.	The Graham Diet becomes popular; it stresses whole grains, fruits, and vegetables and limits animal foods and caffeinated beverages.
Jane E. Locke (1805–1859), poet and newspaper correspondent: *The Recalled, in Voices of the Past, and Poems of the Ideal*.	Hydropathy ("Water Cures") are first prescribed.
Mrs. H. J. Moore: *Anna Clayton; or, The Mother's Trial*, published anonymously.	
Mary Sargeant Nichols: *Mary Lyndon; or, Revelations of a Life*, an autobiographical novel, published anonymously.	
Sara Willis Parton, writing as "Fanny Fern": *Ruth Hall*, a novel.	

TEXTS	CONTEXTS

| 1855 | E.D.E.N. Southworth: *India: The Pearl of Pearl River* and *The Missing Bride; or, Miriam the Avenger*, novels.

Ann Sophia Stephens: *The Old Homestead.*

Harriet Marion Ward Stephens (1823–1858): *Hagar the Martyr; or, Passion and Reality.*

Mary Terhune, writing as "Marion Harland": *The Hidden Path*, a novel.

Anna Warner: *My Brother's Keeper.*

The weekly *Woman's Advocate*, under publisher Anne E. McDowell, becomes the first newspaper operated solely by women. | 1855 | |
| 1856 | Harriette Baker: *The First and the Second Marriages; or, The Courtesies of Wedded Life*, a novel.

Caroline Chesebro': *Philly and Kit* and *Victoria; or The World Overcome*, novels.

Julia Caroline Dorr: *Lanmere*, a novel.

Elizabeth E. Ellet: *Pioneer Women of the West*, compilation of true stories. | 1856 | "Bleeding Kansas": clashes occur between proslavery Border Ruffians and antislavery Free-Staters over whether Kansas will enter the Union as a slave or free state.

The University of Iowa is the first public university to admit female students.

Gregory's Medical School in Boston, originally founded in 1848 to train |

TEXTS		CONTEXTS
1856	Mrs. Benjamin G. Ferris: *The Mormons at Home; With Some Incidents of Travel*, a memoir.	1856 women as midwives, becomes the New England Female Medical College, one of the first medical schools for women.

<table>
<tr><td>

Caroline Lee Hentz: *Ernest Linwood*, a novel, and *Courtship and Marriage; or, The Joys and Sorrows of American Life.*

Mary Jane Holmes: *'Lena Rivers*, a novel.

Jane Elizabeth Hornblower: *Nellie of Truro*, published anonymously.

Maria Jane McIntosh: *Violet; or, The Cross and the Crown*, a novel.

Louise Chandler Moulton (1835–1908), poet, reviewer, novelist, and literary hostess: *Juno Clifford: A Tale*, published anonymously.

Sara Willis Parton, writing as "Fanny Fern": *Rose Clark.*

Mary Pike, writing as "Sydney A. Story, Jr.": *Caste: A Story of Republican Equality*, best-selling novel.

Margaret Junkin Preston (1820–1897), novelist and poet: *Silverwood; A Book of*

</td><td>

When her captain husband falls ill, Mrs. Joshua Patten, only 19 years old, takes command of the clipper *Neptune's Car*, bringing it safely from Cape Horn to San Francisco Bay.

Sixty-six children are killed in a train accident in Philadelphia.

Baking soda is invented.

Gail Borden patents a technique for condensing skimmed milk.

James Buchanan is elected President.

</td></tr>
</table>

TEXTS	CONTEXTS

1856	*Memories*, a novel, published anonymously.	1856	

Anna Cora Mowatt Ritchie: *Mimic Life; or, Before and Behind the Curtain*, collection of novellas.

Eliza Roxey Snow Smith (1804–1886), Mormon poet, hymn writer, and historian: *Poems, Religious, Historical, and Political.*

E.D.E.N. Southworth: *Vivia*, a novel.

Ann Sophia Stephens establishes her own magazine, *Mrs. Stephens' Illustrated New Monthly*. It merges with *Peterson's* in 1858.

Harriet Beecher Stowe: *Dred: A Tale of the Great Dismal Swamp.*

Louisa Caroline Tuthill: *Reality; or, The Millionaire's Daughter*, a novel.

Metta Victoria Fuller Victor: *Mormon Wives.*

Susan Warner: *The Hills of Shatemuc*, published anonymously.

TEXTS	CONTEXTS
1856 Frances Whitcher: *The Widow Bedott Papers*, published posthumously.	**1856**
1857 Harriette Newell Baker, writing as "Mrs. Madeline Leslie": *The Household Angel in Disguise*, a novel.	**1857** In its infamous Dred Scott decision, the Supreme Court upholds the Fugitive Slave Law and denies citizenship to blacks.
Mary Hartwell Catherwood (1847–1902): *A Woman in Armor.*	Mrs. Carl Schurz opens the first private "kindergarten" in America in Watertown, Wisconsin.
Maria Susanna Cummins: *Mabel Vaughan*, a novel, published anonymously.	*Atlantic* magazine (later *Atlantic Monthly*) is first published under James Russell Lowell's editorship; it is later edited by such literary figures as William Dean Howells and James T. Fields and features many prominent women writers among its contributors.
Mary Andrews Denison: *Gracie Amber*, a novel.	
Eliza Ann Dupuy: *The Planter's Daughter: A Tale of Louisiana*, a novel.	
Mrs. Gaugain: *The Lady's Assistant in Knitting, Netting, and Crochet Work.*	
Mary Jane Holmes: *Meadow-Brook.*	The first issue of *Harper's Weekly* appears.
Mrs. H. J. Moore: *The Golden Legacy: A Story of Life's Phases*, published anonymously.	The "Liberty" press, an early mechanized press which would greatly enhance and speed the process of printing, is introduced.
Sara Willis Parton, writing as "Fanny Fern": *Fresh Leaves*, humorous essays.	In the financial panic of this year, John P. Jewett, publisher of such best-sellers as Stowe's *Uncle*

TEXTS		CONTEXTS	
1857	Anna Cora Mowatt Ritchie: *Twin Roses: A Narrative.*	1857	*Tom's Cabin* and Cummins's *The Lamplighter,* fails.
	Mary Seacole (1805?-1881), free-born Jamaican Creole autobiographer: *Wonderful Adventures of Mrs. Seacole in Many Lands.*		
	Catharine Maria Sedgwick: *Married or Single?.*		
	E.D.E.N. Southworth: *Vivia; or, The Secret of Power.*		
	Ann Sophia Stephens: *The Heiress of Greenhurst: An Autobiography.*		
	Mary Terhune, writing as "Marion Harland": *Moss-Side,* a novel.		
1858	"Aunt Sally": *Aunt Sally, or the Cross the Way of Freedom. Narrative of the Slave-Life and Purchase of the Mother of Rev. Isaac Williams of Detroit, Michigan.*	1858	Lucy Stone becomes the first woman to be arrested for civil disobedience by refusing to pay property taxes until women are granted suffrage.
	Mary Andrews Denison: *Old Hepsy,* a novel.		In New York City, 35 women meet and form the Ladies Christian Association, the forerunner of the Young Women's Christian Association (YWCA). The group formed in Boston in 1866 is the first to use the title
	Alice Emilly Bradley Neal, writing as "Alice Haven": *The Coopers; or, Getting Under Way,* a novel.		

TEXTS	CONTEXTS
1858	1858
Mrs. E. N. Gladding: *Leaves from an Invalid's Journal and Poems.*	YWCA.
Mary Pike: *Agnes*, published anonymously.	During a speech in Indiana, activist Sojourner Truth is forced to expose her breasts to prove that she is a woman.
Henrietta Rose: *Nora Wilmot: A Tale of Temperance and Woman's Rights.*	The Mason jar is patented.
Lydia Sigourney: *Lucy Howard's Journal*, a novel.	The first Pullman sleeping car comes into use on trains.
Ann Sophia Stephens: *Mary Derwent*, a novel.	Transatlantic cable is laid.
Virginia Frances Townsend (1836–1920), author of magazine articles, novels for young girls, and this adult novel: *While It Was Morning.*	Activist Anna Reeves Jarvis organizes the first Mother's Day, called Mothers' Work Day.
1859	1859
Lillie Devereux Blake (1833–1913), novelist: *Southwold.*	Abolitionist John Brown leads the Harpers Ferry raid and is later executed.
Alice Cary: *Pictures of Country Life* and *Adopted Daughter and Other Tales.*	The last African slave ship, *Clothilde*, lands in Alabama.
Mary Andrews Denison: *Opposite the Jail*, published anonymously.	Dr. Maria Zakrzewska, former medical associate of Elizabeth Blackwell, joins the staff at the New
Abigail Scott Duniway (1834–1915): *Captain Gray's Company; or, Crossing the Plains and Living in*	England Female Medical College. In 1862, she resigns and goes on to found the soon presti-

TEXTS		CONTEXTS
1859	*Oregon*, a semi-autobiographical novel. Augusta Jane Evans (Wilson): *Beulah*, a novel. Frances Ellen Watkins Harper: "The Two Offers," the first short story published by an African American person in America. Florence Hartley: *The Ladies' Hand Book of Fancy and Ornamental Work*. Mary Jane Holmes: *Dora Deane; or, The East India Uncle*, a novel. Elizabeth King: *Memoir of Elizabeth T. King; with Extracts from Her Letters and Journals*. Phoebe W. Palmer: *Promise of the Father*, arguing for the right of women to preach. Sara Willis Parton, writing as "Fanny Fern": *Folly As It Flies*, humorous essays. E.D.E.N. Southworth: *The Hidden Hand*, one of Southworth's most popular novels. Harriet Beecher Stowe: *The Minister's Wooing*, a novel.	1859	gious New England Hospital for Women and Children. The temporary insanity defense is used for the first time in the U.S. to defend Congressman Dan Sickles, accused of murdering his wife's lover. A patent for "kerosene" is taken out. Mary Edmonia Lewis (1845–1890?), sculptor of Chippewa and African heritage, is admitted to the preparatory school at Oberlin in fall 1859. In addition to busts of Abraham Lincoln, John Brown, and Henry Wadsworth Longfellow, Lewis is known for her statues *The Death of Cleopatra* and *Forever Free*, which shows an African American woman and man removing shackles at the moment of freedom. A controversial divorce reform bill passes the Indiana state legislature, allowing cruelty, desertion, and drunkenness as grounds for divorce.

TEXTS	CONTEXTS
1859 Harriet E. Wilson (1807– 1870): *Our Nig; or, Sketches from the Life of a Free Black, in a Two-Story White House, North. Showing That Slavery's Shadows Fall Even There*, first known novel by an African American.	1859
1860s	1860s Comedienne Lotta Crabtree (1847–1924), who had become a sensation as a child entertaining miners in the California Gold Rush, tours the country in various theater productions and becomes the nation's highest paid female performer.
1860 Margaret Irvin Carrington: *Ab-sa-ra-ka, Home of the Crows: Being the Experiences of an Officer's Wife on the Plains, and Marking the Vicissitudes of Peril and Pleasure During the Occupation of the New Route to Virginia City, Montana, 1866–7, and the Indian Hostilities Thereto; With Outlines of the Natural Features and Resources of the Land, Tables of Distances, Maps and Other Aids to the Traveler; Gathered from Observation and Other Reliable Sources.* Maria Susanna Cummins: *El Fureidis*, published anonymously.	1860 U.S. population totals 31 million, including 3.5 million slaves; 35 percent of the increase in the population since 1851 can be accounted for by immigration. Erastus Beadle's Dime Novels are first published; 321 such novels are issued in the series before it becomes Beadle's New Dime Novels, whose 309 volumes are all reprints from the initial series. This is the first year Native Americans—albeit only "civilized" ones (i.e., residents of reserva-

TEXTS		CONTEXTS	
1860	Caroline Wells Dall (1822–1912), feminist advocate of coeducation and higher education for women: *Woman's Right to Labor; or, Low Wages and Hard Work*.	1860	tions)—are counted by the census.

The first run of the Pony Express takes place.

Mary Andrews Denison: *The Mad Hunter*, a dime novel.

Only five states, all in New England, grant blacks suffrage.

Miriam Coles Harris (1834–1925): *Rutledge*, a gothic novel.

Some 20,000 women shoe workers in Lynn, Massachusetts, go on strike.

Isabella Beecher Hooker: "Shall Women Vote? A Matrimonial Dialogue."

Anna Dickinson, the abolitionist Lyceum lecturer and advocate of women's, laborers', and immigrants' rights, delivers her first speech. Critics have suggested that Bayard Taylor's novel *Hannah Thurston* (1864) and Henry James's *The Bostonians* (1886) both model characters after Dickinson and treat those characters and their position on women's rights with ambiguity if not derision.

Mrs. H. J. Moore: *Wild Nell, the White Mountain Girl*, a novel.

Harriet Prescott Spofford (1835–1921), prolific author of novels, poetry, biographies, children's stories, travel literature, memoirs, and the genre for which she is best known, short stories: *Sir Rohan's Ghost: A Romance*, a novel.

Olympia Brown becomes the first U.S. woman to study theology in full fellowship with men at St. Lawrence University.

Ann Sophia Stephens's *Malaeska: The Indian Wife of the White Hunter* is published as the first issue of Beadle's Dime Novels. It had first appeared as a se-

Elizabeth Palmer Peabody opens the country's first formally organized private kindergarten.

TEXTS		CONTEXTS	
1860	rial in *The Ladies' Companion* in 1839. Metta Victoria Fuller Victor: *Alice Wilde, the Raftsman's Daughter*, Dime Novel No. 4. Anna Warner and Susan Warner, writing as "Susan Wetherell" and "Amy Lothrop": *Say and Seal*. Rhoda Elizabeth White, writing as "Uncle Ben," novelist, humorist, educational reformer: *Mary Staunton; or, The Pupils of Marvel Hall*.	1860	The national network of railroads includes some 30,000 miles of tracks; by 1890 there would be 164,000 miles. Of approximately 35,000 Chinese in America, only 1,784 are women; 85 percent of Chinese women living in San Francisco are prostitutes. Croquet, introduced from England, becomes popular with women and especially with young bourgeois lovers as a courting activity. Abraham Lincoln becomes President and South Carolina immediately secedes from the Union, soon to be followed by other southern states.
1860–1870		1860–1870	With increasing African American in-migration, the urban black population increases by 75 percent overall.
1860–1890		1860–1890	Largely as a result of efforts by the American Medical Association to delegitimize "irregular" practitioners such as midwives, 40 states and territories enact anti-abortion statutes.

* * *

1861   Jane Andrews (1833–
1887): *Seven Little Sisters
Who Live on the Round
Ball That Floats in the Air*,
written to supplement ge-
ography lessons and to
present different cultures
while emphasizing the kin-
ship of children through-
out the world.

Rebecca Harding Davis
(1831–1910), a pioneer in
American literary realism
and naturalism, one of the
most widely read authors
of her day (she produced
at least 11 novels, more
than 260 short stories, 50
essays, and an autobiography): *Life in the Iron Mills*,
appears anonymously in
Atlantic Monthly.

Gail Hamilton (pseud-
onym of Mary Abigail
Dodge, 1833–1896):
*Country Living and Coun-
try Thinking*, urges
women to consider ca-
reers other than marriage,
and especially to consider
writing.

Julia Ward Howe (1819–
1910), poet, dramatist, biographer, travel writer,
and feminist, writes the
lyrics to the "Battle
Hymn of the Republic"
(published in *Atlantic
Monthly*, February 1862).

1861

TEXTS	CONTEXTS
1861 Harriet Jacobs (1813– 1897), writing as "Linda Brent": *Incidents in the Life of a Slave Girl*, the first true full-length slave narrative by a woman published in America. Metta Victoria Fuller Victor: *Maum Guinea and Her Plantation Children*, the most popular of her contributions to the Beadle's Dime Novel series.	**1861**
1861–1865	**1861–1865** U.S. Civil War: When Cuban-born Loreta Janeta Velasquez's husband joins the Confederate Army, Velasquez also enlists under the alias Harry T. Buford, raising "his" own regiment. Velasquez was among some 400 women to fight as Confederates.
1862 Laura Brewster Boquist keeps a journal in 1862 that is published as *Crossing the Plains with Ox Teams* in 1932. Rebecca Harding Davis: *Margaret Howth*, a novel. Emily Dickinson (1830– 1886), at the age of 31, sends four poems to Thomas Wentworth Higginson.	**1862** Abraham Lincoln abolishes slavery. The Union army admits African American troops. Author Louisa May Alcott volunteers as a nurse in the Civil War. In its first annual report, the Department of Agriculture describes the typical farm woman as a "laboring drudge," working

TEXTS		CONTEXTS	
1862	Elizabeth Drew Stoddard (1823–1902), *The Morgesons*, first of several novels and a children's book.	1862	harder than her husband or any other farm hand or hired help.
	Harriet Beecher Stowe: *The Pearl of Orr's Island: A Story of the Coast of Maine.*		
	Jane Gould Tourtillott keeps a diary of her journey from Mitchell, Iowa, to California.		
	Frances Fuller Victor (1826–1902), author of realistic dime novels, short stories, sentimental poetry, satire, history, and travel books: *The Land Claim: A Tale of the Upper Missouri.*		
	Constance Fenimore Woolson (1840–1894), a novelist, short-story writer, poet, and essayist: *Two Women*, a long narrative poem.		
1863	*Memoir of Old Elizabeth, a Coloured Woman*, a slave narrative and spiritual autobiography of a woman born in 1766; she is 97 when her story is recorded.	1863	Anna Callendar Bracket becomes the first woman principal of a normal (teacher-training) school.
			Roller skating is introduced in America.
	Louisa May Alcott (1832–1888), editor of *Merry's Museum*, a magazine for		President Lincoln declares Thanksgiving Day a national holiday.

TEXTS	CONTEXTS
1863 girls; feminist and prolific author of seven novels for girls and two for adults and 16 collections of stories, as well as several Gothic thrillers under the pseudonym "A. M. Barnard": *Hospital Sketches*, an account of her Civil War days working as a nurse in an army hospital until contracting typhoid fever.	1863 The National Woman's Loyal League is founded by Elizabeth Cady Stanton, Susan B. Anthony, Lucy Stone, and Ernestine Rose as a means of assisting the Union in finding an acceptable political solution to the Civil War.
Caroline Chesebro': *Peter Carradine; or, The Martindale Pastoral* and *The Sparrow's Fall*, novels.	Posters recruiting army nurses for the Civil War stipulate that they be at least 30 years old and "very plain-looking."
Augusta Jane Evans (Wilson): *Macaria; or, Altars of Sacrifice*, a novel.	The rights to the paper dress pattern patented by Eleanor and Ebenezer Butterick are preserved in Ebenezer's name.
Mary Jane Holmes: *Marian Grey; or, The Heiress of Redstone Hall*, a novel.	P. T. Barnum stages the marriage of midgets Mercy Warren and Tom Thumb in New York City, causing a sensation.
Fanny Kemble (1809–1893), actress, diarist, and dramatist: *A Journal of a Residence on a Georgia Plantation in 1838–39*, a critical portrayal of the practice of slavery.	
Maria Jane McIntosh: *Two Pictures; or, What We Think of Ourselves, and What the World Thinks of Us.*	
E.D.E.N. Southworth: *Ishmael*, a novel.	

TEXTS	CONTEXTS
1863 Harriet Prescott Spofford: *The Amber Gods and Other Stories.* Ann Sophia Stephens: *The Rejected Wife.* Susan Warner: *The Old Helmet.* Adeline Dutton Train Whitney (1824–1906), novelist, poet, and writer of nonfiction works for children and adults: *Faith Gartney's Girlhood.* It sells over 300,000 copies and establishes the theme she would revisit in many works, the passage of a young woman from child to adult.	1863
1863–1864	1863–1864 Diphtheria becomes a major health concern.
1864 Louisa May Alcott: *Moods,* a novel. Caroline Chesebro': *Amy Carr,* a novel. Jane Cunningham Croly (1829–1901): *Jennie Junei-ana: Talks on Women's Topics.* Maria Susanna Cummins: *Haunted Hearts,* a novel, published anonymously. Mary Andrews Denison: *The Mill Agent,* a novel.	1864 Rebecca Lee becomes the first known African American woman to receive a medical degree, from New England Female Medical College.

TEXTS	CONTEXTS

1864 Eliza Woodson Farnham: *Woman and Her Era*.   **1864**

Caroline Kirkland: *The School-Girl's Garland*.

Mary Ann Webster Loughborough: *My Cave Life in Vicksburg. With Letters of Trial and Travel. By a Lady*.

E.D.E.N. Southworth: *Self-Raised*, a sequel to *Ishmael*.

Harriet Prescott Spofford: *Azarian: An Episode*.

Ann Sophia Stephens: *The Indian Queen*.

Mary Terhune, writing as "Marion Harland": *Husbands and Homes*, a novel.

Susan Warner: *Melbourne House*, a novel.

1865 Alice Cary: *Married Not Mated; or, How They Lived at Woodside and Throckmorton Hall*, a novel.

Caroline Chesebro': *The Fishermen of Gamp's Island* and *The Glen Cabin*.

Mary Mapes Dodge (1830–1905): *Hans Brinker; or, The Silver Skates*.

1865 For every 100 women aged 20, more than five would be dead of tuberculosis by age 30, eight by age 50.

The Thirteenth Amendment to the U.S. Constitution abolishes slavery.

President Lincoln is assassinated; Andrew Johnson becomes President and

TEXTS	CONTEXTS
1865 Julia Deane Freeman, writing as "Mary Forest": *Women of the South Distinguished in Literature*, an anthology of biographical sketches and selections from 34 authors.	1865 survives a trial for impeachment three years later.
Elizabeth Stuart Phelps (Ward, 1844–1911), who adopted her author mother's name, novelist, short-story writer, essayist, and feminist: *Up Hill; or, Life in the Factory*, a novel.	Mary E. Surratt becomes the first woman hanged by the U.S. government; she is sentenced to death for her alleged part in the conspiracy to murder President Lincoln.
Margaret Junkin Preston: *Beechenbrook: A Rhyme of the War*, a long narrative poem popular in the Confederacy.	The Black Codes are passed in the South, designed to replace slavery with a caste system that would differ little from that of antebellum days.
Elizabeth Stoddard: *Two Men*, a novel.	The Ku Klux Klan is founded in Pulaski, Tennessee.
Harriet Beecher Stowe: *House and Home Papers*.	By this date, 29 states have adopted some form of married women's property law.
Adeline Whitney: *The Gayworthys*.	Vassar College in New York opens; it is the first full-program woman's college.
	The Nation is first published; it is still in print.
	The first cylindrical rotary press is invented.
	The first carpet sweeper comes into use.

TEXTS	CONTEXTS
1865	1865 Dr. Ann Preston begins a seven-year tenure as the first woman dean of a medical school.
1865–1899 *Demorest's Monthly Magazine*, edited by Jane C. Croly (known as "Jenny June"), is the first women's magazine to staple tissue-paper dress patterns in each issue.	1865–1899
1866 Augusta Jane Evans (Wilson): *St. Elmo*, a novel. It is staged as a play in 1909, and filmed in 1914.	1866 Dr. Mary Edwards Walker becomes the first woman to win the Congressional Medal of Honor for her service as assistant surgeon during the Civil War.

1866 (TEXTS continued):

Vivian Fine writes "Meeting for Equal Rights 1866," a musical composition celebrating the women's movement.

The Story of Mattie J. Jackson, a slave narrative dictated to Dr. L. S. Thompson.

Mary Lowell Putnam (1810–1898), novelist and abolitionist: *Fifteen Days: An Extract from Edward Colvil's Journal.*

Metta Victoria Fuller Victor, under the pseudonym "Seeley Regester," publishes the first American detective novel: *The Dead Letter: An American Romance.*

1866 (CONTEXTS continued):

Congress enacts a Civil Rights act over President Johnson's veto and puts an official end to the Black Codes.

Lucy B. Hobbs, an African American, is the first known woman to graduate from dental school (Cincinnati, Ohio) and the first practicing female dentist in the U.S.

Elizabeth Cady Stanton becomes the first woman candidate for Congress.

Cholera epidemic.

Whites rob, attack, rape,

TEXTS	CONTEXTS
1866	**1866** and kill blacks and burn their homes in a race riot in Memphis.
	Black laundresses form the Washerwomen of Jackson, Mississippi's first labor organization.
	Sophonisba Breckinridge is born; she becomes an outspoken social worker and advocate for economic equality for women and blacks.
1866–1878	**1866–1878** The New York literary magazine the *Galaxy* is published.
1867 Lydia Maria Child: *A Romance of the Republic*.	**1867** Vermont becomes the last state to pass some sort of child-labor legislation.
Martha Finley (1821–1909): *Elsie Dinsmore*, beginning a series that drew more than 25 million readers.	Dorothea Dix, social reformer who crusades for improvement of the shocking conditions in American prisons and asylums, tours the U.S. investigating mental hospitals and asylums, poor houses, and jails.
Frances "Aunt Fanny" Gage (1808–1884), reformer, editor, author of children's stories: *Elsie Magoon; or, The Old Still-House in the Hollow*.	
Judith W. McGuire: *Diary of a Southern Refugee during the War*.	Howard University in Washington, D.C., is founded.
Sallie A. Putnam: *Richmond During the War:*	The first issue of *Harper's Bazar* appears; in 1929 it changes its name to *Harper's Bazaar*.

TEXTS	CONTEXTS
1867	1867

1867 — *Four Years of Personal Observation.*

Elizabeth Stoddard: *Temple House*, a novel.

Harriet Beecher Stowe: *Daisy's First Winter, and Other Stories.*

Frances Whitcher: *The Widow Spriggins, Mary Elmer, and Other Sketches*, published posthumously.

1867 — Pi Beta Phi, the first national fraternal organization for women, is established at Monmouth College in Illinois.

The cable car is developed.

Emeline Brigham patents a "womb supporter," a type of contraceptive pessary.

1868 — Louisa May Alcott: *Little Women*, a novel modeled on her family.

Alice Cary: *A Lover's Diary.*

Lydia Maria Child: *An Appeal for the Indians.*

Caroline Corbin: *Rebecca; or, A Woman's Secret*, a novel.

Rebecca Harding Davis: *Dallas Galbraith*, a novel, and *Waiting for the Verdict*, a novel.

Martha Finley: *Elsie's Holidays at Roselands.*

Sarah Josepha Hale: *Manners; or, Happy Homes and Good Society All the Year Round.*

1868 — The Fourteenth Amendment grants citizenship to blacks; here black women count only as women and are, as with all other women, denied suffrage.

The first southern Jim Crow laws are passed, devising ways to insure that blacks could not use their new right to vote; many such laws remain on the books until well into the 20th century.

Sorosis, the first women's professional club, is founded in New York City by a group of journalists and other career women when they are barred from attending a New York Press Club dinner for Charles Dickens.

Susan B. Anthony is

TEXTS		CONTEXTS
1868	Isabella Beecher Hooker: "A Mother's Letters to a Daughter on Woman Suffrage."	1868 appointed a delegate to the Democratic presidential convention.

TEXTS

1868   Isabella Beecher Hooker: "A Mother's Letters to a Daughter on Woman Suffrage."

Elizabeth Hobbs Keckley (1824?–1907): *Behind the Scenes; or, Thirty Years a Slave, and Four Years in the White House*, a memoir including her experience as dressmaker to Mary Todd Lincoln.

Estelle Lewis: *Sappho: A Tragedy in Five Acts.*

Elizabeth Parsons Ware Packard: *The Prisoner's Hidden Life; or Insane Asylums Unveiled*, written after Packard's husband, a clergyman, has her committed when she disagrees with him on theological matters. After being a "difficult patient" for three years, she is released into her husband's custody as "incurable" until friends manage to bring the matter to trial. She is found sane after seven minutes of deliberation and spends the rest of her life fighting for the rights of married women and the mentally ill.

Elizabeth Stuart Phelps (Ward): *The Gates Ajar*, a novel.

CONTEXTS

1868   appointed a delegate to the Democratic presidential convention.

South Carolina grants its first divorce.

Mary E. A. Evard patents a Reliance Cook Stove.

Commercial yeast becomes available in stores.

The Pennsylvania Academy of Art offers its first Ladies Life Class with a live nude female model.

Ulysses S. Grant is elected President.

The Working Woman's Association is founded.

The Atlanta *Constitution* begins circulation; it is still Atlanta's newspaper today.

TEXTS	CONTEXTS
1868 Harriet Beecher Stowe: *Oldtown Folks.* Susan Warner: *Daisy*, a novel. Frances Anne Rollins Whipper (1845?–1901), using the pseudonym "Frank A. Rollin": *Life and Public Services of Martin R. Delaney*, first known biography of a free black person.	**1868**
1868–1870 Susan B. Anthony and Elizabeth Cady Stanton publish their woman's rights periodical *The Revolution.*	**1868–1870** *Putnam's Magazine* is in circulation.
1868–1916	**1868–1916** *Lippincott's Magazine*, a monthly literary magazine, is published.
1868–1935	**1868–1935** The San Francisco-based *Overland Monthly* is published.
1869 Harriette Newell Baker, writing as "Mrs. Madeline Leslie": *Juliette; or, Now and Forever.* Sarah Elizabeth Hopkins Bradford: *Scenes in the Life of Harriet Tubman.* Caroline Wells Dall: *Patty Gray's Journey from Boston to Baltimore.*	**1869** The Prohibition Party is founded. St. Louis Law School becomes the first law school to admit women. Belle Mansfield, who read for the law on her own time, becomes the first practicing female attorney in the U.S.

TEXTS		CONTEXTS	
1869	A much-publicized dispute between author Mary Abigail Dodge (pen name Gail Hamilton) and her publisher Ticknor & Fields centers on Dodge's meager royalty rates (7 or 8 percent) compared with the standard author share of 10 percent: as a result of her inquiries into the discrepancy, Dodge is fired as editor of one of the firm's magazines, *Our Young Folks*, and is treated shabbily by her friend and publisher James T. Fields. Dodge appeals to other Ticknor & Fields authors for support and eventually takes the firm to court; she is granted a settlement but, still dissatisfied, decides to contract with Harper Bros. and ultimately writes a book about the brouhaha, *A Battle of Books*.	1869	Elizabeth Cady Stanton and Susan B. Anthony found the National Woman's Suffrage Association (NWSA); that same year Stanton becomes the first woman to testify before a congressional committee.
			Harriet Morrison Irwin becomes the first woman to patent an architectural innovation for a building.
			Disagreeing with the NWSA's tactics and programs, Lucy Stone founds the American Woman Suffrage Association.
			The country's first university press opens at Cornell in 1869.
			The first national women's labor organization, the Daughters of St. Crispin, is founded.
	Frances Ellen Watkins Harper: *Moses: A Story of the Nile*, a collection of poetry.		Donaldina Cameron is born; she becomes a mission superintendent in San Francisco and rescues over 2000 Chinese women and girls from slavery.
	Olive Logan (1839–1909), actress, playwright: *Apropos of Women and the Theater*.		
	Augusta Jane Evans (Wilson): *Vashti; or, "Until*		After the publication of W.H.H. Murray's *Adventures in the Wilderness*, out-

TEXTS		CONTEXTS	
1869	*Death Do Us Part*," a novel. Elizabeth Stuart Phelps (Ward): *Men, Women and Ghosts*, a collection of stories. E.D.E.N. Southworth: *The Fatal Marriage*, a novel. Ann Sophia Stephens: *The Curse of Gold*, a novel.	1869	door camping as a vacation activity for both men and women becomes increasingly popular. The transcontinental railroad is completed.
1870s		1870s	"Grandfather clauses" are added to many voting requirements as a way to keep blacks from voting. Isabella Stewart Gardner (1840–1924) leads a cultural salon sponsoring artists and musicians. Anorexia nervosa is first named and identified. Health reformer Dr. John Harvey Kellogg goes into the cereal business; Battle Creek, Michigan, soon becomes a mecca for those seeking better health through diet.
1870	Rebecca Harding Davis: *Put Out of the Way*, a novel.	1870	U.S. population totals 39 million. Sixty percent of all women workers are em-

TEXTS | CONTEXTS

1870

Abby Morton Diaz (1821–1904), social reformer and prolific author of juvenile fiction: *The William Henry Letters.*

Sara Willis Parton, writing as "Fanny Fern": *Ginger-Snaps*, humor.

Elizabeth Stuart Phelps (Ward): *Hedged In*, a novel.

Rose Porter (1845–1906), religious novelist: *Summer Driftwood for Winter Fire.*

Margaret Junkin Preston: *Old Song and New*, poetry.

Memoir, Letters and Journal of Elizabeth Seton, Convert to the Catholic Faith, and Sister of Charity, Robert Seton, ed.

Lucy Stone begins editing the weekly *Woman's Journal*, a position she holds until her death.

Eliza Ann Youmans (1826– ?), textbook, science, and popular science writer: *The First Book of Botany.*

1870

ployed in domestic service jobs.

Forty percent of black married women in the cotton belt are employed, mostly in field labor; approximately 98 percent of white women in the same region have no gainful occupation. Some 24 percent of black households have one working child under age 16, compared with roughly 14 percent of white households.

The average black mother in the Cotton South has from six to seven children; 80 percent of black households are headed by a married couple.

Smith College is established as a result of a bequest of Sophia Smith; it opens in 1875.

Women represent 21 percent of college graduates.

Esther McQuigg Slack Morris becomes the first woman justice of the peace.

Ellen Swallow, a Vassar graduate, enters the Massachusetts Institute of Technology to pursue an advanced degree in chem-

TEXTS	CONTEXTS
1870	1870

istry. She leaves after obtaining her M.S., claiming that her teachers prevented her from getting her Ph.D. because they did not want the first MIT doctorate in chemistry to go to a woman.

Mary Potts invents a hot iron with a cool hand grip.

Margaret Knight patents a machine that folds and glues paper bags.

In place of the shroud, dead bodies are increasingly arterially embalmed to prevent what had hitherto been seen as natural and unavoidable decay.

Scribner's Monthly is first published; it soon competes with *Harper's* for readers.

Philadelphia Colored Women's Christian Association, thought to be the first black Young Women's Christian Association, is founded.

Kappa Alpha Theta, one of the first sororities, is founded at DePauw University in Greencastle, Indiana.

TEXTS		CONTEXTS	
1870		1870	Ada H. Kepley becomes the first woman to receive a law degree when she graduates from Union College of Law in Chicago.
			The first elevated train appears in New York City.
1870–1910		1870–1910	An average of 6700 southern blacks move north each year.
1871	Louisa May Alcott: *Little Men*, a novel, sequel to *Little Women*.	1871	Frances Elizabeth Willard becomes the first female college president when she is elected to head the Evanston College for Ladies.
	Catharine Beecher: *Woman Suffrage and Woman's Profession*.		"The Great Fire" devastates much of Chicago.
	Alice Cary: *The Born Thrall*.		
	Caroline Chesebro': *The Foe in the Household*, a novel.		P. T. Barnum opens his circus "The Greatest Show on Earth" in New York; ten years later, a merger results in Barnum and Bailey's.
	Olive Logan: *The Mimic World*, an account of backstage life from stage to circus.		
	Elizabeth Stuart Phelps (Ward): *The Silent Partner*, a novel.		
	Harriet Waters Preston (1836–1911), novelist and expert on Provençal literature: *Aspendale*, a novel in		

TEXTS		CONTEXTS

1871	the form of essays and letters.	1871	
	Harriet Prescott Spofford: *New England Legends.*		
	Celia Thaxter (1835–1894), poet: *Poems.*		

1872	Nearly three-fourths of American novels published this year are written by women.	1872	Victoria Woodhull, New York stockbroker, newspaper editor, and champion of female suffrage, runs for the office of President of the United States as the candidate of the Equal Rights Party.
	Louisa May Alcott: *Aunt Jo's Scrap-Bag,* a collection of short stories.		
	Frances Ellen Watkins Harper: *Sketches of Southern Life.*		Sixteen women, including Susan B. Anthony, are arrested in New York for trying to vote in the presidential election.
	Elizabeth Avery Meriwether (1824–1917?), southern novelist, autobiographer, suffragist: *The Master of Red Leaf,* a novel.		
	Sara Willis Parton, writing as "Fanny Fern": *Caper-Sauce.*		An issue of *Woodhull and Claflin's Weekly,* the paper run by suffragist sisters Victoria Woodhull and Tennessee Claflin, is suppressed by Anthony Comstock for obscenity and libel and its editors are imprisoned; the issue describes a sexual scandal involving Congregational minister Henry Ward Beecher of New York.
	Harriet Beecher Stowe: *Oldtown Fireside Stories.*		
	Mary T. Tardy: *The Living Female Writers of the South,* an anthology encompassing 175 authors.		*Publishers' Weekly* first appears. (Originally titled *Publishers' and Stationers' Weekly Trade Circular,* it
	Anna Warner is the first		

TEXTS	CONTEXTS
1872 female author of a do-it-yourself gardening book, *Gardening by Myself.* Susan Warner: *A Story of Small Beginnings.* Sarah Chauncey Woolsey, writing as "Susan Coolidge" (1835–1905): *What Katy Did*, first in a series.	1872 took its shortened name the following year.) Charlotte E. Ray receives her diploma from Howard University's School of Law and becomes the first known practicing African American woman lawyer in the country. A California statute requires that white students and Chinese and Japanese students attend separate schools. Jane Wells patents her invention, the baby jumper. Opium imports increase from 24,000 in 1840 to 416,724 pounds. Women are reported to be its primary users, usually ingesting it in "tonics." Typhoid ravages the Northeast and scarlet fever and measles are rampant. A great fire in Boston devastates, among other things, the plant of publishing firm James R. Osgood & Co. Montgomery Ward & Company opens as the country's first mail-order house.

TEXTS		CONTEXTS
1873	Louisa May Alcott: *Work, a Story of Experience*, a novel.	1873 Financial panic occurs.

1873

TEXTS

Louisa May Alcott: *Work, a Story of Experience*, a novel.

Isabella Beecher Hooker: *Womanhood: Its Sanctities and Fidelities.*

Sarah Gillespie Huftalen, a rural midwestern woman who works as a teacher and writes essays, poetry, and teacher-training guides, begins keeping a diary of her experiences and continues through 1952. In 1994 it is published as *"All Will Yet Be Well."*

Julia C. R. Dorr: *Expiation*, a novel.

Marietta Holley (1836–1926), humorist: *My Opinions and Betsey Bobbet's: Designed as a Beacon Light, to Guide Women to Life, Liberty, and the Pursuit of Happiness, but Which May Be Read by Members of the Sterner Sect, without Injury to Themselves or the Book.*

Eliza Jane Poitevent Nicholson, writing as "Pearl Rivers" (1848–1896), poet and journalist: *Lyrics.*

Harriet Almaria Baker Suddoth, southern novelist writing as "Lumina Sil-

1873

CONTEXTS

Financial panic occurs.

The Comstock Law makes it illegal to send birth control information, branded "obscene," through the mails.

In *Bradwell v. Illinois*, the Supreme Court rules against Myra Bradwell's attempt to gain admittance to the Illinois State Bar, arguing that it is not a privilege of citizenship and justifying its decision with claims of inherent differences between women and men; the case sets a precedent often cited to defend women's exclusion from professional careers.

Susan McKinney is the first black woman to be formally certified as a physician, although Dr. Roberta Cole, who practiced in New York City from 1872 to 1881, is widely considered the country's first black female doctor.

Dr. Edward H. Clarke, in *Sex in Education*, claims intense mental effort by women damages their reproductive capacities.

Fanny Baker Ames cofounds with her husband

TEXTS	CONTEXTS
1873 vervale": *An Orphan of the Old Dominion: Her Trials and Travels, Embracing A History of Her Life Taken Principally from Her Journals and Letters*, about a woman's experience pioneering in the Southwest.	1873 the first visiting social worker service in Pennsylvania.
Celia Thaxter: *Among the Isles of Shoals*, prose.	*McCall's* magazine, under the title *The Queen*, is published by a New York garment maker.
Adeline Whitney: *The Other Girls*, a novel about girls employed on farms and in cities.	The New York *Tribune* begins issuing its "extras," cheap reprints of stories and novels priced from five to fifteen cents.
	After seven years with partners, Henry Holt establishes his own publishing house Henry Holt & Co.
	Susan E. Blow becomes the first woman to open and teach at a public kindergarten.
	Amanda Jones invents a vacuum method for canning food.
	The first convention of women preachers is organized by Julia Ward Howe.
	Suffragists participate in a Centennial Tea Party in Boston to reaffirm that "taxation without representation is tyranny."

*   *   *

TEXTS	CONTEXTS
1874 Catharine Beecher: *Educational Reminiscences and Suggestions.*	1874 Forty people attend the first Chautauqua Assembly held at Lake Chautauqua, New York, marking the beginning of the Chautauqua adult-education movement; its lectures and activities ultimately draw millions when the movement spreads throughout the states and around the world.
Miss H. Burton: *The Lady's Book of Knitting and Crochet.*	
Rebecca Harding Davis: *John Andross,* a novel.	
Julia Ward Howe edits *Sex and Education,* a collection of essays subtitled *A Reply to Dr. E.H. Clarke's "Sex in Education,"* by prominent figures including Howe, Mrs. Horace Mann, Elizabeth Stuart Phelps (Ward), and Caroline Dall.	The Women's Christian Temperance Union (WCTU) is founded; among its leading spokeswomen are Carry Nation and Frances E. Willard.
Elizabeth Dennistoun Wood Kane: *Twelve Mormon Houses Visited in Succession on a Journey through Utah to Arizona.*	The *Woman's Home Companion,* which first appears as *The Home* in Cleveland, Ohio, begins its 82-year run. It goes on to be noted for its fiction, nonfiction, and illustrations before it folds in 1956.
Elizabeth Peake: *Pen Pictures of Europe.*	Mary Outerbridge, who introduced lawn tennis to the U.S., plays the first lawn tennis match on Staten Island.
	The first electric streetcar is in use.

*   *   *

TEXTS	CONTEXTS
1875 Louisa May Alcott: *Eight Cousins; or, The Aunt Hill,* a novel for girls.	1875 *In Minor v. Happersett*, the Supreme Court rules against the case brought by suffragists Virginia and Francis Minor, who argued for Virginia's right to vote under the Fourteenth Amendment.

Mary Baker Eddy: *Science and Health*.

Augusta Jane Evans (Wilson): *Infelice*, a novel.

Margaret Junkin Preston: *Cartoons*, a collection of poetry.

Hannah Whitall Smith (1832–1911), religious writer: *The Christian's Secret of a Happy Life*, a religious bestseller for over 100 years.

The Civil Rights Act passes, extending civil rights for African Americans to gain access to places of public accommodation and transportation; in 1883, after the failure of Reconstruction it is declared unconstitutional by the Supreme Court.

Michigan and Minnesota grant only widowed mothers of school children the right to vote, but solely on school issues.

Maria Mitchell, longtime astronomy professor at Vassar College, becomes president of the American Association for the Advancement of Women.

Wellesley College is founded in Massachusetts.

The Johns Hopkins University is founded in Baltimore, Maryland.

*   *   *

TEXTS	CONTEXTS

1876   Eliza Andrews (1840–1931): *A Family Secret*, a bestseller.

Louisa May Alcott: "Transcendental Wild Oats," a sketch satirizing her experiences 33 years earlier with her family and others at Fruitlands, the Utopian community cofounded by her father.

Anna Dickinson, lecturer and reformer: *A Paying Investment*. In 1878 she makes her brief acting debut in the play *A Crown of Thorns*. She will go on to write her own play, *An American Girl*.

Martha Finley: *Elsie's Motherhood*, continuation of the Elsie Dinsmore series.

Helen Hunt Jackson (1831–1885), novelist and Indian rights activist: *Mercy Philbrick's Choice*, novel possibly based on her knowledge of her friend Emily Dickinson's life.

Frances (Fanny) Raymond Ritter (1840–1890), music educator, translator, singer, poet, and author, publishes a landmark article, "Woman as a Musi-

1876   On July 4, Matilda Joslyn Gage, Susan B. Anthony, Sara Andrews Spencer, Phoebe Couzins, and Lillie Devereux Blake present the Declaration of Rights of Women at the centennial celebration in Philadelphia's Independence Square.

Harriet Purvis becomes the first African American woman elected vice president of the National Woman Suffrage Association.

Mary Baker Eddy founds the Christian Science religion; three years later, she opens the first Christian Science church in Boston.

The American Library Association is first organized.

The Dewey Decimal System is first introduced; it will be widely used as a classification system in libraries.

There are 2500 libraries in the country with 12 million volumes among them. Their growth will be accelerated by Andrew Carnegie's generous endowment that begins this year.

TEXTS	CONTEXTS
1876 cian: An Art-Historical Study," in *Woman's Journal*. In it she details women's largely unacknowledged accomplishments in the history of music.	1876 Alexander Graham Bell invents and patents the telephone.

cian: An Art-Historical Study," in *Woman's Journal*. In it she details women's largely unacknowledged accomplishments in the history of music.

Ella Wheeler Wilcox (1850–1919), poet, novelist, author of over 40 volumes: *Poems of Passion*.

Alexander Graham Bell invents and patents the telephone.

Frank Leslie's Popular Magazine begins publication; it changes its name to the *American Magazine* in 1906 and survives for another 50 years.

Juliet Corson opens the first known U.S. cooking school in New York City.

Lydia Pinkham's Vegetable Compound is widely advertised as "The Greatest Medical Discovery Since the Dawn of History." The compound of black cohosh, liferoot plant, fenugreek seeds, and other herbs in a 21 percent alcohol solution promises to remedy female complaints.

Olivia Flynt patents her "Flynt Waist" or "True Corset," a nonconstricting and thus healthier device than its wasp-waist-inducing sisters.

Maria Spelterini, a professional acrobat, crosses Niagara Falls on a tightrope.

General George Custer is defeated at the Battle of Little Big Horn.

TEXTS	CONTEXTS
1876	1876 Sarah Stevenson, physician and professor, becomes the first woman admitted to the American Medical Association.

TEXTS	CONTEXTS
1877 Parthena Rood Barton: *Experiences of a Practical Christian Life: In Form of a Journal.* Mary Putnam Jacobi (1842–1906), physician and author of fiction and nonfiction: *Question of Rest for Women during Menstruation*, winner of The Boylston Prize from Harvard University for best dissertation. It combines classical background, research into medical literature, and questionnaires to women in all walks of life to demolish myths about menstruation and concludes that only in women have normal functions been considered pathological. Sarah Orne Jewett (1849–1909), novelist, short-story writer, chronicler of New England life: *Deephaven*, a novel. Martha J. Lamb (1826–1893), historian, novelist, and writer of children's stories: *History of the City of New York* (vol. 2, 1880).	1877 Rutherford B. Hayes becomes President. Reconstruction ends and Home Rule is established. Chief Joseph and the Nez Perce launch a four-month running battle to escape to Canada, but are forced to surrender just south of the border. *Puck*, a leading political satire and humor magazine, begins publication and folds in 1918. A nationwide railroad strike occurs. Irish Unionists known as the "Molly Maguires" are hanged in Pennsylvania. Helen Magill (White) completes her dissertation on "The Greek Drama" at Boston University and becomes the first known U.S. woman to earn a Ph.D. The YMCA in New York City offers the first typing

TEXTS		CONTEXTS	
1877	Miriam Squier Leslie (1836–1914), editor, travel writer: *California: A Pleasure Trip from Gotham to the Golden Gate*. Elizabeth Stuart Phelps (Ward): *The Story of Avis*, a novel. E.D.E.N. Southworth: *The Bride's Ordeal*, a novel. Susan Warner: *Diana, Bread and Oranges*, and *Pine Needles*, novels.	1877	training course for women. The first public telephones and first telephone switchboard come into use. The first state reformatory for women opens in Massachusetts; Eudora Clark Atkinson becomes its first superintendent. The Washington *Post* is founded.
1878	Louisa May Alcott: *Rose in Bloom*, a juvenile novel. Lydia Maria Child: *Aspirations of the World*. Rebecca Harding Davis: *A Law unto Herself*, a novel. Martha Finley: *Mildred Keith* and *Signing the Contract and What It Cost*. Anna Katharine Green (1846–1935), novelist, detective story writer, poet: *The Leavenworth Case*, long believed (erroneously) to be the first American detective novel.	1878	A. A. Pope manufactures the first bicycles in the U.S. Over 200 blacks sail from Charleston, South Carolina, to Liberia, West Africa. In *Reynolds v. United States*, the Supreme Court rules against a Mormon defendant and upholds the constitutionality of the Morrill Act of 1862, prohibiting and punishing polygamy in the territories. The American Bar Association is formed.

TEXTS	CONTEXTS
1878 Sarah Orne Jewett: *Play Days: A Book of Stories for Children.* Frances Raymond Ritter: *Some Famous Songs: An Art-Historical Sketch.* Annie Trumbull Slosson (1838–1926), New England short-story writer: *The China Hunter's Club.* Harriet Beecher Stowe: *Poganuc People*, her last novel.	1878 Emma M. Nutt becomes the first woman telephone operator.
1879 Women authors, including Harriet Beecher Stowe, Rose Terry Cooke, Elizabeth Stuart Phelps (Ward), Annie Adams Fields, Julia Ward Howe, Helen Hunt Jackson, and Sarah Orne Jewett, are invited to an *Atlantic Monthly* birthday breakfast (Oliver Wendell Holmes's 70th) for the first time. Elvina Corbould: *The Lady's Knitting Book.* Sarah A. Emery: *Reminiscences of a Nonagenarian.* Elizabeth Stuart Phelps (Ward): *An Old Maid's Paradise*, comic sketches, and *Sealed Orders*, a collection of stories.	1879 There is a great exodus of African Americans from southern states to midwestern and western territories, especially Kansas or Nebraska (whereby the term "exodusters"); many settle as homesteaders or "sodbusters." Lawyer Belva Lockwood becomes the first woman to practice before the Supreme Court. Frances E. Willard is elected president of the Women's Christian Temperance Union and serves until her death in 1898. Mary Eliza Mahoney, the first professionally trained African American nurse in the country, receives her

	TEXTS		CONTEXTS
1879	Maria Stewart, African American author: *Meditations from the Pen of Mrs. Maria Stewart.*	1879	diploma from the school of nursing at the New England Hospital for Women and Children.
	Susan Warner: *My Desire.*		Mary Foot Seymour establishes the first all-female secretary school in the country: the Union School of Stenography in New York.
			The first cardboard container is manufactured.
			The electric light bulb is invented. Within the next five years, electricity will become widely available.
			About 35,000 women are enrolled in various colleges and other institutes of higher learning in the U.S., comprising about one-third of the college student body.
1880s		1880s	The term "Boston marriage" is coined in the late 1800s to refer to a long-term monogamous relationship between two unmarried women.
			Africa is colonized by Britain, Belgium, France, Germany, Italy, Portugal, and Spain.
			Nellie Cashman, known as "the Angel of Tombstone," works against

TEXTS	CONTEXTS
1880s	**1880s** violence, runs a boarding house where she raises several orphans, and campaigns against public hangings.

1880	Martha Finley: *Elsie's Widowhood*, continuation of the Elsie Dinsmore series.	**1880**	U.S. population totals some 50 million, including 2,812,000 immigrants.
	Lucretia Peabody Hale (1820–1900), novelist, humorist, author of children's books: *The Peterkin Papers.*		An estimated 243,000 Native Americans are living in the U.S., representing, according to various historians, from one-fourth to one-tenth of the total population prior to Columbus's arrival. Virtually all surviving Native Americans are now encamped on reservations.
	Jane Grey Swisshelm (1815–1884), journalist, abolitionist: *Half a Century*, autobiography.		
	Metta Victoria Fuller Victor: *A Bad Boy's Diary.*		Some 28.2 percent of the population is urban.
	Susan Warner: *The End of a Coil.*		Two and a half million women are working for wages; only 4 percent of employed women work in offices; most are employed in agriculture.
			By this date there are 2432 registered female doctors in the U.S.
			The Supreme Court overturns a statute prohibiting blacks from jury duty.
			African American workers in North Carolina are perhaps representative in

TEXTS	CONTEXTS
1880	1880 earning from 40 to 80 cents a day, often for 12-hour days; 35 years later, they are taking home less than six dollars a week.

Nine out of ten southern African American married women between the ages of 21 and 30 have at least one child aged three or younger.

Kansas is the first state to include prohibition in its constitution.

Mary Cassatt (1845–1926), noted Impressionist painter who was instrumental in the introduction of that movement to America, first exhibits *Woman in Black at the Opera.*

The publishing house of Houghton Mifflin & Co., which has its origins in the firm of Hurd & Houghton in 1864, is formed.

William Randolph Hearst founds the *San Francisco Examiner.*

The Dial magazine is revived and before it folds in 1929—the poet Marianne Moore is its final editor—it is considered one

TEXTS	CONTEXTS
1880	1880 of the most influential literary monthly magazines.
	Some 850 newspapers are in circulation; by 1900 there are some 2000.
	One in every 21 marriages ends in divorce.
	Canned fruits and meats first appear in stores.
	For the first time, women are permitted to work as U.S. census enumerators.
	James A. Garfield is the first presidential candidate to answer Susan B. Anthony's request for his position on woman suffrage (he was against it).
1880–1910	1880–1910 Life expectancy for rural blacks, both men and women, is only 33 years.
1881 Rose Terry Cooke (1827–1892), short-story writer and poet, social historian of a fading New England culture: *Somebody's Neighbor*. Elaine Goodale Eastman (1863–1953): *Journal of a Farmer's Daughter*, prose and poetry. Martha Finley: *Mildred and Elsie*.	1881 A New York neurasthenist diagnoses an "American nervousness" in the culture at large. Domestic servants in Atlanta, protesting low wages, organize the Washerwoman's Strike. Atlanta Baptist Female Seminary, later Spelman Seminary (College), is founded.

TEXTS	CONTEXTS
1881 Helen Hunt Jackson: *A Century of Dishonor*, tract dealing with the U.S. government's injustices toward Native Americans, circulated at her own expense to every member of Congress. Sarah Orne Jewett: *Country By-Ways*, a collection of stories. Susette La Flesche (1854–1903), Native American writer and orator: "Nedawi," a children's story. Harriet Lothrop, writing as "Margaret Sidney" (1844–1924), children's writer: *Five Little Peppers and How They Grew*.	**1881** James A. Garfield is assassinated shortly after being inaugurated President, and Chester A. Arthur becomes President. Nurse Clara Barton founds the American Red Cross. Marion Talbot establishes the Association of Collegiate Alumnae (later renamed the American Association of University Women). *Century Illustrated Monthly Magazine*—formerly *Scribner's Monthly*—begins publication; five years later Charles Scribner's Sons reenters the magazine business with *Scribner's Magazine*, which folds in 1939. The Boston Symphony Orchestra gives its first performance.
1881–1898 Elizabeth Cady Stanton and Susan B. Anthony, co-founders of the National Woman Suffrage Association, edit with Matilda Joslyn Gage the first three volumes, covering 1848–1885, of *History of Woman Suffrage*.	**1881–1898**

* * *

TEXTS		CONTEXTS	
1882	Emma Lazarus (1849–1887), poet and translator, aroused by Russian pogroms of 1882, writes *Songs of a Semite*, considered her best work; also, *The Dance to Death*, a play.	1882	Emily Edson Briggs becomes the first president of the Women's National Press Association.
	Elizabeth Stuart Phelps (Ward): *Doctor Zay*, a novel.		The Chinese Exclusion Act is passed and bars further immigration of Chinese laborers and families.
	Mary Elizabeth Sherwood (1826–1903), novelist, magazine writer, autobiographer: *A Transplanted Rose*.		The first issue of Lovell's Library series appears; these paperbacks, priced between 10 and 30 cents and printed on better paper and with clearer type than other cheaper reprints, represent social reformer John W. "Book-a-day" Lovell's attempt to bring better quality writing to the masses.
	E.D.E.N. Southworth: *The Unloved Wife*, a novel.		
	Harriet Prescott Spofford: *The Marquis of Carabas*.		
	The *Atlantic Monthly* hosts a 70th-birthday celebration for Harriet Beecher Stowe.		Julia Ward Howe is elected president of the newly formed Woman's Ministerial Conference.
	Susan Warner: *Nobody*, a novel.		
1883	Sherwood Bonner, pseudonym of Katherine McDowell (1849–1883), local color short story writer, novelist: *Dialect Tales*.	1883	The Supreme Court rules that Native Americans are "aliens" and "dependents."
	Sylvia Dubois, at the age of 100, tells her life story to Dr. Cornelius Wilson		Prominent activist Mary Ann Shadd Cary becomes the second known black woman to receive a law

TEXTS	CONTEXTS
1883 Larison, who transcribes it phonetically. It is published as *Sylvia Dubois, a Biografy of the Slav Who Whipt Her Mistres and Gand Her Freedom*. Mary Hallock Foote (1847–1938), novelist and illustrator: *The Led-Horse Claim: A Romance of a Mining Camp*, one of the first novels to depict the West realistically. Sarah Winnemucca Hopkins (1844–1891), *Life among the Piutes* [sic]: *Their Wrongs and Claims*, an autobiographical work by a Paiute princess who gave more than 400 speeches across the U.S. and Europe to gain support for her people. Emma Lazarus's sonnet, "The New Colossus," is inscribed on the pedestal of the Statue of Liberty. Laura Jean Libbey (1862–1925), known as the "working-girl novelist": *A Fatal Wooing*, one of some 80 novels during a 30-year career. Mabel Loomis Todd (1856–1932), co-editor of Emily Dickinson's poems: *Footprints*, a novelette.	1883 degree when she graduates from Howard University. Caroline Earle White founds the American Anti-Vivisection Society. The Brooklyn Bridge in New York opens to traffic. William F. Cody ("Buffalo Bill") opens his Wild West show. *Ladies' Home Journal* is established and edited by the founder's wife, Louisa Knapp Curtis. Joseph Pulitzer purchases the New York *World* and inaugurates the practice of "yellow journalism." Moral crusader Anthony Comstock publishes *Traps for the Young*, which attacks half-dime novels and story papers as promoters of vice.

TEXTS	CONTEXTS
1883 Frances E. Willard (1839–1898), temperance reformer, advocate of women's rights, biographer: *Women and Temperance*. Constance Fenimore Woolson: *For the Major*, a novel.	**1883**
1884 Sherwood Bonner, pseudonym of Katherine McDowell: *Suwanee River Tales*. Anna Davis Hallowell: *James and Lucretia Mott: Life and Letters, by their Granddaughter*. Helen Hunt Jackson: *Ramona*, a fictional plea for the rights of Native Americans. Sarah Orne Jewett: *A Country Doctor*, a novel. Mrs. Edward Mix (1832–1884): *The Life of Mrs. Edward Mix, Written by Herself in 1880*, religious testament by a free black woman from Connecticut. Mary Noailles Murfree (1850–1922), regionalist short-story writer: *In the Tennessee Mountains*, first published under the pseudonym Charles Eg-	**1884** Married couples have an average of 4.24 children. Bryn Mawr College is founded. German scholar Friedrich Engels publishes *Origins of the Family, Private Property, and the State*, which argues that a woman functions in the home much as the proletariat functions in the workplace. Lawyer Belva Lockwood runs for President as the National Equal Rights Party candidate. She runs again in 1888. The country's first million-circulation magazine, *Comfort*, a mail-order journal for the home, offers subscriptions of four years for one dollar; it folds in 1942. The Mississippi Industrial Institute and College for

TEXTS	CONTEXTS

1884

bert Craddock. When her identity is eventually revealed, the event causes national publicity, for her works have been praised for their "masculine" style.

Chicana labor activist Lucy González Parsons publishes "A Word for Tramps," which calls for immediate labor organization and reform, in *Alarm*, the weekly paper of the International Working People's Association.

Eliza Roxey Snow Smith: Mormon poet, hymnwriter, and historian: *The Biography and Family Record of Lorenzo Snow*.

E.D.E.N. Southworth: *Why Did He Wed Her?*, a novel.

Metta Victoria Fuller Victor: *A Naughty Girl's Diary*, a novel.

Susan Warner: *A Red Wallflower*.

1884

the Education of White Girls of the State of Mississippi, later known as the Mississippi State College for Women, becomes the first women's state college.

Martha Carey Thomas, professor at Bryn Mawr, is the first woman's college faculty member to become a college dean.

Annie Oakley, given the nickname "little sure shot" by Sioux chief Sitting Bull, joins Buffalo Bill's *Wild West Show*, and besides Bill, becomes its highest paid performer.

The First Working Girls' Club is founded in New York by Grace Dodge and 12 female factory workers.

Grover Cleveland is elected President.

1885

Jane C. Croly, writing as "Jenny June": *Knitting and Crochet: A Guide to the Use of the Needle and the Hook*.

Elizabeth Bacon Custer (1842–1933): *Boots and*

1885

By this date, one-third of all books published in the U.S. are paperback dime novels.

Bryn Mawr College becomes the first woman's

TEXTS	CONTEXTS
1885	*Saddles; or, Life in Dakota with General Custer.*	1885	college to offer graduate studies.

TEXTS

1885   *Saddles; or, Life in Dakota with General Custer.*

Sarah Orne Jewett: *A Marsh Island.*

Mary Murfree: *The Prophet of the Great Smokey Mountains*, a novel.

Susan Warner: *Daisy Plains.*

CONTEXTS

1885   college to offer graduate studies.

The National Divorce Reform League is formed, designed to put an end to "easy" divorces and "lax" divorce laws.

A group of Boston women create the first organized outdoor play area for children in the U.S.: the playground.

Good Housekeeping is first published.

Edmund Stedman publishes his anthology, *Poets of America.*

The first trolley car is developed.

The Borden Company begins delivering bottles of cold milk.

Balloonist Mary "Carlotta" Myers and her husband patent a steering device for balloons.

More than 1.5 million baby bottles are sold annually.

Sarah E. Goode invents the "Folding Cabinet Bed" and becomes the first known African

TEXTS	CONTEXTS
1885	**1885** American woman to receive a U.S. patent. The publishing house D. C. Heath & Co. is established.
1885–1886 Clarissa Minnie Thompson: *Treading the Winepress; or, a Mountain of Misfortune*, one of the first post-Civil War novels by an African American woman.	**1885–1886**
1886 Louisa May Alcott: *Jo's Boys*, a juvenile novel and sequel to *Little Women* and *Little Men*, and *Lulu's Library*, a collection of stories. Frances Hodgson Burnett (1849–1924), prolific author of novels, short stories, plays, and works for children: *Little Lord Fauntleroy*. Rose Terry Cooke: *The Sphinx's Children*, short stories. Julia A. J. Foote (1823–1900): *A Brand Plucked from the Fire*, autobiography by an African American female evangelist (first copyrighted in 1879). Sarah Orne Jewett: *A*	**1886** Haymarket bombings lead to the hanging of four protestors. Electric railways are first introduced. The American Federation of Labor is founded. The Statue of Liberty is dedicated. By this year there are 266 women's colleges, 207 coed institutions, and 56 technical and professional schools that accept women. Kansas grants women partial suffrage, allowing them to vote in municipal elections. In *Yick Wo v. Hopkins*, the Supreme Court declares

TEXTS	CONTEXTS
1886 *White Heron and Other Stories.*	1886 discrimination against Asians in California illegal.

TEXTS

1886 *White Heron and Other Stories.*

Catherine Owen (Helen Alice Matthews Nitsch): *Ten Dollars Enough; Keeping House on ten dollars a week; how it has been done; how it may be done again.*

Lilla Cabot Perry (1848?– 1933), poet, painter, and lecturer: *Heart of Weed*, a book of verse.

Frances E. Willard: *How to Win: A Book for Girls.*

CONTEXTS

1886 discrimination against Asians in California illegal.

Anna Howard Shaw becomes the first woman in the U.S. to hold both divinity and medical degrees.

Louise "Lulu" Fleming is the first African American woman to be commissioned for career missionary service by the Women's Baptist Foreign Missionary Society of the West.

Julia Richman becomes the first president of the newly established Young Women's Hebrew Association.

The first linotype machine, which spelled the end of laborious manual setting for printing presses, is introduced at the New York *Tribune*.

Some 1500 of the 4500 titles published this year are in paperback; 508 are dime novels.

Coca-Cola, the first cola drink, is invented by a druggist as a remedy for headaches and hangovers.

TEXTS	CONTEXTS
1886	**1886** Josephine G. Cochran patents a dish washing machine.
	Harriet Hubbard Ayer begins marketing her Récamier Preparations skin cream.
	Cosmopolitan magazine appears, selling for 12½ cents an issue.
	The number of divorces rises from 9,937 in 1867 to 25,535 by this year.
1886–1895	**1886–1895** The social purity campaign succeeds in raising the age when women could legally consent to having sex from as low as ten in some states to between 14 and 18 years in 29 states.
1887 Nellie Bly (Elizabeth Cochrane Seaman, 1865–1922): *Ten Days in a Mad-House; or, Nellie Bly's Experience on Blackwell's Island*, based on her undercover work at a female asylum. Her later journalistic stories include exposés on baby-selling and matrimonial agencies and flattering portraits of Emma Goldman and Charlotte Perkins Gilman.	**1887** Congress initiates the allotment system by passing the Dawes Severalty Act, which promises farms and American citizenship to Native Americans willing to detribalize.
	Susanna Medora Salter is elected mayor of Argonia, Kansas, making her the first woman elected mayor in the U.S.
Eliza Southgate Bowne	S. Weir Mitchell, renowned physician and au-

TEXTS		CONTEXTS	
1887	(1783–1809): *A Girl's Life Eighty Years Ago: Selections from the Letters of Eliza Southgate Bowne*.	1887	thor of the "rest cure," proscribes activities like writing for new mother Charlotte Perkins Gilman. Gilman suffers a nervous breakdown after following Mitchell's cure and goes on to write about her experience in "The Yellow Wallpaper."
	Esther Bernon Carpenter (1848–1893), Rhode Island local colorist: *South County Neighbors*, short stories.		
	Augusta Jane Evans (Wilson): *At the Mercy of Tiberius*.		Cecilia Beaux (1855–1942), painter and portraitist, first exhibits *A Little Girl*. She is also known for such works as *Portrait of Bertha Vaughan, Sita and Sarita, Mother and Daughter*, and *New England*.
	Mary E. Wilkins Freeman (1852–1930), author of 20 volumes of adult fiction and six volumes of children's stories, most set in New England: *A Humble Romance and Other Stories*.		
	Alice French (1850–1934), writing essays, short stories, and novels as "Octave Thanet": *Knitters in the Sun*, a collection of short stories.		Anna Connelly patents the fire escape. Maria E. Allen patents a triangle diaper.
	Marietta Holley: *Samantha at Saratoga; or, Flirtin' with Fashion*, a humorous novel.		*Collier's* magazine begins; it survives until 1957.
	Sarah Orne Jewett: *The Story of the Normans, Told Chiefly in Relation to Their Conquest of England*.		
	Harriet Waters Preston: *A Year in Eden*, a novel.		

TEXTS	CONTEXTS

1887

Margaret Junkin Preston: *Colonial Ballads, Sonnets, and Other Verse.*

Lizette Woodworth Reese (1856–1935), poet, memoirist: *A Branch of May,* the first of her 14 collections of poetry.

Harriet Jane Hanson Robinson (1825–1911), novelist, memoirist, suffragist: *Captain Mary Miller.*

1887

1887–1906

1887–1906

Women are the plaintiffs in two-thirds of all divorce cases.

1888

The *Indian's Friend,* founded and edited by Native American women in Philadelphia, begins publication; it includes poetry and essays. The first editor is Amelia S. Quinton, assisted by Helen R. Foote. It continues in print until 1951.

Fannie A. Beers: *Memories: A Record of Personal Experience and Adventure during the Four Years of the War.*

Mary "Molly" Moore Davis (1852–1909), novelist, playwright, short-story writer, and poet who spends much of her life in New Orleans: *In*

1888

Edith Eleanor McLean, weighing two pounds, seven ounces, becomes the first baby ever placed in an incubator.

The Federation of Organized Trades is founded.

Benjamin Harrison is elected President.

The first modern deodorant is introduced.

National Geographic Magazine begins publication.

TEXTS	CONTEXTS
1888 *War Times at La Rose Blanche*, a series of fictionalized autobiographical stories. Margaret Deland (1857–1945), novelist and short-story writer: *John Ward, Preacher*, a novel. Martha Finley: *Christmas with Grandma Elsie*. Parthenia Hague: *A Blockaded Family*. Grace Elizabeth King (1851–1931), New Orleans short-story writer and novelist: *Monsieur Motte*, a collection of stories. Amélie Rives (1863–1945), novelist, playwright, poet: *The Quick or the Dead?*, a novel.	**1888**
1888–1890	**1888–1890** Edmund Stedman and E. M. Hutchinson publish their eleven-volume anthology, *A Library of American Literature*.
1889 Nellie Bly (Elizabeth Cochrane Seaman): *Nellie Bly's Book: Around the World in 72 Days*. Rose Terry Cooke: *Steadfast*, a novel.	**1889** Barnard College is established. College Settlement opens in New York, the first settlement house founded by women.

TEXTS		CONTEXTS
1889	Mary Foot Seymour (1846–1893) launches *Business Woman's Journal*.	1889	Jane Addams establishes Hull House in Chicago with Ellen Gates Starr.

<table>
<tr><td>

Lucy Larcom (1824–1893), poet, abolitionist, anthologist: *A New England Girlhood, Outlined from Memory*, autobiography.

Laura Jean Libbey: *Leonie Locke: The Romance of a Beautiful New York Working Girl*.

Mary Logan (1838–1923), magazine editor, writer of advice books and histories: *The Home Manual*, an advice book.

Matilda Barnes Lukens: *The Inland Passage: A Journal of a Trip to Alaska*.

Bethany Veney, African American author: *The Narrative of Bethany Veney; or, Aunt Betty's Story*.

Katharine Prescott Wormeley (1830–1908): *The Other Side of War*.

</td><td>

Maria Louise Baldwin, superintendent at a predominantly white grammar school in Cambridge, becomes the first African American female principal in Massachusetts and the Northeast.

Susan La Flesche (Picotte), of the Omaha, becomes the first Native American woman to earn a medical degree. She spends the rest of her life practicing medicine on her Nebraska reservation and working for the rights of her people.

Journalist Elizabeth Cochrane Seaman ("Nellie Bly") sets out to beat Jules Verne's fictional "eighty-day" journey around the world and does so, completing her trip in 72 days, 6 hours, and 11 minutes.

Belle Starr, outlaw celebrated in dime novels, is killed.

Street and Smith enter the dime-novel business and soon become Beadle's chief competitors; the for-

</td></tr>
</table>

TEXTS	CONTEXTS
1889	**1889** mer stays in business until 1950, in their final decades as publishers of pulp magazines. The first women's six-day bicycle race comes to an end in Madison Square Garden, New York. *Munsey's Magazine* is first published; it remains in print until 1929 and in 1893 lowers its price to a dime per issue. Lilla Cabot Perry (1848?–1933), poet, painter, and lecturer whose several one-woman shows in Boston and New York are invariably greeted with enthusiasm by critics and the public, paints *Little Angele.* Her style owes much to the Impressionists, whom she works to promote in America, but she retains a great deal of linear clarity and detail.
1889–1890 Miss Garrison, African American author: *A Ray of Light.*	**1889–1890**
1889–1940	**1889–1940** At least 3800 black men and women are lynched in the former Confederacy and its bordering states; many more instances are unreported.

*   *   *

TEXTS	CONTEXTS
1890s	**1890s** Alice Austen (1866–1952), an amateur photographer, provides insights into private experiences of young women during the late nineteenth century. She documents Manhattan street life and Staten Island society in over 8000 photographs.
	The first cafeterias open in America.
	Shirtwaists are the fashion craze.
	The practice of tailing or ad-stripping, where a continued story is printed between columns of advertisements, is perfected in the *Ladies' Home Journal* and soon adopted by other magazines.
1890 A group of women authors in Brooklyn attempt to form an Authors' Protective Union; although the attempt fails, the following year the Society of American Authors is formed.	**1890** Ellis Island opens.
	United Mine Workers is founded.
	At Wounded Knee, U.S. troops kill 200 to 300 unarmed Native Americans.
Mrs. Octavia Rogers Albert: *The House of Bondage; or, Charlotte Brooks and Other Slaves*, a collection of female slave narratives.	Wyoming enters the Union and becomes the first state with full woman suffrage: Esther Morris had led the fight for suffrage in the territory.

TEXTS	CONTEXTS
1890 Eleanor Arnold: *Miss Arnold's Book of Crocheting, Knitting and Drawn Work.*	**1890** Bertha Kaepernick of Wyoming becomes the first female entrant in a rodeo.

Kate Chopin (1851–1904), novelist and short-story writer: *At Fault*, a novel.

Roberts Brothers of Boston publishes *Poems by Emily Dickinson*, a selection of 115 of her verses chosen and heavily edited by Thomas Wentworth Higginson and Mabel Loomis Todd. Although the edition is corrupt, the reception is warm enough to result in the publication of several hundred more poems over the next decade.

Josephine Delphine Heard (1861–1921), African American poet: *Morning Glories.*

Sarah Orne Jewett: *Strangers and Wayfarers* and *Tales of New England*, two collections of short stories.

Amelia Etta Hall Johnson (1858–1922), black religious author, novelist, editor, and poet: *Clarence and Corinne; or, God's Way.* In addition to being the second novel published in

The National American Woman Suffrage Association is formed after the merger of the American and the National Woman Suffrage Associations.

The General Federation of Women's Clubs is established; by 1900 some 150,000 women will join through various local clubs, making it one of the most influential women's organizations in existence.

The National Afro-American League is established.

African American socialist welfare leader Janie Barrett founds the first settlement organization for African American girls in Virginia.

The Daughters of the American Revolution is founded.

The Mormon Church disavows its earlier sanction of polygamy.

The median age of mar-

	TEXTS		CONTEXTS
1890	book form by an African American woman, it was the first Sunday school book written by a black author.	1890	riage is 22.0 years for women and 26.1 for men.

<table>
<tr><td></td><td>Emily Pauline Johnson (1861–1913) begins a two-decade career performing her poetry in the U.S., Canada, and England, under her native name, Tehakionwake.</td><td></td><td>Black female illiteracy in the six largest southern cities is 50 percent.

Literary Digest, featuring condensed versions of mostly newspaper articles, begins its 48-year publication.</td></tr>
<tr><td></td><td>Louise Chandler Moulton: *In the Garden of Dreams*, poetry.</td><td></td><td>*Review of Reviews*, a monthly magazine containing both original and reprinted articles, appears.</td></tr>
</table>

The magazine *The Smart Set* is founded; beginning around 1912 under new editorship, it is a leading journal featuring often derisive columns on "Americana" and selections from writers including F. Scott Fitzgerald, William Butler Yeats, Elinor Wylie, and Harriet Monroe.

Louise Blanchard Bethune, the nation's first known woman architect, is the first woman elected to the American Institute of Architects.

Peanut butter is first patented.

There are approximately 4500 women practicing medicine in the U.S.;

TEXTS		CONTEXTS	
1890		1890	most of them were trained at women's colleges.
1890–1895	Kate Field (1838–1896) founds and edits a weekly newspaper, *Kate Field's Washington*.	1890–1895	
1890–1910		1890–1910	The mass-produced clothing industry takes off.
1891	Sophia Alice Callahan: *Wynema: A Child of the Forest*, possibly the first published novel by a Native American woman. Rose Terry Cooke: *Huckleberries Gathered from New England Hills*, short stories. Lucy A. Delaney: *From the Darkness Cometh the Light or Struggles for Freedom*, a slave narrative. Sarah Barnwell Elliot (1848–1928), southern author of comic fiction, often set in the mountains: *Jerry*. Mary E. Wilkins Freeman: *A New England Nun and Other Stories*. Alice French, writing as "Octave Thanet": *We All*, a novel.	1891	Congress passes a law placing all immigrant decisions into federal hands and adds "polygamists" and "persons suffering from a loathsome or dangerous contagious disease" to its list of inadmissables; the following year it extends its 1882 restriction on Chinese immigration for yet another decade. Stanford University and the University of Chicago announce they are instituting full coeducation at both the undergraduate and graduate levels. Also in the early 1890s, Yale, Columbia, and Brown admit women to graduate work; Yale still refuses to admit women into the undergraduate college, while Columbia and Brown set up coordinate colleges for women undergraduates. Josephine Shaw Lowell is instrumental in founding

TEXTS	CONTEXTS

1891 Helen Hamilton Gardener (1853–1925): *Is This Your Son, My Lord?* and *Pray You Sir, Whose Daughter?* (1892), companion novels that confront and condemn the sexual double standard.

Addie E. Heron: *Dainty Work for Pleasure and Profit.*

Emma Dunham Kelley (Hawkins), African American novelist: *Megda.*

Marguerite Merington (1860–1951), playwright: *Captain Lettarblair.*

Martha Morton (1865–1925), considered "dean of woman playwrights," founds the Society of Dramatic Authors when women are barred from membership in the American Dramatists' Club: *The Merchant.*

Mary Murfree: *The "Stranger People's" Country.*

Lizette Woodworth Reese: *A Handful of Lavender*, poetry.

Annie Trumbull Slosson: *Seven Dreamers*, New England local color stories.

1891 the Consumer's League and serves as its first president.

H. M. Converse, Native American activist, is the first white woman to become an Indian chief; she is named honorary chief of the Six Nations in recognition of her activism.

The word "feminist" is first used, in a book review in the *Athenaeum.*

The first international copyright legislation goes into effect.

Annie Baxter becomes the first female county clerk in the U.S. and the first elected female official in Missouri.

E. S. Edwards is the first woman to design a state seal (Idaho's).

Mary Cassatt's first one-person exhibition in the United States takes place. According to the *New York Times*, "a rude strength, at times out of keeping with the subject, is noticeable, and takes away in a measure from the charm of femininity."

* * *

TEXTS	CONTEXTS
1892 Gertrude Atherton (1857–1948), novelist, biographer, and historian: *The Doomswoman*, a romance set in Old California.	1892 The Populist or People's Party is organized, including woman delegates and speakers.
Anna Julia Cooper (1859?–1964), educator and scholar: *A Voice from the South: By a Black Woman of the South*.	Homestead Steelworkers Strike. Elizabeth Cady Stanton retires from the NAWSA.
Rebecca Harding Davis: *Silhouettes of American Life*.	Ida B. Wells (Barnett), journalist, teacher, and community organizer, becomes a prominent activist in the anti-lynching crusade after three black men are lynched in Memphis.
Mary E. Wilkins Freeman: *The Pot of Gold and Other Stories*.	
Charlotte Perkins Gilman (1860–1935), a leading feminist theorist of her time: "The Yellow Wallpaper."	Composer, pianist, and musical prodigy Amy Mary Cheney Beach (1867–1944) becomes the first woman whose work is performed by the Boston Symphony.
Frances Ellen Watkins Harper: *Iola Leroy; or, Shadows Uplifted*, the first novel by an African American to discuss Reconstruction directly.	In Fall River, Massachusetts, Lizzie Borden is tried and acquitted for the ax murders of her father and stepmother.
Marietta Holley: *Samantha on the Race Problem*, humor.	The publishing house of Putnam is founded.
Grace Elizabeth King: *Tales of a Time and Place*, local color stories set in Louisiana.	*Vogue* magazine is first published. Last year of publication of *Peterson's Magazine*.

TEXTS	CONTEXTS
1892 Annie Nathan Meyer (1867–1951), Jewish champion of higher education for women, novelist, playwright, essayist: *Helen Brent, M.D.*, a novel. Amélie Rives: *Barbara Dering.* Ida B. Wells (Barnett, 1862–1931), newspaper editor and anti-lynching and woman's rights activist: *Southern Horrors: Lynch Law in All Its Phases.*	1892 The Sierra Club is founded. Fannie Farmer opens her School of Cookery in Boston. Lena Sittig patents the first bicycle skirt. The first game of women's basketball is played, at Smith College. Two hundred women in New York City celebrate "Foremothers' Day." Grover Cleveland is elected President (his second term, nonconsecutive). The *Ladies' Home Journal* announces that it will accept no more patent medicine advertisements.
1893 Mary E. Wilkins Freeman: *Jane Field*, a novel. Matilda Joslyn Gage (1826–1898), journalist, editor, and feminist activist: *Woman, Church, and State.* Louise Imogene Guiney (1861–1920), lyric poet, essayist, critic, biographer, journalist: *A Roadside Harp.*	1893 New Zealand becomes the first country to allow women to vote. Colorado's male voters are the first to grant woman suffrage. The First National Purity Congress is held. Queen Liliuokalani, after many attempts to overturn the "Bayonet Consti-

TEXTS	CONTEXTS
1893 Mildred Hill, private kindergarten teacher, and her sister Patty Smith Hill compose "Good Morning to You," which eventually becomes "Happy Birthday to You."	1893 tution" imposed by the U.S. government and restore power to her people, steps down from the Hawaiian throne to, in her words, "avoid any collision of armed forces and perhaps loss of life."
Grace Elizabeth King: *Balcony Stories.*	The World's Columbian Exposition is held in Chicago, featuring a women's exhibition with several buildings designed by and for women; one building includes large murals by Mary Cassatt and Mary MacMonnies.
Victoria Earle Matthews (1861–1907), African American short story writer and essayist: *Aunt Lindy: A Story Founded on Real Life.*	
Mary Alicia Owen (1858–1935), folklorist: *VooDoo Tales, as Told among the Negroes of the Southwest, Collected from Original Sources.*	The frankfurter and the ice cream cone are first introduced to Americans at the Columbian Exposition.
H. Cordelia Ray (1849–1916), African American poet: *Sonnets.*	Financial panic reigns after the stock market collapses.
Annie Trumbull Slosson: *Dumb Foxglove, and Other Stories.*	The Anti-Saloon League (ASL) is formed.
Amanda Berry Smith (1837–1915): *An Autobiography; the Story of the Lord's Dealings with Mrs. Amanda Smith, the Colored Evangelist; Containing an Account of Her Life Work of Faith, and Her Travels in America, England, Ire-*	Hannah Greenebaum Solomon founds the National Council of Jewish Women.
	McClure's Magazine is first published for 15 cents an issue.

TEXTS		CONTEXTS	
1893	*land, Scotland, India and Africa, as an Independent Missionary.* Ruth McEnery Stuart (1852–1917), author of 20 books and more than 80 magazine stories, known primarily for her southern local color and dialect fictions: *A Golden Wedding and Other Tales.* Ida B. Wells (Barnett): *The Reason Why: The Colored American Is Not in the World's Columbian Exposition.* Frances E. Willard: *A Woman of the Century; Fourteen Hundred-Seventy Biographical Sketches Accompanied by Portraits of Leading American Women in All Walks of Life.*	1893	The modern Associated Press (AP) is formed. The first successful American gasoline car is manufactured. Mary Cassatt paints *The Boating Party.*
1894	Kate Chopin: *Bayou Folk,* a collection of stories. Martha Finley: *Elsie at the World's Fair.* Mary E. Wilkins Freeman: *Pembroke,* a novel. Mary Putnam Jacobi: *"Common Sense" Applied to Woman Suffrage.* Sarah Orne Jewett: *Betty Leicester's English Xmas: A*	1894	Anna Lea Merritt (1844–1930), Pre-Raphaelite painter, exhibits *Watchers of the Straight Gate.* Radcliffe College is officially established. The United Daughters of the Confederacy is founded. The *Chap-Book,* a highbrow, expensively printed art magazine lacking ad-

TEXTS	CONTEXTS
1894	1894

TEXTS	CONTEXTS
New Chapter of an Old Story.	vertisements, begins publication and stays in print for four years.
Amelia Etta Johnson: *The Hazeley Family.*	The Immigration Restriction League is founded and sets out to alert the public to the social and economic costs of immigration.
Mrs. N. F. Mossell: *The Work of the Afro-American Woman.*	
Josephine St. Pierre Ruffin becomes the editor of the newly founded *The Woman's Era*, the first black women's newspaper. Founded in Boston by the New Era Club, it would become the official publication of the National Association of Colored Women.	
Harriet Prescott Spofford: *A Scarlet Poppy and Other Stories.*	
Ruth McEnery Stuart: *The Story of Babette* and *Arlotta's Intended,* novels.	
Celia Thaxter: *An Island Garden.*	

TEXTS	CONTEXTS
1895	1895
Katharine Lee Bates, Wellesley College English professor, writes lyrics to "America the Beautiful," which will become an unofficial national anthem.	The *Bookman* begins publishing a list of books in order of demand, listing the six best-selling books in 16 different American cities (works of fiction make up nine-tenths of the list); two years later, it institutes a national summation and in 1899, it be-
Eloise Bibb (Thompson, 1878–1928), African American author: *Poems.*	

TEXTS		CONTEXTS
1895	Sarah Knowles Bolton (1841–1916), worker for temperance, woman suffrage, and higher education, and author of a number of biographies and collections of biographical sketches: *Famous Leaders among Women*.	**1895** gins issuing the list annually.
		The first national conference of African American women, organized by suffragist and activist Josephine St. Pierre Ruffin, is held in Boston.
	Alice M. Brown (1857–1948), novelist, short-story writer, dramatist, and poet: *Meadow-Grass: Tales of New England Life*, local color stories.	With her appointment to the Washington, D.C., Board of Education, Mary Church Terrell becomes the first African American woman to sit on a board of education.
	Maria Louise Burgess, African American author: *Ave Maria*, fiction.	Cecilia Beaux becomes the first woman professor of art at the Pennsylvania
	Letitia M. Burwell: *A Girl's Life in Virginia before the War*.	Academy of Fine Arts Faculty.
	Mary "Molly" Moore Davis: *Under the Man-Fig*, a novel set in the Southwest.	Sears, Roebuck & Co., incorporated in 1894, opens its mail-order business; its first catalog totals 786 pages; by the turn of the century the company is
	Alice Ruth Moore Dunbar-Nelson (1875–1935), African American short-story writer, poet, journalist, political and social activist: *Violets and Other Tales*.	selling approximately $10 million worth of merchandise a year. William Randolph Hearst purchases the New York *Journal*.
	Mary E. Wilkins Freeman: *The Long Arm*, a mystery novella.	New Hampshire is the first state to make the establishment and support of public libraries compulsory.

TEXTS		CONTEXTS	
1895	Sarah Orne Jewett: *The Life of Nancy*, a collection of stories.	1895	Charles Dana Gibson's drawings make popular the image of the "Gibson Girl"—upper-class, lush-figured, pinned-up long hair, pure white com-plexion.
	Emily Pauline Johnson, a.k.a. Tehakionwake: *The White Wampum*, a collec-tion of poems.		
	Josephine Lazarus, Jewish American poet and essay-ist: *The Spirit of Judaism*.		Due to the bicycling craze (first in vogue in 1868 al-though bikes were not manufactured in the U.S. until 1878) skirt lengths go up an inch or two above the ankle.
	Elizabeth Stuart Phelps (Ward): *A Singular Life*, a novel.		
	Elizabeth Cady Stanton (1815–1902): *The Woman's Bible*, a critique of masculine bias in the Judeo-Christian tradition.		
	Elizabeth Stoddard: *Poems*.		
	Ida B. Wells (Barnett): *A Red Record: Tabulated Sta-tistics and Alleged Causes of Lynchings in the United States, 1892–1893–1894*.		
	Constance Fenimore Woolson: *Horace Chase*.		
1895–1899	Rosa Sonneschein edits *American Jewess*, the first national Jewish women's magazine in the United States.	1895–1899	

*   *   *

TEXTS		CONTEXTS
1896	Mary Eileen Ahern (1868–1938) begins editorship of *Public Libraries*, serving until 1931.	**1896** Utah and Idaho allow women the vote.

<table>
<tr><td>

Rebecca Harding Davis: *Doctor Warrick's Daughters* and *Frances Waldeaux*, novels.

Fannie Farmer (1857–1915), prolific cookbook author, publishes the extremely popular *Boston Cooking School Cook Book*, the first cookbook to emphasize accurate measurements.

Mary E. Wilkins Freeman: *Madelon*, a novel.

Sarah Orne Jewett: *The Country of the Pointed Firs.*

Annie Fellows Johnston (1863–1931): *The Little Colonel*, first in a series of 13 books for children.

Elizabeth Stuart Phelps (Ward): *Chapters from a Life*, autobiography.

Katherine E. Purvis writes lyrics for "When the Saints Go Marching In," with music by James M. Black.

Ruth McEnery Stuart: *Sonny*, a novel set in Ar-

</td><td>

Plessy v. Ferguson rules "separate but equal" is a valid justification for segregation.

The National Association of Colored Women, the result of a merger of the National Federation of Afro-American Women and the Colored Women's Clubs, is founded in Washington, D.C. Mary Church Terrell becomes its first president.

William McKinley is elected President.

Oxford University Press opens its American branch in New York City.

In *Savage v. Neely*, the New York Supreme Court rules that authors may demand that their publishers give them access to sales records of their books.

Pulp magazines are invented. Cheaply printed weeklies or monthlies offering fiction, quizzes, articles, and reader letters with prices starting at a dime, their popularity

</td></tr>
</table>

TEXTS

CONTEXTS

1896   kansas, one of her many
about farming life, considered one of the best of
the dialect fictions.

Maria E. Ward: *Bicycling
for Ladies.*

Emmeline B. Wells
(1828–1921), Mormon
poet and journalist: *Mus-
ings and Memories,* collection of poetry.

1896   takes off after World War
I when they begin to spe-
cialize (e.g., one of the
most popular would be
Street and Smith's *West-
ern Story Magazine*).

New York City stages the
first public exhibition of
motion pictures.

May Irwin (1862–1938),
known as Madame Laugh-
ter, appears in a brief film
sequence that becomes
known as *The Kiss.* Her
filmed kiss with costar
John C. Rice offends
many people and gener-
ates the first debate over
screen censorship. One of
the most popular comedi-
ennes of the late 1880s, Irwin often spoke out
against the exploitation of
animals by entertainers.

The first national
women's tennis champion-
ships are held in Pennsylvania.

Johnson and Johnson pro-
duces the first commercial
disposable sanitary pads,
called "Lister's Towels."

Amy Mary Cheney Beach
writes *Gaelic Symphony,*
the first symphony com-
posed by an American
woman.

TEXTS	CONTEXTS
1896	**1896** Bicycling through New York City, Evylyn Thomas becomes the first person known to be run over by a car; she survives the crash with a broken leg to show for it.
1897 Gertrude Atherton: *Patience Sparhawk and Her Times*. Margaret Jane Blake: *Memoirs of Margaret Jane Blake of Baltimore, Md. and Selections in Prose and Verse by Sarah R. Leavering*. Kate Chopin: *A Night in Acadie*, a collection of stories. Mary "Molly" Moore Davis: *An Elephant's Track, and Other Stories*, short fiction. Mary Weston Fordham: *Magnolia Leaves*, poetry. Mary E. Wilkins Freeman: *Once upon a Time, and Other Child-Verses* and *Jerome, a Poor Man*, a novel. Mary A. H. Gay: *Life in Dixie during the War*. Ellen Glasgow (1873–1945), southern novelist,	**1897** Lutie Lytle, upon completion of her law degree and admission to the Tennessee bar, begins practicing as one of the first black women lawyers in the United States. The first subway opens in Boston. The Alaskan gold rush is under way. Havelock Ellis publishes *Studies in the Psychology of Sex: Sexual Inversion*, which pathologizes same-sex love between women as "inverted." Alice McLellan Birney founds the Parent-Teacher Association (then known as the National Congress of Mothers) and becomes its first president. The American Negro Academy is founded, and Anna Julia Cooper is the only elected female member.

TEXTS	CONTEXTS
1897 essayist, and short-story writer: *The Descendant,* her first novel, published anonymously.	1897 Victoria Earle Matthews (novelist) founds the White Rose Mission in New York City to provide African American women with lodging and to teach them self-help and survival skills.

<table>
<tr><td>

Anna Katharine Green: *The Affair Next Door,* a mystery introducing Miss Amelia Butterworth, the prototype for the elderly female sleuth.

Lucretia P. Hale: *Plain Needlework, Knitting, and Mending for All at Home and in Schools.*

Josephine Preston Peabody (1874–1922), poet, playwright: *Old Greek Folk Stories.*

Lucy Maynard Salmon (1853–1927), historian: *Domestic Service,* analysis of household employment within a historical perspective.

Harriet Prescott Spofford: *An Inheritance,* a novel.

Ruth McEnery Stuart: *In Simpkinsville,* a local color collection.

Lilian Whiting (1847–1942), prolific biographer of women, travel writer: *After Her Death: The Story of a Summer.*

</td><td>

Gertrude Stein begins attending Johns Hopkins School of Medicine; she leaves in 1901 without attaining her degree.

Maude Adams (1872–1953), one of the most popular actresses of her time, makes her first appearance in *The Little Minister,* a work authored by playwright James Barrie; they continue to collaborate until his death in 1937.

McCall's Magazine is first published.

The publishing house of Doubleday, McClure & Co. is established; in 1900 Doubleday splits with McClure to start his own firm.

</td></tr>
</table>

*   *   *

TEXTS	CONTEXTS
1898 Jane Cunningham Croly: *History of the Woman's Club Movement in America.* Margaret Deland: *Old Chester Tales.* Kate Drumgoold: *A Slave Girl's Story, Being an Autobiography of Kate Drumgoold.* Alice Morse Earle (1851–1911), social historian: *Home Life in Colonial Days.* Sarah Barnwell Elliot: *The Durket Sperret*, a comic novel. Mary E. Wilkins Freeman: *Silence and Other Stories.* Charlotte Perkins Gilman: *Women and Economics: A Study of the Economic Relation between Men and Women as a Factor in Social Evolution.* Ellen Glasgow: *Phases of an Inferior Planet.* Ida Husted Harper (1851–1931), journalist and suffragist, co-editor of *History of Woman Suffrage* with Anthony and Stanton: *The Life and Work of Susan B. Anthony.*	1898 The Spanish-American War gives the U.S. Guam, the Hawaiian Islands, the Philippines, and Puerto Rico; William Randolph Hearst's New York *Journal* and Joseph Pulitzer's *World* are credited and take credit for helping to incite the country to war. The Anti-Imperialist League is founded. Utah women become the first in the country to qualify for jury service. In Wilmington, North Carolina, white mobs murder some 20 to 100 blacks and terrorize the community. The first advice-to-the-lovelorn column is written by Marie Manning for the New York *Evening Journal.* The publishing house Dunlap & Grosset (later Grosset & Dunlap) is established. The Michigan Board of Health estimates that one-third of all in-state pregnancies are artificially terminated.

TEXTS	CONTEXTS
1898	**1898**

Louise Eleanor Hogan: *A Study of a Child*, a diary.

Julia Ward Howe: *From Sunset Ridge; Poems Old and New*.

Emma Dunham Kelley (Hawkins): *Four Girls at Cottage City*, a combination of spiritual autobiography and sentimental novel.

Harriet Jane Hanson Robinson: *Loom and Spindle; or, Life among the Early Mill Girls*.

| **1899** | **1899** |

TEXTS	CONTEXTS
Mary Antin (1881–1949), a Russian Jewish immigrant, writes of traveling through Russia and Germany to settle in Boston in *From Plotzk to Boston*.	The concept of lying-in disappears when the New York Asylum for Lying-In Women merges with the New York Infant Asylum.
Gertrude Atherton: *A Daughter of the Vine*.	The National Institute of Arts and Letters is founded.
Alice Brown: *Tiverton Tales*.	Ellen Swallow Richards hosts a series of conferences devoted to domestic sciences at which the term "home economics" is used for the first time.
Olivia Ward Bush (1869–1944), African American poet, playwright, and journalist: *Original Poems*.	
Kate Chopin: *The Awakening*, a novel that results in scandal and controversy due to its exploration of a woman's search for ful-	Florence Kelley, influential advocate of labor reform and protective labor legislation, becomes the executive secretary of the newly established

TEXTS		CONTEXTS
1899	fillment; its author is shunned and she finds it difficult to publish af- · terward.	1899	National Consumer's League.

1899   fillment; its author is shunned and she finds it difficult to publish af- · terward.

Alice Ruth Moore Dunbar-Nelson: *The Goodness of St. Rocque and Other Stories.*

Martha Finley: *Elsie in the South.*

Mary E. Hitchcock: *Two Women in the Klondike: The Story of a Journey to the Goldfields of Alaska.*

Sarah Orne Jewett: *The Queen's Twin and Other Stories.*

Harriet Prescott Spofford: *The Maid He Married*, a novel.

Onoto Watanna (Winnifred Eaton, 1875–1954), Chinese American novelist, autobiographer, biographer, and screenwriter: *Miss Nume of Japan.*

1899   National Consumer's League.

Generva Mudge, driving in a New York City race, is the first woman automobile racer; her car spins out of control into several spectators.

Thorstein Veblen publishes his *The Theory of the Leisure Class*, which describes an era of "conspicuous consumption" and the wife's role as conspicuous consumer.

By the end of the century, the book trade is spending $5 million a year on book advertising.

late 1890s

late 1890s   Nine out of ten African Americans live in the South, 80 percent in rural areas; African Americans represent one-third of the southern population.

Jackets for books first appear.

*   *   *

TEXTS		CONTEXTS
1900	Isabella Bird: *A Lady's Life in the Rocky Mountains*, a memoir.	1900 An average of 3.56 children are born to each American woman.

In the January, February, and March issues of *Atlantic Monthly*, Gertrude Simmons Bonnin, a.k.a. Zitkala-Ša, or Redbird (1876–1938), Native American rights activist and daughter of a Sioux mother, publishes "Impressions of an Indian Childhood," "The School Days of an Indian Girl," and "An Indian Teacher among Indians."

Charlotte Perkins Gilman: *Concerning Children.*

Frances Ellen Watkins Harper: *Poems.*

Pauline E. Hopkins (1859–1930), African American novelist, playwright, and biographer whose works often appeared in serial form in publications such as *Colored American Magazine: Contending Forces: A Romance Illustrative of Negro Life North and South.*

Mary Johnston (1870–1936), feminist and author of 23 novels, mostly historical romances: *To Have and to Hold*, the best-

Women equal one-fifth of the American labor force, numbering some five million workers.

Total population is 76,094,000; 3,688,000 immigrants have arrived since 1891. Women represent approximately half of the total U.S. black population of 8,883,994.

Thirty-eight percent of native-born white working women, 21 percent of foreign-born working women, and 3 percent of black working women are employed in manufacturing.

Women represent 60 percent of high-school graduates.

Each year 55,000 divorces are granted; the divorce rate is approximately 4 per 1000 marriages. Two-thirds of these divorces are granted to women, and the U.S. rate is more than double the highest European rate.

There are nearly 5000

	TEXTS		CONTEXTS
1900	selling novel of 1900 and the first best-seller of the 20th-century.	1900	libraries in the country with total holdings of some 40 million volumes.

Harriet Prescott Spofford: *Old Madame, and Other Tragedies*, a collection of stories.

Priscilla Jane Thompson (1871–1942), African American poet: *Ethiope Lays*.

Emma Wolf, Jewish American novelist and short-story writer: *Heirs of Yesterday*.

The first known female proprietor of a publishing firm, Caro M. Clark, inaugurates C. M. Clark Publishing Company by issuing Charles Felton Pidgin's *Quincy Adams Sawyer*, which sells nearly a quarter of a million copies thanks to her extensive advertising campaign.

The Foraker Act makes Puerto Rico the first U.S. territory not granted the promise of statehood or the protection of the Constitution.

The 18-year-long policy suspending Chinese immigration becomes a permanent exclusion.

W.E.B. Du Bois reports that 252 African American women have received baccalaureate degrees, 65 of whom earned them at Oberlin College.

Carrie Chapman Catt is elected to succeed Susan B. Anthony as president of the National American Woman Suffrage Association. She serves for four

TEXTS	CONTEXTS
1900	1900 years, then is elected to a second term in 1915, serving until successful ratification of the Nineteenth Amendment in 1920.

With 6374 working actresses in the U.S., women constitute 43 percent of the acting profession.

One servant to every 15 households: domestic service jobs account for one-third of female employment, a drastic drop from 60 percent in 1870, precipitated by the boom in factory, office, and retail jobs.

Half of all U.S. working women are farmhands or domestic servants.

The General Federation of Women's Clubs refuses to accept Josephine St. Pierre Ruffin's credentials as a delegate from the black woman's organization the Era Club.

For every 1000 white women there are 124 live births, down from 278 a century earlier.

The Cake Walk becomes the most fashionable dance.

TEXTS	CONTEXTS
1900	1900 Zelda Fitzgerald, one half of "the couple" of the Roaring Twenties, is born.
	"(She Was Only) A Bird in a Gilded Cage" is a popular U.S. song.
	The U.S. has approximately 5000 women doctors, 1500 female medical students, and seven medical schools exclusively for women.
	Infant mortality in the U.S. is 122 per 1000 live births. Average age at death is 47.
	Half of all births are attended by midwives.
1900–1920	1900–1920 The first electric appliances are marketed— including dishwashers, sewing machines, vacuum cleaners, refrigerators, toasters, and irons.
1900–1921	1900–1921 The number of silk stockings sold in America rises from 12,000 pairs to 18 million pairs.
1900–1930	1900–1930 With the rise of gynecology/obstetrics as a medical specialty and the passage of laws in many states outlawing mid-

TEXTS	CONTEXTS
1900–1930	**1900–1930** wifery, midwives virtually disappear by 1930.
1901 Gertrude Simmons Bonnin, a.k.a. Zitkala-Ša, or Redbird: *Old Indian Legends.*	**1901** McKinley is assassinated shortly after election to his second term; Theodore Roosevelt becomes President.
Elizabeth Duane Gillespie: *A Book of Remembrance.*	Eugene Debs's Socialist Party is formed.
Sarah Orne Jewett is made a Doctor of Letters by Bowdoin College. She publishes *The Tory Lover* this same year.	The American Federation of Labor announces its support for federal control over child labor.
Evelyn Key's *The Century of the Child* popularizes modern child development principles.	A treaty establishes U.S. supervision over the building of the Panama Canal.
Lillian Pettengill: *Toilers of the Home: The Record of a College Women's Experience as a Domestic Servant,* written by the author about her experiences as an undergraduate at Vassar, doing domestic work for tuition money.	Educator Mary Woolley begins her 36-year tenure as president of Mount Holyoke College. In 1930 she is named one of 12 greatest living women in America. Woolley maintains a longstanding and widely acknowledged "romantic friendship" with another Mount Holyoke professor, Jeannette Marks, which lasts from their meeting in 1895 when Marks was a student until Woolley's death in 1947.
Alice Hegan Rice (1870–1942), novelist, particularly of the urban poor: *Mrs. Wiggs of the Cabbage Patch.*	
Onoto Watanna (Winnifred Eaton): *A Japanese*	Physician Anita McGee

TEXTS		CONTEXTS	
1901	*Nightingale*, a novel.	1901	founds the Army Nurse Corps.
	Mabel Osgood Wright (1859–1934), nature writer, novelist: *The Garden of a Commuter's Wife*.		Sarah Jane Farmer, on a trip through Persia, converts to Ba'hai and founds the American Ba'hai movement upon her return to the States.
	Edith Franklin Wyatt (1873–1958), novelist and short-story writer, advocate of working-class women, child labor laws, and woman suffrage: *Every One His Own Way*.		Anna Edson Taylor is the first woman to go over Niagara Falls in a barrel and survive.
			The Everleigh sisters open the world-famous brothel the Everleigh Club in Chicago.
1901–1902	Pauline E. Hopkins: *Hagar's Daughters, a Story of Southern Caste Prejudice* and *Winona: A Tale of Negro Life in the South and Southwest*.	1901–1902	
1902	Gertrude Atherton: *The Splendid Idle Forties*.	1902	Sieh King King, a 16-year-old foreign student at the University of California, delivers a speech condemning the Chinese slave girl system and foot-binding, and declaring men and women equal; she is thus the first known public voice for Chinese women's emancipation in the U.S.
	Augusta Jane Evans (Wilson): *A Speckled Bird*, a novel.		
	Ellen Glasgow: *The Battle-Ground*, a novel.		
	Sarah Raymond Herndon: *Days on the Road Crossing the Plains in 1865*.		
	Isabella Beecher Hooker:		Martha Washington is the first American woman to

TEXTS	CONTEXTS
1902 *An Argument on United States Citizenship.*	1902 be depicted on a postage stamp.
Helen Keller (1880–1968): *The Story of My Life.*	Women in Australia are enfranchised.
Mary MacLane: *The Story of Mary MacLane, By Herself.*	U.S. ends its occupation of Cuba and the Republic of Cuba is founded.
Helena Arkansas Mason, African American autobiographer: *Life of Mrs. Helena Arkansas Mason.*	"Bill Bailey, Won't You Please Come Home" is a popular song.
Georgia Wood Pangborn: *Roman Biznet.*	
Ruth McEnery Stuart: *Napoleon Jackson: The Gentleman of the Plush Rocker.*	
Journalist Ida Tarbell's exposé on the Standard Oil company for *McClure's* magazine serves as an exemplar for "muckraking" journalism.	
Susie King Taylor (1848–1912), African American autobiographer and nurse: *Reminiscences of My Life with the 33d United States Colored Troops Late 1st S.C. Volunteers.*	
Onoto Watanna (Winnifred Eaton): *The Wooing of Wisteria.*	

TEXTS	CONTEXTS
1902 Carolyn Wells (1869–1942), anthologist, author of 170 books, including children's books and over 70 detective novels: *A Nonsense Anthology*. Edith Wharton (1862–1937), prolific novelist and short-story writer whose works include novels of manners, gothic fiction and ghost stories, psychological realism, and social analysis: *The Valley of Decision*, a novel.	**1902**
1902–1903 Pauline E. Hopkins: *Of One Blood; or, The Hidden Self*.	**1902–1903**
1903 Mary Austin (1868–1934): ardent and vocal feminist and spokesperson for Native American and Hispanic traditions, publishes first and most famous book, *The Land of Little Rain*. Mary "Molly" Moore Davis: *The Little Chevalier*, an historical novel. Mary E. Wilkins Freeman: *The Wind in the Rose-Bush and Other Stories of the Supernatural* and *Six Trees*, collections of stories.	**1903** Ford Motor Company is founded. Henry Ford introduces the Model T in 1908, priced at $850 (the price subsequently decreases); by 1909, 19,000 Model T's have been produced. Mary Kenney (O'Sullivan), active in the American Federation of Labor and co-founder of the Union for Industrial Progress (1894), co-founds the National Women's Trade Union League. Agnes Nestor becomes the first woman president

TEXTS	CONTEXTS
1903 Charlotte Perkins Gilman: *The Home: Its Work and Influence.*	**1903** of an international labor union when she is elected president of the women's local of the International Glove Workers Union.
Ella Rhoads Higginson (1860–1940), poet, travel writer, short-story writer, and novelist of the Pacific Northwest: *The Voice of April-Land, and Other Poems.*	Maggie Lena Walker becomes the first African American woman and very likely the first woman president of a bank, Saint Luke Penny Savings Bank in Richmond, Virginia, which she also founded.
Mrs. Fremont Older (1875–1968), author of social melodramas and magazine articles: *The Socialist and the Prince.*	Ethyl Smith's *Der Wald*, the first opera composed by a woman, premieres at the Metropolitan Opera.
Belle Owen: *A Prairie Winter, by an Illinois Girl.*	Orville and Wilbur Wright achieve their first successful flight at Kitty Hawk, North Carolina.
Josephine Preston Peabody: *The Singing Leaves*, poetry.	Gertrude Käsebier (1852–1934), an early woman photographer who often uses female subjects: *The Sketch*, a platinum print.
Onoto Watanna (Winnifred Eaton): *The Heart of Hyacinth*, a novel.	
Kate Douglas Wiggin (1856–1923), children's author: *Rebecca of Sunnybrook Farm.*	Eva Watson-Schütze (1867–1935), another early woman photographer who often photographs women: *Woman with Lily*, a platinum print.
Edith Wyatt: *True Love: A Comedy of the Affections*, a novel.	Nettie Stevens, biologist and geneticist, is the first

TEXTS		CONTEXTS
1903	1903	woman to show that gender is tied to a specific chromosome.
1904 Mary Austin: *The Basket Woman*. Alice Brown: *High Noon*, a collection of stories. Rebecca Harding Davis: *Bits of Gossip*, a collection of stories. Charlotte Perkins Gilman: *Human Work*. Ellen Glasgow: *The Deliverance*, a novel. Mary Johnston: *Sir Mortimer*, a romance. Helen Reimensnyder Martin (1868–1939), novelist and short-story writer who chronicles the lifestyle of the Mennonites: *A Mennonite Maid*, a novel. Mary Alicia Owen: *Folklore of the Musquakie Indians*, anthropological study by woman made a tribal member in 1892. Elizabeth Stuart Phelps (Ward): *Trixy*, a novel. Gene Stratton Porter, (1863–1924), Indiana nat-	1904	Anna Howard Shaw becomes president of the National American Woman Suffrage Association (NAWSA); she serves until 1915, when she becomes president emeritus. Deaf mute Helen Keller graduates *cum laude* from Radcliffe. Mary Cassatt, the Impressionist painter, receives the Chevalier of French Legion of Honor. Mabel Boardman begins her 40-year tenure as head of the Red Cross. Evangeline Booth, daughter of the British founders of the Salvation Army, becomes the first woman commander of the U.S. Salvation Army. Mary McLeod (Bethune) opens the school that would eventually become Bethune-Cookman College in Florida with only six students—her son and five girls—attending. The American Academy of Arts and Letters is founded.

TEXTS	CONTEXTS
1904 uralist and novelist: *Freckles.* Jessie B. Rittenhouse (1869–1948), poet, critic, editor, teacher, and a founder of the Poetry Society of America, edits *The Younger American Poets.* Elizabeth Robins (1862–1952), actress, feminist, and novelist: *The Magnetic North.* Bertha Muzzy Sinclair (1871–1940), writing as "B. M. Bower," prolific writer of Westerns: *Chip of the Flying U.* Ida Tarbell (1857–1944), biographer, journalist, historian: *The History of the Standard Oil Company.* Effie Waller: *Songs of the Months.* Onoto Watanna (Winnifred Eaton): *Daughters of Nijo* and *The Love of Azalea,* novels. Edith Wharton: *The Descent of Man and Other Stories.* *Tryphena Ely White's Journal: Being a Record, Written One Hundred Years*	1904 The first offset press is invented and introduced in the U.S. The National Child Labor Committee is formed. The first public vocational school for young women, Trade School for Girls, opens in Boston. Theodore Roosevelt is elected to his first full term as President. A woman is arrested on New York City's Fifth Avenue for smoking a cigarette in an open-air car. The Broadway subway opens in New York City.

TEXTS	CONTEXTS

| 1904 | *Ago, of the Daily Life of a Young Lady of Puritan Heritage, 1805–1905*, Fanny Kellog, ed. | 1904 | |

| 1905 | Frances Hodgson Burnett: *A Little Princess.*

Mary Boykin Chesnut (1823–1886): *A Diary from Dixie*, published posthumously, covers the experiences of a Confederate woman from 1861–1865.

Martha Finley: *Elsie and Her Namesakes.*

Mary E. Wilkins Freeman: *The Debtor*, a novel.

Pauline E. Hopkins: *A Primer of Facts Pertaining to the Early Greatness of the African Race and the Possibility of Restoration by Its Descendants—with Epilogue.*

Helen Reimensnyder Martin: *Sabina: A Story of the Amish*, a novel.

Emma Bell Miles, an Appalachian woman who spent her life in the mountains, publishes a collection of the folk songs and music of the mountains, the first of its kind: *Spirit of the Mountains.* | 1905 | The Niagara movement is organized on the Canadian side of Niagara Falls because U.S. hotels deny its black leaders, including W.E.B. Du Bois, rooms; it is the forerunner of the National Association for the Advancement of Colored People (NAACP), founded in 1909.

The social hygiene movement is launched in New York City with the formation of the Society of Sanitary and Moral Prophylaxis.

Pond's Extract is first marketed for cosmetic purposes.

Wellesley College Professor of Psychology Mary Whiton Calkins becomes the first woman elected president of the American Psychological Association; when in 1918 Calkins becomes president of the American Philosophical Association, she becomes one of just three persons and the first woman ever to hold both positions. |

TEXTS	CONTEXTS
1905 Margaret Prescott Montague, Richmond novelist, short-story writer, poet, and essayist: *The Poet, Miss Kate and I.* Lillian Mortimer (?–1914), playwright, vaudevillian: *No Mother to Guide Her.* Marie Van Vorst (1867–1936), social reformer, novelist: *Amanda of the Mill.* Edith Wharton: *The House of Mirth*, the novel that makes her famous. Ellen G. White (1827–1915), writer on religious issues and advocate of temperance and dress, diet, prison, and education reform: *The Ministry of Healing.*	**1905** Jessie Tarbox Beals (1870–1942), considered America's first female photojournalist, also known as a portraitist and architectural photographer, moves to New York City and establishes a studio from which she works to record "the soul of New York" through pictures of Greenwich Village, Chinatown, the Lower East Side, Central Park, and the downtown city. She also travels to photograph scenes in other states and contributes to publications including the *Ladies' Home Journal, Vogue, Town and Country,* and the *New York Herald.* International Workers of the World (IWW) is formed.
1906 Mary Austin: *The Flock.* Rachel Crothers (1878–1958), playwright and director: *The Three of Us.* Mary E. Wilkins Freeman: *By the Light of the Soul.* Ellen Glasgow: *Wheel of Life.*	**1906** By this date, an estimated 150,000 women have had ovariotomies, the surgical removal of ovaries also known as "female castration." A devastating earthquake hits San Francisco, resulting in widespread fires. The first radio program is broadcast.

	TEXTS		CONTEXTS
1906	Emma Goldman (1869–1940), essayist, autobiographer, editor, lecturer, anarchist, and feminist, founds *Mother Earth*, a magazine that publishes political, philosophical, and literary writing, usually from a radical perspective.	1906	The National League for the Protection of Colored Women is established.
			The Pure Food and Drug Act and Meat Inspection Act is enacted, largely as a result of public outcry following Upton Sinclair's *The Jungle*.
	Onoto Watanna (Winnifred Eaton): *A Japanese Blossom*, a novel.		Women in Finland are enfranchised.
			Geraldine Farrar (1882–1967), world-acclaimed opera singer, makes her first appearance before an American audience.
			Mary Abastemia St. Leger Eberle (1878–1942), influenced by the Ash Can school of painting, which relies on realistic techniques but takes everyday and "lower" urban life as its subjects, exhibits her first New York street scene sculpture: *Roller Skating*.
1906–1909		1906–1909	U.S. troops occupy Cuba.
1907	The *Colored Woman's Magazine* (1907–20) is first published and becomes one of the longest-running periodicals edited by black women.	1907	Immigration from southern and eastern Europe reaches its highest level: 1,285,349.
			Oklahoma includes prohibition in its constitution;

TEXTS	CONTEXTS
1907	1907

TEXTS

1907 Virginia W. Broughton, black religious author: *Twenty Year's Experience of a Missionary.*

Elizabeth Parsons Channing: *Autobiography and Diary of Elizabeth Parsons Channing: Gleanings of a Thoughtful Life.*

Mary "Molly" Moore Davis: *His Lordship: Romantic Comedy for 5 Males and 6 Females* and *The New System: Comedy for 4 Males and 4 Females*, satirical plays.

Augusta Jane Evans (Wilson: *Devota.*

Priscilla Jane Thompson: *Gleanings of Quiet Hours,* poetry.

Onoto Watanna (Winnifred Eaton): *The Diary of Delia: Being a Veracious Chronicle of the Kitchen with Some Sidelights on the Parlour.*

Edith Wharton: *The Fruit of the Tree*, a novel.

CONTEXTS

1907 by this date only Maine, Kansas, Nebraska, North Dakota, and Oklahoma remain prohibition states.

Mary Emma Woolley becomes the first woman senate member of Phi Beta Kappa.

Florence Lawrence (1886–1938) begins her screen career at Vitograph Company. After joining Biograph when D. W. Griffith becomes their director, she becomes known as the "Biograph Girl." Lawrence is considered the first motion-picture actress to receive star treatment, thus initiating the studio star system.

Kate Barnard becomes the first woman to be elected to a major state office— Commissioner of Charities & Corrections for Oklahoma.

When her husband deserts her and her three children, Alice Foote Mac-Dougall enters the wholesale coffee business. By 1928 her enterprises are worth an estimated $2 million.

Feminist Harriet Stanton Blanch is refused service

TEXTS	CONTEXTS
1907	1907 at a New York restaurant because she is unaccompanied by a male escort.
	The modern United Press (UP) is formed; in 1958 as a result of a merger with William Randolph Hearst's International News Service it becomes United Press International (UPI).
	By this date, one in ten American homes have electricity.
	Gertrude Stein and Alice B. Toklas meet in Paris and become lifelong companions.
1907–1908	1907–1908 The Gentleman's Agreement between Japan and the United States bars further entry of Japanese, and later Korean, laborers into the U.S.
1907–1912 Lavinia Lloyd Dock and Mary Adelaide Nutting: *History of Nursing*, a 4-volume feminist project.	1907–1912
1907–1917	1907–1917 Sixteen states pass sterilization laws preventing procreation among those deemed "unfit" and "undesirable": mostly non-Anglo-Saxons.

*   *   *

TEXTS	CONTEXTS
1908	**1908**
Eliza Andrews: *The Wartime Journal of a Georgia Girl*, a diary begun in December 1864.	*Muller v. Oregon* restricts the workday for women employed in laundries to ten hours. The decision is based on the assumption of women's inferior physical capacity as a justification for differences in legislation dealing with women and with laborers in general.
Mary Baker Eddy founds the *Christian Science Monitor*.	
Mary E. Wilkins Freeman: *The Shoulders of Atlas*, a novel.	
Julia Ward Howe becomes the first woman elected to the American Academy of Arts and Letters.	Helen Turner (1858–1958), Impressionist painter, shows *Mother and Child*.
Helen Reimensnyder Martin: *The Revolt of Anne Royle*, a novel about a Mennonite woman.	The National Association of Colored Graduate Nurses, the first professional black women's organization, is founded. It dissolves in 1950 when the American Nursing Association admits black nurses.
Kate Alma Orgain: *Southern Authors of Poetry and Prose*, containing selections by 11 women and 15 men.	
Agnes Repplier (1855–1950), essayist, biographer, historian: *A Happy Half-Century*.	The National College Women's Equal Suffrage League is established, with faculty and graduates of Barnard, Bryn Mawr, Mt. Holyoke, Radcliffe, Smith, and the universities of Chicago, California, and Wisconsin as delegates.
Mary Roberts Rinehart (1876–1958), prolific novelist, detective fiction writer, and playwright: *The Circular Staircase*, the first in the "Had-I-But-Known" mystery novel	William Howard Taft is elected President.
	The Bureau of Investiga-

	TEXTS		CONTEXTS
1908	tradition. From 1910 to 1940, she is America's most successful popular writer.	1908	tions (later the FBI) is founded.
	Clara Ann Thompson (1869–1949), African American poet: *Songs from the Wayside*.		Mary Pennington, chemist and refrigeration specialist, becomes chief of the Food Research Laboratory of the Department of Agriculture. She had received a Ph.D. from the University of Pennsylvania in 1895, although, because of her sex, she was denied the B.S. she had earned. Her research leads to new, safer standards for food processing, storage, and shipment.
	Margaret Floy Washburn, psychologist: *The Animal Mind*.		
	Edith Wharton: *The Hermit and the Wild Woman and Other Stories*.		
			With the death of Mrs. William Waldorf Astor — famous for her "Mrs. Astor's ball" — "old society" in New York City virtually ends.
			Florence Nightingale Graham (Elizabeth Arden) opens her first beauty salon in New York City.
			General Motors is founded.
			Carrie Kilgore is the first known woman in the U.S. to ascend alone in a balloon.
1909	Jane Addams (1860–1935), social activist and autobiographer, winner of	1909	Sigmund Freud visits the U.S.

TEXTS	CONTEXTS
1909	1909

TEXTS

1909 — the 1931 Nobel Peace Prize: *The Spirit of Youth and the City Streets.*

Mary Austin: *Lost Borders,* a collection of stories set in the West.

Annie L. Campbell Burton: *Memories of Childhood's Slavery Days,* a slave narrative.

Frances Boyd Calhoun (1867–1909): *Miss Minerva and William Green Hill.*

Sui Sin Far (Edith Maud Eaton, 1865–1914): "Leaves from the Mental Portfolio of an Eurasian," the first known autobiographical piece by an Asian American woman.

Rose O'Neill (1874–1944), novelist, poet, illustrator: *The Lady in the White Veil,* a novel.

Elizabeth Stuart Phelps (Ward): *The Oath of Allegiance, and Other Stories.*

Gene Stratton Porter: *A Girl of the Limberlost,* a novel.

Gertrude Stein (1874–1946), novelist, short-story writer, poet, autobi-

CONTEXTS

1909 — The U.S. flag is planted at the North Pole.

A group of social workers in Philadelphia publish their study *Women and the Trades: Pittsburgh, 1907–1908,* which shows, contrary to cultural assumptions, that the majority of women need to work to survive economically and that working conditions are far from safe.

The largest women's strike in American history begins when 20,000 shirtwaist makers join to protest oppressive "sweatshop" conditions, long hours, and low wages; Mary Beard, feminist historian and suffragist, helps organize the strike.

The American Home Economics Association is founded.

Alice Huyler Ramsey becomes the first woman, along with three other female passengers, to complete a transcontinental automobile journey.

Mrs. Ralph Henry Van Deman takes a four-minute flight, with Wilbur Wright serving as pilot, and becomes the first

TEXTS		CONTEXTS
1909	ographer, playwright, important in initiating the linguistic experimentation that characterizes much of Modernism: *Three Lives*, published privately. Carolyn Wells: *The Clue*, the first of 82 mystery novels, most of which feature Fleming Stone, an academic sleuth. Helen Maria Winslow (1851–1938), novelist, poet, children's author, advocate of women's clubs: *A Woman for Mayor*.	**1909**	woman airline passenger in the country. The suntanned "Outdoor Girl" replaces the paler "Gibson Girl" as the fashion ideal as more and more women take up automobile driving. The Negro National Committee is established; the following year, it chooses the name National Association for the Advancement of Colored People (NAACP). *The Progressive* magazine begins publication.
1910s		**1910s**	Cabarets become popular night spots.
1910	Edith Abbott (1876–1957), social reformer and educator: *Women in Industry*. Jane Addams: *Twenty Years at Hull-House*. Helen M. Angle: *The Log or Diary of Our Automobile Voyage through Maine and the White Mountains, Written by One of the Survivors*. Rheta Childe Dorr (1866–1948), journalist, war correspondent, feminist: *What Eight Million*	**1910**	Total U.S. population is 92,407,000; 8,795,386 immigrants have arrived since 1901. Eight million women are working outside the home. Women represent 40 percent of college graduates by this year. One in every nine marriages ends in divorce. Only 26 of the country's

TEXTS	CONTEXTS
1910 *Women Want*, which argues that the fulfillment of demands for women's economic, social, and political freedom is in the best interest of a democratic society.	**1910** 193 trade schools are for women.
Mary E. Wilkins Freeman: *The Green Door*, a novel.	Women's participation in trade unions reaches a low of 1.5 percent.
Charlotte Perkins Gilman: *What Diantha Did*, a novel.	The first woman suffrage parade is held in New York City.
Corra Harris (1869–1935), Georgia novelist who portrays the South in a realistic fashion: *A Circuit Rider's Wife*, a novel critical of the hierarchy of the Methodist Church.	The National Association of University Women is founded.
	Ella Flagg Young becomes the first woman president of the National Education Association.
	Only 1500 women attorneys are practicing in the United States.
Maggie Pogue Johnson, African American poet: *Virginia Dreams: Lyrics for an Idle Hour; Tales of the Time Told in Rhyme*.	Nora Bayes, Irene Franklin, Elsie Janis, and Eva Tanguay become known as the Big Four of women headlining vaudeville acts; they earn nearly $2000 a week, in contrast to regular laborers who are making about $15 a week.
Theresa Malkiel (1874–1949), journalist, novelist, feminist, socialist: *Diary of a Shirtwaist Striker*.	
Margaret Prescott Montague: *Mary Cary*, filmed as *Nobody's Kid* in 1921.	The White-Slave Traffic Act (the Mann Act) is passed, outlawing the transportation of women across state lines for "immoral purposes."
Christina Moody, African American poet: *A Tiny Spark*.	

TEXTS	CONTEXTS
1910	**1910**

TEXTS	CONTEXTS
Josephine Preston Peabody: *The Piper*, a play.	Congress enacts legislation prohibiting the entrance of immigrants employed as prostitutes or procurers into music or dance halls or into any other arena "where prostitutes gather."
Elizabeth Stuart Phelps (Ward): *The Empty House, and Other Stories.*	
Lavinia Honeyman Porter: *By Ox Team to California: A Narrative of Crossing the Plains in 1860.*	Ellen Emmet Rand (1875–1941), at age 18 a successful fashion illustrator for *Vogue*, becomes known for her portraits, such as *In the Studio.*
Emily James Putnam (1865–1944), classics scholar and feminist: *The Lady.*	
Dora Knowlton Thompson Ranous: *Diary of a Daly Debutante: Being Passages from the Journal of a Member of Augustin Daly's Famous Company of Players.*	Eva Watson-Schütze, photographer, prints *Woman Playing Piano*, a platinum print.
	The premarital pregnancy rate rises 23 percent since 1880.
H. Cordelia Ray: *Poems.*	A Kinsey survey finds that only one out of ten non-college women rely on withdrawal for birth control, while over one-third use diaphragms.
Katherine Davis Tillman, African American dramatist: *Fifty Years of Freedom; or, From Cabin to Congress; a Drama in Five Acts.*	
Onoto Watanna (Winnifred Eaton): *Tama*, a novel.	Twice as many urban blacks are likely to die from tuberculosis as whites.
Edith Wharton: *Tales of Men and Ghosts.*	In the southern states, 17,266 black women work as schoolteachers, outnumbering their male counterparts by more than three to one.

TEXTS	CONTEXTS
1910	1910 The Camp Fire Girls is formed, becoming the first national interracial and nonsectarian organization for girls.

Madame C. J. (Sarah Breedlove) Walker, black entrepreneur, founds the Madame C. J. Walker laboratories in Indianapolis and soon becomes the richest self-made woman in the U.S. through sales of hair straighteners and pomades to blacks.

Atlantic Monthly magazine and *Putnam's Monthly and the Critic* merge.

The first U.S. newsreel is produced.

The saying "bring home the bacon" is coined.

Fanny Brice (1891–1951), comic actress and singing star of theater, vaudeville, movies, and radio, begins appearing in the Ziegfeld Follies; she will star there until 1936.

Congress is petitioned by 404,000 women demanding woman suffrage.

Factory-made biscuits and quick cereals begin to be

TEXTS		CONTEXTS
1910	1910	a feature in many American homes.
		Nan Jane Aspinall becomes the first woman to ride a horse alone across the country.
		With her first solo flight, Blanche Scott becomes the first U.S. woman to pilot a plane.
		Halley's Comet appears.
1911 Jane Addams: *A New Conscience and an Ancient Evil.*	1911	A fire in the Triangle Shirtwaist Company (New York City) kills 147 mostly female, immigrant employees.
Frances Hodgson Burnett: *The Secret Garden*, a novel for children.		The National Urban League is founded.
Carrie Williams Clifford (1882–1958), African American poet: *Race Rhymes.*		Theresa West Elmendorf becomes the first woman president of the American Library Association.
Anna Botsford Comstock (1854–1930), naturalist who writes many nature books for children and for popular audiences, as well as serving as illustrator and junior author on many of her husband's college textbooks: *Handbook of Nature Study.*		Marie Curie wins her second Nobel Prize in medicine.
		Harvard philosopher George Santayana coins the term "genteel tradition" to describe premodernist culture and letters.
Alice French, writing as "Octave Thanet": *Stories That End Well.*		*Publishers' Weekly* begins

TEXTS	CONTEXTS
1911 Charlotte Perkins Gilman: *The Man-Made World; or Our Androcentric Culture; The Crux*, a novel; and *Moving the Mountain*, a novel.	1911 publishing its "Best Seller Consensus."

Emma Goldman: *Anarchism and Other Essays.*

Constance Cary Harrison (1843–1920), southern author of local color and satiric fictions: *Recollections Grave and Gay*, an autobiography.

Mary Johnston: *The Long Roll*, a novel of the Civil War.

Elizabeth Lindley: *The Diary of a Book Agent.*

Mary White Ovington (1865–1951), author and civil rights worker: *Half a Man: The Status of the Negro in New York.*

Edith Wharton: *Ethan Frome*, a novel.

Edith Wyatt and Sue Ainslie Clark: *Making Both Ends Meet: The Income and Outlay of New York Working Girls*, which documents through case studies the unfair working

The first successful movie magazine, *Motion Picture*, begins publication.

The leftist magazine *The Masses* begins publication; in 1917, when it is barred from the mails during the war, it folds and quickly reappears as the *Liberator* (1918–24).

The National Council of Women Voters is formed.

The National Association Opposed to Woman Suffrage is established.

Jovita Idar de Juarez, educator and journalist, becomes president of the Mexican Feminist League, an organization working against lynching and for equal rights and education for women.

TEXTS		CONTEXTS
1911	conditions and poverty under which young work-ing women were struggling.	1911

1912	Edith Abbott and Sopho-nisba Breckinridge: *The Delinquent Child and the Home.*	1912

Mary Antin: *The Promised Land*, story of a young Jewish girl's odyssey from Russia to life in America.

Mary Austin: *A Woman of Genius*, a novel.

Willa Cather (1873–1947), novelist and short-story writer concerned with life on the frontier, the life of the artist, and questions of female iden-tity: *Alexander's Bridge*, her first novel, published when she was 38 years of age.

Sui Sin Far (Edith Maud Eaton): From the late 1890s through 1914, short stories and articles signed Sui Sin Far appear in pop-ular and prominent na-tional magazines. In 1912, many of the stories by this first Chinese Ameri-can author are collected in *Mrs. Spring Fragrance.*

Suffrage passes by state referendum in Arizona, Kansas, and Oregon; it is defeated in Michigan and Ohio.

Mabel Normand (1894–1930), comedienne and di-rector, joins Mack Sen-nett and the Keystone Film Company, of which she will be the most popu-lar female actress, later fre-quently pairing with Char-lie Chaplin. In 1916 she forms the Mabel Nor-mand Feature Film Company.

With her appointment as director of the newly formed U.S. Children's Bureau, Julia Clifford Lathrop becomes the first woman head of a major government bureau.

Juliette Low's Girl Guides becomes the Girl Scouts of America.

Margaret Murray Wash-ington, co-principal—along with her husband Booker T.—and director of Industries for Girls at

TEXTS	CONTEXTS
1912 Corra Harris: *The Recording Angel.*	1912 the Tuskegee Institute in Alabama, becomes president of the National Association of Colored Women.

1912   Corra Harris: *The Recording Angel.*

Mary Logan and Mary Logan Tucker, mother and daughter historians: *The Part Taken by Women in American History,* including 2000 biographical sketches.

Ethel Louise McLean: *A Gentle Jehu in Japan,* a memoir.

Harriet Monroe (1860–1936), poet, editor, founds the important literary magazine *Poetry: A Magazine of Verse* in October. It provides the first major forum in the U.S. for debating issues regarding poetry. Monroe serves as editor for the next 24 years. Among its contributors are Edna St. Vincent Millay and Marianne Moore; it is still being published in Chicago by the Modern Poetry Association.

Leila Amos Pendleton: *A Narrative of the Negro.*

Nell Speed, journalist and author of pulp fiction and several series for children: *Molly Brown's Sophomore Days.*

1912   the Tuskegee Institute in Alabama, becomes president of the National Association of Colored Women.

On its first voyage, the British ocean liner *Titanic* sinks and more than 1500 die.

Sixty-one-year-old American Annie Peck is the first person ever to climb Mount Coropuna (21,250 feet) in Peru; when she reaches the top she plants a banner proclaiming "Votes for Women."

Woodrow Wilson is elected President.

The first electric washing machine is marketed.

Musical theater actress Lillian Russell patents her design for a custom dresser-trunk.

Harriet Quimby, the first licensed U.S. female pilot, becomes the first woman to fly a plane across the English Channel.

Texan Katherine Stinson, 19 years old, earns her pilot's license and goes on to earn fame for, among

TEXTS	CONTEXTS
1912 Gertrude Stein does "word portraits" of Picasso and Matisse for Alfred Stieglitz's *Camera Work*. Onoto Watanna (Winnifred Eaton): *The Honorable Miss Moonlight*, a novel. Jean Webster (1876–1916), novelist and author of children's books: *Daddy-Long-Legs*. Edith Wharton: *The Reef*, a novel.	**1912** other things, being the first woman to fly the mail, "loop the loop," and barnstorm in Japan and China.
1913 Willa Cather: *O Pioneers!*, a novel. L. Louise Elliott: *Six Weeks on Horseback through Yellowstone Park*. Mrs. Frances Joseph Gaudet: *He Leadeth Me: An Autobiography by Mrs. Frances Joseph Gaudet*. Ellen Glasgow: *Virginia*, a novel. Maud Cuney Hare (1874–1936), African American musician, poet, biographer, and playwright: *Norris Wright Cuney: A Tribune of the Black People*.	**1913** Grace Drayton, originator and illustrator of the "Campbell Kids," the highly successful icons of the Campbell Soup advertising campaign, begins the Dolly Dingle paperdoll series in *Pictorial Review*; it continues there until 1933. Fifty years after emancipation, black literacy has risen from 5 percent to 70 percent and black wealth is estimated at $700 million. Nonetheless, racism is still pervasive, if evidenced only by the fact that at least 51 blacks are lynched in 1913.

TEXTS | CONTEXTS

1913   Mary Johnston: *Hagar*, a novel.

Mary Logan: *Reminiscences of a Soldier's Wife*.

Mary White Ovington: *Hazel*, advertised as a novel written specifically for African American girls.

Eleanor H. Porter (1868–1920), novelist: *Pollyanna*.

Nell Speed: *Molly Brown's Senior Days*.

Anna Garlin Spencer (1851–1931), journalist, professor, and feminist: *Woman's Share in Social Culture*.

Carolyn Wells: *The Technique of the Mystery Story*, the first book of instruction for writers of mysteries.

Edith Wharton: *The Custom of the Country*, a novel.

1913   The militant Congressional Union for Woman Suffrage is formed by Lucy Burns, Crystal Eastman, and Alice Paul; they lead a march of 5000 women on Washington, D.C., and are attacked by mobs.

Mahatma Gandhi, leader of the Indian Passive Resistance movement, is arrested.

Pancho Villa gains notoriety as a bandit leader in Mexico.

Rose Schneiderman, a Jewish immigrant, leads the "Uprising of the Twenty Thousand"; she later serves as president of the National Women's Trade Union League from 1926 to 1950.

The Paterson Silk Strike occurs in New Jersey; Elizabeth Gurley Flynn and other members of the Industrial Workers of the World (IWW) are involved.

The International Exhibition of Modern Art, known as the "Armory Show," is credited with introducing modernism to the American public.

TEXTS	CONTEXTS
1913	1913 F. W. Woolworth builds the country's first sky-scraper, the Woolworth Building in New York City, out of the proceeds of the millions he has earned through his five-and-dime stores; the building is 58 stories high.

Vanity Fair magazine begins publication; it folds in 1936 and is not reissued until 1983.

Kate Gleason invents mass-produced affordable tract housing.

Georgia "Tiny" Broadwick becomes the first woman to free-fall parachute from an airplane.

Cartoonist Rose O'Neill patents the Kewpie doll, which makes her a millionaire.

What might be deemed the world's first nude calendar appears. It features a reproduction of a nude painting and incites calls for censorship and removal.

The Southern States Woman Suffrage Conference is founded.

	TEXTS		CONTEXTS
1913		1913	The first act of the new Alaska territory's legislature is to pass a woman suffrage bill.
			When British suffragist Emmeline Pankhurst arrives in the U.S., the Ellis Island Board orders her to be deported; President Wilson intervenes.
1914	Margaret Anderson (1886–1973) founds *Little Review* with the aim of publishing creative criticism that is "fresh and constructive, and intelligent from the artist's point of view"; the first number features articles on feminism, Nietzsche, and psychoanalysis. Contributors would include Amy Lowell, Emma Goldman, Dorothy Richardson, T. S. Eliot, James Joyce, Gertrude Stein, and H.D. (Hilda Doolittle), among others. Anderson continues as editor until 1923.	1914	Montana and Nevada pass state referendums on woman suffrage; Missouri, Ohio, Nebraska, and North and South Dakota defeat similar referendums.
	Mary Antin: *They Who Knock at Our Gates: A Complete Gospel of Immigration*.		Mrs. Frank Leslie, publisher of *Leslie's Weekly*, leaves Carrie Chapman Catt $2 million to help further the woman suffrage cause.
			The Panama Canal opens.
			The Smith-Lever Act establishes federal funding for the teaching of home economics in coeducational state colleges and universities.
			World War I begins.
	Effie T. Battle, African American author: *Gleanings from Dixie Land in Ten Poems*.		The U.S. Children's Bureau publishes and distributes its enormously influential pamphlet *Infant*

TEXTS	CONTEXTS
1914 Alice Brown: *Children of the Earth: A Play of New England*, winner of the Winthrop Ames Prize.	1914 *Care*, describing women's responsibility for their family's health and well-being and stressing that they could insure this only by following to the letter the instruction of experts. The pamphlet is still in print today.
Olivia Ward Bush: *Driftwood*, poetry and prose.	
Alice Ruth Moore Dunbar-Nelson: *Masterpieces of Negro Eloquence: The Best Speeches Delivered by the Negro from the Days of Slavery to the Present Time.*	A group of publishers launches a "Revival of Reading" Campaign, one of the most successful cooperative book advertising efforts to date.
Emma Goldman: *The Social Significance of the Modern Drama.*	Polish-born Helena Rubinstein, who studied both medicine and dermatology, opens her first beauty salon in New York. With salons in that city and in London and Paris, Rubenstein eventually becomes one of the wealthiest women in the world.
Inez Haynes Irwin (1873–1970), novelist, writer of stories for girls, and suffragist: *Angel Island*, one of the earliest science fiction novels by a U.S. woman.	
Mary Johnston: *The Witch*, a novel promoting religious and intellectual freedom for women.	The 4-H Club—Head, Heart, Hands, and Home (later Health)—becomes a national organization.
Maria Cristina Mena, a.k.a. Maria Chambers, Chicana short-story writer: "The Vine Leaf," one of several short stories and sketches of Mexican life she publishes in	The first national figure-skating tournament is held in Connecticut. *The New Republic* magazine begins publication.

	TEXTS		CONTEXTS
1914	*The Century* and *American* in the early 1900s.	1914	Cosmetic industry sales total $17 million.
	Louella Parsons (1881–1972) becomes the first woman to serve as movie critic for a major paper, the New York *Morning Telegraph*.		The waltz and the two-step replace the cotillion as the most popular dances in America's ballrooms; with "ragtime" music comes the craze for "animal" dances—including the fox trot, the grizzly bear, the turkey trot, the bunny hug—which scandalize conservatives and are execrated in press and pulpit.
	Margaret Sanger edits *The Woman Rebel*, a monthly journal covering socialist and anarchist concerns.		
	Elsie Singmaster (1879–1958), novelist of the Pennsylvania Dutch: *Katy Gaumer*.		The daughter of the woman who organized the first Mother's Day persuades Congress to designate the second Sunday in May as Mother's Day.
	Gertrude Stein: *Tender Buttons*.		
			Polly Jacob patents her invention, the "backless brassiere."
1915	Annie Heloise Abel (1873–1947): *The American Indian as Slaveholder and Secessionist: An Omitted Chapter in the Diplomatic History of the Confederacy*.	1915	Anarchist Emma Goldman is arrested in Portland, Oregon, for lecturing on sexual freedom and contraception; a circuit court judge sets aside her conviction and condemns the "prudery" he believes so evident throughout the U.S.
	Willa Cather: *The Song of the Lark*, a novel.		
	Adelaide Crapsey (1878–1914), inventor of the cinquain, a five-line poetic		A federal prosecutor drops charges against Margaret Sanger for violating

TEXTS	CONTEXTS

1915	form: *Verse*, published posthumously.	1915	the Comstock Law by distributing pamphlets on birth control through the mail; she is arrested again in 1916 in Brooklyn for opening a birth control clinic and this time is sent to jail.
	Isabel Alice Hartley Crawford: *Kiowa: The History of a Blanket Indian Mission*, a memoir.		
	Alice Gerstenberg (1885–1972), playwright: *Overtones* opens as a one-act play in New York. Expanded to three acts in 1922, it is seen as a forerunner of later psychological drama.		Sixty-one women die for every 10,000 live births.
			Theda Bara (1885–1955) appears in *A Fool There Was*, which establishes her as a star and brings a new word, "vamp," into use. Bara goes on to play the vamp in 39 more films.
	Charlotte Perkins Gilman: *Herland*, utopian novel.		
	Anna Katharine Green: *The Golden Slipper and Other Problems for Violet Strange*, a collection of mystery stories introducing Violet Strange, the prototype for girl detectives such as Nancy Drew.		Nevada passes its "quickie" divorce law.
			Mary Coffin (Ware) Dennett founds the National Birth Control League, the first American birth control organization. It becomes the Voluntary Parenthood League in 1918.
	Onoto Watanna (Winnifred Eaton): *Me*, anonymously published autobiography.		
			Jane Addams, of Hull House fame, forms a nationwide Woman's Peace Party, arguing that women need the vote and equal government representation in order to oppose war effectively.

TEXTS	CONTEXTS
1915	**1915** Two influential books appear that, among other things, help to shape the "canon" of American literature, defining its great writers as predominantly white male New Englanders: Fred Lewis Pattee's *History of American Literature Since 1870* and Van Wyck Brooks's *America's Coming of Age.*
	Anne W. Brigman (1868–1950), photographer who often focuses on women subjects, produces *The West Wind*, a gelatin silver print.
	Geraldine Farrar becomes the first opera star to appear in Hollywood films, including *Carmen.*
	Susan Glaspell, her husband George Cram Cook, and Mary Heaton Vorse found Provincetown Players, an influential, often experimental drama group. Together they write and stage numerous plays, including in this year *Suppressed Desires*, a satiric look at marriage and the fascination with Freud.
	Alfred A. Knopf, Inc., is founded; Willa Cather is to become Knopf's favor-

TEXTS	CONTEXTS
1915	1915 ite author (perhaps because she never requested an advance and only once asked for a [1 percent] royalty raise).
	A German U-boat sinks the British passenger ship *Lusitania*, arousing American public indignation.
	The Women's International League for Peace and Freedom, now the oldest active peace organization in the U.S., is established.
	The first transcontinental phone call occurs.
	A marketing campaign begins in *Harper's Bazar* (as it was known then) to get women to shave underarm hair when sleeveless dresses come into style (leg-shaving comes later and is cemented during World War II when Betty Grable's "pin-up" shows off her smooth-shaven legs).
	With the invention of the metal lipstick container, the mass production and purchase of lipsticks begins.
	The NAACP petitions the Supreme Court and

TEXTS	CONTEXTS
1915	1915 wins when the court rules unconstitutional the grandfather clause used to prevent blacks from voting.
	D. W. Griffith's film *The Birth of a Nation* opens; the NAACP protests its stereotypical representation of African Americans.
1915–1920	1915–1920 African Americans migrate to northern cities in great numbers.
1916 Jane Addams: *The Long Road of Woman's Memory*.	1916 Suffragists Alice Paul and Lucy Burns establish the National Woman's Party in the 12 states that have already given women presidential suffrage. This militant outgrowth of the NAWSA and the Congressional Union opposes Woodrow Wilson and the Democratic ticket in that year's election because its leaders blame Wilson for the failure to pass a federal suffrage amendment.
Alice Stone Blackwell, editor of *Woman's Journal* and a nationwide newspaper columnist, prepares notes for Woodrow Wilson's speech declaring support for woman suffrage.	
H.D. (Hilda Doolittle, 1886–1961): *Sea Garden*, volume of imagist poetry.	
Ellen Glasgow: *Life and Gabriella: The Story of a Woman's Courage*, described by many as her most feminist work.	Margaret Sanger opens the first U.S. birth control clinic in New York City.
Susan Glaspell (1876–1948), prolific author of plays and fiction, feminist, co-founder of the Provincetown Playhouse:	The journal *The Seven Arts* begins publication. Wilson is re-elected President on a peace platform.

TEXTS	CONTEXTS
1916 *Trifles*, the first play in which Glaspell uses the technique she makes famous of the "off-stage protagonist," in this case a woman accused of murdering her harsh husband but protected by a female community.	1916 Pancho Villa attacks the U.S., which retaliates by invading Mexico.

Corra Harris: *A Circuit Rider's Widow*.

Grace Elizabeth King: *The Pleasant Ways of St. Medard*, a novel.

Eve Merriam's *The Inner City Mother Goose*, a book of satirical adult nursery rhymes, is investigated by a grand jury in New York; it also undergoes censure in Baltimore, San Francisco, and Minneapolis.

Margaret Sanger (1879–1966), pioneer birth control advocate, establishes *Birth Control Review*.

Edith Wharton: *Xingu and Other Stories*.

The first general federal legislation on child labor is passed; the act prohibits interstate shipments of goods manufactured in places where children under age 14 have been employed or where children between the ages of 14 and 16 have labored more than eight-hour days or five-day weeks or at night; in 1918, the Supreme Court rules that it represents an undue infringement on states' rights.

Mary B. Talbert becomes president of the National Association of Colored Women.

Henrietta "Hetty" Green, known as the "Witch of Wall Street," possibly the nation's richest woman, dies; although she had inherited a large sum of money, she substantially increased it through savvy investments and speculations.

Hazel Hook Walt invents the bobby pin, although a manufacturer slightly al-

TEXTS	CONTEXTS
1916	1916 ters the design and beats her to the patent.
	Shalimar perfume is invented.
	A group of authors, artists, editors, illustrators, and publishers form "The Vigilantes," war supporters who volunteer their skills on behalf of disseminating "patriotic publicity"; Gertrude Atherton is one of the few women associated with the organization.
1917 Elsa Barsaloux: *Priscilla War Work Book: Comforts for Soldiers and Sailors.*	1917 Congress passes an immigration law over President Wilson's veto, which excludes adults unable to read some language and maps out an "Asiatic Barred Zone" that completely excludes all Asiatic people excepting those already excluded (the Chinese) or severely restricted (the Japanese). It also excludes members of revolutionary organizations and demands the immediate deportation of resident aliens who are caught speaking about revolution or sabotage at any point after entry.
Dorothy Canfield Fisher (1879–1958), novelist, short-story writer, critic, translator, and advocate of Montessori education: *Understood Betsy*, a children's book.	
Mary Hallock Foote: *Edith Bonham.*	
Thetta Quay Franks: *Household Organization for War Service: America Expects Every Woman to Do Her Duty.*	
Grace Livingston Hill (1865–1947), author of 107 works, including con-	Three women from Canada, Mrs. Spinks, Mrs. W. C. Tyler, and Mrs.

TEXTS	CONTEXTS
1917	1917

TEXTS

1917 temporary romance, historical romance, mystery, and nonfiction: *The Witness.*

Mary Johnston: *The Wanderers*, a novel promoting women's rights.

Jeanette Lee: *The Green Jacket*, the first of several mysteries featuring Millicent Newberry, possibly the first female fictional sleuth to head her own detective agency.

Edna St. Vincent Millay (1892–1950), poet, fiction writer, and dramatist associated with the Provincetown Players; also a social activist considered by her generation the epitome of the "New Woman": *Renascence and Other Poems.*

Elsie Clews Parsons (1875?-1941), anthropologist: *Notes on Zuni* and *Social Rule.*

Laura E. Richards and Maud Howe Elliott: *Julia Ward Howe*, winner of the first Pulitzer Prize given for biography.

Elizabeth G. Stern, Jewish American author: *My Mother and I.*

CONTEXTS

1917 Wylie, become the first women delegates to the electoral college.

Jeannette Pickering Rankin, suffragist and pacifist, is sworn in as the first woman ever to serve in Congress.

U.S. enters World War I.

American Women's Hospitals Service is founded; it is a WWI organization designed to utilize the skills of female doctors.

One thousand women picket the White House demanding suffrage as part of the National Woman's Party's campaign of militancy.

Beginning in this year, as many as 216 suffragists are illegally arrested for their protest activities; 97 of them are sentenced to as many as six months in either the infamous D.C. jail or the equally infamous Occoqua, Virginia, workhouse. In 1918, the D.C. Court of Appeals overturns their convictions and sentences.

Indiana, Michigan, Nebraska, Ohio, Rhode Island, and Arkansas state

TEXTS	CONTEXTS
1917 Sara Teasdale (1884–1933), poet: *Love Songs.* Edith Wharton: *Summer,* a novel. Edith Wyatt: *Great Companions,* a collection of essays by the novelist and social activist.	1917 legislatures grant woman suffrage. By state referendum, New York passes woman suffrage; also by state referendum Ohio rescinds the suffrage the legislature had granted previously. North Dakota's legislature grants presidential suffrage only. Women in Russia and Mexico are enfranchised. At a small bookshop in New York, 21 women employed in the book and publishing business meet and organize the Woman's National Association of Booksellers and Publishers. When Margaret Anderson, editor of *The Little Review,* runs an antiwar story by Wyndham Lewis, the issue is seized by U.S. postal authorities. Ten thousand African Americans march in New York City in an NAACP-sponsored silent protest of racial discrimination and violence. Lucy Diggs Slowe wins the women's single title at the first national American Tennis Association championship, be-

TEXTS	CONTEXTS
1917	1917 coming the first African American woman athletic champion.

Kate Gleason becomes the first white woman to be president of a national bank.

Highly paid and well-respected film director Lois Weber (1882–1939) establishes her own production house, releasing films through Universal Pictures. Over the course of her career, she directs and produces between 200 and 400 films, fewer than 50 of which survive today. Weber's work is so popular in her day that Universal Studios builds her her own studio and eventually pays her $2500 a week.

The Bolshevik Revolution occurs in Russia.

Thomas Edison, in his essay "The Woman of the Future," predicts that the American woman will be liberated by such new inventions as the washing machine, refrigerator, stove, iron, and carpet sweeper, transforming her from a "domestic laborer" to a "domestic

TEXTS	CONTEXTS
1917	1917 engineer" and freeing her energy for "broader, more constructive fields." Mary Lathrop is the first woman member admitted to the American Bar Association. Horace Brisbin Liveright begins his publishing career; among those employed with his firm are Lillian Hellman and Edith W. Stern.
1917–1921	1917–1921 The 4-volume *Cambridge History of American Literature* is published.
1918 Louise Bryant (1887–1936), journalist, author, suffragist: *Six Red Months in Russia.* Willa Cather: *My Ántonia,* a novel. Rose Cohen, Jewish American author: *Out of the Shadow.* Sarah Lee Brown Fleming (1875–1963), African American novelist and poet: *Hope's Highway,* a novel. Mary E. Wilkins Freeman: *Edgewater People.*	1918 Annette Abbott Adams becomes the first woman district attorney, serving in Northern California; in 1920, she becomes the first woman to be an assistant attorney general in the U.S.; in 1950 she becomes the first woman to sit on the California Supreme Court. Anne Martin of Nevada is the first woman to run for the Senate. World War I ends; the peace treaty is signed in Versailles in 1919.

TEXTS	CONTEXTS
1918 Elizabeth Hasanovitz, Jewish American author: *One of Them.*	1918 Women in Great Britain over 30 years old as well as householders or wives thereof are enfranchised. Women are also enfranchised in Austria, Canada, Czechoslovakia, Germany, Hungary, Poland, Scotland, and Wales.
Florence Marian Howe: *Memories Grave and Gray.*	
Georgia Douglas Johnson (1886–1966), African American poet: *The Heart of a Woman and Other Poems*, first African American female to receive national recognition since Frances E. W. Harper.	Woman suffrage passes by state referendum in Michigan and South Dakota but is defeated in Louisiana.
Lulu Hunt Peters: *Diet and Health with a Key to the Calories*, which introduces "calorie counting" to numbers of Americans.	Despite President Wilson's plea, the Senate fails to provide the necessary two-thirds majority vote to pass the federal woman suffrage amendment.
Lola Ridge (1873–1941), poet, political activist: *The Ghetto and Other Poems.*	Writer Katherine Anne Porter begins her involvement in Mexican politics.
Jessie B. Rittenhouse: *The Door of Dreams.*	The radical Marxist journal *The Liberator* begins publication.
Emma Speed Sampson (1868–1947): *Billy and the Major.*	
	Gladys Dick founds the Cradle Society in Evanston, Illinois, the first professional adoption organization in the country.
	Linda A. Eastman becomes the head of the Cleveland public library system, making her the

TEXTS	CONTEXTS
1918	1918 first woman head librarian for a major metropolitan area.
	Canned foods are no longer limited to just peas, corn, and succotash but include numerous ready-made meals, from lobster à la Newburg to Heinz's spaghetti in meat sauce.
	Margaret B. Owen sets a typewriting speed record in New York City by typing 170 words per minute with no errors.
	Installment-credit plans are introduced.
1919 Annie Heloise Abel: *The American Indian as Participant in the Civil War.*	1919 The Eighteenth Amendment (Prohibition) is ratified, largely as the result of women's, and especially female temperance supporters', efforts.
Zoe Akins (1886–1958), poet, dramatist, screenwriter: *Déclassé*, a play.	
Mildred Aldrich (1853–1928), journalist and author of four firsthand accounts of life in wartime France: *When Johnny Comes Marching Home*, a novel.	Congress passes the Volstead Act, which, among other things, defines intoxicating liquor as any drink with 0.05 percent alcohol content, establishes penalties and injunctions, and allows for search-and-seizure.
Delilah L. Beasley, African American historian: *The Negro Trail Blazers of California.*	Lady Astor, née Nancy Witcher Langhorne, takes her oath of membership

TEXTS	CONTEXTS
1919 Gertrude Barrows Bennett, under the pen name "Francis Stevens": *The Cerberus Heads*, a science-fiction novel.	1919 to the British House of Commons, becoming the first American-born woman to serve as a Member of Parliament.
Charlotte Hawkins Brown (1882?–1961), African American fiction writer, educator, and club-woman: *"Mammy": An Appeal to the Heart of the South*, a short story published as a book.	After her husband, Woodrow, suffers a stroke, Edith Bolling Wilson is credited with operating as acting President of the United States.
Mamie Jordan Carver, African American author: *As It Is; or, The Conditions under Which the Race Problem Challenges the White Man's Solution*.	Alice Hamilton, physician, reformer, and a founder of occupational health, becomes Harvard's first woman professor when she is hired to teach in its new industrial hygiene program.
Mary Hallock Foote: *The Ground-swell*.	The National Federation of Business and Professional Women's Clubs, Inc., of the United States of America is established by Lena Madeson Phillips.
Maggie Shaw Fullilove, African American novelist: *Who Was Responsible?*.	
Susan Glaspell: *Bernice*, a full-length play in which the characters try to understand a woman now dead.	Fannie (Mooney) Sellins, socialist labor union organizer, is shot and killed during a skirmish with sheriffs of the Allegheny Coal Company over miners' rights.
Elsie Janis (1889–1956), vaudeville actress, producer, and memoirist: *The Big Show: My Six Months with the American Expeditionary Forces*.	During the first "Red Scare," anarchist author and lecturer Emma Goldman is among those de-

TEXTS		CONTEXTS
1919	Mary Johnston: *Michael Forth*.	1919

ported to the Soviet Union.

Amy Lowell (1874–1925), poet: *Pictures of the Floating World*, which firmly establishes her reputation as a leading Imagist poet.

Chicago race riots leave 23 blacks and 15 whites dead and over 1000 homeless; race riots occur in other cities across the country that summer, including Knoxville, Tennessee; Omaha, Nebraska; and Longview, Texas.

Alice Rostetter: *Widow's Veil*, a play.

Alice Applegate Sargeant: *Following the Flag: Diary of a Soldier's Wife*.

A white mob in Oklahoma lynches African American Marie Scott after her brother kills the white man who raped her.

Laura Eliza Wilkes, African American historian: *Missing Pages in American History, Revealing the Services of Negroes in the Early Wars in the United States of America, 1641–1815*.

By this year, 38 presses have been established at the country's universities.

Sylvia Beach opens her Paris bookshop, Shakespeare and Company, as a meeting place for expatriate American writers; among those who live in Paris for several months or years after the First World War are Djuna Barnes, Katherine Anne Porter, Gertrude Stein, and Edith Wharton.

Harcourt, Brace & Howe publishing company is established after the first two men leave Henry Holt & Co.; Ellen

TEXTS	CONTEXTS
1919	1919 Knowles Eayres, Vassar graduate and Harcourt's future wife, is instrumental in helping to get the firm off the ground.

The New York *Daily News* is established, considered the first picture-text tabloid newspaper and a forerunner of Sunday supplement magazines.

The first sensational "true story" magazine, aptly named *True Story*, begins publication.

The first celebration of the annual National Children's Book Week is held.

Julia Morgan (1872–1957), architect of over 1000 buildings, is chosen by William Randolph Hearst to be the designer for his huge mansion, San Simeon, in California.

Louise Seaman (Bechtel) becomes editor of children's books at Macmillan.

Seven million people purchase automobiles.

Mary Church Terrell, human rights activist and

TEXTS	CONTEXTS
1919	1919 head of many progressive activist organizations, including the Colored Women's League of Washington, D.C., the National Association of Colored Women, and the International Council of Women of the Darker Races, receives international recognition at the International Peace Congress in Zurich. The state legislatures in Iowa, Maine, Minnesota, Missouri, Ohio, and Wisconsin grant women presidential suffrage. Women in Belgium, British East Africa, Holland, Iceland, Luxembourg, Rhodesia, and Sweden are enfranchised. The federal woman suffrage amendment passes the House, fails initially in the Senate, but passes on the second vote and is sent to the states for ratification.
1919–1920	1919–1920 Chicago "Black Sox" scandal.
1920s African American women's voices play a large part in the burgeoning of creative activ-	1920s Georgia O'Keeffe (1887– 1986), one of the most original painters of the 20th century, creates

TEXTS	CONTEXTS
1920s	**1920s**
ity known as the Harlem Renaissance. Gwendolyn Bennett, Marita Bonner, Anita Scott Coleman, Alice Ruth Moore Dunbar-Nelson, Jessie Redmon Fauset, Angelina Weld Grimké, Zora Neale Hurston, Georgia Douglas Johnson, Nella Larsen, Eloise Bibb Thompson, and Dorothy West, among others, are publishing poetry, short stories, and essays in publications such as *Opportunity*, *The Crisis*, the *Saturday Evening Quill*, and the *Messenger*.	bold, semi-abstract, and vibrant paintings that often deal with huge close-up details of flowers and bleached bones, as well as abstract views of clouds, rocks, mountains, and seascapes.
	Through his caricatures for *Vanity Fair* magazine, John Held invents the figure of the "flapper" as an icon for the "Roaring Twenties."
Georgia Douglas Johnson, African American playwright and poet in Washington, D.C., presides over the Saturday Nighters'—all of whom are contributors to or associated with the New Negro Renaissance—discussions of art, politics, and their own poetry and fiction.	Nell Brinkley leads women cartoonists of the era with her drawings of flappers. Other important women cartoonists of the 1920s and 1930s include Ethel Hays, Virginia Huget, and Gladys Parker.
	Lillian Evanti (1890–1967) becomes the first African American woman to develop a professional career in grand opera.
Anne Spencer (1882–1975), African American lyric poet, is publishing in the major anthologies of her time.	
1920	**1920**
S. Josephine Baker, medical inspector and pioneer in health education: *Healthy Mothers, Healthy Babies, Healthy Children.*	The Nineteenth Amendment (Woman Suffrage) is ratified. Tennessee is the necessary 36th state to ratify.

TEXTS	CONTEXTS
1920 Alice Brown: *The Wind Between the Worlds*, a novel.	1920 The League of Women Voters is formed to continue the work of the now defunct National American Woman Suffrage Association.

TEXTS

1920

Alice Brown: *The Wind Between the Worlds*, a novel.

Alice Ruth Moore Dunbar-Nelson: *The Dunbar Speaker and Entertainer: Containing the Best Prose and Poetic Selections by and about the Negro.*

Sarah Lee Brown Fleming: *Clouds and Sunshine*, poetry.

Zona Gale (1874–1938), novelist, short-story writer, dramatist, poet, and pacifist: *Miss Lulu Bett*, a novel, her dramatization of which wins a Pulitzer Prize in 1921.

Marie Ganz, Jewish American author: *Rebels into Anarchy—and Out Again.*

Angelina Weld Grimké (1880–1958), poet, dramatist, and short-story writer: *Rachel*, first drama to be published by a black woman and to be performed professionally by black actors.

Addie W. Hunton and Kathryn M. Johnson: *Two Colored Women with the American Expeditionary Forces.*

CONTEXTS

1920

The League of Women Voters is formed to continue the work of the now defunct National American Woman Suffrage Association.

Total population numbers 106,461,000; 5,735,811 immigrants have arrived since 1911; black population numbers 10,463,131, the first time it has dipped below 10 percent of the total population.

For the first time, more than half of the population live in cities (51.2 percent).

Nearly half of all bookkeepers and accountants are women; more than 90 percent of all typists and stenographers are women.

Almost 12 percent of all female workers are professional.

Of those black women who are not field laborers, 80 percent are maids, washerwomen, and cooks.

Some 21.3 percent of all gainfully employed adult females are white.

More than 47 percent of the total

TEXTS	CONTEXTS
1920 Edna St. Vincent Millay: *Aria da Capo*, an antiwar one-act play first performed in 1919.	1920 college enrollment is female.
Lizette Woodworth Reese: *Spicewood*, a collection of poetry.	The U.S. Department of Labor establishes the Woman's Bureau to oversee wage-earning women's rights and interests. Mary Anderson becomes its first director.
Sally Nelson Robins, southern novelist and journalist: *Romances of Illustrious Virginians*.	Black and white women meet in Memphis and form the Women's Committee of the Commission on Interracial Cooperation.
Margaret Sanger: *Woman and the New Race*, a treatise on the benefits of voluntary motherhood; over 200,000 copies are sold.	Palmer Raids; the "Red Scare" continues.
Evelyn Scott (1893–1963), novelist, poet, and playwright: *Precipitations*, poems.	Labor activist Elizabeth Gurley Flynn helps to establish the American Civil Liberties Union.
Harriet Prescott Spofford: *The Elder's People*, a collection of stories.	Five thousand radios are in use in American homes.
Edith Wharton: *The Age of Innocence*, wins the Pulitzer Prize for novel/fiction in 1921.	The Sears, Roebuck catalog has 92 illustrated pages of women's clothing, compared with none in 1894.
Zara Wright, African American novelist: *Black and White Tangled Threads* and *Kenneth*.	Five percent of the physicians in the U.S. are women.
Anzia Yezierska (1882?–1970), Polish-born novelist and short-story writer, chronicler of the	Marie Luhring is elected to the Society of Automotive Engineers, becom-

TEXTS	CONTEXTS
1920 experience of Jewish immigrants: *Hungry Hearts*, a collection of stories.	1920 ing its first woman member.
	Social worker Edith Abbott helps establish the School of Social Service Administration at the University of Chicago, the first graduate school in social work within a university.
	Warren G. Harding is elected President; he dies in 1922 and his Vice President, Calvin Coolidge, is sworn in.
	Ethelda Bleibtrey becomes the first American woman to win a gold medal in the Olympic games.
	The National Association of Book Publishers is formed.
	Doubleday is the first publisher to run full-page ads for a single work in the *New York Times Book Review*.
	F. Scott Fitzgerald publishes his short story "Bernice Bobs Her Hair," detailing the interest in the fashion of hair bobbing in his day.
	Bessie Smith (1898?– 1937), who will come to

TEXTS		CONTEXTS
1920	1920	be known as the "empress of the blues" for hits such as "St. Louis Blues" and "Nobody's Blues But Mine," begins her recording career.
		Literary Review, a supplement to the Saturday section of the New York *Evening Post*, begins publishing.
		Librarian Sarah Byrd Askew designs the bookmobile, a traveling library for those who lack easy access to books.
1920–1921	Jessie Redmon Fauset (1884?–1961), African American novelist and editor, writes and edits *Brownie's Book*, a magazine for African American children.	1920–1921
1921	Gertrude Simmons Bonnin (Zitkala-Ša): *American Indian Stories.*	1921	Oklahoma Congresswoman Alice M. Robertson becomes the first woman to preside over the House of Representatives.
	Faith Baldwin (1893–1978): *Mavis of Green Hill*, first of many popular romances for women that will sell well over ten million copies.		Nicola Sacco and Bartolomeo Vanzetti are convicted of murder; they are executed in 1927; on the eve of the execution, writers including Edna St. Vincent Millay and Katherine Anne Porter keep vigil.
	Rachel Crothers: *Nice People*, a play.		

TEXTS	CONTEXTS
1921 Carrie Law Morgan Figgs, African American poet and playwright: *Nuggets of Gold*, poetry.	1921 Margaret Anderson, editor of *The Little Review*, is fined $50 for printing excerpts of James Joyce's *Ulysses*.
Susan Glaspell: *Inheritors*, a play.	European immigration is limited by law to 3 percent of the number of foreign-born of each nationality present in the country at the time of the 1910 census.
Hazel Hall (1886–1924), poet: *Curtains*.	
Elizabeth Ross Haynes, African American author: *Unsung Heroes*.	
Edna St. Vincent Millay: *Second April*, poetry.	Margaret Sanger founds the American Birth Control League.
Marianne Moore (1887–1972), poet, editor, and critic: *Poems*.	Alice Paul, president of the National Women's Party, revokes Mary Talbert's invitation to speak at one of its meetings, claiming that as an NAACP representative, Talbert represents a group that advocates racial equality, not gender equality.
Louise Pound (1872–1958), teacher, sportswoman, editor, linguist: *Poetic Origins and the Ballad*.	
Mary Roberts Rinehart: *The Confession*, a gothic mystery novel.	
Jessie B. Rittenhouse: *The Lifted Cup*.	The Women's Peace Union is founded, disbanding in 1941.
Evelyn Scott: *The Narrow House*, a novel.	The Association of Collegiate Alumni becomes the American Association of University Women; Ada Comstock becomes its first president, a position she holds until she becomes Radcliffe College's
Mary Etta Spencer, African American novelist and short-story writer: *The Resentment*, a novel.	

TEXTS	CONTEXTS
1921 Elinor Wylie (1885–1928), poet and novelist: *Nets to Catch the Wind*, very successful volume of poetry.	1921 first full-time woman president in 1923.

Georgianna R. Simpson at the University of Chicago, Sadie Tanner Mossell at the University of Pennsylvania, and Eva Dykes at Radcliffe College, are the first known black women in the country to earn Ph.D. degrees.

Dual pricing of books is inaugurated when the publishers of Gertrude Atherton's new novel, *Sisters-in-Law*, announce that the book will cost $2 in cloth and $1.50 in paper.

Little Blue Books are introduced; cheaply produced, cheap in price, they enable vast numbers of readers across the country to order classics in philosophy, literature, psychoanalysis, and socialism through the mail at cut-rate prices.

The Publishers AdClub is formed; through it, publishers purchase cooperative display advertising in newspapers across the country.

Bessie Coleman becomes the first licensed black pi-

TEXTS	CONTEXTS
1921	1921 lot in the world. She is featured on a 1995 postage stamp.
	The first Miss America Pageant is held in Atlantic City; Margaret Gorman of Washington, D.C., wins.
	Kotex "sanitary napkins" are first marketed.
	Knee-length skirts for women become the standard fashion.
	Former President Grover Cleveland's baby daughter, Ruth, gets a candy bar named after her.
1921–1938	1921–1938 Summer sessions are held at Bryn Mawr College to educate working women.
1922 Jane Addams: *Peace and Bread in Time of War*.	1922 The USSR is formed.
	Mussolini becomes dictator in Italy.
Willa Cather: *One of Ours*, winner of the Pulitzer Prize for novel/fiction.	The Cable Act insures women will no longer be deprived of citizenship upon marriage to an alien.
Carrie Williams Clifford: *The Widening Light*, poetry.	Rebecca Latimer Felton, 88, becomes the first woman appointed to the United States Senate; she serves one day then
Janet Ayer Fairbank (1878–1951), novelist: *The Cortlandts of Washington Square*, first in a series	

TEXTS	CONTEXTS
1922 focusing on the life of a woman.	1922 resigns so that the newly elected senator can take her place.

TEXTS

1922 focusing on the life of a
woman.

Helen R. Hull (1888–
1971), lesbian novelist,
short-story writer, and, in
her youth, political activist: *Quest*. She produces
17 novels and at least 65
short stories.

Georgia Douglas Johnson:
Bronze: A Book of Verse.

Jeanette Lee: *The Mysterious Office*, a mystery.

Kathleen Norris (1880–
1966), prolific novelist,
short-story writer, mem-
oirist: *Certain People of Importance*.

Emily Post (1872–1960):
*Etiquette in Society, in Busi-
ness, in Politics, and at
Home*.

Olive Higgins Prouty
(1882–1974), novelist:
Stella Dallas, later made
into a well-known
film starring Barbara
Stanwyck.

J. Pauline Smith, African
American poet: *"Exceeding
Riches" and Other Verse*.

Gertrude Stein: *Geography
and Plays*.

CONTEXTS

1922 resigns so that the newly
elected senator can take
her place.

The Permanent Commit-
tee for the Abolition of
Child Labor is formed.

Claude McKay publishes
his *Harlem Shadows*, which
is credited with launching
the decade of black cre-
ative talent referred to as
the "Harlem Renais-
sance."

For the first time, the
Spingarn Medal award, es-
tablished by the NAACP
in 1911, is given to a
woman, Mary B. Talbert.

Meta Warrick Fuller
(1877–1968), African
American sculptor, exhib-
its a life-size sculpture,
Awakening Ethopia. She becomes known for using Af-
rican Americans as models
for her sculptures.

The trend toward produc-
ing "blurbs" on book jackets (and of critics re-
sponding to blurbs more
than to the book itself)
has grown so pervasive
that when publisher
George Duran attempts
to bring out its January
1923 books in plain ma-
nila wrapping paper, sales

TEXTS	CONTEXTS
1922 Onoto Watanna (Winnifred Eaton): *Sunny-san*, a novel. Lillian E. Wood, African American novelist: *"Let My People Go."*	1922 drop and the firm soon returns to "blurbed" jackets. May Massee becomes editor of children's books at Doubleday, Doran. The word "obey" is deleted from marriage vows in the Protestant Episcopal service. More than 40 million Americans buy movie tickets. Women's razors and depilatories are first advertised in Sears, Roebuck catalogs. The "flapper" costume—a chemise with dropped waist and raised hem—comes into style. The American Social Hygiene Association begins a sex education campaign to prevent the spread of venereal diseases. *Better Homes and Gardens* magazine begins publication. *Reader's Digest* is first published. By this date, over 100 novels have been made into movies.

	TEXTS		CONTEXTS
1922		1922	Blanche Yurka (1887–1974), stage and screen actress best known for classical drama and for roles as strong-willed women, plays Gertrude to John Barrymore's Hamlet for 125 performances.

By this date there are 30 radio broadcasting stations nationwide; a year later there are 556. |
| 1923 | S. Josephine Baker: *The Growing Child.*

Louise Bogan (1897–1970), poet and longtime poetry critic for *The New Yorker: Body of This Death*, first book of poetry.

Willa Cather: *A Lost Lady*, a novel.

Carrie Chapman Catt (1859–1947): *Woman Suffrage and Politics.*

Thelma Duncan (1902–1988?), African American playwright: *The Death Dance.*

Hazel Hall: *Walkers*, a collection of poetry.

Mary Johnston: *The Slave Ship*, a novel promoting racial justice. | 1923 | An Equal Rights Amendment is presented to Congress by Alice Paul of the National Woman's Party.

Adkins v. Children's Hospital makes a minimum wage law for women unconstitutional, thus basically, as labor reformer Florence Kelly noted, insuring "the inalienable right of women to starve."

Margaret Sanger establishes the Clinical Research Bureau to investigate establishing clinical services for women seeking birth control information.

Microbiologist and physician Gladys Henry Dick and her husband isolate the bacterial cause of scarlet fever. |

TEXTS	CONTEXTS
1923 Edith Summers Kelley (1884–1956), Canadian-born novelist who lived most of her life in the U.S.: *Weeds*.	1923 "Yes, We Have No Bananas" is a popular song.

Edith Summers Kelley (1884–1956), Canadian-born novelist who lived most of her life in the U.S.: *Weeds*.

Flora Klickman: *The Popular Knitting Book*.

Mina Loy (1882–1986), Modernist poet, playwright, and painter: *Lunar Baedecker*, collection of poems.

Edna St. Vincent Millay wins a Pulitzer Prize for *The Ballad of the Harp-Weaver*, *A Few Figs from Thistles*, and 8 sonnets in *American Poetry, 1922, a Miscellany*.

Jessica Nelson North (1894–?): *A Prayer Rug*, poetry.

Sally Nelson Robins: *Love Stories of Illustrious Virginians*.

Lucy Maynard Salmon, historian: *The Newspaper and the Historian* and *The Newspaper and Authority*.

Genevieve Taggard (1894–1948): *Hawaiian Hilltop*, poems.

Mary Evaline Wolff, (1877–1964), also known

"Yes, We Have No Bananas" is a popular song.

Josephine Baker (1906–1975), African American entertainer known for her dance techniques and daring costumes and, later, as one of France's most beloved performers, starts her illustrious career in the chorus of the Broadway show *Shuffle Along*.

Alma Cummings becomes the first person to win the first dance marathon held in the United States, setting a world record by dancing for 27 hours.

Maidenform, Inc., founded by Ida Rosenthal, manufactures its first bra.

Time magazine begins publication.

An attempt by a New York Supreme Court Justice to impose a "Clean Books" bill—which would censor publishers—is defeated.

By this date, some 500 communities produce competing daily newspapers.

W. W. Norton founds his own publishing firm.

TEXTS		CONTEXTS
1923	as Sister Mary Madeleva, scholar and first of the modern nun-poets: *Knights Errant, and Other Poems.* Elinor Wylie: *Black Armour*, poetry. Anzia Yezierska: *Children of Loneliness.*	1923	D. H. Lawrence publishes his *Studies in Classic American Literature*, which focuses on male-authored classics exclusively. Bessie Smith's "Downhearted Blues/Gulf Coast Blues" becomes the first record by an African American to sell over a million copies.
1924	Dorothy Day (1897–1980), journalist, activist, co-founder of many missions and of *The Catholic Worker*, novelist, and autobiographer: *The Eleventh Virgin*, a novel. Jessie Redmon Fauset: *There Is Confusion*, a novel. Edna Ferber: *So Big*, winner in 1925 of the Pulitzer Prize for novel/fiction. Emma Goldman: *My Disillusionment with Russia.* Dorothy Guinn, African American playwright: *Out of the Dark.* Marianne Moore: *Observations*, a book of poetry which receives *The Dial* magazine award in 1925.	1924	An act of Congress grants Native Americans citizenship. "Ma" Miriam Amanda Ferguson of Texas, an active suffragist and prohibitionist, succeeds her husband and becomes the nation's first woman governor. Calvin Coolidge is elected to his first full term as President. Sociologists Robert and Helen Lynd embark on their study of life in a small American city that results in the publication of *Middletown*, which documents the new autonomy, mobility, and sexuality of Muncie, Indiana's, youth.

TEXTS

CONTEXTS

1924

Frances Newman (1883–1928), Atlanta novelist, short-story writer, critic, and librarian: *The Short Story's Mutations: From Petronius to Paul Morand* and "Rachel and Her Children," winner of an O. Henry Memorial Award.

Julia Peterkin (1880–1961), novelist and specialist in the life and language of the Gullahs of South Carolina: *Green Thursday*.

Dorothy Scarborough (1878–1935), Texas novelist and scholar: *In the Land of Cotton*.

Margaret Wilson: *The Able McLaughlins*, Pulitzer Prize for novel/fiction.

1924

Bertha Mahoney and Elinor Whitney begin publishing the *Horn Book Magazine*, the first magazine devoted to reviewing children's literature.

The average cost of hardcover nonfiction books ranges from $5 to $10.

The *Saturday Review of Literature* is founded.

Florence Rood becomes the first woman president of the American Federation of Teachers.

Mary McLeod Bethune becomes president of the National Association of Colored Women.

There are 2,500,000 radios in American homes.

J. Edgar Hoover is appointed head of the Bureau of Investigations (later the FBI).

Polly Adler, a discouraged businesswoman, sets out to become "the best goddamn madam in America." Her clients include wits of the Algonquin Round Table, motion-picture stars, Mafia figures, and business tycoons.

TEXTS	CONTEXTS
1924	1924 U.S. citizens consume 245 million ice cream cones annually.
	H. L. Mencken and George Jean Nathan begin publishing *The American Mercury*.
	Simon & Schuster is established; its first book is the first *Cross Word Puzzle Book*.
	When Putnam publishers runs a crossword puzzle contest in the New York *World*, promising prizes to the first three contestants to deliver correct solutions to the Putnam office, crowds of possible winners begin to gather after midnight of the day the puzzle is issued. By the time the office opens the following day, police have to be called in to restore order.
	From 1924 to 1930, no Chinese women are allowed into the U.S.
	The Vassar Board of Trustees creates an Interdisciplinary School of Euthenics to teach development and care of the family, offering courses such as "Husband and Wife" and "Motherhood."

* * *

TEXTS

CONTEXTS

1925   Annie Heloise Abel: *The American Indian under Reconstruction.*

S. Josephine Baker: *Child Hygiene.*

Hallie Quinn Brown (1845–1949), African American author and biographer: *Our Women: Past, Present, and Future* and *Tales My Father Taught Me.*

Sue M. Wilson Brown: *The History of the Order of the Eastern Star among Colored People.*

Willa Cather: *The Professor's House*, a novel.

Babette Deutsch (1895–1982), poet and critic: *Honey Out of the Rock.*

Ellen Glasgow: *Barren Ground*, a novel.

Georgia Douglas Johnson: *A Sunday Morning in the South*, a drama protesting lynching.

Aline Kilmer (1888–1941), poet, essayist, author of children's books: *The Poor King's Daughter, and Other Poems.*

1925   Nellie Taylor Ross of Wyoming becomes the second American woman to succeed her husband as governor of a state.

Anatomist Florence Sabin becomes the first female member of the National Academy of Sciences. Margaret Washburn is the second (1931).

A young Zora Neale Hurston wins a scholarship to Barnard College, where she is the only black student and where she studies with anthropologist Franz Boas.

Marian Anderson (1902–1993), African American woman known as one of the world's greatest contraltos, first gains public renown in an appearance as soloist at the New York Philharmonic.

Schoolteacher John Scopes is tried in Tennessee for teaching evolution in violation of both a state law making such teachings illegal and fundamental religious values.

President Calvin Coolidge proclaims that the "business of America is business."

TEXTS	CONTEXTS
1925	**1925**

<table>
<tr><td>

Amy Lowell: *What's O'Clock*, wins Pulitzer Prize for poetry in 1926.

Anita Loos (1893–1981), novelist, script writer: *Gentlemen Prefer Blondes*.

Poet Marianne Moore becomes editor of the revamped former transcendentalist journal *The Dial* and serves as its editor until it folds in 1929.

Beatrice Witte Ravenel (1870–1956), South Carolina poet: *Arrow of Lightening*.

Mary Roberts Rinehart: *The Red Lamp*, a gothic mystery.

Cornelia Otis Skinner (1901–1979), playwright, humorist, actress, biographer: *Captain Fury*, a play.

Gertrude Stein: *The Making of Americans*; the work had been finished in 1919.

Etsu Inagaki Sugimoto, Japanese American novelist: *A Daughter of the Samurai*, followed by *A Daughter of the Narikin* (1932), and *A Daughter of the Nohfu* (1935).

</td><td>

American medical schools institutionalize a 5 percent quota on female applicants.

Cosmetic industry sales total $141 million, up $124 million from 1914.

The Women's World Fair, the first fair ever devoted exclusively to women's accomplishments, is held in Chicago.

Modern Library, Inc., is founded; it is expanded and renamed Random House two years later.

Viking Press is formed.

The New Yorker magazine begins publication.

Crossword puzzles are the latest rage.

The "Charleston" becomes a popular dance step.

Ku Klux Klan membership is 3 million.

Artist Marguerite Thompson Zorach (1887–1968) founds the New York Society of Women Artists and becomes its first president.

</td></tr>
</table>

	TEXTS		CONTEXTS
1925	Onoto Watanna (Winnifred Eaton): *His Royal Nibs*.	1925	The strip-tease is accidentally invented at New York's Minsky's Burlesque House due to the audience's enthusiastic response when a dancer's shoulder strap breaks during a police raid.
	Edith Wharton: *The Writing of Fiction*.		
	Anzia Yezierska: *Bread Givers: A Struggle between a Father of the Old World and a Daughter of the New*.		
1926	Ellen Glasgow: *The Romantic Comedians*, a novel.	1926	Georgia O'Keeffe paints *Black Iris*.
	Frances Newman: *The Hard-Boiled Virgin*, a novel banned in Boston for its mention of menstruation, venereal disease, and female sexuality.		Martha Graham, (1894–1991), influential dancer and choreographer, forms her first independent dance company.
	Dorothy Parker (1893–1967), leader of the Algonquin Round Table wits: *Enough Rope*, her first volume of poetry, which becomes a bestseller.		Gertrude Bonnin (Zitkala-Ša), the author of autobiographical accounts of her Sioux childhood published in *The Atlantic Monthly*, founds and becomes the first president of the National Council of American Indians.
	Elizabeth Madox Roberts (1881–1941), novelist, poet: *The Time of Man*.		Violette N. Anderson argues a case before the U.S. Supreme Court, the first black woman to do so.
	Margaret Sanger: *Happiness in Marriage*.		
	Elsie Singmaster: *Keller's Anna Ruth*, a novel.		Gertrude Ederle of New York becomes the first woman to swim the English Channel.
	Leonora Speyer: *Fiddler's Farewell*, which wins the		

TEXTS		CONTEXTS
1926	1927 Pulitzer Prize for poetry.	1926	Evangelist Aimee Semple McPherson's questionable tales of torture at the hands of kidnappers fill the tabloid papers.

TEXTS

1926

1927 Pulitzer Prize for poetry.

Elizabeth G. Stern: *I Am a Woman—and a Jew*.

Edith Wharton: *Here and Beyond*, short stories.

CONTEXTS

1926

Evangelist Aimee Semple McPherson's questionable tales of torture at the hands of kidnappers fill the tabloid papers.

The Book-of-the-Month Club is established.

New Masses magazine begins publication; it folds in 1948.

Irita Bradford Van Doren, former literary editor of the *Nation,* begins her long and distinguished career as director/editor of the New York *Herald Tribune's Book Review*.

William Morrow starts his publishing company.

Don Juan is the first talking movie.

The National Broadcasting Company (NBC) is founded.

Mae West (1892–1980), who had been appearing in Broadway shows since 1911, has her first big success when she writes, produces, and stars in the play *Sex,* which runs for almost a year before being closed down by the local vice squad.

*   *   *

TEXTS	CONTEXTS
1926–1965 Louella Parsons, influential Hollywood gossip columnist, begins appearing in the *Los Angeles Examiner*.	**1926–1965**

TEXTS	CONTEXTS
1927 Willa Cather: *Death Comes for the Archbishop*, a novel.	**1927** Charles Lindbergh flies from New York to Paris, the first solo transatlantic flight.
Claire Winger Harris becomes the first woman writer to appear in the science fiction pulps, winning a prize for "Fate of the Poseidonia" in *Amazing Stories*.	Minnie Buckingham-Harper becomes the first African American woman to serve in the U.S. legislature when she is appointed to fill her husband's West Virginia congressional seat.
Mourning Dove, also known as Hum-Ishu-Ma (1888–1936), member of Okanogan tribe, one of the first Native American women to publish a novel: *Cogewea the Half-Blood: A Depiction of the Great Montana Cattle Range*.	Columbia Broadcasting System (CBS) is founded. Isadora Duncan (1878–1927), a founder of modern dance, is killed in a tragic car accident.
Dorothy Parker begins writing stories and a book-review column signed "Constant Reader" for *The New Yorker*.	The movie *It* gives its star Clara Bow (1905–1965) her nickname "the *It* girl."
Julia Peterkin: *Black April*, a novel set in South Carolina.	The country music industry is born when the Carter Family, led by "Mother Maybelle" Carter, records the first nationally popular records about rural life.
Nettie Arnold Plummer, African American author: *Out of the Depths; or, The Triumph of the Cross*.	

TEXTS	CONTEXTS
1927 Elizabeth Madox Roberts: *My Heart and My Flesh*, a novel. Dorothy Scarborough: *Impatient Griselda*, a novel. Evelyn Scott: *Migrations*, a novel. Eulalie Spence (1894–1981), African American dramatist: *Fool's Errand: A Play in One Act* and *Foreign Mail*. Marjorie Wilson, African American author: *Vagrant Love*. Mary Alice Wyman, biographer: *Two American Pioneers, Seba Smith and Elizabeth Oakes Smith*.	**1927** Lilian Westcott Hale (1881–1963), an important American Impressionist, is elected an associate member of the National Academy of Design; she is promoted to full membership four years later. Garnering many awards, she is known both for her portraits and for her many pictures of woods and gardens.
1927–1928	**1927–1928** Janet Gaynor (1906–1984) wins the first Best Actress Oscar for *Seventh Heaven, Sunrise,* and *Street Angel.* Gaynor is thus the only actress to win for silent film roles.
1928 Bess Streeter Aldrich (1881–1954), author of several novels about life in the Plains states: *A Lantern in Her Hand*. Djuna Barnes (1892–1982), experimentalist au-	**1928** Trotsky is exiled; Stalin rises to power in the USSR. African American inventor Marjorie Joyner patents a permanent waving machine.

TEXTS	CONTEXTS
1928	1928

TEXTS

1928

thor of journalism, plays, and stories, as well as two novels: *Ryder*, described by its author as "a female *Tom Jones.*"

Viña Delmar, novelist, playwright, short-story writer: *Bad Girl*, a best-selling novel.

Isa Glenn, southern novelist: *Southern Charm*.

Hazel Hall: *Cry of Time*, posthumously published volume of poetry.

Josephine Herbst (1897–1969), proletarian novelist: *Nothing Is Sacred*.

Eleanor Johnson, working with American Education Publications, begins publishing *Weekly Reader*, a newspaper for school children. Its circulation in the first year reaches 100,000; in the 1990s it has more than 9 million subscribers.

Georgia Douglas Johnson: *An Autumn Love Cycle*, poetry.

Nella Larsen (1891–1963), novelist and first African American author to receive a Guggenheim fellowship for creative writing: *Quicksand*.

CONTEXTS

1928

Graciela Olivarez, the first woman to chair the Mexican-American Legal Defense and Education Fund, is born in New York City.

Ethel Barrymore (1879–1959) is the first living actress to have a theater named after her (New York City).

Fanny Brice makes her film debut in *My Man*.

Mae West appears in *Diamond Lil*.

This year marks the peak of community newspapers, which number 14,000.

The average hardcover novel increases in price to $3.

Skywriting is used for the first time to promote a book: Evelyn Johnson and Gretta Palmer's *Murder*.

Carole Lombard (born Jane Alice Peters, 1908–1942) begins one of the most successful careers as a female comic in the history of films. She will make 42 talking pictures, specializing in screwball

TEXTS	CONTEXTS
1928	**1928**

1928 · Gladys Li, Asian American playwright: *The Submission of Rose Moy.*

Anne O'Hare McCormick (1880–1954), journalist: *The Hammer and the Scythe: Communist Russia Enters the Second Decade.*

Margaret Mead (1901–1978), anthropologist: *Coming of Age in Samoa.*

Frances Newman: *Dead Lovers Are Faithful Lovers,* a novel.

Carol Norton: *Bobs, a Girl Detective.*

Julie Peterkin: *Scarlet Sister Mary,* Pulitzer Prize-winning novel.

Edith Everett Taylor Pope, southern novelist: *Not Magnolia.*

The first selection of Doubleday's Crime Club is Kay Cleaver Strahan's *The Double Moon Mystery.*

Sophie Treadwell, playwright: *Machinal.*

Edith Wharton: *The Children,* a novel.

1928 · comedies, between 1928 and her death in 1942 on a war bond tour. Known as a consummate professional, one of the highest paid performers of her day, and a voracious reader, she stars in two films considered among the best comedies ever produced, *My Man Godfrey* and *Nothing Sacred.*

Socialite Mrs. Jerome Napoleon Bonaparte is the first person depicted in a testimonial ad for a book; she is shown holding a Borzoi Book and is described as an ardent admirer in an ad that runs in *The New Yorker*, the *New York Times Book Review*, and *Publishers' Weekly.*

The teletypesetter is first demonstrated. Unlike the telegraph, it sends along with news stories impulses that deliver encoded instructions to linotype machines so that they automatically prepare pages for print.

Greek-American physician George Nicholas Papanicolau develops the "Pap" or vaginal smear test at Cornell University; in

TEXTS	CONTEXTS
1928 Elinor Wylie: *Trivial Breath*, poetry.	**1928** 1943 the medical establishment recognizes the "Pap" smear as a method of detecting cervical cancer. Herbert Hoover is elected President.
1929 Léonie Adams (1899–1988), poet: *High Falcon and Other Poems.* Gertrude Berg, who performs as Molly Goldberg, writes all of the 4500 scripts for the 20-year run of *The Rise of the Goldbergs*, a popular radio program that begins this year. Louise Bogan: *Dark Summer*, poetry. Anna Hempstead Branch (1875–1937), poet with an interest in mysticism and social service: *Sonnets from a Lock Box.* Viola Irene Cooper: *Windjamming to Fiji*, a memoir. Rachel Crothers: *Let Us Be Gay*, a play about divorce. Maud Cuney Hare: *Antar of Araby.*	**1929** By this date, 80 percent of families' needs are purchased by women. By this date, nearly seven in ten homes have electricity. The Women's Air Derby, the first transcontinental race for women pilots, is held July 29 with participants flying from Santa Monica, California, to Cleveland, Ohio. Shortly thereafter, 99 of the 126 licensed women pilots in the U.S. form the "Ninety-Nines," "dedicated to assist women in aeronautical research, air racing events, the acquisition of aerial experience, and the administration of aid through aerial means in times of emergency." Some 27 million people purchase automobiles. More than 100 million people buy movie tickets.

TEXTS	CONTEXTS

1929   Katherine Bement Davis: *Factors in the Sex Lives of Twenty-two Hundred Women.*

Mignon Eberhart: *The Patient in Room 18*, her first of approximately 70 detective novels.

Anne Ellis (1875–1938): *The Life of an Ordinary Woman*, her first of three autobiographical works set in the mining areas of the West.

Pearl Ellis publishes *Americanization through Homemaking*, a handbook emphasizing health, hygiene, and education written expressly, Ellis suggests, for assimilating Mexican American girls and other immigrants into white culture and customs.

Jessie Redmon Fauset: *Plum Bun: A Novel without a Moral.*

Josephine Herbst: *Money for Love*, a novel.

Helen Keller: *Midstream: My Later Life.*

Nella Larsen: *Passing*, a novel.

1929   Since 1920, there has been a 60 percent increase in book production, attributed to a growth in public interest and in the number of best-sellers.

The American publishers of Radclyffe Hall's lesbian novel, *The Well of Loneliness*, are tried and convicted of obscenity, although an appeals court overturns the verdict later in the year.

British feminist and author Virginia Woolf (1882–1941) publishes her highly influential *A Room of One's Own.*

The publishing firm of Farrar & Rinehart is established; Margaret Sanger will be among its authors.

Nina Mae McKinney (1913–1967) becomes the first black female motion-picture star when she appears in King Vidor's *Hallelujah*. She receives rave reviews and an unprecedented five-year contract from MGM, but her success is short-lived as there are almost no roles available for black actresses.

TEXTS	CONTEXTS
1929 Helen Merrell Lynd (1896–1982), sociologist: *Middletown: A Study in Contemporary Culture*, with her husband, Robert S. Lynd; followed by *Middletown in Transition: A Study in Cultural Conflicts* (1935) and *Update: Middletown Families: Fifty Years of Change and Continuity* (1982).	1929 Dorothy Arzner (1900–1979) directs *The Wild Party*. From the late 1920s through the 1940s she will be the most prominent woman director and producer in Hollywood. She is openly lesbian and other directors claim she is accepted because her lesbianism "made her one of the boys."
Dorothy Reed Mendenhall, researcher in child and maternal health: *Midwifery in Denmark*, based on her study of childbirth in Denmark, argues that the American tendency toward intervention in the birth process is damaging and advocates midwifery and reliance on natural processes.	The first national study of sexual attitudes and experiences is conducted by Katherine Bement Davis. She finds that, among women "assumed to be normal" before interviewed, "50.4% of them had experienced intense emotional relations with other women." About half of these relations were accompanied by sex or "were recognized as sexual in character."
May Miller, African American playwright and poet: *Graven Images* and *Riding the Goat*. She is considered by some one of the parents of black drama; her first play was published when she was 15. Many of her works are in a folk idiom and focus on figures from the Bible or from black history.	Margaret Sanger forms the National Committee on Federal Legislation for Birth Control. Her New York birth control clinic is raided and three nurses and two doctors are arrested; the case against them is later dismissed.
Lola Ridge: *Firehead*, a sonnet sequence responding to the execu-	Dorothy Eustis becomes president of the Seeing Eye organization, which

TEXTS	CONTEXTS
1929 tions of Sacco and Van-zetti. Mary Roberts Rinehart: *This Strange Adventure*, novel. Dorothy Scarborough: *Can't Get a Redbird*, a novel. Evelyn Scott: *The Wave*, an experimental novel. Agnes Smedley (1892–1950), *Daughter of Earth*, an autobiographical novel. Leane Zugsmith (1903–1969), Jewish: proletarian novelist and feminist: *All Victories Are Alike*.	1929 she had founded when she came up with the idea of training dogs to lead the blind. The U.S. stock market crashes, launching the Great Depression.
late 1920s Women writers such as Sophie Wenzel Ellis, L. Taylor Hansen, Lilith Lorraine, and Leslie F. Stone are publishing science-fiction stories in the popular science-fiction pulps of the day, such as *Amazing Stories.* For the next few decades, many women who publish in the science-fiction pulps will do so under male pseudonyms.	late 1920s Margaret Sanger's birth control clinic conducts a study of 10,000 mostly working-class clients and finds that one out of five pregnancies have been intentionally terminated.
1930s	1930s Ma Barker and her sons gain notoriety for their criminal activities.

TEXTS	CONTEXTS
1930s	1930s Amphetamine "diet pills" are first introduced for clinical treatment of obesity.
	Comic books begin to become popular; at their height in the 1950s, some 35 million copies are sold each month.
	As sound pictures become the norm and large studios come to the fore, Hollywood enters its Golden Age. Among the actresses who will achieve stardom during this decade are Claudette Colbert, Joan Crawford, Bette Davis, Irene Dunne, Greta Garbo, Katharine Hepburn, Carole Lombard, and Myrna Loy.
	Katherine Dunham, African American dancer, choreographer, anthropologist, teacher, and initiate of Haitian voodun, is the first to bring African and Caribbean dance styles to Broadway and Hollywood.
	Ethel Waters (1900–1977), African American singer, comedienne, and actress, becomes the first widely acknowledged female jazz singer; among her best known songs are "Dinah," "Heat Wave," and "His Eye Is on the

TEXTS	CONTEXTS
1930s	**1930s** Sparrow." Her 1939 Broadway performance in the drama *Mamba's Daughter* marks the first time a black woman appears in a Broadway drama.
1930 Jane Addams: *The Second Twenty Years at Hull House.*	**1930** Four million Americans are unemployed.
Thelma Duncan: *Sacrifice.*	From 34 to 44 percent of black households in the largest northern cities have at least two employed workers in them.
Susan Glaspell: *Alison's House*, a play based on the life of Emily Dickinson, wins Pulitzer Prize for drama in 1931.	Some 27.1 percent of foreign-born, 19 percent of native-born white, and 5.5 percent of black working women are employed in manufacturing.
Edith Hamilton: *The Greek Way*, a scholarly study.	More than 14 percent of all female workers are in professional occupations.
Dorothy Parker: *Laments for the Living*, stories.	
Julia Peterkin's *Scarlet Sister Mary* is dramatized by Daniel Reed, with a white cast, headed by Ethel Barrymore, in blackface.	U.S. census records 1,998,000 servants.
Katherine Anne Porter (1890–1980), Texas author of 27 works of short fiction and one novel: *Flowering Judas, and Other Stories.*	Black women represent approximately 25 percent of all women employed in steam laundries.
Lizette Woodworth Reese: *White April and Other Poems.*	Twenty-nine percent of black households are headed by a woman.

Of the 45,200 Filipinos in America, 2500 are women. |

TEXTS

CONTEXTS

1930   Jessie B. Rittenhouse: *The Secret Bird.*

Elizabeth Madox Roberts: *The Great Meadow*, a historical novel set in Kentucky.

Bernadotte E. Schmitt: *The Coming of War: 1914*, winner of Pulitzer Prize for history in 1931.

Edith Wharton: *Certain People*, a collection of stories.

Mildred Wirt Benson begins ghostwriting the Nancy Drew Mystery Stories for the Stratemeyer syndicate. Under the pseudonym Carolyn Keene, she authors most of the first 25 volumes in the series, which begins with *The Secret of the Old Clock*. By the mid-1990s, the Nancy Drew series has sold over 80 million copies and has been translated into at least 17 foreign languages. Later revisions of the series have taken away much of the girl detective's independence and cleverness. Wirt Benson also ghostwrote volumes in several other Stratemeyer series, including the Ruth Field-

1930   There are 55 birth control clinics in 23 cities in 15 states.

There are roughly 30 million households and 26 million registered automobiles in the U.S.

Four-fifths of all households have electricity.

Largely as a result of the Depression, publishing houses including Simon & Schuster and Farrar & Rinehart release their new lists, originally scheduled as hardbacks for $2 to $3 apiece, in paper for a dollar.

Factory-made breads are commonplace.

"Mother" Jones (Mary Harris), renowned labor organizer and agitator who helped found both the Social Democratic Party and the Industrial Workers of the World, turns 100; her birthday and her accomplishments are celebrated throughout the land .

Annie Jump Cannon, known as the "Census Taker of the Heavens," completes a project she be-

	TEXTS		CONTEXTS
1930	ing, Kay Tracey, and Dana Girls series; for many years she received a flat rate of $125 per book.	1930	gan in 1897: cataloging and classifying approximately 400,000 astronomical objects.
			Ellen Church becomes the first airline stewardess, an idea she herself suggested to a manager at Boeing Air Transport.
			Norma Shearer (1900–1983) receives the Academy Award for Best Actress for her starring role in *The Divorcee.*
			Jessie Daniel Ames founds the Association of Southern Women for the Prevention of Lynching and serves as its director until 1942.
			Elsie Janis, at one time a popular comedienne, becomes the first woman to produce a Hollywood talking picture, *Paramount on Parade.*
			Author Sinclair Lewis becomes the first American author to win the Nobel Prize for literature.
			Fortune magazine is first published.
1930–1978	Harriet Stratemeyer Adams (1892–1982), working under a variety of pen	1930–1978	.

TEXTS	CONTEXTS
1930–1978 names, takes over from her father the Stratemeyer Syndicate and pens or supervises the production of hundreds of novels in these series: the Nancy Drew Mysteries, the Hardy Boys Mysteries, the Tom Swift Series, the Bobbsey Twins Series, the Honey Bunch Series, the Dana Girls Series, the Barton Books for Girls Series, and the Linda Craig Series.	**1930–1978**
1931 *Readings from Negro Authors, for Schools and Colleges, with a Bibliography of Negro Literature*, the first known anthology to be edited by black women— Otelia Cromwell, Lorenzo Dow Turner, and Eva B. Dykes. Margaret Ayer Barnes (1886–1967), novelist and dramatist: *Years of Grace*, Pulitzer Prize for novel/fiction. Mary Ritter Beard (1876–1958), historian, writer, and activist: *On Understanding Women.* Kay Boyle (1902–1992), novelist, short-story writer, poet, memoirist, and political activist:	**1931** Gertrude Vanderbilt Whitney, promoter, patron, and sculptor, opens the Whitney Museum of American Art, devoted to America's avant-garde. Jane Addams becomes the first woman awarded the Nobel Peace Prize. Eight African American "Scottsboro boys" are convicted for the rape of two white women in Alabama; their death sentences are later overturned by the Supreme Court. *Story* magazine, the only "little magazine" exclusively devoted to the short story, begins publication.

TEXTS	CONTEXTS
1931	*Plagued by the Nightingale,* a novel.	1931

Pearl S. Buck (1892–1973): *The Good Earth,* winner of the 1932 Pulitzer Prize for novel/fiction.

Willa Cather makes an exception in her opposition to book clubs and allows the Book-of-the-Month Club to offer *Shadows on the Rock* to its members after Dorothy Canfield, one of the club's judges, writes Cather; it sells more than 65,000 copies through the club.

Chona (1841?–1935): At 90 years of age, Chona relates her autobiography to Ruth M. Underhill, an anthropologist; it is published as *The Autobiography of Chona, a Papago Woman.*

Emily Clark, longtime columnist of "Browsings in an Old Book Shop": *Innocence Abroad,* a history of the *Reviewer.*

Sadie Iola Daniel, African American author: *Women Builders.*

Jessie Redmon Fauset: *The Chinaberry Tree: A Novel of American Life.*

TEXTS	CONTEXTS
1931	1931

1931

Hallie Flanagan and Margaret Ellen Clifford: *Can You Hear Their Voices?*, an agitprop drama about the plight of farmers.

Fannie Hurst (1889–1968), Jewish American novelist: *Back Street.*

Emma Goldman: *Living My Life*, her autobiography.

Caroline Gordon (1895–1981), southern fiction writer and critic, associated with the Fugitives: *Penhally.*

Elizabeth Miele, Jewish American playwright: *Did I Say No?.*

Dorothy Parker: *Death and Taxes*, verse.

Mary Roberts Rinehart: *My Story*, autobiography.

Constance Rourke (1885–1941), biographer, historian, and critic: *American Humor: A Study of the National Character.*

Evelyn Scott: *A Calendar of Sin*, a novel.

Vida Dutton Scudder, literary scholar and social ac-

	TEXTS		CONTEXTS
1931	tivist: *Franciscan Adventure*.	1931	
	Phoebe Atwood Taylor (1909–1976), prolific mystery novelist: *The Cape Cod Mystery*.		
1932	Mary Austin: *Earth Horizon*, autobiography.	1932	Although Louise Stokes and Tydie Pickett are the first African American women ever selected to compete in the Olympics, they are replaced by two white athletes in the actual competition; Stokes is allowed to compete in the 1936 Olympics.
	Kay Boyle: *Year Before Last*, an experimental, lyrical novel.		
	Fielding Burke (Olive Tilford Dargan, 1869–1968): *Call Home the Heart*, a proletarian novel.		
	Elaine Sterne Carrington (1892–1958), playwright and short-story writer, begins writing radio serials with the *Red Adams* series. A primary shaper of the soap-opera genre, she fought to provide positive self-images for women.		Mildred Ella "Babe" Didrikson Zaharias wins two Olympic gold medals in the eight-meter hurdles and javelin and ties for first place in the high jump; "Babe" will break records in track, tennis, basketball, baseball, bowling, diving, and golf.
	Mazie Earhart Clark, African American poet: *Garden of Memories*.		The Lindbergh baby kidnapping case captures the attention of millions.
	Rachel Crothers: *When Ladies Meet*, a play.		Fifty-two writers sign an open letter backing the Communist party ticket for President.
	Ella Cara Deloria (1889–1971), Dakota/Sioux author and scholar: *Dakota Texts*.		Frances Steloff, owner of New York's famous Gotham Book Mart, is ar-

TEXTS	CONTEXTS
1932 Zelda Fitzgerald (1899–1948): *Save Me the Last Waltz*, a novel.	**1932** rested for selling "pernicious" literature; the grand jury fails to indict her although 40 books are seized from her store during the arrest and never returned.
Ellen Glasgow: *The Sheltered Life*, a novel.	
Jovita Gonzalez, Chicana short-story writer: "Among My People," in J. Frank Dobie, ed., *Tone the Bell Easy*.	Painter Isabel Bishop (1902–1988) opens a one-woman show at the Midtown Galleries in New York City. Among her subjects are young working women seen on the streets of the city.
Helen R. Hull: *Heat Lightning*, a bestselling novel.	
Grace Elizabeth King: *Memories of a Southern Woman of Letters*, an autobiography published a few months after the New Orleans local colorist's death.	Gracie Allen (1905–1964) and George Burns begin their 19-year radio show with Burns playing straight man to Allen's comedy. In addition to her career as a comedienne, Allen paints surrealistic works with titles such as *Man Builds Better Mousetrap and Buys Mohair Toupe* and writes a widely syndicated newspaper column.
Janet Lewis, novelist, poet, librettist, and short-story writer: *The Invasion: A Narrative of Events Concerning the Johnston Family of St. Mary's*, a novel.	
Grace Lumpkin, novelist of the southern poor: *To Make My Bread*.	Florence Beatrice Smith Price (1888–1933), the first successful black woman composer, wins first place in the Wanamaker Music Contest for her *Symphony in E Minor*.
Dorothy Myra Page: *Gathering Storm*, fictional dramatization of significant events in American labor history.	
	Franklin Delano Roosevelt is elected President.

TEXTS	CONTEXTS
1932 Julia Peterkin: *Bright Skin*, a novel. Elizabeth Madox Roberts: *The Haunted Mirror*, a collection of short stories. Sarah Royce: *A Frontier Lady: Recollections of the Gold Rush and Early California*, a posthumously published journal, begun in 1849, chronicling her experiences in the California gold rush. Gertrude Stein: *The Autobiography of Alice B. Toklas;* serialized in *Atlantic Monthly* and a Book-of-the-Month Club selection, it is the first work to earn Stein money and popular recognition. Margaret Sutton publishes the first of the Judy Bolton series, chronicling the adventures of a girl detective from age 15 to age 22. Over the course of the 38 books in the series, Judy Bolton grows up and marries an FBI agent, but continues solving mysteries. The series ends in 1967, when it is canceled by Grosset & Dunlap. Kathleen Eldridge Tamagawa, Japanese American	1932 Hattie O. W. Caraway becomes the first woman elected to a full term in the United States Senate. *Family Circle* magazine begins publication.

	TEXTS		CONTEXTS
1932	autobiographer: *Holy Prayers in a Horse's Ear.* Dorothy Thompson (1894–1961), journalist: *I Saw Hitler;* this work, along with her widely syndicated column "On the Record," helps to alert the English-speaking world to the menace of the Hitler regime. Mae West (1893–1980), playwright, actress, humorist: *Diamond Lil,* also titled *She Done Him Wrong.* Edith Wharton: *The Gods Arrive,* a novel. Laura Ingalls Wilder (1867–1957): *Little House in the Big Woods,* first in a series of seven semi-autobiographical Little House books about growing up on the frontier. Elinor Wylie: *Collected Poems,* published posthumously.	1932	
1932–1934		1932–1934	Drought makes the Great Plains a "dust bowl."
1933	Sophonisba Preston Breckinridge (1866–1948): *Women in the Twentieth Century: A Study of*	1933	Katharine Hepburn receives for *Morning Glory* her first of four Best Actress Oscars.

	TEXTS		CONTEXTS
1933	*Their Political, Social and Economic Activities.*	1933	U.S. Congress votes that the Philippines should be independent.
	Elizabeth Lindsay Davis, African American author: *Lifting as They Climb.*		Thirteen million Americans are unemployed.
	Jessie Redmon Fauset: *Comedy, American Style,* a novel.		Hitler becomes chancellor of Germany and inaugurates the widescale persecution of Jews.
	Josephine Herbst: *Pity Is Not Enough,* first in her Depression-era trilogy.		Japan resigns from the League of Nations.
	Fannie Hurst: *Imitation of Life,* later filmed in two popular versions.		Frances Perkins is named Secretary of Labor and becomes the first woman to hold a cabinet post.
	Claire Kummer, playwright: *Her Master's Voice.*		Ruth Bryan Owen (Rohde) becomes the first woman diplomat to represent the U.S. abroad; she serves in Denmark and Iceland as envoy extraordinary and minister plenipotentiary.
	Cornelia Meigs (1884–1973), writer of biographies and novels targeted at young women: *Invincible Louisa: The Story of the Author of "Little Women".*		
	Caroline Miller: *Lamb in His Bosom,* Pulitzer Prize-winning novel.		Dorothy Day plays a principal role in founding the "Catholic Worker" movement, which produces an anti-capitalist, anti-communist newspaper and numerous facilities providing food, shelter, and clothing for the poor.
	Mourning Dove: *Coyote Stories.*		
	Julia Ross Newberry: *Julia Newberry's Diary.*		
	Hortense Powdermaker, anthropologist: *Life in Lesu.*		The Tennessee Valley Authority is created to con-

	TEXTS		CONTEXTS
1933	Eleanor Roosevelt (1884–1962), First Lady, social activist, and autobiographer: *It's Up To the Women*, detailing her Progressive, social feminist views.	1933	trol floods and sell cheap electricity.

<table>

1933 — TEXTS

Eleanor Roosevelt (1884–1962), First Lady, social activist, and autobiographer: *It's Up To the Women*, detailing her Progressive, social feminist views.

Evelyn Scott: *Eva Gay*, an autobiographical novel.

Agnes Smedley: *Chinese Destinies: Sketches of Present-Day China*.

Sara Teasdale: *Strange Victory*, a posthumously published volume of poetry. Teasdale committed suicide earlier in the year.

Molly Day Thacher: *Blocks*, an antiwar verse drama.

1933 — CONTEXTS

trol floods and sell cheap electricity.

Newsweek magazine begins publication.

U.S. News magazine is launched; it becomes *U.S. News and World Report* in 1948.

Perhaps the first men's fashion magazine, *Esquire*, begins publication as a medium for advertising men's clothing.

By this date two-thirds of American homes possess at least one radio.

Disposable Tampax tampons are marketed.

Ruth Wakefield bakes the first chocolate chip cookie at her Toll House Inn in Massachusetts.

Jean Harlow (1911–1937), actress known for her platinum blonde hair and sexy roles, appears in *Bombshell*, considered by many her best film. A talented comic actress also acclaimed for her performances in *Platinum Blonde* (1931) and *Red Dust* (1932), among others, Harlow dies at age 26 of a mysterious illness.

TEXTS	CONTEXTS
1933	**1933** I. Rice Pereira (1907–1971), known for her distinctive geometric abstractions, opens her first one-woman exhibition at the A.C.A. Gallery.
	Agnes Tait (1897–1981) works as an easel painter for the Public Works of Art Project in New York. Interested in narrative and figural painting, she was involved in the "Art for the Millions" movement. Her paintings include *Skating in Central Park* and *Olive Grove, Mallorca*, as well as a mural frieze, *Fruits of the Land*. After World War II, she turns her attention to lithographs and illustrations for children's books.
	Cartoon characters Blondie and Dagwood marry.
1933–1934	**1933–1934** The Twenty-first Amendment repeals prohibition.
1933–1935	**1933–1935** FDR institutes the first "New Deal."
1934 Zoe Akins: *The Old Maid*, winner of Pulitzer Prize for drama in 1935, an adaptation of a novella by Edith Wharton.	**1934** Polish-German nonagression pact is signed.
	Nationwide textile strike.

TEXTS	CONTEXTS
1934 Ruth Benedict (1887–1948), one of the first U.S. women to become a professional anthropologist, and teacher and friend to Margaret Mead: *Patterns of Culture*, a standard anthropological text for 25 years.	**1934** Florence Allen, judge, lawyer, suffragist, and spokesperson for world peace, is appointed to the Sixth Circuit Court of Appeals, the first woman at that rank in the federal court system.

Jessie Bernard, sociologist, with her husband Luther Lee Bernard: *Sociology and the Study of International Relations*. She will go on to author or co-author over twenty works of sociology, including many that examine women's roles.

The Catholic Church forms the Legion of Decency in an attempt to improve the moral standards of Hollywood films.

Clair Blank begins the Beverly Gray "College Mysteries."

The Hays Code is adopted to prevent Hollywood films from displaying open sensuality.

Kay Boyle: *My Next Bride*, a novel.

Cissy Patterson becomes the first female publisher of a modern large city daily newspaper.

Sophonisba Breckinridge: *The Family and the State*.

Eva Emery Dye: *The Soul of America: An Oregon Iliad*.

Gertrude Atherton becomes the first woman president of the National Academy of Literature.

Mignon G. Eberhart: *The Cases of Susan Dare*, stories featuring a mystery writer as sleuth.

The first strike in a publishing firm occurs after Dorothy Rimmer, a bookkeeper with the firm of Macaulay Company, is fired for trying to enlist fellow workers to join the Office Workers Union; although the strike is called off after all the workers, including Rimmer, are re-

Caroline Gordon: *Aleck Maury, Sportsman*, a novel.

TEXTS		CONTEXTS	
1934	Lillian Hellman (1905–1984), playwright and autobiographer: *The Children's Hour*, a play, runs for 691 performances on Broadway.	1934	hired and the firm agrees to collective bargaining, three months later, four female employees, all members of the Office Workers Union, are fired; another strike is called and by the time of its resolution, the drive toward organization is sweeping through all the major publishing houses.
	Josephine Herbst: *The Executioner Waits*, second in her Depression-era trilogy.		
	Zora Neale Hurston (c. 1901–1960), African American anthropologist, novelist, and short-story writer: *Jonah's Gourd Vine*.		The influential journal *Partisan Review* is founded; it folds in 1936 and is reorganized in 1937.
	Alice James (1848–1892): *The Diary of Alice James*, recording her shrewd observations of her famous brothers, her awareness of her impending death from breast cancer, and her philosophical ruminations, appears posthumously after being suppressed by the James family for many years.		The first coin-operated laundry—called a "washateria"—opens in Fort Worth, Texas.
			Bonnie Parker and her partner-in-crime Clyde Barrow are gunned down in Louisiana.
	Josephine Winslow Johnson, novelist, short-story writer, and painter: *Now in November*, Pulitzer Prize-winning novel of life on a Midwestern farm.		Actress Bette Davis (1908–1989) receives her first Oscar nomination for *Of Human Bondage*; by the time she leaves Warner Brothers in 1949 she has made 49 films for the studio and is still to star in such acclaimed films as *All About Eve* (1950) or *Whatever Happened to Baby Jane?* (1961).

TEXTS		CONTEXTS	
1934	Mary Johnston: *Drury Randall*, a novel.	1934	Jazz singer Billie Holiday (1915–1959) teams up with saxophonist Lester Young and together they produce some of the most highly regarded jazz recordings ever.
	Jessie B. Rittenhouse: *My House of Life*, an autobiography.		
	Tess Slesinger (1900–1975), novelist, short-story writer, and screenwriter: *The Unpossessed*, a Modernist novel.		
	Betty Smith (1904–1972), novelist, playwright: *A Tree Grows in Brooklyn*.		
	Gertrude Stein: *Portraits and Prayers*.		
	Ruth Suckow (1892–1960), regionalist (Midwest) novelist and short-story writer: *The Folks*.		
	Genevieve Taggard: *Not Mine to Finish*, a collection of poetry.		
	Edith Wharton: *A Backward Glance*, a memoir.		
	Audrey Wurdemann (1911–1960), poet: *Bright Ambush*, winner of the 1935 Pulitzer Prize for poetry.		
1934–1935		1934–1935	Italian-Ethopian War.

*   *   *

TEXTS	CONTEXTS
1935	**1935**

<table>
<tr><td>

Pearl Buck becomes the first U.S. woman to be awarded a Nobel Prize in literature.

Olive Dargan: *A Stone Came Rolling*, a novel.

Josefina Excajeda, Chicana short-story writer: "Tales from San Elizario," in J. Frank Dobie, ed., *Puro Mexico*.

Charlotte Perkins Gilman: *The Living of Charlotte Perkins Gilman*, a posthumous autobiography.

Ellen Glasgow: *Vein of Iron*, a novel.

Zora Neale Hurston: *Mules and Men*, a collection of folktales, songs, children's games, prayers and sermons, and hoodoo practices.

Haruto Ishimoto, Japanese American autobiographer: *Facing Two Ways: The Story of My Life*.

Rose Wilder Lane (1886–1968), novelist, short-story writer, political essayist: *Old Home Town*, a collection of stories about

</td><td>

The National Council of Negro Women is established, and Mary McLeod Bethune is elected president; the following year Bethune becomes director of the Division of Negro Affairs for the National Youth Administration.

Theater Director Hallie Flanagan (1889–1969) is chosen to head the New Deal's Federal Theater Project (FTP), which loses funding in 1939. Employing 12,000 to 15,000 people, the organization produces more than 900 works seen by over 15 million people across the country. Several other women, including Rosamond Gilder, Madalyn O'Shea, Kate Drain Lawson, Susan Glaspell, and Rose McClendon, hold important administrative jobs in the project.

Romaine Brooks (1874–1970), portraitist, exhibits at the Arts Club of Chicago. Longtime companion of Natalie Barney, Brooks lives for many years as an expatriate in Paris. Many of her portraits have lesbians as their subject. Titles include *Una, Lady Trou-*

</td></tr>
</table>

TEXTS	CONTEXTS
1935 women in a midwestern town.	1935 *bridge, The Crossing, The Masked Archer,* and *Miss Natalie Barney,* "*L'Amazone.*"

TEXTS

1935 women in a midwestern town.

Meridel LeSueur, novelist, journalist, poet closely associated with prairie populists and Marxists: "Annunciation," a story in which an expectant mother meditates on her pregnancy and the world awaiting the child.

Mabel Dodge Luhan (1879–1962), memoirist: *Winter in Taos.*

Grace Lumpkin: *A Sign for Cain*, a proletarian novel.

Marianne Moore: *Selected Poems.*

Lola Ridge: *Dance of Fire*, a volume of poetry.

Muriel Rukeyser (1913–1980), poet and political activist: *Theory of Flight*, a collection of poems, winner of the Yale Younger Poets award.

Mari Sandoz (1896–1966), whose writings are characterized by a mingling of biography, autobiography, history, and fiction, begins her six-

CONTEXTS

1935 *bridge, The Crossing, The Masked Archer,* and *Miss Natalie Barney,* "*L'Amazone.*"

Patsy Montana's "I Want to be a Cowboy's Sweetheart" becomes the first million-selling country song by a woman.

Aunt Molly Jackson, who claimed to be the inspiration for "Pistol Packin' Mama," begins recording folk songs for the Library of Congress Archive of Folk Song. The union organizer and acclaimed ballad singer eventually records 150 songs for the project.

The Social Security Act provides federal employment, old age insurance, and social welfare for dependent women and children.

The communist League of American Writers is founded.

Harlem race riots occur.

Senator Huey Long is assassinated.

Penguin Books is founded.

TEXTS		CONTEXTS
1935	volume Great Plains series with *Old Jules*. Tess Slesinger: *On Being Told That Her Second Husband Has Taken His First Lover and Other Stories*. Gertrude Stein: *Lectures in America* and *Narration*. Anna Louise Strong (1885–1970), radical journalist and autobiographer: *I Change Worlds: The Remaking of an American*. Etsu Inagaki Sugimoto: *Grandmother O Kyo*, an autobiography. Mary Heaton Vorse (1874–1966), journalist and correspondent who reports extensively on labor issues, novelist: *A Footnote to Folly*, autobiography. Gale Wilhelm: *We Too Are Drifting*, a novel about a young lesbian artist's relationships.	1935	Sophie Tucker (1884?–1966), best known for her work in vaudeville, becomes the first woman president of the American Federation of Actors. Comedienne Marian Jordan (1898–1961) begins 17 years as Molly on the popular radio show *Fibber McGee and Molly*.
1935–1938		1935–1938	Second New Deal.
1935–1941		1935–1941	Under the Works Progress Administration, especially through the Federal Writers', Arts, and Theater Projects, women find

TEXTS	CONTEXTS
1935–1941	1935–1941 economic relief from the Depression. Overall; however, less than 20 percent of all WPA workers are female; 3 percent are African American females.

TEXTS	CONTEXTS
1936 Harriette Arnow (1908–1986), Appalachian novelist and social historian: *Mountain Path*. Djuna Barnes: *Nightwood*, a novel. Kay Boyle: *Death of a Man*, a novel indicting Nazism. Anne Frierson: *Quagmire*, a Gullah drama. Frances Parkinson Keyes (1885–1970), novelist, magazine contributor, political analyst ("Letters from a Senator's Wife"): *Honor Bright*, a novel. Clare Boothe Luce (1903–1987), playwright, diplomat, feminist: *The Women*, a social satire, runs for over 500 performances. Margaret Mitchell (1900–1949), Southern novelist: *Gone With the Wind*. The novel is released by Macmillan at a list price of $3; department stores of-	1936 The American Labor Party is formed. A Gallop poll finds that 82 percent of those questioned say women with employed husbands should not be allowed to work. Of the women surveyed, 75 percent agree. Reva Beck Bosons becomes Utah's first woman judge and is later elected congresswoman. In *West Coast Hotel v. Parrish*, the Supreme Court reverses earlier decisions and rules that women are entitled to a minimum wage. In *United States v. One Package*, a federal appeals court overturns the Comstock law's provisions against contraception. Mary McLeod Bethune, black school founder, civic leader, club woman, is appointed director of minority affairs in the

TEXTS	CONTEXTS
1936	1936

TEXTS

1936

fer the volume for less, setting off a huge price war. It sells a million copies in six months, 50,000 in a single day. The runaway best-seller wins the Pulitzer Prize in 1937.

Kathleen Moore Morehouse: *Rain on the Just*, a novel of Appalachia.

Josefina Niggli (1910–1983), Mexican American playwright, short-story writer, and folklorist: *Soldadera: A One-Act Play of the Mexican Revolution*.

Anaïs Nin (1903–1977), novelist and memoirist: *House of Incest*, a novel.

Dorothy Parker: *Not So Deep as a Well*, poetry.

Irna Phillips (1901–1973), as writer and creator of dozens of radio and television soap operas, earns the title "Queen of the Soaps."

Gertrude Stein: *The Geographical History of America*.

Mary Dallas Street, poet and novelist: *At Summer's End*.

CONTEXTS

1936

New Deal's National Youth Association.

Max Factor, a Hollywood cosmetic organization that created the "make-up for the stars," goes international when it opens a salon in London.

Life magazine begins publication.

Margaret Bourke-White (1906–1971) is one of the first women and among the most notable of photojournalists. A creator of the photographic essay genre, she does *Life*'s first cover photo and photo essay.

FDR is re-elected.

Ella Fitzgerald becomes one of the country's top jazz vocalists while still a teenager.

Dorothea Lange (1895–1965), photographer, documents effects of the Depression in rural areas in such works as *Migrant Mother, California, 1936*.

* * *

TEXTS	CONTEXTS
1936–1937	1936–1937 Luise Rainier wins the Best Actress Oscar two years in a row for *The Great Ziegfeld* and *The Good Earth*.
1936–1939	1936–1939 The Spanish Civil War begins; it ends in 1939 with the beginning of Franco's dictatorship.
1937 Anita Blackmon: *Murder à la Richelieu*. Rachel Crothers: *Susan and God*, her final play. Dorothy Fields (1904–1974), lyricist, becomes the first woman to win an Oscar for songwriting; she receives it for "The Way You Look Tonight," from the movie *Swing Time*. Caroline Gordon: *None Shall Look Back* and *The Garden of Adonis*, novels. Karen Horney (1885–1952), psychiatrist and psychoanalyst specializing in female sexuality and psychology: *The Neurotic Personality of Our Time*. Zora Neale Hurston: *Their Eyes Were Watching God*, an extremely influential novel.	1937 North Carolina becomes the first state to fund the provision of contraceptives with tax dollars; racism is said to have played a major role in the decision. Amelia Earhart, record-breaking pilot, is lost en route in her attempt to fly westbound around the world. The American Association of University Presses adopts its constitution. *Woman's Day* magazine appears in October. It begins as a three-cent monthly women's service magazine published by A&P grocery for distribution in its stores. Augusta Savage (1892–1962), African American sculptor and one of the most important artists of the Harlem Renaissance,

TEXTS		CONTEXTS	
1937	Margaret Morse Nice (1883–1974), ornithologist: *Studies in the Life of the Song Sparrow*, an influential two-volume work, the second of which appears in 1943.	1937	is named the first director of the Harlem Community Art Center. Two years later she is the only black artist asked to contribute art to the World's Fair, at which she exhibits *The Harp*.
	Charlotte Murray Russell: *Tiny Diamond*, the first of several mysteries featuring Jane Edwards, an unmarried midwestern woman sleuth in her forties.		Billie Holiday performs with the Count Basie band.
	Evelyn Scott: *Background in Tennessee*, a memoir.		*Public Opinion Quarterly*, the principal journal of the polling industry, is founded.
	Gertrude Stein: *Everybody's Autobiography*.		
	Gladys Bagg Taber (1899–1980), novelist and magazine columnist, writes "Diary of Domesticity" for the *Ladies' Home Journal*.		
	Sara Teasdale: *Collected Poems*, posthumously published.		
	Dorothy Thompson, outspoken anti-Nazi, begins writing regular columns for the *Ladies' Home Journal*.		
	Edith Wharton: *Ghosts*, a collection of short stories.		

TEXTS		CONTEXTS
1937	Marguerite Young (1908–1995), novelist, poet, historian, and editor: *Prismatic Ground*, poetry.	1937	
1938	Kay Boyle: *Monday Night* and *Bridegroom's Body*, novels.	1938	Some 10.4 million Americans are unemployed.
	Dorothy Day: *From Union Square to Rome*, autobiography.		Three hundred birth control clinics are in operation across the country.
	Marion Rice Hart: *Who Called That Lady a Skipper? The Strange Voyage of a Woman Navigator*, a memoir.		A gender-neutral Fair Labor Standards Act is passed; it also indirectly establishes the government's right to legislate child labor.
	Helen McCloy, writer of mystery fiction combined with social satire: *Dance of Death*. She creates one of the first psychiatrist detectives.		Crystal Dreda Bird Fauset is elected to the Philadelphia state legislature and becomes the first known African American woman in the U.S. to so serve.
	Josefina Niggli: *Mexican Folk Plays*.		The House of Representatives establishes a special committee to investigate un-Americanism; it becomes a regular committee in 1945.
	Marjorie Kinnan Rawlings (1896–1953): *The Yearling*, winner of 1939 Pulitzer Prize for fiction.		
	Laura Riding (1901–1991), poet, novelist, critic: *Collected Poems*.		Chicana feminist, librarian, and civil rights activist Martha Cotera is born.
	Elizabeth Madox Roberts: *Black Is My Truelove's Hair*, a novel.		Edith Head, fashion and set designer, becomes the head of the design department at Paramount, the first woman to head such

TEXTS	CONTEXTS
1938	1938

Eleanor Roosevelt: *My Days*, an autobiography.	a department at a major studio. She earns more than 1000 screen credits, 32 Academy Award nominations, and eight Academy Awards.
Margaret Sanger: *Margaret Sanger*, an autobiography.	
Emma L. Shields and Helen D. Wemple: *Knit One, Purl One: A Little Girl's Knitting and Crochet Book*.	Billie Holiday tours with the all-white Artie Shaw band; she is met with so much racism and segregation — forced to use service elevators, to stay in separate hotels — she finally quits.
Agnes Smedley: *China Fights Back: An American Woman with the Eighth Route Army*.	Beatrice Fox Auerbach becomes president of G. Fox & Company in Hartford, Connecticut, a position she holds through 1965. She increases the business tenfold, making it the largest privately owned department store in the country, and pioneers such labor programs as the five-day week, retirement plans, medical and nonprofit lunch facilities for employees, and a revolving fund to lend employees interest-free money in times of personal crisis. Fox's is also the first large department store to hire black employees for positions which offered advancement.
Gertrude Stein: *Picasso*.	
Gale Wilhelm: *Torchlight to Valhalla*, a novel.	
Marya Zaturenska wins the Pulitzer Prize for poetry for *Cold Morning Sky*.	
Leane Zugsmith: *The Summer Soldier*, a novel.	
	Black women trade unionists form the International

TEXTS	CONTEXTS
1938	**1938** Ladies' Auxiliary of the Brotherhood of Sleeping Car Porters, the first black women's international labor organization.
	Sixteen African American women in Philadelphia found Jack & Jill of America to sponsor cultural events and opportunities for children.
	A *Ladies' Home Journal* poll finds that 79 percent of American women approve of contraceptive use.
	The National Organization for Decent Literature is founded to raise the standards of print media.
	Orson Welles broadcasts H. G. Wells's *The War of the Worlds* over the radio, causing a panic.
	Claire McCardell designs a tent dress ("the Monastic"), which soon becomes a fashion hit and launches "the American Look."
1939 Dorothy Day: *House of Hospitality*, autobiography. Elizabeth Dean: *Murder Is a Collector's Item*, the first of several mysteries featuring Emma Marsh, an ama-	**1939** The Birth Control Federation of America, later Planned Parenthood of America, proposes a "Negro Project," believing that "the mass of Negroes . . . particularly in the

TEXTS		CONTEXTS
1939	teur detective who enjoys New York's nightlife.	1939	South, still breed carelessly and disastrously."

TEXTS

1939

teur detective who enjoys New York's nightlife.

Anne Walter Fearn, worker for social reform in both the American South and China: *My Days of Strength*.

Muriel Follett: *New England Year: A Journal of Vermont Farm Life*.

Rose Franken (1895–1988), playwright, novelist, short-story writer, and scriptwriter: *Claudia: The Story of a Marriage*, first of eight in a very popular series; first dramatized in 1941.

Shirley Graham (1907–1977), African American biographer, playwright, and advocate of human rights: *It's Morning*.

Lillian Hellman: *The Little Foxes*, a play.

Josephine Herbst: *Rope of Gold*, the third volume in her Depression-era trilogy.

Karen Horney: *New Ways in Psychoanalysis*.

Zora Neale Hurston: *Moses, Man of the Mountain*.

CONTEXTS

1939

South, still breed carelessly and disastrously."

Sixty-four percent of white southerners surveyed think lynching is justified in cases of sexual assault.

Eleanor Patterson founds the Washington *Times-Herald*; four years later it becomes the city's largest paper, although what many considered her ruthlessness leads *Time* magazine to label her "the most hated woman in America."

The Kenyon Review, a quarterly magazine at Kenyon College under John Crowe Ransom's editorship, begins publishing and is an influential purveyor of the "New Criticism."

Approximately 48 million radio sets have been sold.

Pocket Books is founded.

Cup-sizing for brassieres is designed by Warners' employee Leona Gross Lax.

The "Lambeth Walk," first performed in 1909 by

	TEXTS		CONTEXTS
1939	Cleofas Jaramillo, Chicana writer, autobiographer, and folklorist: *The Genuine New Mexico Tasty Recipes.*	1939	dancer Daphne Polk, becomes a popular dance step.

Agnes Newton Keith, travel writer and memoirist on experiences in Asia and Africa: *Land Below the Wind*, bestseller describing life in Borneo.

Adet, Anor, and Meimei Lin: *Our Family*, memoir by Chinese American sisters aged 16, 13, and 8, respectively.

Grace Lumpkin: *The Wedding*, a social comedy.

Josephine Miles (1911–1985), poet and scholar: *Lines at Intersection*, poetry.

Dorothy Parker: *Here Lies*, a collection of her short stories.

Katherine Anne Porter: *Pale Horse, Pale Rider: Three Short Novels.*

Craig Rice, the pen name of Georgiana Ann Randolph Craig (1908–1957), who also writes under the names of Michael Ven-

Hattie McDaniel (1895?–1952), radio comedy star and film actress, becomes the first African American to win an Academy Award; she is awarded the Oscar for Best Supporting Actress for her work in *Gone With the Wind.*

Among the exhibits at the World's Fair in New York are two extremely popular futuristic ones: "Democracity," which envisions an increase in leisure time and a highly structured means of organizing it, and the General Motors building, which represents American life in 1960 as an era defined by its ingenious technological innovations.

World War II begins. Hitler invades Czechoslovakia and Poland; the German-Russian non-aggression pact is signed.

A border war is ongoing between Japan and Russia in Manchuria.

When African American opera singer Marian

TEXTS	CONTEXTS
1939 ning and Daphne Saunders, and ghost-writes novels for several actors, including Gypsy Rose Lee and George Sanders: *8 Faces at 3*, the first of 20 mysteries. She also writes more than 60 short stories, a true-crime book, a gothic, and many radio scripts. She is especially known for her screwball comedy mysteries.	**1939** Anderson's concert is canceled by the Daughters of the American Revolution, Eleanor Roosevelt resigns her DAR membership and arranges a new concert for Anderson at the Lincoln Memorial. Anderson's concert transforms an ugly racial incident into an affirmation of human rights.
May Sarton (1912–1995), poet, playwright, novelist, memoirist: *Inner Landscape*, poetry.	Jane Matilda Bolin is appointed to a judgeship in New York City, becoming the first African American female appointed judge in the U.S.
Gertrude Stein: *The World Is Round*, her first book for children.	Maria Montoya Martinez (1884–1981), a Pueblo Indian artist, works backward from pottery shards found at archaeological sites in order to recreate pottery designs of her ancestors.
Jean Thomas, folklorist who becomes known as "The Traipsin' Woman," founder of the American Folk Song Festival: *Ballad Makin' in the Mountains of Kentucky*.	
1940s *Vice Versa*, probably the first lesbian journal in the United States, is typed and mimeographed by a secretary during regular working hours; she uses the anagram Lisa Ben.	**1940s** Plucked eyebrows and bright red lips are a popular look, fashioned after movie stars such as Marlene Dietrich.

*   *   *

TEXTS	CONTEXTS
1940 Kay Boyle: *Crazy Hunter*, a novel.	1940 Battle of Britain.
Janet Flanner (1892–1978), journalist and essayist: *An American in Paris.*	Trotsky is assassinated in Mexico.
Inglis Fletcher (1879–1969), historical novelist: *Raleigh's Eden*, the beginning of her Carolina series.	Total population is 132,122,000; 33 percent (44 million people) live at or below poverty level.
Frances Gaither: *Follow the Drinking Gourd.*	Some 85.9 percent of all adult female workers are nonwhite.
Mildred Haun (1911–1966), Appalachian writer: *The Hawk's Done Gone*; reissued in 1967 with previously unpublished stories.	There are 2,412,000 servants in the U.S. Thirty three percent of all white working women hold clerical jobs, compared with only 1.3 percent of all black female workers.
Dorothy B. Hughes, mystery writer named a Grand Master by the Mystery Writers of America: *The So Blue Marble.*	Dorothy Arzner directs her best-known film, *Dance, Girl, Dance.*
Helena Kuo (Kuo Chin ch'iu), Chinese American essayist, novelist, and autobiographer: *Peace Path*, essays about women and Chinese culture.	"Grandma" Anna Mary Moses (1860–1961), primitivist painter, has her first one-woman show at 80 years of age. She is an immediate popular success.
Gypsy Rose Lee (1914?–1970), well-known striptease entertainer: *The G-String Murders*, a bestselling murder mystery, filmed in 1943.	Thirty-one percent of all black households are headed by a woman. Life expectancy is up to an average of 64 years from 49 years in 1900.

TEXTS

CONTEXTS

1940

1940

Meridel LeSueur: *Salute to Spring*, collection of journalism and stories.

Frances and Richard Lockridge introduce their extremely popular husband-and-wife detective team Pam and Jerry North in *The Norths Meet Murder*. It is later turned into a popular radio series.

Carson McCullers (1919–1967), southern novelist, short-story writer, playwright: *The Heart Is a Lonely Hunter*, a novel.

Elizabeth Madox Roberts: *Songs in the Meadow*, a collection of poetry.

Beryl Simons: *Jane Carberry: Detective*.

Gertrude Stein: *Ida, a Novel*.

Gladys Bagg Taber: *Harvest at Stillmeadow*.

Mary Church Terrell (1863–1896), African American author and civil rights leader: *A Colored Woman in a White World*, autobiography.

Ola Elizabeth Winslow: *Jonathan Edwards*, winner

Diethylstilbestrol (DES) is approved for human use and prescribed for women to prevent complications during pregnancy; some 2 to 3 million mothers take this drug, especially during the 1940s and 1950s; in 1971, studies reveal that it can cause vaginal and cervical cancer, especially in the daughters born to these mothers.

A little more than half of American households have some sort of built-in bathing equipment; one-third are still cooking with wood or coal; and only one-third have central heating.

Since 1910, high school enrollment has increased by 540 percent, college enrollment by 321 percent.

Black women in the northern cities have an average of 3 children and white women have 2; in the rural South, 5.5 children are born to black women and 5 to white women.

Ida Fuller of Vermont becomes the first recipient of a Social Security check.

Sarah Ophelia Colley begins her long career as

TEXTS		CONTEXTS	
1940	of the Pulitzer Prize for biography in 1941.	1940	"Minnie Pearl," the "Queen of Country Comedy" and a favorite on the Grand Ole Opry. She is named Nashville Woman of the Year in 1965 and is elected to the Country Music Hall of Fame in 1968.
			Dale (Dalia) Messick begins the long-running cartoon strip *Brenda Starr*.
			FDR is elected to a third term.
			First appearing under the title *Calling All Girls*, the country's first successful magazine for teenaged girls appears and undergoes several name changes, including *Polly Pigtails* and *Young Miss*, before settling on *YM* in 1992.
1940–1947		1940–1947	The name "Rosie the Riveter" is coined to refer to women employed in the American defense industries during World War II; out of the peak figure of 19.5 million "Rosies," 15.9 million had been employed before the war.
1940–1950		1940–1950	White women's employment increases from 24.5 percent to 28.4 percent;

TEXTS	CONTEXTS
1940–1950	**1940–1950** black women's remains stable at 32 percent.
1941 Grace Abbott (1878–1939), social activist and head of the U.S. Children's Bureau from 1921 to 1934: *From Relief to Social Security*.	**1941** Fifty-two percent of American families have mechanical refrigerators and/or washing machines.
Sally Benson (1900–1972): *Junior Miss*, slice-of-life story focusing particularly on the socialization of a young girl.	Avon Pocket-Size Books first appear.
	Hitler begins the systematic extermination of Jews in Europe.
Louise Bogan: *Poems and New Poems*.	President Roosevelt forms the Fair Employment Practices Committee.
M.F.K. Fisher (1908–1992), autobiographer who emphasizes culinary experience: *Consider the Oyster*.	In *United States v. Classic*, the Supreme Court rules that the right to vote in primaries as well as general elections is extended to blacks by the Constitution.
Ellen Glasgow: *In This Our Life*, winner of 1942 Pulitzer Prize for fiction.	
Bernice Kelly Harris (1893–1973), novelist of rural and small-town life: *Portulaca*.	Lena Horne, African American singer, actress, and activist, becomes the first black woman to sign a term contract in film.
Lillian Hellman: *Watch on the Rhine*, wins New York Drama Critics Circle Award for best American drama of the season.	Louise Nevelson (1900–1988), known for her surrealist collages and as a pioneer of environmental sculpture, has the first of her five one-woman shows in New York City.
Karen Horney founds the *American Journal of Psychoanalysis*.	Black civil rights activist Irene Gaines leads the

TEXTS	CONTEXTS
1941 Margaret Leech: *Reveille in Washington*, winner of Pulitzer Prize for history in 1942.	1941 fight for an executive order banning discrimination in federal employment.

Janet Lewis: *The Wife of Martin Guerre*, historical fiction.

Pearl Harbor is bombed by Japan; the U.S. declares war on Japan; Germany and Italy declare war on the U.S.

Adet, Anor, and Meimei Lin: *Dawn over Chungking*, memoir.

The Victory Book Campaign is launched shortly after the bombing of Pearl Harbor and under the slogan "We Want Books" begins a drive to collect books for men and women in the armed forces.

Carson McCullers: *Reflections in a Golden Eye*, a novel.

Helen MacInnes (1907–1985), suspense novelist: *Above Suspicion*.

Edna St. Vincent Millay: *Collected Sonnets*.

Isabel Bishop is known for the complex painting *Dante and Virgil in Union Square* (1932) and for her paintings of secretaries and shopgirls on their lunchbreaks, such as *Tidying Up*. In 1946 she becomes the first woman officer of the National Institute of Arts and Letters.

Sumie Seo Mishima, Japanese American autobiographer: *My Narrow Isle: The Story of a Modern Woman in Japan*.

Mary O'Hara (1885–1980), novelist, screenwriter: *My Friend Flicka*.

Tarpe Mills begins her *Miss Fury* comic strip. When it begins appearing in comic book form, it sells over a million copies per issue.

Coincident with escalating tensions with Japan, Mary Oyama, a Japanese American newspaper columnist and co-founder of the League of Nisei Artists and Writers, stops writing her advice to the lovelorn

TEXTS	CONTEXTS
1941 column for the San Francisco *New World Sun.* The column, which she began writing in the mid-1930s, often served as a forum for Oyama's reflections on what it meant to be Nisei (second generation immigrant) in the U.S. Josephine Pinckney (1895–1957), novelist, poet, much of whose work focuses on life in Charleston, S.C.: *Hilton Head.* Elizabeth Madox Roberts: *Not By Strange Gods.* Anya Seton (1916–1990), author of historical/biographical novels: *My Theodosia.* Sophie Treadwell: *Hope for a Harvest*, a drama of bigotry and environmental waste set in California. Janet Camp Troxell: *The Home Front: Five Hundred Ways to Save Time, Labor, and Money.* Eudora Welty, prolific southern author of novels, short stories, and memoirs: *A Curtain of Green*, collection of stories.	1941

*   *   *

TEXTS	CONTEXTS
1942 Charlotte Armstrong (1905–1969), after writing poems and two plays, goes on to produce numerous—and very popular—mystery and suspense novels: *Lay On, Mac Duff!* is her first in this genre.	**1942** President Roosevelt issues Executive Order 9066, ordering the military to handle the evacuation of all Japanese from the Pacific Coast and their placement in internment camps; some 110,000 Japanese Americans are interned on the West Coast.
Sally Benson: *Meet Me in St. Louis*, short stories about a young girl and her family at the time of the 1904 Louisiana Purchase Exposition.	More than 800 birth control clinics exist across the country.
Margaret Farrar (1897–1942), the first woman to write a crossword puzzle book, becomes the first woman editor of the *New York Times* crossword puzzles.	The WAVES (Women Accepted for Volunteer Emergency Service), the U.S. Navy's Women's Corps, and SPAR (from the Coast Guard motto, *Semper Paratus*, "Always Ready") the U.S. Coast Guard's Women's Corps, are formed.
Esther Forbes (1891–1967), novelist and biographer, first woman member of the American Antiquarian Society: *Paul Revere and the World He Lived In*, winner of 1943 Pulitzer Prize for history; her *Johnny Tremaine*, a fictionalized retelling of *Paul Revere*, is published in 1943.	The Women's Army Auxiliary Corps (WAAC) is formed; in 1943, WAAC is abolished and the Women's Army Corps (WAC) is established. While WAAC granted women partial military status, WAC gives women the opportunity to attain the same rank, titles, and pay as their male counterparts.
Zora Neale Hurston: *Dust Tracks on a Road*, autobiography.	Nancy Harker Love becomes squadron com-

TEXTS	CONTEXTS
1942	1942

1942   Emily Kimbrough (1899–1989), editor *(Ladies' Home Journal)*, humorist, travel writer: *Our Hearts Were Young and Gay*, with Cornelia Otis Skinner, actress, humorist, and biographer.

Helena Kuo: *I've Come a Long Way*, autobiography.

Susanne K. Langer (1895–1985), philosopher: *Philosophy in a New Key: A Study in the Symbols of Reason, Rite, and Art*, best-selling and influential study of aesthetics.

Mary McCarthy (1912–1989), essayist and fiction writer: *The Company She Keeps.*

Margaret Millar, Canadian-born novelist known for psychological mysteries: *The Devil Loves Me.*

Marjorie Kinnan Rawlings: *Cross Creek*, a memoir.

Han Suyin, Chinese American novelist, autobiographer, and biographer: *Destination Chungking.*

1942   mander of the Women's Auxiliary Flying Services, founded on September 10, 1942. In 1943 it merges with the Women's Flying Training Detachment to form Women's Airforce Service Pilots (WASP).

Jacqueline Cochrane—the first woman to fly faster than the speed of sound (1953)—heads the WASPs, which ferries planes across the U.S. during the War.

The Congress of Racial Equality (CORE) is founded.

Margaret Bourke-White becomes the first woman war correspondent.

Clare Boothe Luce is elected to the House of Representatives. In 1953, she is appointed ambassador to Italy.

Peggy Guggenheim opens the "Art of This Century" gallery in New York City, a showplace for modern art.

Dell Books is formed; all the book divisions of Delacorte publishing, including Dell, Delta, Yearling, Candlelight, Purse, Heri-

	TEXTS		CONTEXTS
1942	Margaret Walker, African American poet and novelist: *For My People*, first book of poetry by an African American to receive the Yale Younger Poets Award.	1942	tage Press, and Dial Press, are presided over by Helen Meyer, who becomes president of Delacorte in 1979.
			Dover Publications is established.
			Movie star Carole Lombard, wife of actor Clark Gable, is killed along with her mother and 20 other passengers in a plane crash near Las Vegas while on a tour promoting war bonds.
			The American Birth Control League changes its name to Planned Parenthood Federation of America, Inc. (PPFA), hoping that "parenthood" would appeal to a larger segment of the population than did the controversial "birth control."
1943	Jane Bowles (1917–1973), fiction writer and playwright: *Two Serious Ladies*, a novel. Vera Caspary (1899?–1987), novelist, screenplay writer, and journalist: *Laura*, a mystery novel; it is made into a classic Hollywood film the next year. Caspary is blacklisted during the McCarthy era.	1943	For the first time, the U.S. Army commissions female doctors. Race riots occur in Mobile, Alabama; Detroit, Michigan; and the Harlem section of New York City, among other places. Nellie Nelson becomes the first woman elected

TEXTS	CONTEXTS
1943	M.F.K. Fisher: *The Gastro-nomical Me*, a collection of food-centered autobio-graphical essays. Ellen Glasgow: *A Certain Measure: An Interpretation of Prose Fiction.* Elizabeth Janeway, short-story writer, novelist, fem-inist: *The Walsh Girls*, a novel. Hui-lan Koo, Chinese American autobiogra-pher: *Hui-lan Koo: An Au-tobiography.* Janet Lewis: *Against a Darkening Sky.* Adet Lin: *Flame from the Rock*, a novel. Edna St. Vincent Millay: *Collected Lyrics.* Jeanette Covert Nolan: *Final Appearance*, a mystery. Ayn Rand (1905–1982), Russian-born novelist: *The Fountainhead.* Craig Rice: *Having Won-derful Crime*, one of her most noted comic mys-teries.	1943 president of the American Historical Association. The All-American Girl's Professional Baseball League is formed due to the depletion of male base-ball players in World War II. Among its most noted players were Doro-thy "Kammie" Kamen-shek, of the Rockford Peaches, a seven-time All-Star; Doris Sams of the Muskegon-Kalamazoo Lassies; and Jean Faut, of the South Bend Blue Sox. The league is particularly popular in the Midwest; play continues into the mid-'50s. A fictionalized version of their story is told in the popular 1993 film, *A League of Their Own.* The Council on Books in Wartime announces that it will send some 35 mil-lion fictional and nonfic-tional works—Armed Ser-vices Editions—to men and women in the armed forces overseas during the following year: among those included in the first shipment is Margaret Car-penter's mystery, *Experi-ment Perilous*; by war's end, more than 108,500,000 copies of

	TEXTS		CONTEXTS
1943	Lin Tai-yi, Chinese American novelist: *War Tide*.	1943	these editions have been produced.
	Eudora Welty: *The Wide Net*, collection of stories, and *The Robber Bridegroom*.		The war-induced fabric shortages lead to simple, practical fashions.
	Phyllis Whitney, popular and sophisticated author of children's mysteries, adult mysteries, and Gothic romances: *The Red Carnelian*.		The "Jitterbug" and variations like the "Lindy Hop" are the most popular dances of the year.
	Tan Yun, Chinese American novelist: *Flame from the Rock*.		
1943–1944		1943–1944	Actress Betty Grable (1916–1973) is the only woman to appear on two consecutive annual *Motion Picture Herald*'s polls of the top movie box-office attractions. In the mid-'40s, she will become the highest salaried American woman of her time, earning $300,000 a year.
1944	Doris Bell Collier Ball, physician and mystery novelist writing under the pseudonym Josephine Bell: *Death at the Medical Board*.	1944	Margaret O'Brien receives a special Academy Award for the "outstanding child actress of the year."
	Mary Coyle Chase (1907–1981), Colorado play-		Nell Blaine, painter known for her brilliantly colored landscapes and still lifes, becomes the

TEXTS		CONTEXTS
1944	wright: *Harvey*, featuring an invisible rabbit, begins a run of 1775 perfor- mances; it wins the Pulit- zer Prize for drama in 1945. A popular movie based on the play appears in 1950.	1944 youngest member of the American Abstract Artists.

TEXTS

1944 wright: *Harvey*, featuring an invisible rabbit, begins a run of 1775 performances; it wins the Pulitzer Prize for drama in 1945. A popular movie based on the play appears in 1950.

Alice Mary Ross Colver: *Fourways: A Novel.*

Frances Gaither: *The Red Cock Crows.*

Jean Garrigue (1914–1972), poet: *Thirty-six Poems, and a Few Songs.*

Ruth Gordon (1896–1985), dramatist and comic actress: *Over Twenty-one*, a farce.

Helena Kuo: *Westward to Chungking*, a novel, and *Giants of Earth*, a collection of biographical sketches.

Rose Pesotta (1896–1965), Jewish American author and labor organizer: *Bread upon the Waters.*

Katherine Anne Porter: *The Leaning Tower and Other Stories.*

CONTEXTS

1944 youngest member of the American Abstract Artists.

Normandy Invasion.

Paper shortages caused by the war force publishers to take a 25 percent cut in their supply; books are released on lighter paper with narrower margins and more words per page; many older titles go out of print because of the shortage.

Sue S. Dauser becomes the first woman appointed captain in the U.S. Navy.

Roosevelt is elected to a fourth term; he dies in 1945 and Harry S. Truman becomes President.

In *Smith v. Allwright*, the Supreme Court finds the all-white political primary unconstitutional.

Helen Mary (Gahagan) Douglas (1900–1980), former Broadway star and opera singer and wife of actor Melvyn Douglas, is elected to Congress from California.

Sixty percent of domestic workers are black women; the 13 percent increase since 1940 can largely be

TEXTS		CONTEXTS	
1944	Craig Rice: *Home Sweet Homicide*, a combined mystery and autobiography. Anya Seton: *Dragonwyck*. Lillian Smith (1897–1966), novelist, civil rights advocate: *Strange Fruit*, banned in Boston and Detroit for its treatment of miscegenation and abortion. The next year the Superior Court of Massachusetts declares the novel a menace to young people's morals. Mai-mai Sze: *China*. Kathleen Winsor, novelist: *Forever Amber*, an enormous best-seller set in Restoration England. It is banned in Massachusetts due to its sexual content; the ban is lifted by a high court in 1947. Marguerite Young: *Moderate Fables*, poetry.	1944	accounted for by white women quitting such jobs with the end of the Depression. For the first time, Chinese women are allowed to enter the country with no restrictions. The first large-scale automatic digital computer, conceived in 1937, is finally completed; between 1943 and 1945, an army team develops the first all-electronic general purpose computer. *Seventeen* magazine begins publication. "Don't Fence Me In" is a popular song.
1944–1945	H.D. (Hilda Doolittle): *Trilogy*, epic poem.	1944–1945	
1945	Grace Abbott: *The Child and the State*, a study of child welfare issues. Vera Caspary: *Bedelia*, a novel	1945	Three million to 3.5 million women union members are active in the U.S. Harry S. Truman becomes President.

TEXTS		CONTEXTS
1945	Susan Glaspell: *Judd Rankin's Daughter*, a novel.	1945 U.S. drops atomic bombs on Hiroshima and Nagasaki.

<table>
<tr><td>

TEXTS

1945

Susan Glaspell: *Judd Rankin's Daughter*, a novel.

Elizabeth Hardwick, critic, editor, and novelist: *The Ghostly Lover*.

Bernice Kelly Harris (1892–1973), playwright and novelist: *Sage Quarter*.

Bowen Ingram, pen name of Mildred Prewett Ingram (1925–1981), Tennessee novelist and short-story writer: *If Passion Flies*.

Betty MacDonald (1908–1958), humorist: *The Egg and I*, which was filmed in 1947, the first picture to feature Ma and Pa Kettle.

Josefina Niggli: *Mexican Village*, a collection of stories and perhaps the first work of fiction by a Mexican American to reach a large audience.

Santha Rama Rau, Indian American autobiographer and novelist: *Home to India*.

Gertrude Stein: *Wars I Have Seen*, her final memoir.

</td><td>

CONTEXTS

1945

U.S. drops atomic bombs on Hiroshima and Nagasaki.

WWII ends; a peace conference is held in Paris in 1946.

The United Nations is founded.

Alaska passes an Anti-Discrimination Bill, legislating against unfair treatment of Alaskan Natives, largely due to the efforts of Elizabeth Peratrovich, a member of the Raven clan of the Tlingit Indians of Southeast Alaska.

A study conducted by economists at Bryn Mawr college finds that, per week, farm women spend 60.55 hours on housework, women in smaller cities spend 78.35 hours, and in larger cities, women spend 80.57 — this despite the alleged benefits of urban electrification and advanced technology.

For the first time, Harvard Medical School admits women (12) to its freshman class.

Ebony magazine is founded.

</td></tr>
</table>

TEXTS	CONTEXTS
1945 Goldie Stone, Jewish American author: *My Caravan of Years: An Autobiography*. Mai-mai Sze: *Echo of a Cry*, autobiography. Jessamyn West (1902?–1984), novelist, short-story writer: *The Friendly Persuasion*. Jade Snow Wong: *Fifth Chinese Daughter*, autobiography by a Chinese American woman. Marguerite Young: *Angel in the Forest*, a history of two early-19th-century utopian communities.	**1945** Bantam Books is organized. Dorothy Rodgers, married to composer Richard Rodgers, patents the "Jonny Mop" toilet cleaning device. Mahalia Jackson (1911–1972), African American singer known as the "Queen of Gospel Music," achieves fame with "Move on Up a Little Higher," which sells over a million copies. She is later active in the civil rights movement. Twelve-year-old Elizabeth Taylor is acclaimed for her starring role in the film *National Velvet*.
1946 Mary Ritter Beard: *Woman as Force in History*. Ruth Benedict: *The Chrysanthemum and the Sword*, a study of Japan. Elizabeth Bishop (1911–1979), poet: *North & South*, winner of Houghton Mifflin Poetry Award. Kay Boyle: *A Frenchman Must Die*, a novel about the French Resistance.	**1946** Federal support of child-care facilities, vital during wartime for women workers, is abruptly cut off. A Roper poll indicates that 25 percent of women would rather have been born male. In *Irene Morgan v. Commonwealth of Virginia*, the Supreme Court rules that states cannot segregate on interstate buses.

TEXTS	CONTEXTS
1946 Eleanor Clark, novelist, short-fiction writer, essayist, and memoirist: *The Bitter Box*, a novel.	1946 When women department store workers in Oakland, California, walk out, it precipitates a city-wide general strike involving 120,000 workers.

Eleanor Clark, novelist, short-fiction writer, essayist, and memoirist: *The Bitter Box*, a novel.

Fannie Cook (1893–1949), novelist and painter: *Mrs. Palmer's Honey*, winner of the first George Washington Carver Memorial Award.

Helen Eustis, Edgar-winning author: *The Horizontal Award*.

Shirley Graham: *Paul Robeson, Citizen of the World*.

Dorothy B. Hughes: *Ride the Pink Horse*, a mystery novel, later turned into a successful film.

Denise Levertov, poet and activist: *The Double Image*, poetry.

Anita Loos: *Happy Birthday*, a play.

Carson McCullers: *The Member of the Wedding*, a novel.

Patricia McGerr: *Pick Your Victim*.

Flannery O'Connor (1925–1964), southern, Catholic novelist and

When women department store workers in Oakland, California, walk out, it precipitates a city-wide general strike involving 120,000 workers.

Emily Greene Balch, peace advocate, social reformer, and economist, is awarded the Nobel Peace Prize.

Frances Xavier Cabrini becomes the first U.S. citizen declared a saint by the Roman Catholic Church. She was born in Italy but, after working in the U.S. since 1889, became a naturalized U.S. citizen in 1909.

Dr. Benjamin Spock publishes *Baby & Child Care*.

Television is introduced.

The "Breck Girl" makes her first appearance.

Agnes De Mille (1905–1993), choreographer noted for her work in musicals and films including *Carousel*, *Oklahoma!*, *Paint Your Wagon*, and *Brigadoon*, is named Woman of the Year by the American Newspaper Woman's Guild.

TEXTS | CONTEXTS

1946   short-story writer, publishes her first story, "The Geranium."

Mine Okuba, Japanese American autobiographer: *Citizen 13660.*

Ann Petry, African American novelist: *The Street.*

Craig Rice is the first woman mystery writer to be featured on the cover of *Time* magazine.

Jo Sinclair, Jewish American novelist and journalist: *Wasteland,* a novel.

Mary Dallas Street: *Christopher Holt.*

Mai-mai Sze: *The Tao of Painting: A Study of the Ritual Disposition of Chinese Painting,* two-volume study.

Genevieve Taggard: *Slow Music,* a collection of poetry.

Lin Tai-yi: *The Golden Coin,* a novel.

Julia Weber: *My Country School Diary: An Adventure in Creative Teaching.*

Eudora Welty: *Delta Wedding,* a novel.

1946   Vivian Leigh, British actress, makes the "Cleopatra" look—black silky hair, black eyeliner and long eyelashes, red lips—popular; in 1961, Elizabeth Taylor's portrayal of the Egyptian queen on film revitalizes this look.

Maya Deren (1917–1961), emigré from the Ukraine and experimentalist filmmaker known especially for her films of voodoo ceremonies, becomes the first woman to be granted a Guggenheim fellowship in motion pictures.

TEXTS	CONTEXTS
1946–1964	**1946–1964** Baby boom (76,441,000 children born).
1947 Margaret Clapp: *Forgotten First Citizen: John Bigelow*, winner of Pulitzer Prize for biography in 1948. Ruth Gordon: *The Leading Lady*, a play. Laura Z. Hobson (1900–1986), Jewish American novelist: *Gentleman's Agreement*. Frances Parkinson Keyes: *Came a Cavalier*. Janet Lewis: *The Trial of Soren Qvist*, a novel. Josefina Niggli: *Step Down, Elder Brother*. The National Council of Teachers in English publishes black educator, author, and librarian Charlemae Rollins's *We Build Together*, a guide to children's literature that avoids stereotypical portrayals of African Americans. Gertrude Stein: *The Mother of Us All*, a play based on the life of Susan B. Anthony.	**1947** Maria Tallchief, the first Native American prima ballerina, begins dancing with the New York City Ballet; she will perform with them through 1960. Cold War begins; the House Un-American Activities Committee investigates suspected Communists, including prominent Hollywood celebrities and literary figures. The Central Intelligence Agency (CIA) is founded. Ethel Percy Andrus founds the National Retired Teachers Association. Within nine years Andrus and NRTA establish the first health insurance plan for people over 65; the organization also creates an inexpensive mail-order prescription program, a retirement home, and a travel service, among other programs. Gerty T. Cori, M.D., is the first woman awarded the Nobel Prize in medicine or physiology.

TEXTS		CONTEXTS
1947	Agnes Sligh Turnbull (1888–1982), novelist, short-story writer: *The Bishop's Mantle*, a novel.	1947

		Rosa Lee Ingram, a widowed tenant farmer in Georgia and mother of 12, is convicted of murdering the white farmer who allegedly assaulted her. An international amnesty campaign, spearheaded by a group of prominent African American women, ends with her pardon in 1959.
		Elizabeth Short, a would-be actress, is found murdered in a vacant lot in Los Angeles, launching the famous Black Dahlia murder case, which triggers the biggest criminal hunt in L.A. history. The case remains unsolved.
1948	Judy Campbell introduces the Trixie Belden series, featuring a girl detective who differs from Nancy Drew and Judy Bolton in coming from a poor family and living in the country rather than a city. Kathryn Kenny authors some of the later volumes in the series. Anita Scott Coleman (1890–1960), African American author active during the Harlem Renaissance: *Reason for Singing*, poetry.	1948

		As chair of the Commission on Human Rights for the United Nations, Eleanor Roosevelt creates the Universal Declaration of Human Rights.
		Harry Truman signs the Women's Armed (Services) Integration Act, which grants women the opportunity to pursue careers in the military.
		Nancy C. Leftenant becomes the first African American nurse in the Army Nurse Corps.

TEXTS	CONTEXTS
1948	1948

TEXTS

1948

Ethel Collins Dunham: *Premature Infants: A Manual for Physicians.*

Inglis Fletcher: *Roanoke Hundred.*

Lucille Fletcher writes the highly praised radio play *Sorry, Wrong Number.*

Martha Gellhorn, journalist and novelist: *The Wine of Astonishment.*

Zora Neale Hurston: *Seraph on the Suwanee*, a novel.

Shirley Jackson (1916–1965), novelist, memoirist, and short-story writer: "The Lottery" appears in *The New Yorker.*

Fay Kanin: *Goodbye, My Fancy*, a comic play.

Frances Parkinson Keyes: *Dinner at Antoine's*, a bestseller.

Lucy Robins Lang: *Tomorrow Is Beautiful.*

Charlotte Murray Russell: *Ill Met in Mexico.*

Cornelia Otis Skinner: *Family Circle.*

CONTEXTS

1948

Accompanying Harry Truman's campaign train, Alice Dunnigan becomes the first African American woman journalist to travel with a President.

The last known clitoridectomy is performed in the U.S on a five-year-old girl to cure her of masturbation.

Truman beats Dewey.

Some 4 percent of the national labor force is made up of young workers aged 14 through 18.

Architect Eleanor Raymond and chemist/engineer Maria Telkes invent and build the first solar-heated house, in Dover, Massachusetts.

New American Library (NAL), under two imprints, Signet and Mentor, issues its first book.

The influential 3–volume *Literary History of the United States*, by Robert E. Spiller et al., eds., appears.

The Chicago *Times* and the Chicago *Sun* merge to form the daily Chicago *Sun-Times.*

	TEXTS		CONTEXTS
1948	Elizabeth Spencer, southern novelist: *Fire in the Morning*.	1948	Gretchen Fraser becomes the first U.S. skier to win an Olympic medal for skiing.
	Mai-mai Sze: *Silent Children*.		Alice Trumbull Mason (1904–1971), an active member of the American Abstract Artists group, paints *L'Hasard*, an oil on masonite.
	Dorothy West, African American novelist, short-story writer, and editor active in the Harlem Renaissance: *The Living Is Easy*, a novel.		Israel is founded.
1949	Harriette Arnow: *Hunter's Horn*, a novel.	1949	West Germany is formed.
	Gwendolyn Brooks: *Annie Allen*, awarded the 1950 Pulitzer Prize for poetry. Brooks is the first African American recipient of the award.		NATO is established. Mao Tse-Tung is victorious; the People's Republic of China is founded.
	M.F.K. Fisher: *An Alphabet for Gourmets*.		Eugenie Moore Anderson becomes the first U.S. woman ambassador.
	Frances Gaither: *Double Muscadine*.		Burnita S. Matthews, a Truman appointee, becomes the first woman federal district judge.
	Barbara Howes, poet and editor for several years of *Chimera: The Undersea Farmer*.		Harry Truman appoints Georgia Neese Clark as the first woman treasurer of the United States.
	Muriel Rukeyser: *Orpheus*, poetry.		The Women's Political Council (WPC), a grassroots organization of black professional women, is formed in Montgom-
	Lillian Smith: *Killers of the Dream*, nonfiction.		

TEXTS		CONTEXTS
1949	Eudora Welty: *The Golden Apples*, collection of inter-related stories.	1949	ery, Alabama, to address the city's racial problems.

Hisaye Yamamoto, Japanese-American writer: "Seventeen Syllables," chosen as one of the best short stories of the year.

French feminist philosopher and author Simone de Beauvoir (1908–1986) publishes *Le deuxième sexe;* in 1953, it is translated and published in English as *The Second Sex* and helps to provide the philosophical underpinnings of the emergent "Second Wave" of feminist activity in the U.S.

Grove Press is first formed.

Harlequin Enterprises is founded.

The first bikini bathing suit makes its appearance.

Ida Lupino (1918–1995), with her husband Collier Young, founds the Filmmakers, an independent production company. A highly successful film actress, Lupino becomes the only woman to direct a large body of work in the American commercial cinema of the 1950s as well as to direct dozens of television series episodes and pilots. Films such as *Hard, Fast, and Beautiful, The Bigamist,* and *The Hitch-*

TEXTS		CONTEXTS	
1949		1949	*hiker* critique consumerism and tensions between home life and careers.
1950s		1950s	Twenty percent of unmarried women have had intercourse by the age of nineteen.
1950	Margaret Louise Coit: *John C. Calhoun: American Portrait*, winner of Pulitzer Prize for biography in 1951.	1950	Willie May "Big Mama" Thornton, blues singer and songwriter, records her own composition "Hound Dog," which later becomes a huge hit for Elvis Presley.
	Viña Delmar, after two decades without publishing any novels, begins the second phase of her career with *About Mrs. Leslie*.		Some 27 percent of the population (41 million people) are living at or below the poverty level.
	Patricia Highsmith (1921–1995), writer of psychological suspense novels: *Strangers on a Train*.		Aid to Dependent Children programs become known as Aid to Families with Dependent Children.
	The Chicago Police Bureau of Censorship bans *A Diary of Love*, by Maude Hutchins, the estranged wife of the president of the University of Chicago.		Fawcett begins to publish original paperbacks, the first to do so.
			There is one servant to every 42 households.
	Abigail Lewis: *An Interesting Condition: The Diary of a Pregnant Woman*.		Ethel Waters, blues singer, comedienne, and actress, wins the New York Drama Critics Circle Award for playing Berenice in *Member of the Wedding* on stage; she is
	Judith Merril, science-fiction novelist and short-		

TEXTS		CONTEXTS	
1950	story writer: *The Shadow on the Hearth*.	1950	later nominated for an Academy Award for the movie version of the same role.
	Anaïs Nin: *The Four-Chambered Heart*.		Kay Sage, poet and Surrealist painter who often played with architectural forms in her works, exhibits *Page 49*, an oil on canvas.
	Hortense Powdermaker, anthropologist: *Hollywood: The Dream Factory*.		
	Anzia Yezierska: *Red Ribbon on a White Horse*.		The 41 percent of black females who are domestic workers still receive no benefits from national worker legislation, such as minimum wage or hour laws, social security, or unemployment compensation.
			Some 25 percent of all black wives and 10 percent all white wives are either separated, divorced, or widowed; for both groups, approximately 40 percent are heads of households including children.
			African American Chicago lawyer Edith Sampson is appointed an alternate delegate to the United Nations.
			The gay rights organization the Mattachine Society is founded by a group of gay men in Los Angeles.

TEXTS	CONTEXTS
1950	1950 Republican Senator Margaret Chase Smith, the first woman to be elected to both houses of Congress, is the first and one of few in the Senate to denounce Senator Joseph McCarthy for basing his campaign to rid the nation of communism in "fear, ignorance, bigotry, and smear." During the McCarthy era, women including Marya Mannes, Mary McCarthy, Lillian Hellman, and Diana Trilling speak out against McCarthyism.

The George Burns and Gracie Allen Show makes a successful transition from radio to television.

Mahalia Jackson makes her first appearance at Carnegie Hall.

Fifty-seven percent of black women work outside the home, compared with 37 percent of white women. Some 42 percent of employed black women work as domestics. During the 1950s, they will receive an average weekly pay of $13.

Charlotte Klein, one of the first female public relations executives, is instru-

TEXTS	CONTEXTS
1950	1950 mental in launching the "first anthropologically correct Negro Doll" ever mass-marketed in the U.S. Ideal Toy, which creates the doll, establishes a jury including Eleanor Roosevelt to determine the doll's exact shade. The doll is the biggest selling toy in the South during the Christmas shopping season that year.
1950–1953	1950–1953 Korean War.
1951 Hannah Arendt (1906–1975), German-born philosopher and political activist: *The Origins of Totalitarianism.* Louise Bogan: *Criticism: Achievement in American Poetry, 1900–1950.* Kay Boyle: *The Smoking Mountain: Stories of Germany During the Occupation.* Rachel Carson: *The Sea Around Us*, winner of the National Book Award for nonfiction in 1952. Lillian Hellman: *The Autumn Garden*, a play. Marguerite "Maggie" Higgins (1920–1966), foreign correspondent, wins a Pu-	1951 The first color televisions are available. Paula Ackerman, acting on an interim basis after her husband's death, becomes the first woman to fulfill a rabbi's duties. Marion Donovan begins marketing the product she created "out of a shower curtain and absorbent padding": disposable diapers. Lucille Ball (1911–1989), actress and comedienne, with her husband Desi Arnaz, launches the long-running and extremely popular television show *I Love Lucy.* Cartoon artist Hilda Terry becomes the first

TEXTS	CONTEXTS
1951	1951

litzer Prize for her coverage of the Korean War, becoming the first woman to win a Pulitzer for journalism.

Hazel Ai Chun Lin, Chinese American novelist: *The Physicians.*

Helen McCloy becomes the first female president of the Mystery Writers of America.

Carson McCullers: *The Ballad of the Sad Cafe,* a novella and short stories.

Catherine Marshall (1914–1983), religious writer: *A Man Called Peter,* spiritual autobiography, bestseller.

Marianne Moore: *Collected Poems.* In 1952 she receives the National Book Award, the Pulitzer Prize, and the Bollingen Prize for this collection.

Shelley Ota, Japanese American writer: *Upon Their Shoulders.*

Adrienne Rich, influential feminist poet and essayist: *A Change of World,* chosen by W. H. Auden for the Yale Younger Poets Award.

woman member of the National Cartoonist Society.

Lee Krasner (1908–1985), Abstract Expressionist and avant-garde artist, has her first one-woman show at the Betty Parsons Gallery. She is known for paintings such as *Red, White, Blue, Yellow, Black*; it combines Cubist structure with explosive color. Earlier in her career she was famous for her "little image paintings," but after the death of her husband Jackson Pollock she moved to larger canvases.

TEXTS		CONTEXTS	
1951	Jessamyn West: *The Witch Diggers*, a novel.	1951	
1952	Dorothy Day: *The Long Loneliness*, autobiography. Patricia Highsmith, writing as Claire Morgan: *The Price of Salt*, one of the bestselling lesbian novels of all time. Mary McCarthy: *The Groves of Academe*. Yoko Matsuoka, Japanese American autobiographer: *Daughter of the Pacific*. Edna St. Vincent Millay: *The Collected Poems*, published posthumously. Flannery O'Connor: *Wise Blood*, a novel. Naomi Replansky: *Ring Song*, a collection of poetry. Han Suyin: *A Many Splendored Thing*, autobiographical novel. Hilary Waugh: *Last Seen Wearing*, an early classic of the police procedural genre. Su-ling Wong and Earl Herbert Cressy: *Daughter*	1952	Helen Frankenthaler develops stain (Color Field) painting, stretching large, unsized canvases on the floor, thinning oil paint to the consistency of water, and pouring and pushing it into patterns. Her first major work in this mode is *Mountains and Sea*. Abstract Expressionist artist Joan Mitchell has her first solo show. Elizabeth II becomes Queen of England. Some 87 percent of southern black women have never voted. The House of Representatives sanctions an investigation of paperback books, magazines, and comics to assess the extent of "immoral, obscene, or otherwise offensive matter." When playwright Lillian Hellman is called before the House Un-American Activities Committee, she is blacklisted after refusing to "name names."

	TEXTS		CONTEXTS
1952	*of Confucius*, autobiography.	1952	Rear Admiral Grace Murray Hopper invents the computer "compiler," which enables the first automatic programming for computers. She is also responsible for developing COBOL, the first computer language to use English.
	Hisaye Yamamoto: "Yoneko's Earthquake," chosen as one of the best stories of the year.		
			St. Martin's Press is established.
			Kitty Wells records the hit "It Wasn't God Who Made Honky-Tonk Angels," in answer to Hank Thompson's condemnation of women, "The Wild Side of Life." Her song makes her the first woman in country music to have a number one record.
1953	Jane Bowles: *In the Summer House*, a play.	1953	Ethel Greenglass Rosenberg and her husband Julius are executed in the electric chair at Sing Sing prison for allegedly passing atomic secrets to the Soviet Union.
	Gwendolyn Brooks: *Maud Martha*, bildungsroman of African American womanhood.		
	Vera Caspary: *Thelma*, a novel.		The Kinsey Report *Sexual Behavior in the Human Female*, is published (four years after the publication of *Sexual Behavior in the Human Male*) to much criticism; it finds that almost 50 percent of
	Su Hua Ling Chen: *Ancient Melodies*, autobiography by Chinese American woman.		

TEXTS	CONTEXTS
1953 Dorothy Johnson, Montana novelist, short-story writer, and essayist: *Indian Country*, a collection of stories. Ann Petry: *The Narrows*, a novel. Monica Sone, Japanese American autobiographer: *Nisei Daughter*. Gertrude Stein: *Patriarchal Poetry*. Jessamyn West: *Cress Delehanty*, sketches of the life of an adolescent girl.	**1953** American women have had premarital sex, 62 percent masturbate, 26 percent have had an extramarital affair, and 20 percent have had at least some homosexual experience. President Eisenhower issues an executive order prohibiting gay men and lesbians from obtaining federal employment. Oveta Culp Hobby is appointed the first secretary of Health, Education, and Welfare. Ann Davidson is the first woman to sail solo across the Atlantic Ocean. Anchor Books, a trade paperback division of Doubleday, is introduced. Hugh Hefner's *Playboy* magazine is founded. *TV Guide* magazine is first published. The "Italian" haircut—a carefully casual closely cropped cut—becomes the fashion for women. Clothes designer Coco Chanel introduces her Chanel Suit; it becomes popular with "working girls" of the '50s.

TEXTS		CONTEXTS
1953		1953	Tennis player Maureen Connolly—"Little Mo"—becomes the first U.S. woman to win the "grand slam," taking championship honors in Australia, France, the U.S., and at Wimbledon.
			Dwight D. Eisenhower becomes President.
			Soviet military intervention in Germany.
			Stalin dies.
1954	Harriette Arnow: *The Dollmaker*, a novel.	1954	A nuclear explosion occurs on Bikini Island.
	Doris Betts: *The Gentle Insurrection, and Other Stories.*		The Senate condemns Senator Joseph McCarthy.
	Louise Bogan: *Collected Poems, 1923–1953.*		*Brown v. Board of Education of Topeka* finds racial discrimination unconstitutional in schools; the suit is brought on behalf of Linda Brown, a student from Topeka, Kansas.
	Ellen Glasgow: *The Woman Within*, posthumously published autobiography in which she reveals a long, secret affair with a married man and claims her best work was done when love was over.		After a history of NAACP work in the South, civil rights activist Ella Baker becomes president of the Manhattan NAACP; her later involvement with SCLC and SNCC includes her delivery of the keynote address in 1964 at the Mississippi Freedom Democratic Party convention.
	Bowen Ingram: *Light in the Morning.*		
	Frances Gray Patton, North Carolina novelist: *Good Morning, Miss Dove.*		

TEXTS   CONTEXTS

1954   May Swenson (1919–   1954   Three out of five house-
        1989), poet: *Another*   holds — about 29 million —
        Animal.   own television sets.

        Alice B. Toklas (1877–   Ninety percent of adult
        1967): *The Alice B. Toklas*   Americans drink 3 to 4
        Cook Book.   cups of coffee a day; 70
                                              percent of men and 58
        Eudora Welty: *The Ponder*   percent of women drink
        Heart, a novel.   beer, wine, or liquor.

        Maria Yen, Chinese Amer-   Thirty percent of women
        ican writer: *The Umbrella*   and 60 percent of men
        Garden, nonfiction.   smoke.

                                              Actress Audrey Hepburn
                                              (1929–1993) receives the
                                              Best Actress Award for *Ro-*
                                              man Holiday. She goes on
                                              to star in numerous films,
                                              including *Sabrina*, *My*
                                              Fair Lady, and *Breakfast at*
                                              Tiffany's, and to serve as
                                              spokesperson for
                                              UNICEF.

                                              Jane Freilicher, known for
                                              her cityscapes that com-
                                              bine realism and abstract
                                              expressionism, exhibits
                                              Early New York
                                              Evening.

                                              Disc jockey Alan Freed
                                              coins the term "rock 'n'
                                              roll" to describe the new
                                              music hitting the air
                                              waves.

                                              The first "TV dinners"
                                              are introduced, purport-
                                              edly to help lighten the

TEXTS	CONTEXTS
1954	**1954** load of working mothers and their "baby boom" children.
	Dorothy Dandridge (1922–1965) is the first African American woman nominated for an Academy Award for best actress, for her performance in *Carmen*.
	Leontyne Price, African American opera singer, makes her concert debut as a soprano at Town Hall in New York.
1955 Eileen Chang, Chinese American novelist: *The Rice Sprout Song*, a novel.	**1955** Rosa Parks is arrested after refusing to give up her seat to a white passenger on a Montgomery bus. The outrage and organized protests her treatment stirred lead many to hail her as the "mother of the Civil Rights movement."
Alice Childress, African American playwright: *Trouble in Mind*, a play.	
The first reliable edition of Emily Dickinson's poems is published.	There are two female senators and 16 congresswomen.
Elizabeth Gurley Flynn (1890–1964), political activist and feminist: *I Speak My Own Piece: Autobiography of "The Rebel Girl."*	Eight women in San Francisco found the Daughters of Bilitis, a group advocating social and civil rights for lesbians.
Isabella Gardner (1915–1981), poet: *Birthdays from the Ocean*.	
Patricia Highsmith: *The Talented Mr. Ripley*, the	The U.S. joins the Universal Copyright Convention; each member coun-

TEXTS		CONTEXTS
1955	first in a popular mystery series featuring the morally bankrupt Tom Ripley.	1955	try agrees to treat works by citizens of other countries as it would those of its own citizens.

TEXTS	CONTEXTS
Cleofas Jaramillo: *Romance of a Little Village Girl*.	Seventy percent of American Catholics follow Church teachings on birth control.
Anne Morrow Lindbergh, novelist and autobiographer: *Gift from the Sea*.	Louise A. Boyd becomes the first woman to fly over and around the North Pole.
Mary McCarthy: *A Charmed Life*, a novel.	
Margaret Millar: *Beast in View*, winner of the Best Novel award from the Mystery Writers of America.	Frances Gabe begins working on her invention, the self-cleaning house, "equipped with a general Cleaning, Drying, Heating, and Cooling apparatus in each room."
Flannery O'Connor: *A Good Man Is Hard to Find, and Other Stories*.	Leontyne Price appears in Puccini's *Tosca* with the NBC Opera; she is the first black singer to appear in a televised opera.
Ann Petry: *Harriet Tubman: Conductor on the Underground Railway*.	
Eudora Welty: *The Bride of Innesfallen*, collection of stories.	AFL and CIO merge.
	Myra Adele Logan is the first woman surgeon to operate on the human heart.
Liang Yen, also known as Margaret Briggs: *Daughter of the Khans*, autobiography by Chinese American woman.	Jane Wilson, who began as an Abstract Expressionist, in the mid-1950s turns to "memoryscapes" of the Midwest.

*   *   *

TEXTS	CONTEXTS
1956	1956

TEXTS

1956   *The Ladder*, a lesbian magazine, begins publication. It closes in 1972.

Marian Anderson (1902–1993), the premier contralto of her generation and the first African American woman soloist to perform at the Metropolitan Opera house: *My Lord, What a Morning*, her autobiography.

Elizabeth Bishop: *Poems: North & South—A Cold Spring*, Pulitzer Prize-winner.

Diana Chang, Chinese American novelist: *The Frontiers of Love*.

Eileen Chang, Chinese American novelist: *The Naked Earth*.

Hsin-hai Chang, Chinese American novelist: *The Fabulous Concubine*.

Caroline Gordon: *The Malefactors*, a novel.

Billie Holiday (born Eleanora Fagan, 1915–1959), singer and autobiographer: *Lady Sings the Blues*.

Grace Metalious (1924–1964): *Peyton Place*, best-selling novel.

CONTEXTS

1956   Soviet military intervention in Hungary.

Grace Kelly (1929–1982), actress known for performances in *High Noon* and *Rear Window*, marries Prince Rainier of Monaco.

Bette Nesmith starts selling her invention, Liquid Paper, out of her garage.

TEXTS	CONTEXTS
1956	**1956**

1956   Marcia Nardi (born Lillian Massell, 1901–1990), whose letters to William Carlos Williams are excerpted in his *Paterson*, publishes *Poems*.

Helen Waite Papashvily: *All the Happy Endings*, perhaps the first social and psychological study of popular 19th-century American fiction written by, for, and about women.

Mary Lee Settle, southern writer: *O Beulah Land*, the first in her series of novels about the coal-mining region of West Virginia.

Jo Sinclair: *The Changelings*, a novel.

Elizabeth Spencer: *The Voice at the Back Door*, a novel.

Han Suyin, Chinese American novelist: *And the Rain My Drink*.

1957   Ann Bannon, lesbian "pulp" novelist: *Odd Girl Out*.

Catherine Drinker Bowen, biographer: *The Lion and the Throne: The Life and Times of Sir Edward Coke, 1552–1634*,

1957   A Civil Rights Bill is passed, the first one since the 1875 bill (which was overturned by the Supreme Court in 1883).

Under the leadership of Daisy Bates of the National Association for the

TEXTS		CONTEXTS
1957	winner of the National Book Award in 1958. Dorothy Johnson: *The Hanging Tree*, a novel. Jean Kerr, playwright and novelist known for her semi-autobiographical comedies about family life: *Please Don't Eat the Daisies.* Mary McCarthy: *Memories of a Catholic Girlhood.* Ayn Rand: *Atlas Shrugged.* Kay Sage (1898–1963), poet and Surrealist painter: *The More I Wonder.*	1957	Advancement of Colored People, protesters help insure the safe integration of nine African American teens ("The Little Rock Nine") into Central High School in Arkansas. Althea Gibson, who broke the color barrier in tennis in 1949, wins consecutive Wimbledon and U.S. Open titles and is the Associated Press poll's "Woman Athlete of the Year" for 1957 and 1958. She later becomes the first black woman to win all the world's singles titles for women. Harlequin Enterprises begins focusing production on romance fiction. The "Sack," an unfitted dress, comes into fashion. The Soviets launch *Sputnik I* into outer space.
1957–1975		1957–1975	During the Vietnam era, approximately 261,000 women serve in the U.S. Armed Forces, over 7500 in Vietnam itself.
1958	Hannah Arendt: *The Human Condition.* Djuna Barnes: *The Antiphon*, verse drama.	1958	The U.S. launches *Explorer I* into space, several months after *Sputnik.*

	TEXTS		CONTEXTS
1958	Janet Lim: *Sold for Silver*, autobiography by a Chinese American woman.	1958	At the urging of retired persons from a variety of professions, 74-year-old Ethel Percy Andrus founds the American Association of Retired Persons (AARP). Later this same year she creates *Modern Maturity* magazine, which by the 1990s has one of the highest circulations of magazines in publication.
	Hazel Ai Chun Lin: *The Moon Vow*, novel.		
	Rose Pesotta: *Days of Our Lives*, autobiography.		
	Balachandra Rajan, Indian American novelist: *The Dark Dancer*.		
	Louisa Revell: *See Rome and Die*.		Atheneum Publishers is formed.
	Han Suyin: *The Mountain Is Young*, novel.		Cheryl Crane, 14-year-old daughter of actress Lana Turner, stabs and kills her mother's boyfriend, Johnny Stompanato. She is later acquitted of the crime.
	May Swenson: *A Cage of Spines*, poetry.		
			Fernand Lamaze introduces his method of natural childbirth, which soon becomes popular in the U.S.
1959	Ann Bannon: *I Am a Woman* and *Women in the Shadows*.	1959	Joan Baez, musician and social activist, first receives national attention at the Newport Folk Festival.
	Sylvia Beach (1887–1962), bookseller who first published Joyce's *Ulysses* in France: *Shakespeare & Co.*, memoir of her bookshop.		Fidel Castro overthrows the Batista regime in Cuba.

TEXTS		CONTEXTS	
1959	Diana Chang: *A Woman of Thirty*, a novel.	1959	With her election to a judgeship in Philadelphia, Juanita Kidd Stout becomes the first African American woman elected judge in the U.S.
	Katherine Dunham, African American dancer: *A Tale of Innocence: Memoirs of Childhood*, an autobiography.		
	Lorraine Hansberry (1930–1965): *A Raisin in the Sun*. The first African American woman to have a play on Broadway, where *Raisin* runs for 538 performances, and the first African American and youngest American to win the New York Drama Critics Circle Award for Best Play of the Year. A film version is made in 1960.		Ruth Handler, wife of Mattel co-founder, invents the Barbie doll, named after her daughter. She later invents the first breast prosthesis for mastectomy patients.
	Shirley Jackson: *The Haunting of Hill House*, a novel.		
	Margaret Leech: *In the Days of McKinley*, winner of the Pulitzer Prize for history in 1960, the second such award for Leech.		
	Denise Levertov: *With Eyes at the Back of Our Heads*, poetry.		
	Janet Lewis: *The Ghost of Monsieur Scarron*, a novel.		

TEXTS	CONTEXTS
1959 Mary Margaret McBride (1899–1976), newspaper and radio journalist: *A Long Way from Missouri*.	1959

Paule Marshall, African American novelist and short-story writer: *Brown Girl, Brownstones*, a novel.

Grace Paley, Russian Jewish American short-story writer and poet: *The Little Disturbances of Man. Stories of Men and Women at Love*.

Kate Simon (1912–1990), Polish-born but raised in the Bronx, travel writer and memoirist: *New York Places and Pleasures*.

Ruth Stone, poet: *In an Iridescent Time*.

Lin Tai-yi: *The Eavesdropper*.

Mona Van Duyn, poet: *Valentines to the Wide World*.

Jessamyn West: *Love Is Not What You Think* and *Love, Death, and the Ladies' Drill Team*, a collection of short stories.

Mae West: *Goodness Had Nothing to Do With It*, autobiography.

*   *   *

TEXTS	CONTEXTS
1960s	**1960s** Manufacturing of infant formulas to supplant breast-feeding begins.

TEXTS	CONTEXTS
1960 Harriette Arnow: *Seedtime on the Cumberland*, social history. Ann Bannon: *Journey to a Woman*, a lesbian novel. Charlotta Spears Bass (1880?–1969), civil rights activist, 40-year editor of the oldest African American newspaper on the West Coast, and autobiographer: *Forty Years: Memoirs from the Pages of a Newspaper*. Kay Boyle: *Generation without Farewell*, a novel. Gwendolyn Brooks: *The Bean Eaters*, poetry. Vera Caspary: *Evvie*, a novel of a young woman working in a city in the 1920s. H.D. (Hilda Doolittle) becomes the first woman to receive the Award of Merit Medal for Poetry from the American Academy of Arts and Letters. Margaret Harada, Japanese American novelist: *The Sun Shines on the Immigrant*.	**1960** Civil Rights Act passed. Some 45.7 percent of the country's population is urban. Twenty-one percent of the population (39 million people) live at or below poverty level. There are 3 million recipients of Aid to Families with Dependent Children benefits. In the labor force, 23,272,000 women constitute 32.3 percent of the total work force and 38 percent of all women of working age; 30.5 percent of all working women are married. Some 24.2 percent of college professors are women (down from 31.9 percent in 1930); 36.6 percent of editors and reporters are women (up from 12.2 percent in 1910); 6.9 percent of physicians are women (up from 5 percent in 1920); and 6.9 percent of industrial managers are women (up from 1.7 percent in 1910).

TEXTS	CONTEXTS
1960 Lillian Hellman: *Toys in the Attic*, winner of New York Drama Critics Circle Award and Gold Medal for drama from the National Institute of Arts and Letters.	1960 Four-fifths of all whites and three-fifths of all nonwhites use or have used contraception; 93 percent of all college-educated women have done so.
Jean Kerr: *The Snake Has All the Lines.*	*Redbook* magazine asks its readers "Why Young Mothers Feel Trapped"; over 24,000 women respond.
Gussie Kimball, Jewish American author: *Gitele.*	The birth control pill is introduced in the U.S.
Harper Lee: *To Kill a Mockingbird*, winner of the Pulitzer Prize in 1961.	John F. Kennedy is elected President.
Virginia Lee, Chinese American novelist: *The House That Tai Ming Built.*	Abstract Expressionist Grace Hartigan is cited as the most celebrated woman painter in America for her gestural paintings.
Hazel Ai Chun Lin: *House of Orchids.*	
Phyllis McGinley (1905–1978), poet: *Times Three: Selected Verse from Three Decades with Seventy New Poems*, winner of 1961 Pulitzer Prize for poetry.	Patsy Cline (1932–1963), country and crossover singing artist, joins the Grand Ole Opry. Although her career is cut short when she dies in a 1963 plane crash, her music remains extremely popular. By 1992, her *Greatest Hits* album will be the only album from the 1960s still on the charts.
Flannery O'Connor: *The Violent Bear It Away*, a novel.	
Sylvia Plath (1932–1963): *The Colossus and Other Poems.*	Some 58,900,000 newspapers are circulated daily.

TEXTS		CONTEXTS
1960	Mary Lee Settle: *Know Nothing*, a novel.	1960	The Student Nonviolent Coordinating Committee (SNCC) is formed.

	TEXTS		CONTEXTS
1960	Mary Lee Settle: *Know Nothing*, a novel. Anne Sexton (1928–1974): *To Bedlam and Part Way Back*, poetry. Jo Sinclair: *Anna Teller*. Elizabeth Spencer: *The Light in the Piazza*, winner of the McGraw-Hill Fiction Award. Lin Tai-yi: *The Lilacs Overgrown*, a novel.	**1960**	The Student Nonviolent Coordinating Committee (SNCC) is formed.
1960–1970		**1960–1970**	The reported rape rate rises 95 percent.
1961	Diana Chang: *A Passion for Life*, a novel. Anita Scott Coleman: *Singing Bells*. H.D. (Hilda Doolittle): *Helen in Egypt*, epic poem. Maureen Howard, novelist and memoirist: *Not a Word about Nightingales*, a novel. Carolyn Kizer, poet: *The Ungrateful Garden*. Adet Lin: *The Milky Way and Other Chinese Folk Tales*.	**1961**	The Peace Corps is established. The Berlin Wall is built. "Freedom Rides" begin throughout the South, with both black and white civil rights activists riding buses throughout the segregated South to test the region's commitment to federal law. Elizabeth Gurley Flynn, political activist known as "The Rebel Girl of the Industrial Workers of the World [IWW]," becomes the first woman chair of

TEXTS	CONTEXTS
1961 Carson McCullers: *Clock without Hands*, a novel.	1961 the United States Communist Party.
Paule Marshall: *Soul Clap Hands and Sing*, a collection of novellas.	President Kennedy forms the President's Commission on the Status of Women, chaired by Eleanor Roosevelt.
Tillie Olsen, feminist, social activist, fiction writer, and retriever of many "lost" works by women: "Tell Me a Riddle," novella, winner of O. Henry Award for best short story of the year.	Bay of Pigs Invasion in Cuba. Kennedy sends troops to Vietnam.
Grace Paley, is awarded a Guggenheim fellowship in fiction.	Americans send their first man into space less than a month after the Soviets accomplish the first manned space flight.
Santha Rama Rau: *Gifts of Passage: An Autobiography*.	Only 3.6 percent of law students are women.
	Some 76.1 percent of all high-school-age workers are simultaneously enrolled in school.
	A *Ladies' Home Journal* poll of young women 16 to 21 years of age finds that "most" want four kids and "many" want five.
	At age 18, Billie Jean King becomes the youngest player to win at Wimbledon. She goes on to win 20 Wimbledon titles, a record number.

TEXTS	CONTEXTS
1961	**1961** Charity Davis (born in 1842), believed to be the longest-living American woman, dies at 119 years and 160 days.
	Soprano diva Leontyne Price debuts at the Metropolitan Opera singing Leonora in *Il Trovatore*.
1962 Ann Bannon: *Beebo Brinker*, a lesbian novel.	**1962** An estimated 552,000 Native Americans, including "Eskimos," are living in the U.S.
Helen Gurley Brown publishes *Sex and the Single Girl*.	Cuban missile crisis.
Rachel Carson (1904–1964), marine biologist and writer: *The Silent Spring*, awakens people to the dangers of insecticides for the environment.	Manpower Development and Training Act.
	The U.N. posthumously awards Eleanor Roosevelt its first Human Rights Prize.
Anna Chennault: *A Thousand Springs: The Biography of a Marriage*, autobiography by a Chinese American woman.	Dolores Huerta becomes vice president and chief negotiator for the United Farmworkers Union.
Wilma Dykeman, novelist, biographer, and historian of Appalachia: *The Tall Woman*, a novel.	Attorney Edith Spurlock Sampson becomes the second African American woman elected judge in America.
Joyce Johnson, memoirist and novelist: *Come and Join the Dance*.	Some 46.5 million viewers watch on all three networks as Jacqueline Kennedy leads a tour of the White House.
Madeleine L'Engle, writer of fantasy for children, au-	

TEXTS	CONTEXTS
1962	1962

TEXTS

1962 tobiographer: *A Wrinkle in Time*, winner of the Newbery Prize.

Anne Morrow Lindbergh: *Dearly Beloved: A Theme and Variations*.

Andre Norton, science-fiction author, begins her Witch World series, which continues into the 1990s.

Rochelle Owens, playwright: *Futz*.

Sylvia Plath, in the last year of her life, begins to break out of conventional poetic patterns in ways that will influence many poets to follow.

Katherine Anne Porter: *Ship of Fools*, a novel.

Balachandra Rajan: *Too Long in the West*.

Anne Sexton: *All My Pretty Ones*, poetry.

Anna Louise Strong begins publishing her *Letter from China*.

Han Suyin: *Two Loves*, two novellas.

Barbara Tuchman (1912–1989), journalist and histo-

CONTEXTS

1962 Beulah Louise Henry, known as "Lady Edison" for her numerous inventions, receives her 45th patent.

Sprinter Wilma Rudolph is the first African American woman awarded the James E. Sullivan memorial trophy as outstanding athlete of the year.

The "Twist" becomes a national dance craze.

Wigs come into fashion.

Marilyn Monroe (1926–1962), legendary movie star and "sex symbol," dies from an apparent overdose of sleeping pills.

TEXTS	CONTEXTS
1962 rian: *The Guns of August*, a Pulitzer Prize-winning history of the beginnings of World War I.	**1962**
1963 Hannah Arendt: *On Revolution*. Harriette Arnow: *Flowering on the Cumberland*, a social history. Margaret Bourke-White (1904–1971), noted photojournalist and autobiographer: *Portrait of Myself*. Diana Chang: *The Only Game in Town*, a novel. Dorothy Day: *Loaves and Fishes*. Betty Friedan: *The Feminine Mystique*. Royalties from this bestseller are used to found the National Organization for Women, for which she serves as president, 1966 to 1970. Elizabeth Hardwick founds the *New York Review of Books*. Virginia Lee: *The House That Tai Ming Built*.	**1963** Cicely Tyson is the first African American person to appear regularly in a television series (*East Side, West Side*). Minimalist sculptor Anne Truitt has her first one-person show. During the Civil Rights March on Washington, Martin Luther King delivers his "I Have a Dream" speech. Civil rights leader Medgar Evers is murdered in Mississippi. Four young black girls are killed when the church they attend in Birmingham, Alabama, is bombed by white racists. Meta Warrick Fuller sculpts *The Crucifixion* in memory of the four African American girls killed in the Birmingham church bombing. The Equal Pay Act bans wage discrimination based solely on sex.

TEXTS		CONTEXTS
1963	Mary McCarthy: *The Group*, a novel.	1963 Feminist Gloria Steinem goes undercover as a Playboy Bunny in Hugh Hefner's Playboy empire.

1963   Mary McCarthy: *The Group*, a novel.

Jessica Mitford: *The American Way of Death*, an exposé of the funeral industry.

Lucille M. Nixon and Tomoe Tama collect poems by Japanese American housewives, gardeners, maids, farmers, and business people in *Sounds from the Unknown*.

Joyce Carol Oates, prolific novelist, short-story writer, poet, essayist, and playwright, who also writes suspense novels under the name Rosamond Smith: *By the North Gate*, a collection of short stories.

Sylvia Plath: *The Bell Jar*, a novel published under the pseudonym Victoria Lucas. She commits suicide a few weeks after its publication.

Adrienne Rich: *Snapshots of a Daughter-in-Law*, poetry.

Gloria Steinem's undercover exposé of Hugh Hefner's Playboy empire, "I Was a Playboy Bunny," appears.

1963   Feminist Gloria Steinem goes undercover as a Playboy Bunny in Hugh Hefner's Playboy empire.

Homosexuality is considered illegal (and frequently "sick" and "sinful") in every state except Illinois.

"Hootenannies," group folk concerts with audience participation, become popular.

Mary Ann Fischer becomes the first U.S. woman to give birth to quintuplets.

Katherine Dunham becomes the first black choreographer to work with the Metropolitan Opera (on a production of *Aida*).

President John F. Kennedy is assassinated in Dallas; Sarah Tilghman Hughes swears in Lyndon B. Johnson aboard Air Force One following Kennedy's assassination, becoming the first woman federal judge to swear in a President.

Artist Elaine de Kooning, known for her still lifes, portraits, and abstracts, is commissioned by

TEXTS	CONTEXTS
1963 Han Suyin: *The Four Faces*, a novel. May Swenson: *To Mix with Time*, poetry. Alice B. Toklas: *What Is Remembered*, a memoir. Linda Ty-Casper, Filipina American fiction writer: *"The Transparent Sun" and Other Stories.* Charlotte Zolotow, influential and prolific author of children's literature: *The Quarreling Book.*	**1963** ex-President Harry S. Truman to paint a portrait of President John F. Kennedy; the project is disrupted when Kennedy is assassinated.
1964 Marion Zimmer Bradley, science-fiction and fantasy writer, begins her Darkover series, which continues into the 1990s. Eleanor Clark: *The Oysters of Locmariaquer*, combining essay genre with travel book and novel techniques, winner of National Book Award for nonfiction. Louise Fitzhugh: *Harriet the Spy*, the beginning of a popular children's series with a somewhat controversial (anti)heroine who keeps a journal in which she records brutally frank	**1964** The Economic Opportunity Act (President Johnson's "War on Poverty") leads to projects such as the Job Corps and Neighborhood Youth Corps. The Civil Rights Act is passed; Title VII bans sex discrimination in employment. Martin Luther King, Jr., wins the Nobel Peace Prize. At a meeting of the Student Nonviolent Coordinating Committee (SNCC), Stokely Carmichael utters his notorious

TEXTS	CONTEXTS
1964 assessments of the adults around her.	1964 remark that the best position for women in the organization is "prone."
Shirley Ann Grau, novelist and short-story writer: *The Keepers of the House*, Pulitzer Prize-winning novel.	Freedom Summer: voter registration drive in Mississippi.
Ada Louise Huxtable, an internationally known architecture critic for the *New York Times* and winner of the first Pulitzer Prize for architecture criticism (1970): *Classic New York*.	Fannie Lou Hamer leads the Mississippi Freedom Democratic Party to the Democratic convention. Lyndon B. Johnson is elected to his first full term as President.
Adrienne Kennedy, experimental playwright: *Funnyhouse of a Negro*.	Kitty Genovese, a 28–year old woman, is beaten to death on a corner in Queens, New York; at least 38 neighbors look on but do nothing.
Jane Langton, mystery novelist who illustrates her own works: *Transcendental Murder*, the first featuring New England sleuth Homer Kelly.	Hattie Elizabeth Alexander, acclaimed for her work in theoretical biology, becomes the first woman president of the American Pediatric Society.
Denise Levertov: *O Taste and See*, poetry.	
Bette Bao Lord, Chinese American novelist and biographer: *Eighth Moon*, biography.	Physicist Chien-Shiung Wu becomes the first woman ever to win the prestigious Comstock Prize from the National Academy of Sciences.
Qoyawayma Polingaysi: *No Turning Back*, autobiography of life as a Hopi and leader in the education of Native Americans.	Jerrie Mock becomes the first woman to fly around the world alone.

TEXTS		CONTEXTS
1964	Jane Rule, novelist, short-story writer, essayist, and critic: *Desert of the Heart*, a lesbian novel.	1964	Donyale Luna is featured on the cover of *Harper's Bazaar* and becomes the first African American cover girl for a mainstream U.S. fashion magazine.

1964	Jane Rule, novelist, short-story writer, essayist, and critic: *Desert of the Heart*, a lesbian novel. Lin Tai-yi: *Kampoor Street*, a novel. Dorothy Uhnak: *Police-woman: A Young Woman's Initiation into the Realities of Justice*, fictionalized autobiography.	1964	Donyale Luna is featured on the cover of *Harper's Bazaar* and becomes the first African American cover girl for a mainstream U.S. fashion magazine. The "Watusi" and "Frug" are popular rock 'n' roll dances. California becomes the most populous state. *The Sonny and Cher Show* begins its ten-year stint; Cher goes on to become an outspoken singer, actress, and celebrity.
1965	Sally Carrighar, naturalist: *Wild Heritage*. Jean Harlow, actress: *Today Is Tonight*, posthumously published novel. Diane Johnson, novelist: *Fair Game*. Pauline Kael, film critic and author: *I Lost It at the Movies*. Flannery O'Connor: *Everything That Rises Must Converge*, a posthumous collection of short stories. Sylvia Plath: *Ariel*, posthumously published poems.	1965	The U.S. Air Force begins bombing North Vietnam. Four nurses serving in Vietnam receive Purple Hearts. Before the U.S. withdraws from the war, eight nurses are killed. President Lyndon Johnson endorses birth control in his State of the Union address. *Griswold v. Connecticut* is noteworthy for fully overturning legislation that made using birth control or giving out information about its use illegal.

TEXTS	CONTEXTS
1965 Katherine Anne Porter: *The Collected Stories of Katherine Anne Porter*, wins Pulitzer Prize in 1966. May Sarton: *Mrs. Stevens Hears the Mermaids Singing*, a novel. Han Suyin: *The Crippled Tree*, autobiography. Marguerite Young: *Miss MacIntosh, My Darling*, an experimental novel in imagistic prose, appears in its entirety. It had been published in sections periodically since 1947.	1965 The Voting Rights Act outlaws voting discrimination. The federal program Project Head Start is established to assist and educate impoverished children. Race riots occur in the Watts section of Los Angeles; throughout the late '60s, riots break out in cities including Chicago, Newark, Detroit, and Washington, D.C. The Moynihan Report, entitled "The Negro Family: The Case for National Action," locates the blame for the poverty and alleged pathology of the black community largely on black single mothers. Black activist Malcolm X is murdered. A study conducted in New York state finds that in the years before abortions are decriminalized, African American and Puerto Rican women represent 80 percent of all deaths from illegal abortions. The Naturalization Act passes, establishing an an-

TEXTS	CONTEXTS
1965	1965 nual quota of 20,000 immigrants from each country; entry is favored for family reunification, skilled and professional labor, and refugee resettlement.

Toni Morrison begins her publishing career as an editor for a subsidiary of Random House; three years later, she is promoted to Senior Editor and transferred to the New York office where she helps to advance the careers of many novelists—including African American women writers such as Toni Cade Bambara—until she leaves the firm in 1985.

A national survey finds that the average American woman across socioeconomic levels spends four hours a day on housework and three and a half hours a day caring for children.

Patsy Mink becomes the first Japanese American woman in Congress.

Stephanie Kwolek invents and patents "Kevlar," a high-tech material used in epoxy resins and as a reinforcement for laminates and tire treads, for Du Pont chemicals.

TEXTS	CONTEXTS
1965	**1965** Helen Gurley Brown becomes editor of *Cosmopolitan*.
	The Beatles' "Help!" is a popular song.
	The "Mod" look is in fashion; bell-bottoms are especially popular with the youth of both sexes.
1966 Alice Adams, novelist and short-story writer: *Careless Love*.	**1966** Twenty-eight feminists found the National Organization for Women (NOW).
Silveria Baltasar, Filipina American writer: *Your House Is My House*, nonfiction.	"Last of the Red Hot Mamas" Sophie Tucker dies at age 79.
Under the pseudonym Amanda Cross, literary critic and feminist scholar Carolyn Heilbrun begins the Kate Fansler series of mystery novels with *In the Final Analysis*.	Lawyer and New York state senator Constance Baker Motley becomes the first African American woman to serve as federal judge following her appointment by President Johnson.
Wilma Dykeman: *The Far Family*, a novel about life in Appalachia.	Stokely Carmichael coins the slogan "black power" for the emerging militant black separatist movement.
Dorothy Gilman: *The Unexpected Mrs. Pollifax*, the first of many mysteries featuring a middle-aged widow as spy/sleuth.	The Black Panther Party for Self-Defense is founded in Oakland, California.
Maureen Howard: *Bridgeport Bus*, a novel.	

TEXTS		CONTEXTS
1966	Berry Morgan, southern novelist: *Pursuit*.	1966

<table>
<tr><td>

Berry Morgan, southern novelist: *Pursuit*.

Anaïs Nin begins the publication of *The Diary of Anaïs Nin, 1931–1966,* a record of avant-garde life in Paris and New York. The seventh and last volume appears in 1980.

Joyce Carol Oates: *Upon the Sweeping Flood*, short stories.

Cynthia Ozick, Jewish American novelist, poet, and essayist: *Trust*, a novel.

Jane Roberts, fiction writer, poet, medium: *How to Develop Your ESP Power*, reissued in 1976 as *The Coming of Seth*.

Mary Lee Settle: *All the Brave Promises: Memoirs of Aircraft Woman 2nd Class 2146391.*

Anne Sexton: *Live or Die*, Pulitzer Prize-winner for poetry in 1967.

Susan Sontag, cultural critic, novelist, and short-story writer: *Against Interpretation, and Other Essays*.

</td><td>

Blanche Knopf, wife and silent partner of publisher Alfred A. Knopf, dies unexpectedly in her sleep; a whole issue of the *Borzoi Quarterly* is dedicated to her and filled with tributes, telegrams, cables, and letters of sympathy, many from noted writers, editors, and other public figures from around the world.

The miniskirt is in fashion, with skirt lengths rising four to seven inches above the knee.

Janis Joplin (1943–1970), singer and songwriter, gives her first big concert in San Francisco; she dies four years later of a drug overdose.

Carol Burnett becomes one of the country's most popular comediennes, starring in *The Carol Burnett Show* through 1977.

</td></tr>
</table>

TEXTS	CONTEXTS
1966 Jacqueline Susann (1921–1974), popular novelist: *The Valley of the Dolls*, filmed in 1967. Han Suyin: *A Mortal Flower*, autobiography. Megan Terry, playwright: *Viet Rock: A Folk War Movie*, a play written for Off-Broadway theaters, the first rock musical and the first anti-war play about the Vietnam War. Margaret Walker, African American novelist and poet: *Jubilee*, epic novel. Jessamyn West: *A Matter of Time*, a novel. Sylvia Wilkinson: *Moss on the North Side*. Wakako Yamauchi, Japanese American author: "And the Soul Shall Dance."	**1966**
1967 Eileen Chang: *The Rouge of the North*, a novel. Nikki Giovanni, African American poet and essayist: *Black Feeling, Black Talk*. Karen Horney: *Feminine Psychology*.	**1967** The National Organization of Women holds its first national conference in Washington, D.C., and drafts its "Bill of Rights for Women." Florence Beaumont becomes the first woman in the U.S. to protest a

TEXTS	CONTEXTS
1967 Catherine Marshall: *Christy*, a religious novel.	1967 war by immolating herself.

TEXTS

1967 Catherine Marshall: *Christy*, a religious novel.

Marianne Moore: *The Complete Poems.*

Joyce Carol Oates: "Where Are You Going, Where Have You Been?," acclaimed short story, and *A Garden of Earthly Delights*, a novel.

Rose Schneiderman: *All for One.*

Elizabeth Spencer: *No Place for an Angel*, a novel.

Betty Lee Sung: *Mountain of Gold.*

Han Suyin: *China in the Year 2001.*

Diane Wakoski, poet: *The George Washington Poems.*

Sylvia Wilkinson: *A Killing Frost.*

CONTEXTS

1967 war by immolating herself.

Rita Mae Brown helps to form the first Student Homophile League while attending New York University.

The National Welfare Rights Organization is founded to educate and agitate on behalf of persons eligible for welfare.

Helen Natalie Jackson Claytor becomes the first African American woman national president of the YWCA.

The Work Incentive Program is designed to reduce the number of AFDC recipients and requires many women to register for job training and placement services.

President Lyndon Johnson appoints a Commission on Obscenity and Pornography; its report in 1970 declares that it could find no harmful effects resulting from viewing obscene materials and recommends repealing legislative restrictions on them for consenting adults (then-President Nixon rejects its findings).

TEXTS	CONTEXTS

1967

1967

In *Loving v. Virginia*, the Supreme Court allows interracial marriage and revokes anti-miscegenation laws.

"The Boston Strangler," Albert De Salvo, confesses to strangling 13 women and is sentenced to life in prison.

Richard Speck is convicted for murdering eight Chicago nurses in 1966.

The 100 millionth telephone is installed.

British fashion model Twiggy tours the U.S.

Cosmetic styles emphasize "natural" looks and faces devoid of color.

Approximately 7000 women work as strippers in the U.S.

Peggy Fleming wins the Women's World Figure Skating Championships for the second year in a row.

The photographs of Diane Nemerov Arbus (1923–1971) are featured at the Museum of Modern Art; she is known for

TEXTS	CONTEXTS
1967	**1967** her images of the grotesque and for unusual juxtapositions, and for her pictures of many celebrities, including Mae West, Andy Warhol, Norman Mailer, and Susan Sontag.

TEXTS	CONTEXTS
1968 Folksinger Joan Baez, publishes her autobiography: *Daybreak*.	**1968** The Fair Housing Act makes it illegal to discriminate in housing matters on the basis of race, color, religion, or nationality; it is not until 1974, under the Housing and Community Development Act, that this prohibition is extended to cover sex discrimination.
Louise Bogan: *The Blue Estuaries: Poems 1923–1968*.	
Jane Cooper, poet: *The Weather of Six Mornings*.	
Mary Daly: *The Church and the Second Sex*.	
Joan Didion, California novelist and nonfiction writer: *Slouching Towards Bethlehem*, essays.	Shirley Chisholm is the first African American woman elected to the U.S. House of Representatives.
Nikki Giovanni: *Black Judgment*.	Ex-congresswoman and octogenarian Jeannette Rankin leads 5000 women in a march on Capitol Hill in protest of the Vietnam War.
Louise Glück, poet: *Firstborn*.	
Chuang Hua, Chinese American novelist: *Crossings*, experimental novel.	Only 1.6 percent of all law school professors are women.
Diane Johnson: *Loving Hands at Home*, a novel.	Seneca Falls, New York, site of the first convention on women's rights, becomes the site of the National Women's Hall of Fame.
Ursula K. Le Guin's science fiction Earthsea trilogy begins with *A Wizard*	

TEXTS	CONTEXTS
1968 *of Earthsea. The Tombs of Atuan* appears in 1971, followed by *The Farthest Shore* in 1973. Alma Lutz (1890–1973), journalist and biographer of many women, including Elizabeth Cady Stanton, Susan B. Anthony, Emma Willard, Mary Baker Eddy: *Crusade for Freedom*, a study of women's roles in antislavery campaigns. Helen MacInnes: *The Salzburg Connection*, a suspense novel. Anne Moody: *Coming of Age in Mississippi*, a memoir of her experiences as a civil rights activist. Sonia Sanchez, African American poet and scholar: *Black Fire*, a collection of poetry. Lee Smith: *The Last Day the Dogbushes Bloomed*, first novel by the prolific southern novelist and short-story writer. Han Suyin: *Birdless Summer*, autobiography. Linda Ty-Casper: *The Three-Cornered Sun*, a novel.	1968 Ten African American intellectuals and writers respond to William Styron's *The Confessions of Nat Turner*, setting off a controversy over, among other things, whether white authors could effectively or ethically assume African American voices in their writing. Feminists gain national media attention by protesting the sexism of the Miss America Pageant. Elizabeth Duncan Koontz is the first African American president of the National Education Association (NEA). Jacqueline Kennedy marries Greek shipping magnate Aristotle Onassis. Ruth Eisman-Schier, who helped kidnap an Emory University student, becomes the first woman on the FBI's Ten Most Wanted list; she is captured in 1969. Civil rights leader Martin Luther King, Jr., is assassinated in Memphis, Tennessee. Coretta Scott King leads a silent march of 50,000

TEXTS	CONTEXTS
1968	1968 in Memphis after her husband's murder. She is voted Woman of the Year and Most Admired Woman by college students.

Tet offensive by North Vietnam.

Soviets occupy Czechoslovakia.

Robert Kennedy is assassinated.

Richard Nixon is elected President.

Swimmer Debbie Myer becomes the first female to win three gold medals in the Olympics.

Race riots in 168 towns and cities.

Jogging emerges as a popular exercise activity.

Pantsuits for women come into fashion.

Laugh-In is the most popular TV show.

Actress Eartha Kitt disrupts Lady Bird Johnson's luncheon at the White House with her protest of the Vietnam War.

TEXTS	CONTEXTS
1968	**1968** Silent screen star Mae Marsh, famous for her role as Little Sister in D. W. Griffith's *The Birth of a Nation*, dies at age 72.
1969 Alta founds Shameless Hussy Press, the first feminist publishing house in the U.S.	**1969** For the second year in a row, Katharine Hepburn earns the Best Actress Oscar: 1968 for *Guess Who's Coming to Dinner* and 1969 for *The Lion in Winter*.
Elizabeth Bishop: *The Complete Poems*, winner of the National Book Award.	
Lucille Clifton, African American poet, memoirist, children's writer: *Good Times*.	The group "Diana Ross and the Supremes" breaks up; Ross goes on to a successful solo career.
Ann Cornelisen, social activist, memoirist, and novelist: *Torregreca: Life, Death, Miracles*, winner of a special award from the National Institute of Arts and Letters.	The first Women's Studies baccalaureate degree program is offered at San Diego State University. New York Radicalesbians is formed.
Emily Hahn, nonfiction writer: *Times and Places*, a memoir.	New York City hosts the First Congress to Unite Women.
Lorraine Hansberry: *To Be Young, Gifted, and Black*, published posthumously.	Stonewall riots in New York City mark the beginning of the gay liberation movement and the founding of the Gay Liberation Front (GLF).
Lillian Hellman: *An Unfinished Woman*, memoir, winner of the National Book Award.	Clara McBride Hale, known as "Mother," opens the Hale House for babies born to drug-

TEXTS	CONTEXTS
1969 Elisabeth Kübler-Ross: *On Death and Dying*.	1969 addicted mothers in Harlem.
Mary Lee, Chinese American poet: *Tender Bough*.	American astronauts Neil Armstrong and Buzz Aldrin land on the moon, the first humans to do so.
Nancy Howell Lee: *The Search for an Abortionist*, a memoir.	
Ursula K. Le Guin, science fiction and fantasy writer, essayist: *The Left Hand of Darkness*.	The Woodstock Music and Art Fair, held August 15 to 18 on a farm in upstate New York, draws some 300,000 to 400,000 people.
Isabel Miller: *Patience and Sarah*.	*Penthouse* magazine appears.
Kate Millett, scholar and feminist: *Sexual Politics*, ground-breaking analysis of gender.	Diane Crump becomes the first woman jockey to race at a U.S. parimutuel track; the same year, Barbara Jo Rubin becomes the first winning woman jockey in the U.S. and the first to ride two winners in the same day; also that year the first all-woman jockey field in a horse race occurs in Boston.
Arthenia J. Bates Millican: *Seeds Beneath the Snow*, a collection of stories.	
Joyce Carol Oates: *them*, winner of the National Book Award in 1970.	
Marge Piercy, novelist and poet: *Going Down Fast*, a novel.	Sharon Sites Adams becomes the first woman to sail alone across the Pacific Ocean.
Norma Rosen, Jewish American novelist: *Touching Evil*.	Actress Sharon Tate and four others are murdered in Los Angeles by members of Charles Manson's cult.
Adela Rogers St. Johns, novelist, journalist, first American woman sports	

	TEXTS		CONTEXTS
1969	writer, author of a Depression series on unemployed women: *The Honeycomb*, autobiography. Anne Sexton: *Love Poems*. Jean Stafford, novelist and short-story writer: *Collected Stories*, winner of Pulitzer Prize in 1970. May Wong, Chinese American poet: *A Bad Girl's Book of Animals*.	1969	Sixty-eight percent of Americans surveyed believe "it is wrong for people to have sexual relations before marriage." Yoko Ono and John Lennon wed.
1970s		1970s	Some 24 percent of all Native American women of child-bearing age are sterilized, 35 percent of Puerto Rican women are sterilized; in federally subsidized programs, black women represent 43 percent of those sterilized. The first articles begin appearing in medical journals on the possibilities of *in vitro* fertilization. Women Against Pornography and Women Against Violence are formed. Women's "consciousness-raising" groups spring up across the nation. Median income for Native American women is $1,697.

TEXTS	CONTEXTS
1970s	**1970s** Fifty-two million pounds of white bread are consumed annually.

TEXTS	CONTEXTS
1970 The New York-based Radicalesbians publishes "The Woman-Identified Woman," outlining their belief that patriarchy can only truly be challenged when women identify and relate only with other women.	**1970** Invasion of Cambodia.
	Total U.S. population is 203,211,926.
The *Redstockings Manifesto* appears in *Notes from the Second Year: Women's Liberation—Major Writings of the Radical Feminists.* The authors claim, "We cannot rely on existing ideologies as they are all products of male supremacist culture."	Women's employment is 31.2 million, compared with 18.4 million in 1950.
	Eleven percent (23 million people) are living at or below poverty level.
	Women's median income is $5,440 compared with men's $9,184.
Maya Angelou, African American actress, singer, poet, and autobiographer: *I Know Why the Caged Bird Sings*, an autobiography of the author's life through her midteens.	While Anglo-American women earn only about 65 percent of what white men earn, Filipino American women earn 47.5 percent, Japanese American women 43.7 percent, Chinese American women 39.6 percent, and Korean American women 37 percent of white men's wages.
Hannah Arendt: *On Violence.*	Some 57 percent of all Chinese American women workers are employed as seamstresses or in food services.
Judy Blume, popular children's author: *Are You There God? It's Me, Margaret.*	
Rosellen Brown, poet and novelist: *Some Deaths in*	Six years after the passage of Title VII of the Civil Rights Act, northern black women's wages

TEXTS		CONTEXTS
1970	*the Delta*, a collection of poems.	1970

CONTEXTS (1970): equal about 95 percent of white women's.

The Voting Rights Act lowers the minimum voting age from 21 to 18.

California enacts the Western world's first completely no-fault divorce law.

The Association of American Law Schools becomes a front-runner in banning sex discrimination in admission, employment, and placement at affiliated institutions.

New York City hosts the first organized political anti-rape action, a "Rape Speak Out" organized by the city's Radical Feminists.

Author Rita Mae Brown helps lead the "lavender menace," in which lesbians dressed in lavender spread themselves throughout the crowd at the Second Congress to Unite Women in order to prove that lesbians are a presence that cannot be ignored in, nor feared by, the women's movement.

Fifty-eight percent of all married couples use either the pill, the IUD, or steril-

TEXTS (1970):

Mignon G. Eberhart, prolific practitioner of the "Had I But Known" style of gothic mystery, is named a Grand Master by the Mystery Writers of America.

Mari Evans: *I Am a Black Woman*, collection of poetry.

Shulamith Firestone: *The Dialectic of Sex: The Case for Feminist Revolution*.

Nikki Giovanni: *Re:Creation*, poetry.

Gail Godwin, novelist: *The Perfectionists*.

Germaine Greer, journalist and critic: *The Female Eunuch*, influential feminist study.

Ada Louise Huxtable: *Will They Ever Finish Bruckner Boulevard?*.

Momoko Iko, Japanese American playwright and novelist: *The Old Man*.

Frances Kakugawa, Japanese American poet: *Sand Grains*, poet.

	TEXTS		CONTEXTS
1970	Denise Levertov: *Relearning the Alphabet*, poetry.	1970	ization as methods of birth control.
	Audre Lorde (1934–1992), black lesbian feminist poet, essayist, and activist: *The First Cities*, poetry.		Sixty-eight percent of American Catholics defy Church teachings proscribing birth control.
	Louise Meriwether, African American novelist and biographer: *Daddy Was a Number Runner*, a novel.		Some 17 percent of white women and 6 percent of black women hold college degrees.
	Robin Morgan: *Sisterhood Is Powerful*.		Four students at Kent State University are shot.
	Toni Morrison, African American novelist and critic: *The Bluest Eye*.		For every 1000 married women, 169 get divorces.
	Pauli Murray, poet and legal scholar: *Dark Testament, and Other Poems*.		Florence Howe founds the Feminist Press.
	Lorine Niedecker (1903–1970), poet: *My Life by Water*, collection of her works.		Dancer and choreographer Trisha Brown forms the Trisha Brown Dance Company.
			Women's Strike for Equality.
	Joyce Carol Oates: *The Wheel of Love*, a collection of short stories, and *Love and Its Derangements*, poetry.		Elizabeth P. Hoisington and Anna Mae Hays become the first women promoted to the rank of brigadier general in the U.S. Army.
	Grace Paley receives a National Council on the Arts grant and a National Institute of Arts and Letters award for short-story writing.		Alice Neel (1900–1985), whose work with portraiture in the American realist tradition shows a strong influence from

TEXTS	CONTEXTS
1970 Santha Rama Rau: *The Adventuress: A Novel.*	1970 Expressionism, exhibits *Andy Warhol.*

Ninotchka Rosca, Filipina American short-story writer: *"Bitter Country" and Other Stories.*

Time magazine publishes an article entitled "Women's Lib: A Second Look," publicizing feminist author Kate Millett's bisexuality and casting doubts on feminists' "maturity, morality and sexuality."

Jane Rule: *This Is Not for You*, a novel.

Sonia Sanchez: *We a BaddDDD People*, poetry.

May Sarton: *Kinds of Love*, a novel.

Essence magazine is first published.

The American Book Publishers Council and the American Textbook Publishers Institute merge to become the Association of American Publishers.

Carolyn See: *The Rest Is Done with Mirrors*, a novel.

Mona Van Duyn: *To See, to Take*, winner of the National Book Award.

New York state law permits abortion on demand, provided the woman and her physician consent.

Alice Walker, African American poet, novelist, essayist, and biographer: *The Third Life of Grange Copeland*, her first novel.

On April 22, the first Earth Day is held.

Eudora Welty: *Losing Battles*, a novel.

Jockey Diane Crump becomes the first woman to ride in the Kentucky Derby.

The Mary Tyler Moore Show begins. The long-running sitcom features "Mary Richards," a single career woman who fights for equal pay and lives a

	TEXTS		CONTEXTS
1970		1970	full life without marriage. Spin-off shows such as *Phyllis* and *Rhoda* also feature women characters. Moore goes on to win acclaim as a dramatic actress.
1971	The Women's Press Collective in Oakland prints Judy Grahn's *Edward the Dyke and Other Poems*, and Violet Press in New York publishes Fran Winant's	1971	Bella Abzug, women's rights advocate and leader in the fight against sexual harassment, is elected to the House of Representatives.
1971	*Looking at Women*; these works mark the beginning of a published lesbian poetry tradition in the United States. *Our Bodies, Ourselves* is published by Boston Women's Health Book Collective. Daphne Athas: *Entering Ephesus*, a novel. Mei-Mei Berssenbrugge, Chinese American poet and dramatist: *Fish Souls*. Joan Didion: *Play It as It Lays*, a novel. Katherine Dunn: *Truck*, a novel. Nikki Giovanni: *Gemini: An Extended Autobiographical Statement on My First Twenty-five Years of Being*	1971	Bella Abzug, Shirley Chisholm, Betty Friedan, and Gloria Steinem organize the National Woman's Political Caucus to challenge Democratic and Republican procedures for selecting delegates to their conventions. Washington state's ban on sexual discrimination, the nation's first, goes into effect. Anne L. Armstrong becomes the first woman to be named national co-chair of the Republican Party; the following year, she becomes the first woman to give a keynote speech at a major party's national convention. Margaret Arnstein, public health nurse and nursing

TEXTS		CONTEXTS
1971	*a Black Poet* and *Spin a Soft Black Song.*	1971	educator, becomes the first woman to be awarded the Sedgwick Memorial Medal, the highest honor of the American Public Health Association; in 1965 she becomes the first woman to receive the Rockefeller Public Service Award.
	Shirley Ann Grau: *The Condor Passes*, a novel.		
	Momoko Iko: *The Gold Watch.*		
	Elizabeth Janeway: *Man's World, Woman's Place: A Study in Social Mythology.*		Female journalists are allowed to join the National Press Club for the first time; Esther Tufty becomes the first woman member. It is at the Press Club that presidential press conferences are usually held.
	Maxine Kumin, poet, novelist: *The Abduction*, a novel.		
	G. M. Lee, Chinese American dramatist: *One in Sisterhood.*		
	Ursula K. Le Guin: *The Lathe of Heaven*, science fiction.		Lucinda Franks becomes the first woman to receive a Pulitzer Prize for national reporting.
	Louise Meriwether: *The Freedom Ship of Robert Smalls*, a biography.		The average age for onset of menopause is 49.
	Eve Merriam: *Growing Up Female in America: Ten Lives.*		*Ms.* magazine is launched in Gloria Steinem's living room in New York City.
	Bharati Mukherjee, novelist: *The Tiger's Daughter.*		Women are recruited as Secret Service Agents for the first time.
	Cynthia Ozick: *The Pagan Rabbi and Other Stories.*		
	Ann Petry: *Miss Muriel*, collection of stories.		Margery Ann Tabankin becomes the first female president of the National Student Association.

TEXTS		CONTEXTS	
1971	Anne Sexton: *Transformations*, poetry.	1971	Aileen Hernandez becomes the first African American woman president of the National Organization for Women (NOW).
	Ruth Stone: *Topography and Other Poems.*		
	Barbara Tuchman: *Stilwell and the American Experience in China, 1911–1945*, the historian's second Pulitzer Prize for general nonfiction.		Jeanne Holm becomes the first woman Air Force general.
			"Hot pants" are the latest rage.
	Marta Vidal: *Chicanas Speak Out.*		
	Eudora Welty: *One Time, One Place: Mississippi in the Depression*, a collection of her photographs with text.		
1972	*The Furies: Lesbian-Feminist Monthly* begins publication.	1972	The Women's Equity Action League, a nonprofit national organization founded in 1968 that lobbies for a broad range of feminist issues, opens its office in Washington, D.C.
	Literatura Chicana: Texto and Contexto.		
	Ms. magazine begins publication.		Twelve percent of law school students are women.
	Women's Studies: An Interdisciplinary Journal begins publication.		Shirley Chisholm seeks a presidential nomination on the Democratic party ticket.
	Toni Cade Bambara (1939–1995), African American short-story writer and novelist: *Gorilla, My Love*, a collection of stories.		
			Joann Pierce and Susan Lynn Roley become the first woman FBI agents.
	Doris Betts: *The River to Pickle Beach*, a novel.		

TEXTS	CONTEXTS
1972 Lucille Clifton: *Good News about the Earth*, poetry.	1972 A burglary at the Watergate Hotel in Washington, D.C., becomes news.

TEXTS

1972 Lucille Clifton: *Good News about the Earth*, poetry.

Mary Hallock Foote: *A Victorian Gentlewoman in the Far West: The Reminiscences of Mary Hallock Foote*, posthumously published autobiography.

Gail Godwin: *Glass People*, a novel.

Caroline Gordon: *The Glory of Hera*, a novel.

Jessica Hagedorn, Filipina fiction writer, poet, and dramatist: *Chiquita Banana*.

Willyce Kim, Korean American poet: *Eating Artichokes*.

Maxine Kumin: *Up Country: Poems of New England*; collection wins Pulitzer Prize in 1973.

Madeleine L'Engle: *The Crosswicks Journal: A Circle of Quiet*, autobiography about the multiple roles of women; first in a trilogy.

Margaret Mead: *Blackberry Winter: My Earlier Years*.

Louise Meriwether: *The Heart Man: Dr. Daniel*

CONTEXTS

1972 A burglary at the Watergate Hotel in Washington, D.C., becomes news.

Nixon is re-elected, but continued investigations into the scandal surrounding the Watergate crisis culminate in his resignation in 1974, at which time Gerald R. Ford becomes President.

After a sensational 20–month-long trial for her alleged involvement in a bombing designed to free "black political prisoners," black Communist revolutionary and writer Angela Davis is cleared of all charges.

The Education Amendments are ratified, disallowing gender discrimination in schools that receive federal support.

The Equal Rights Amendment passes in Congress and is sent to the states for ratification.

The Supreme Court decides that a state can require a woman to use her husband's surname on certain documents, including driver's licenses.

TEXTS	CONTEXTS
1972 *Hale Williams*, a biography.	1972 Sally Jane Preisand is the first woman rabbi to be ordained in the U.S.
Joyce Carol Oates: *Marriages and Infidelities*, a collection of short stories.	The Department of Health, Education, and Welfare claims that approximately 16,000 women have been sterilized through federal programs that year alone. Within two years, the 1972 figures are revised upward to show that between 100,000 and 200,000 sterilizations have been funded.
Flannery O'Connor: *The Complete Stories* (posthumous collection), wins the National Book Award.	
Mary Howell Raugust, the first woman ever hired as a dean at Harvard Medical School, publishes her *Why Would a Girl Go into Medicine?*, which exposes discrimination against female medical students and patients.	Some 46,497 forcible rapes are reported; estimates suggest that only one out of ten rapes is ever reported.
Anya Seton: *Green Darkness*, a novel.	The first rape crisis center opens in Washington, D.C.; five years later, 150 centers operate nationwide.
Anne Sexton: *The Book of Folly*, poetry.	
Alix Kates Shulman, novelist: *Memoirs of an Ex-Prom Queen*.	In St. Paul, Minnesota, the first battered women's shelter opens; six years later, 300 shelters have opened and the National Coalition Against Domestic Violence has been formed.
Elizabeth Spencer: *The Snare*, a novel.	
Han Suyin: *The Morning Deluge: Mao Tsetung and the Chinese Revolution, 1893–1954*; vol. 2, *Wind in the Tower*, published in 1976.	Warner Books is established.

TEXTS		CONTEXTS	
1972	Margaret Tsuda, Japanese American poet: *Cry Love Aloud*. Margaret Walker: *How I Wrote Jubilee*. Eudora Welty: *The Optimist's Daughter*, Pulitzer Prize-winning novel. Kathleen E. Woodiwiss: *The Flame and the Flower*, influential popular romance.	1972	Actress Jane Fonda shocks many patriotic Americans by touring North Vietnam and speaking out against the war. The National Conference of Puerto Rican Women is formed. Alene Duerk becomes the first woman Navy rear admiral. Barbara Jordan, attorney and politician, becomes the first African American woman from the South (Texas) elected to the U.S. House of Representatives. Women newscasters Jane Pauley, Lesley Stahl, and Judy Woodruff make their first appearances on the air. Gelsey Kirkland becomes the principal dancer for the New York City Ballet.
1973	Ai, African American/Japanese American poet: *Cruelty*. Rita Mae Brown, novelist, poet, humorist, screenwriter, and mystery writer: *Rubyfruit Jungle*, extremely popular novel about a young woman growing up lesbian.	1973	Annie Leibovitz, photographer, publishes *Shooting Stars*, a collection of her acclaimed pictures of well-known figures. Judy Chicago begins work on *The Dinner Party*, which includes sculpture, painting, ceramics, needlework, plastics, and china-painting. The three-dimensional traveling

TEXTS	CONTEXTS
1973 Sally Carrighar: *Home to the Wilderness*, an autobiography of her life as a naturalist.	1973 installation celebrates 39 women from history, legend, and myth.

Jinsie K. S. Chun, Chinese American novelist: *I Am Heaven*, biographical novel.

Margaret Craven (1901–1980), novelist, short-story writer, and journalist: *I Heard the Owl Call My Name*, a novel.

Mary Daly: *Beyond God the Father*.

Sylvia Maida Dominquez, Chicana dramatist: *La Comadre Maria: una comedia*.

Wilma Dykeman: *Return the Innocent Earth*, a novel.

Barbara Ehrenreich, feminist journalist and social historian: *Complaints and Disorders: The Sexual Politics of Sickness*.

Julia Fields: *East of Moonlight*, poetry.

Nancy Friday: *My Secret Garden: Women's Sexual Fantasies*.

Nikki Giovanni: *My House, Ego-Tripping and*

The Pennsylvania Academy of Fine Arts hosts the first major exhibition of the paintings and photographs of Susan Hannah (MacDowell) Eakins (1851–1938). In her own day, Eakins's artist husband, Thomas, received the lion's share of critical attention.

Roe v. Wade strikes down all state laws prohibiting abortion on any grounds during the first trimester. Norma McCorvey, "Jane Roe," delivers her baby and gives it up for adoption before the case even goes to court.

The Comprehensive Employment and Training Act program provides funds for services and training for displaced homemakers.

Sex-segregated help-wanted ads are outlawed by the Supreme Court.

The Supreme Court rules in *Frontiero v. Richardson* that military women cannot be discriminated against in family benefits but does not enforce anti-

TEXTS		CONTEXTS
1973	*Other Poems for Young People.*	1973	sex-discrimination policies commensurate to those already in place for race.

Vivian Gornick, feminist and memoirist, longtime writer for *Village Voice*: *In Search of Ali Mahmoud: An American Woman in Egypt.*

Shirley Ann Grau: *The Wind Shifting West*, short stories.

Lillian Hellman: *Pentimento: A Book of Portraits.*

Jeanne Wakatsuki Houston, Japanese American autobiographer: *Farewell to Manzanar.*

Erica Jong, novelist and poet: *Fear of Flying*, a novel.

Pauline Kael, movie critic: *Deeper into Movies*, winner of National Book Award in 1974.

Mary Lee: *The Guest of Tyn-y-Coed Cae: Poems and Drawings.*

Denise Levertov: *The Poet in the World*, essays.

Audre Lorde: *From a Land Where Other People Live*, poetry.

American Telephone and Telegraph (AT&T) is ordered to pay $15 million in back pay to its female employees because of discriminatory salary practices.

The Vietnam cease-fire agreement is reached.

Female office workers across the country organize, forming groups like Boston's 9 to 5, New York's Women Office Workers, and Chicago's Women Employed.

The Women's Caucus, founded by Betsy Wade, Joan Cook, and Grace Glueck, protests gender-based salary inequities at their employer, the *New York Times*. When their efforts prove fruitless, they hire civil rights lawyer Harriet Rabb to represent all 550 women employed at the paper. *Boylan v. Times*, settled out of court in 1978, results not only in a small cash settlement for each of the women but the establishment of an affirmative action plan at the paper.

TEXTS	CONTEXTS
1973	1973

TEXTS

1973

Joyce Maynard: *Looking Back: A Chronicle of Growing Up Old in the Sixties.*

Louise Meriwether: *Don't Ride the Bus on Monday: The Rosa Parks Story*, a biography.

Nicholasa Mohr: *Nilda*, semi-autobiographical story of a Puerto Rican girl growing up in the Bronx, illustrated by the author. *Nilda* is named the *New York Times* Outstanding Book of the Year.

Toni Morrison: *Sula*, a novel.

Joyce Carol Oates: *Do With Me What You Will*, a novel, and three volumes of poetry—*Angel Fire, A Posthumous Sketch*, and *Dreaming America and Other Poems.*

Francine Prose, novelist: *Judah the Pious.*

Adrienne Rich: *Diving into the Wreck*, winner of the National Book Award in 1974.

Wendy Rose, Native American woman of Hopi tribe: *Hopi Roadrunner Dancing.*

CONTEXTS

1973

The Government Printing Office approves "Ms." as an acceptable title for women.

Lelia Kasensia Smith Foley becomes the first black female mayor in the U.S. (in Taft, Oklahoma).

Marian Wright Edelman founds the Children's Defense Fund; Edelman was the first black woman admitted to the Mississippi Bar.

The National Black Feminist Organization is formed.

Los Angeles hosts the First National Lesbian Feminist Conference.

Women make up 44.7 percent of the nation's work force.

The Feminist Federal Credit Union is formed in Detroit.

The U.S. coal industry hires the first woman miner.

The National Organization for Non-Parenthood is formed to combat pervasive pronatalism.

TEXTS	CONTEXTS
1973 Rose Marie Royball, Chicana poet: *From La Llorona to Envidia . . . A Few Reflections.*	**1973** The abortion rights group Catholics for a Free Choice is formed.

<table>
<tr><td>

Sonia Sanchez: *A Blues Book for Blue Black Magical Women*, poetry.

Alice Sheldon, writing as James Tiptree, Jr., publishes her influential science-fiction story, "The Women Men Don't See."

Jacqueline Susann: *Once Is Not Enough*, a novel.

Alice B. Toklas: *Staying on Alone*, a collection of letters written after Gertrude Stein's death.

</td><td>

Terry Williams becomes the first woman offered an athletic scholarship (at the University of Miami at Coral Gables).

Forty-eight percent of Americans say "it is wrong for people to have sexual relations before marriage."

Call Off Your Old Tired Ethics (COYOTE), the first organized group of female prostitutes, is formed.

Advertising Age claims it costs Americans more to eat at home than to eat out; one in three meals are eaten outside the home.

Billie Jean King defeats "male chauvinist pig" Bobby Riggs in a celebrated tennis match.

Bonnie Tiburi is hired as the first female pilot to fly for a major airline.

In an episode of the sitcom *All in the Family*, menstruation is discussed for the first time on television.

</td></tr>
</table>

TEXTS	CONTEXTS
1973	1973 Revlon introduces its "Charlie" perfume with an ad campaign that features women assuming traditionally "male" roles and attitudes.
1974 *WomanSpirit* magazine, one of the first magazines devoted to women's spirituality and the Goddess, is first published. Kathy Acker, postmodernist novelist: *I Dreamt I Was a Nymphomaniac.* Alice Adams: *Families and Survivors*, a novel. Jane Chambers, possibly the first self-identified lesbian to be out in mainstream theater: *A Late Snow.* Diana Chang: *Eye to Eye*, a novel. Lucille Clifton: *An Ordinary Woman*, poetry. Elizabeth Colson, anthropologist: *Autobiographies of Three Pomo Women*, from stories she gathered in the 1930s and 1940s. Annie Dillard, essayist, poet, and naturalist: *Tickets for a Prayer Wheel.*	1974 The Census Bureau classifies 19,440,000 families as poor; 10,877,000 are male-headed and 8,563,000 are female-headed. Janet Gray Hayes becomes the first woman to be elected mayor of a major U.S. city (San Jose, California). Ellen Burstyn wins the Academy Award for Best Actress for her role in the consciousness-raising classic *Alice Doesn't Live Here Anymore.* Democratic candidate Ella Grasso wins by a landslide in the gubernatorial election in Connecticut, becoming the first woman ever elected governor who did not follow her husband into office. Elaine Noble, Massachusetts state legislator, becomes the first "out" lesbian to win state office.

	TEXTS		CONTEXTS
1974	Gloria Flores, Chicana poet: *And Her Children Lived*.	1974	The minimum wage is extended to domestic workers.
	Gail Godwin: *The Odd Woman*, a novel.		Equal Credit Opportunities Act.
	Sylvia Alicia Gonzales, Chicana poet: *La Chicana Piensa*.		President Gerald Ford signs legislation allowing girls to play Little League baseball.
	Marilyn Hacker, poet: *Presentation Piece*, winner of the National Book Award.		The American Psychiatric Association removes homosexuality from its list of mental disorders.
	June Jordan, African American poet, novelist, essayist: *New Day: Poems of Exile and Return*.		The Lesbian Herstory Archives is founded in New York.
	Edith Summers Kelley: *The Devil's Hand*, a female bildungsroman published posthumously, almost 50 years after its composition.		Black lesbian feminists in Boston form the Combahee River Collective.
			The Passport Office begins accepting the use of a married woman's birth name.
	Toni Kosover: *The Diary of a New York Career Girl*.		The U.S. Merchant Marine Academy becomes the first service academy to admit women.
	Ursula K. Le Guin: *The Dispossessed*, science fiction.		
	Madeleine L'Engle: *The Summer of the Great-Grandmother*, the second in an autobiographical trilogy.		Nuclear fuel facility laboratory technician Karen Silkwood, 28, dies in an automobile crash near Oklahoma City on her way to meet with a *New York Times* reporter and a

TEXTS	CONTEXTS
1974 Alison Lurie: *The War between the Tates*, a novel.	**1974** union official. She had planned to document her allegations that Kerr-McGee Nuclear Corporation had falsified quality control reports and that 40 pounds of highly dangerous plutonium were missing from the plant.
Josephine Miles: *To All Appearances: New and Selected Poems*.	
Kate Millett: *Flying*, an autobiographical novel.	
Berry Morgan: *The Mystic Adventures of Roxie Stoner*.	The Coalition of Labor Union Women is formed.
Tillie Olsen: *Yonnondio: From the Thirties*.	The Mexican American Women's National Association is founded.
Grace Paley: *Enormous Changes at the Last Minute*, collection of stories.	Barbara Ann Allen Rainey becomes the first woman naval aviator.
Rosemary Rogers, popular romance novelist: *Sweet Savage Love*.	*Hustler* magazine begins publication.
May Sarton: *Collected Poems*.	*People* magazine is first published.
Susan Fromberg Schaeffer: *Anya*, a novel, and *Granite Lady*, a collection of poetry.	As a result of the "Tidal Basin Affair," in which Congressman Wilbur Mills is caught with stripper Fannie Foxe, Mill's political career ends and Foxe's show business career effectively begins.
Anne Sexton: *The Death Notebooks*, poetry. She commits suicide this same year.	
Ann Allen Shockley: *Loving Her*, a novel.	Fifteen billion frankfurters are eaten by Americans.
Leslie Marmon Silko, Native American poet and	Americans buy 107 billion bottles of soft drinks.

	TEXTS		CONTEXTS
1974	novelist: *Laguna Woman*, poetry. Jessamyn West: *The Secret Look*, poetry. Kathleen E. Woodiwiss: *The Wolf and the Dove*, romance novel.	1974	
1975	*Signs: Journal of Women in Culture and Society* is first published. Gothic thrillers published in various magazines by Louisa May Alcott under the pseudonym A. M. Barnard are collected and published as *Behind a Mask: The Unknown Thrillers of Louisa May Alcott*. Lisa Alther: *Kinflicks*, a novel. Susan Brownmiller: *Against Our Will*, a study of rape. Ana Castillo, Chicana poet and novelist: *Otro Canto*. Yuan-lin Chi, Chinese American novelist: *A Shadow of Spring*. Judy Chicago, multimedia artist: *Thru the Flower: My Struggle as a Woman Artist*.	1975	U.N. International Women's Year conference is held in Mexico City with 6300 women attending; it leads to the pronouncement of the U.N. Decade for Women. There are 11.4 million recipients of Aid to Families with Dependent Children benefits. The 109,377,000 women in the U.S. outnumber men (103,760,000), in part due to longer female life expectancy. In *Taylor v. Louisiana*, the Supreme Court outlaws automatic exclusion of women from jury duty. Carla Hills becomes the first woman secretary of the Department of Housing and Urban Development. Milicent Fenwick of New Jersey is the first known

TEXTS		CONTEXTS	
1975	Laurie Colwin (1944–1992), novelist and short-story writer: *Shine on, Bright and Dangerous Object*, a novel.	1975	grandmother elected to Congress.
	Margarita Cota-Cardenas, Chicana poet and novelist: *Noches despertando inconciencias*.		Jacqueline Kennedy Onassis joins Viking Press as a consulting editor; she stays for two years, then resigns and joins Doubleday.
	Annie Dillard: *Pilgrim at Tinker Creek*, which wins the Pulitzer Prize for nonfiction.		Country music and movie star Dolly Parton, known for writing and singing songs about women's lives, pays Porter Wagoner a million dollars in order to leave his show and gain control over her career. She goes on to build a multimillion-dollar entertainment industry.
	Nikki Giovanni: *The Women and the Men*, poetry.		
	Jessica Hagedorn: *Dangerous Music: Poetry and Prose*.		
	Joy Harjo, Creek poet: *The Last Song*.		Pregnant women are no longer automatically discharged from the armed services.
	Maureen Howard: *Before My Time*, a novel.		Military academies are required by Congress to admit women.
	Angela de Hoyos, Chicana poet: *Arise Chicano* and *Chicano Poems for the Barrio*.		The U.S. Civil Service Commission removes its ban on the employment of gays and lesbians.
	Gayl Jones, African American novelist and poet: *Corregidora*, a novel.		The First Women's Bank opens in New York City.
	Carol Lem, Chinese American poet: *Grassroots*.		*Business Week* publishes a special issue on "The Corporate Woman."

TEXTS	CONTEXTS
1975	**1975**

<table>
<tr><td>

Bobbie Ann Mason, Southern novelist, short-story writer, and critic: *The Girl Sleuth: A Feminist Guide to the Bobbsey Twins, Nancy Drew, and Their Sisters.*

Ella May Miller: *The Joy of Housekeeping.*

Nicholasa Mohr: *El Bronx Remembered: A Novel and Stories.*

Dorinda Moreno, Chicana poet: *La Mujer es la tierra: la tierra de vida*, poetry and sketches.

Bharati Mukherjee: *Wife,* a novel.

Berta Ornelas, Chicana novelist: *Come Down from the Mound.*

Linda Pastan, poet: *Aspects of Eve.*

Sylvia Plath: *Letters Home: Correspondence, 1950–1963*, posthumously published.

Estela Portillo Trambley, Chicana fiction writer and playwright: *Rain of Scorpions*, short stories.

Judith Rossner: *Looking for Mr. Goodbar*, a novel.

</td><td>

Tish Sommers founds the Displaced Homemakers League; in 1980 she founds the Older Women's League.

In a much-discussed controversial case, JoAnne Little, an African American, is acquitted of the murder of the guard who raped her in her North Carolina jail cell.

The Roman Catholic Church canonizes Elizabeth Bayley Seton, the first woman born in the U.S. (in 1774) to be deemed a saint. In 1809, she founded the first U.S. Catholic order, the Sisters of Charity of St. Joseph.

Women sports reporters first enter men's locker rooms.

Saturday Night Live premieres on NBC; comic Gilda Radner becomes immediately popular with characters such as clumsy Lisa Loopner, confused Roseanne Roseannadana, and reporter Baba Wawa.

1800 women attend the first women's spirituality conference in Boston.

</td></tr>
</table>

	TEXTS		CONTEXTS
1975	Gayle Rubin: "The Traffic in Women: Notes on the Public Economy of Sex" appears in *Towards an Anthropology of Women*, Rayna Rapp, ed.	1975	Ruth Siems develops Stove Top Stuffing for General Foods.
	Joanna Russ, novelist and short-story writer, especially of science fiction: *The Female Man*.		
	Anne Sexton: *The Awful Rowing Toward God*, poetry, published posthumously.		
	Eileen Simpson: *The Maze*, a novel.		
	Marcela Trujillo Gaitan, Chicana poet: *Chicano Themes: Manita Poetry*.		
	Wendy Wasserstein, playwright: *Uncommon Women and Others*.		
	Betty Siao-meng Waungling, Chinese American novelist: *Days of Joy*, memoir.		
	Jade Snow Wong: *No Chinese Stranger*, Chinese American autobiography.		
1976	Ann Beattie: *Chilly Scenes of Winter*, a novel.	1976	United Nations Decade for Women begins.
	Martha Boesing, playwright: *Love Song for an*		The first women are admitted to the U.S.

TEXTS	CONTEXTS
1976 *Amazon*, a one-act play that presents a ceremony celebrating women's friendships.	1976 Military Academy in West Point, New York.

TEXTS

1976 *Amazon*, a one-act play that presents a ceremony celebrating women's friendships.

Erma Bombeck, humorist, with a newspaper column syndicated since 1965: *The Grass Is Always Greener over the Septic Tank*.

Miriam Bornstein-Samoza, Chicana poet: *Bajo Cubierta*.

Rosellen Brown: *The Autobiography of My Mother*.

Lucille Clifton: *Generations*, a memoir.

Ann Cornelisen: *Women of the Shadows*, nonfiction.

Janice Delaney, Mary Jane Lupton, and Emily Toth: *The Curse: A Cultural History of Menstruation*.

Julia Fields: *A Summoning a Shining*, a collection of poetry.

Carolyn Forché: *Gathering the Tribes*, winner of the Yale Series of Younger Poets Award.

Gail Godwin: *Dream Children*, a collection of stories.

CONTEXTS

1976 Military Academy in West Point, New York.

Twenty-seven percent of white and 45 percent of black sexually active unmarried girls are pregnant before they turn 18.

By this year, 24 percent of all Native American women have been sterilized.

Pauli Murray becomes the first African American woman to be ordained as an Episcopal priest.

Award-winning novelist Toni Morrison begins teaching classes in black literature and creative writing at Yale University and Bard College before eventually taking a position at Princeton University.

Of physicians practicing in the U.S., 8.6 percent are women.

The National Alliance of Black Feminists is founded.

The Organization of Pan Asian American Women is formed.

Barbara Walters becomes the first woman co-anchor

TEXTS		CONTEXTS
1976	Lillian Hellman: *Scoundrel Time*.	1976	of a daily evening news program.

<table>
<tr><td>

Lillian Hellman: *Scoundrel Time*.

Lori Higa, Japanese American dramatist: *Calamity Jane Meets Suchi Mama and the BVD Kid; or, . . . Lady Murasaki Rides the Wild Wild West*.

Shere Hite, cultural historian, publishes the first *Hite Report: A Nationwide Study of Female Sexuality*.

Gayl Jones: *Eva's Man*, a novel.

Frances Kakugawa: *Golden Spike* and *Path of Butterflies*, books of poetry.

Maxine Hong Kingston, Chinese American writer: *The Woman Warrior*, winner of National Book Critics' Circle Award for nonfiction.

Denise Levertov: *Collected Poems, 1960–1974*.

Hazel Ai Chun Lin: *Rachel Weeping for Her Children Uncomforted*.

Joyce Carol Oates: *Childwold*, a novel.

Cynthia Ozick: *Bloodshed and Three Novellas*.

</td><td>

of a daily evening news program.

Singer Anita Bryant leads the "Save Our Children" campaign in Florida, which ends with voters rejecting gay rights; Bryant later recants her strict anti-gay position.

News analyst and correspondent Pauline Frederick becomes the first woman to moderate a presidential debate, which she does for Gerald Ford and Jimmy Carter.

Barbara Jordan becomes the first African American keynote speaker for a major party's national political convention, delivering a commanding address before fellow Democrats.

Jimmy Carter is elected President.

The first Michigan Womyn's Music Festival is held.

Janet Guthrie becomes the first woman driver in the Indianapolis 500.

Marilyn Levine, ceramic sculptor known for her work in the *trompe l'oeil* tradition, specializes in imitating objects made of

</td></tr>
</table>

	TEXTS		CONTEXTS
1976	Marge Piercy: *Woman on the Edge of Time*, a novel.	1976	leather, exemplified by her piece *Rick and Marga-ret's Suitcase*, created this year.

Anne Rice, novelist who also writes erotica under the pen names "A. N. Ro-quelaire" and "Anne Ram-pling": *Interview with the Vampire*, first in the ex-tremely popular Vampire Chronicles.

Adrienne Rich: *Of Woman Born: Motherhood as Institu-tion and Experience*, essays, winner of the National Book Award.

Isabella Rios, Chicana novelist: *Victuum*.

Ntozake Shange, poet, playwright, novelist, and performance artist: *for col-ored girls who have consid-ered suicide when the rain-bow is enuf*, a choreopoem; and *Sassafrass, Cypress & Indigo*, a novel.

Gail Sheehy: *Passages: Pre-dictable Crises of Adult Life*.

Han Suyin: *Wind in the Tower: Mao Tse-tung and the Chinese Revolution, 1954–1975*, biography.

Alice Walker: *Meridian*, a novel.

Charlie's Angels first airs on network television.

Singer, actress, director Barbra Streisand becomes the first Oscar-winning ac-tress also to win an Oscar for Best Song with "Ever-green" from the film *A Star Is Born*.

African American artist and educator Alma Thomas receives the Inter-national Women's Year Award for Outstanding Contributions and Dedica-tion to Women and Art.

	TEXTS		CONTEXTS
1976	Mitsuye Yamada, Japanese American poet: *Camp Notes and Other Poems.*	1976	
	Bernice Zamora: *Restless Serpents*, poetry by a Chicana author.		
1976–1984		1976–1984	Sex-related murders rise 160 percent.
1977	The influence of the Women's Movement and the development of Women's Studies programs leads feminist scholars to begin the work of recovering "lost" women authors and analyzing the role of gender in literature by women and men, as well as studying how gender dynamics influenced the writing of literary history. In this year, Ann Douglas publishes the influential *The Feminization of American Culture.* It is followed in 1978 by Nina Baym's *Woman's Fiction: A Guide to Novels by and about Women in America, 1820–1870* and Judith Fetterley's *The Resisting Reader: A Feminist Approach to American Fiction*, and, in 1979, by Sandra M. Gilbert and Susan Gubar's *The Madwoman in the Attic: The Woman Writer and the Nineteenth-*	1977	Bette Davis becomes the first woman to receive the American Film Institute's Life Achievement Award.

Compared with only 13 percent in 1952, 72 percent of southern black women have voted in an election.

Hyde Amendment prohibits Medicaid-funded abortions.

Of AFDC recipients, 52.6 percent are white, 43 percent are black, and the rest are "American Indian and other."

The National Women's Studies Association (NWSA) is founded.

The First National Women's Conference is held in Houston, Texas. |

TEXTS	CONTEXTS
1977 *Century Literary Imagination.*	1977 Azie Taylor Morton becomes the nation's first African American woman treasurer.
Meena Alexander, Indian American poet, novelist, playwright, and scholar: *I Root My Name* and *Without Place*, poetry, and *In the Middle Earth*, a one-act play.	In this, the first year women are allowed to earn Rhodes scholarships, 24 of the 77 recipients are women.
Toni Cade Bambara: *The Sea Birds Are Still Alive*, stories.	The Women's Caucus of the National Gay Task Force is established.
Peg Bracken: *I Hate to Housekeep Book.*	Economist Juanita Morris Kreps, a Carter appointee, becomes the first woman Secretary of Commerce; five years earlier, she was chosen the first woman governor of the New York Stock Exchange.
Olga Broumas: *Beginning with O*, a book of poetry selected for the Yale Younger Poets Series.	
Mary Higgins Clark, popular author of thrillers: *A Stranger Is Watching.*	Carter-appointee Patricia Roberts Harris becomes the first African American female officially to serve on a president's cabinet when she becomes Secretary of Housing and Urban Development; later, she becomes Secretary of Health and Human Services.
Wanda Coleman, African American poet: *Poems.*	
Margaret Craven: *Walk Gently This Good Earth.*	
Joan Didion: *A Book of Common Prayer*, a novel.	
Annie Dillard: *Holy the Firm*, essays in nature and philosophy.	Eleanor Holmes Norton becomes the first female chair of the Equal Employment Opportunity Commission (EEOC) and authors federal guidelines
Dorothy Dinnerstein: *The Mermaid and the Mino-*	

TEXTS		CONTEXTS	
1977	*taur: Sexual Arrangements and Human Malaise*, a feminist analysis of the objectification of the female body through history.	1977	on sexual harassment in the workplace.

<table>
<tr><td>Marilyn French, feminist novelist: *The Women's Room*.</td><td>Virginia Dill McCarty is nominated as the first female U.S. Attorney.</td></tr>
</table>

TEXTS (continued):

Marilyn French, feminist novelist: *The Women's Room*.

Nancy Friday: *My Mother/My Self: The Daughter's Search for Identity*.

Shirley Ann Grau: *Evidence of Love*, a novel.

Beverly Lowry, novelist: *Come Back, Lolly Ray*.

Kate Millett: *Sita*, autobiographical novel.

Nicholasa Mohr: *In Nueva York*, short stories.

Toni Morrison: *Song of Solomon*, wins National Book Critics' Circle Award and National Book Award.

Bharati Mukherjee: *Days and Nights in Calcutta*, memoir.

Marcia Muller introduces Sharon McCone, a female private detective, in *Edwin of the Iron Shoes*. She will go on to inspire the flood

CONTEXTS (continued):

Virginia Dill McCarty is nominated as the first female U.S. Attorney.

Women employees begin a three-year strike for fair wages from a Minnesota bank; the group comes to be called the "Willmar 8."

A Wisconsin judge is recalled for the first time in the state's history after giving a lenient sentence to the teenaged rapist of a 16-year-old girl; in announcing his sentence, the judge claimed the rape to be a normal response to "sexual permissiveness and provocative clothing."

The Army reinstates the Medal of Honor to Civil War surgeon Dr. Mary Edwards Walker. It had been revoked sixty years earlier for "insufficient evidence of gallantry."

Rosalyn Yalow wins the Nobel Prize in Medicine for developing the process of radioimmunoassay.

Some 36 million women use tranquilizers; 16 million take sleeping pills,

TEXTS		CONTEXTS	
1977	of female detective novels that creates a new "Golden Age" of the mystery novel in the 1980s and 1990s.	1977	and 12 million take amphetamines. Between 1977 and 1980, Valium is the most prescribed drug in the country.
	Anaïs Nin: *The Delta of Venus*, a book of erotica originally written in the 1940s.		John T. Molloy publishes *The Woman's Dress for Success Book*.
	Francine Prose: *Marie Laveau*, a novel.		Former Peace Corps volunteer Ann Moore patents the "Snugli," fashioned after the fabric harnesses the Togolese use to carry their children.
	Marina Rivera, Chicana poet: *Sobra* and *Mestiza*.		
	Wendy Rose: *Academic Squaw: Reports to the World from the Ivory Tower*.		
	Patsy Sumie Saiki, Japanese American autobiographer: *Sachi: A Daughter of Hawaii*.		
	Anne Sexton: A Self-Portrait in Letters, edited by Linda Gray Sexton and Lois Ames.		
	Leslie Marmon Silko: *Ceremony*, a novel.		
	Susan Sontag: *On Photography*, winner of National Book Critics' Circle Award.		
	Han Suyin: *Llasa, the Open City: A Journey to Tibet*, nonfiction.		

TEXTS	CONTEXTS
1977	**1977**

Ines Hernandez Tovar, Chicana poet: *Con Razon, Corazon: Poetry.*

Dorothy Uhnak: *The Investigation*, a mystery novel.

Alma Luz Villanueva, Chicana poet: *Bloodroot* and *Poems: Third Chicano Literary Prize.*

Sylvia Wilkinson: *Shadow of the Mountain.*

Nellie Wong, Chinese American poet: *Dreams in Harrison Railroad Park.*

| **1978** | **1978** |

Our Right to Love, edited by Ginny Vida, is the first anthology of lesbian essays published by a mainstream press (Prentice-Hall).

Two important laws concerning Native Americans are passed: the American Indian Religious Freedom Act and the Indian Child Welfare Act, the latter an attempt to halt the practice of fracturing families by placing children in foster homes or up for adoption.

Kathy Acker: *Kathy Goes to Haiti*, a novel.

Marilou Awiakta, Cherokee poet from Appalachia: *Abiding Appalachia: Where Mountain and Atom Meet.*

Women of All Red Nations (WARN) holds its founding conference, representing women from over thirty Native nations. They call for the decolonization of all Indian peoples and identify sterilization abuses, political prisoners, the restoration of an Indian land base,

Judy Blume: *Wifey: an Adult Novel.*

E. M. Broner: *A Weave of Women*, lyric novel by a Jewish American author.

TEXTS		CONTEXTS
1978	Rosellen Brown: *Tender Mercies*, a novel.	1978

<table>
<tr><th>TEXTS</th><th>CONTEXTS</th></tr>
</table>

TEXTS | CONTEXTS

1978

Rosellen Brown: *Tender Mercies*, a novel.

Diana Chang: *A Perfect Love.*

Suzy McKee Charnas, science-fiction writer: *Motherlines.*

Nancy Chodorow, feminist psychologist: *The Reproduction of Mothering.*

Laurie Colwin: *Happy All the Time.*

Mary Daly, radical feminist philosopher and theologian: *Gyn/Ecology: The Metaethics of Radical Feminism.*

Toi Derricotte, poet: *The Empress of the Death House.*

Harriet Doerr: *Stones for Ibarra*, a novel.

Barbara Ehrenreich and Deirdre English: *For Her Own Good: 150 Years of the Experts' Advice to Women.*

Phyllis Eisenstein, author of science-fiction and fantasy short stories and novels: *Born to Exile,* winner of the Balrog Award.

1978

education, and the survival of the family as target issues.

In *Santa Clara Pueblo v. Martinez*, the Supreme Court finds that the federal government has no right to interfere in intra-tribal affairs, even when women's rights are at issue.

An anti-gay ordinance (the Briggs initiative) is defeated in California through the organization and efforts of gay activists.

San Francisco's mayor, George Moscone, and openly gay city supervisor Harvey Milk are assassinated.

For the first time all seven sister colleges—Barnard, Bryn Mawr, Mount Holyoke, Radcliffe, Smith, Vassar, and Wellesley—have female presidents.

Toxic Shock Syndrome is identified and named and, in 1980, connected to tampon use. Between 1979 and 1985, 2814 cases, resulting in 122 deaths, are reported.

TEXTS	CONTEXTS
1978	1978

TEXTS

1978

Nikki Giovanni: *Cotton Candy on a Rainy Day*, poetry.

Mary Gordon: *Final Payments*, winner of the Kafka Prize.

Elizabeth Forsythe Hailey: *A Woman of Independent Means*, a novel.

Patricia Hampl, poet and memoirist: *Woman Before an Aquarium*, poetry.

Barbara Grizzuti Harrison: *Visions of Glory: A History and a Memory of Jehovah's Witnesses*.

Beth Henley: *Crimes of the Heart*, winner of the Pulitzer Prize for drama in 1981.

Maureen Howard: *Facts of Life*, a memoir.

Dorothy B. Hughes, one of the first women to write mysteries in the hard-boiled tradition, is named a Grand Master by the Mystery Writers of America.

Kristin Hunter, African American novelist: *The Lakestown Rebellion*.

CONTEXTS

1978

Faye Wattleton is the first black president of Planned Parenthood Federation of America.

Phyllis Grann becomes publisher (later president) of G. P. Putnam's Sons; Grann is the first woman to hold the post of publisher of any major publishing house in modern times.

The term "feminization of poverty" is coined by sociologist Diana Pearce.

The National Coalition Against Domestic Violence is founded.

The first "Take Back the Night" march is held, in San Francisco.

A Chicago-based study finds that black women are 18 times more likely to be raped than white women.

Harriet Tubman becomes the first African American woman to appear on a postage stamp.

U.S. District Court finds that female sportswriters cannot be prevented from entering major league baseball locker rooms.

TEXTS   CONTEXTS

1978   Patricia Ikeda, Japanese   1978
        American poet: *House of
        Wood, House of Salt.*

        Joyce Johnson: *Bad Con-
        nections*, a novel.

        Judith Krantz, best-selling
        romance novelist and the
        highest paid author of the
        early 1980s: *Scruples.* As
        have many of her works,
        Scruples has been made
        into a television mini-
        series.

        Meridel LeSueur: *The
        Girl*, a chronicle of
        women's lives written in
        1939.

        Beverly Lowry: *Emma
        Blue.*

        Janice Mirikitani: *Awake
        in the River*, poetry by Jap-
        anese American woman.

        Tillie Olsen: *Silences*,
        essays.

        Linda Pastan: *The Five
        Stages of Grief*, poetry.

        Juanita Ponce-Montoya,
        Chicana poet: *Grief
        Work.*

        Adrienne Rich's influen-
        tial essay "Compulsory
        Heterosexuality and Les-
        bian Existence" first ap-

TEXTS	CONTEXTS
1978 pears in *Signs: A Journal of Women in Culture and Society*.	1978

1978   pears in *Signs: A Journal of Women in Culture and Society*.

Muriel Rukeyser: *Collected Poems*.

Joanna Russ: *The Two of Them*, science-fiction novel.

Mary Lee Settle: *Blood Tie*, winner of a National Book Award.

Alice Sheldon, writing as James Tiptree, Jr.: *Up the Walls of the World*, science fiction.

Alix Kates Shulman: *Burning Questions*, a novel.

Susan Sontag: *Illness as Metaphor*.

May Swenson: *New and Selected Things Taking Place*, poetry.

Eleanor Wong Telemaque, Chinese American novelist: *It's Crazy to Stay Chinese in Minnesota*.

Evangelina Vigil, Chicana poet: *Nade y nade*.

Michele Wallace: *Black Macho and the Myth of the Superwoman*.

TEXTS	CONTEXTS
1978 Eudora Welty: *The Eye of the Story*, essays. May Wong, Chinese American poet: *Superstitions: Poems.*	**1978**
1979 Barbara Taylor Bradford: *A Woman of Substance*, a popular novel. Kate Braverman: *Lithium for Medea*, a novel. Barbara Brinson-Pineda, Chicana poet: *Noctorno.* Octavia E. Butler, African American writer of science fiction: *Kindred.* Vera Caspary: *The Secrets of Grown-ups*, autobiography. Fay Chiang, Chinese American poet: *In the City of Contradictions.* Judy Chicago: *The Dinner Party: A Symbol of Our Heritage*, a volume describing the creation, history, and people involved in her multi-media exhibit, *The Dinner Party.* Kiana Davenport, Hawaiian novelist and short-story writer: *A Desperate Season.*	**1979** Nuclear accident at Three Mile Island. Jane Byrne is elected Chicago's first woman mayor. The Reverend Jerry Falwell establishes the "Moral Majority." Beverly LaHaye founds Concerned Women of America, a conservative woman's organization; by 1995 membership is estimated at 600,000. For the first time, more women than men enter college in the U.S. The National Archives for Black Women's History opens in Washington. Historian and author Barbara Tuchman becomes the first woman elected president of the American Academy and Institute of Arts and Letters. U.S. Treasury issues the Susan B. Anthony dollar, making Anthony the first woman to appear on a

TEXTS	CONTEXTS
1979 Joan Didion: *The White Album*, essays. Phyllis Eisenstein: *Sorcerer's Son.* Sally Miller Gearhart, science-fiction writer: *The Wanderground.* Gail Godwin: *A Mother and Two Daughters*, a novel. Anne Halley, poet and fiction writer: *The Bearded Mother*, poetry. Elizabeth Hardwick: *Sleepless Nights*, a novel. Alice Hoffman: *The Drowning Season*, a novel. Angela de Hoyos: *Selected Poems.* Clara Kubojiri, Japanese American dramatist: *Country Pie, Talk Story.* Mary Wong Lee, Chinese American poet: *Through My Windows*; *Book II* published 1980. Denise Levertov: *Collected Earlier Poems, 1940–1960.* Ruthanne Lum McCunn: *An Illustrated History of the Chinese in America.*	1979 U.S. coin; it stops minting the coin two years later. Bette Midler, known for her raunchy humor and raucous stage personality, appears in *The Rose*, a film biography of rock singer Janis Joplin, and opens on Broadway in *Bette! Divine Madness.* A *Navajo Times* story contends that rape is the crime occurring most frequently on the Navajo Reservation. The National Weather Service stops naming all storms for women and begins giving half of them men's names. In a much-publicized case, Greta Rideout charges her husband John with marital rape; when he is acquitted, the couple attempts a reconciliation. However, after the couple separates a few months later, John is arrested and found guilty of trespassing in Greta's home and verbally and physically threatening her. Lesbians and gays march for their rights in Washington, D.C.

	TEXTS		CONTEXTS
1979	Colleen McElroy, African American poet and short-story writer: *Poems*. Nicholasa Mohr: *Felita*, a juvenile novel. Eleanor Munro, art historian and memoirist: *Originals: American Women Artists*. Barbara Noda, Japanese American poet: *Strawberries*. Jayne Anne Phillips, short-story writer, novelist: *Black Tickets*, stories. Adrienne Rich: *On Lies, Secrets, and Silence: Selected Prose 1966–1978*. Eileen Simpson: *Reversals: A Personal Account of Victory over Dyslexia*. Ellease Southerland, African American novelist: *Let the Lion Eat Straw*. Luz Maria Umpierre, Puerto Rican poet: *Una Puertorriquena en penna*.	1979	The Shah of Iran is exiled to the U.S. Two of the 52 U.S. hostages in the U.S. Embassy in Teheran, Iran, are women: Kathryn Koob and Elizabeth Ann Swift. Beverly Kelley becomes the first woman commander of a Coast Guard ship. Soviet troops invade Afghanistan.
1980s		1980s	Between 80 and 90 percent of heterosexual women engage in premarital sex; for white women

TEXTS	CONTEXTS
1980s	**1980s** in their 20s, the average is four to five partners.
	Fifty percent of American women diet and almost 80 percent of prepubescent girls restrict their eating for fear of getting fat.
1980 Alice Adams: *Rich Rewards*, a novel.	**1980** The U.S. census allows that the "head of the household" need not be the husband, but is determined by who rents or owns the home.
Jean M. Auel, novelist: *The Clan of the Cave Bear*, the first in her popular Earth's Children series featuring as the central character a strong woman.	
Toni Cade Bambara: *The Salt Eaters*, a novel.	There are approximately 1.9 million Asian American women in the U.S, constituting 51 percent of the total Asian American population.
Ann Beattie: *Falling in Place*, a novel.	Approximately 1 million Native Americans live in the U.S., down from an estimated pre-contact population of between 25 and 45 million; researchers estimate the life expectancy of contemporary Native Americans to average 45 years and unemployment to be between 60 and 90 percent.
Elaine Becker, Japanese American dramatist: *The Best of Both Worlds*.	
Irene Blea, Chicana poet: *Celebrating, Crying, and Cursing*.	
Gwendolyn Brooks: *Primer for Blacks*.	
Octavia E. Butler, African American science-fiction writer, begins her gender-bending Patternist series with *Wild Seed*.	Some 25 percent of all black men and women between the ages of 25 and 54 are divorced; the rate is roughly 10 percent for whites.

TEXTS		CONTEXTS
1980	Olivia Castellano, Chicana poet: *Blue Mandolin, Yellow Field.*	1980	Almost 50 percent of black households are female-headed. Of the one-third that fall below the poverty line, 70 percent are female-headed.

<table>
<tr><td>1980</td><td>Olivia Castellano, Chicana poet: Blue Mandolin, Yellow Field.</td><td>1980</td><td>Almost 50 percent of black households are female-headed. Of the one-third that fall below the poverty line, 70 percent are female-headed.</td></tr>
<tr><td></td><td>Jane Chambers: Last Summer at Bluefish Cove.</td><td></td><td></td></tr>
<tr><td></td><td>Suzy McKee Charnas: The Vampire Tapestry.</td><td></td><td>Over 40 percent of the total work force is female; women with children at home constitute 20 percent of the total work force.</td></tr>
<tr><td></td><td>Yuan-tsung Chen: The Dragon's Village.</td><td></td><td></td></tr>
<tr><td></td><td>Anna Chennault: The Education of Anna, autobiography.</td><td></td><td>The Supreme Court rules in Harris v. McRae that Medicaid and other funds for abortion can be cut off within individual states.</td></tr>
<tr><td></td><td>Judy Chicago: Embroidering Our Heritage: The Dinner Party Needlework.</td><td></td><td></td></tr>
<tr><td></td><td>Sandra Cisneros, Chicana poet and fiction writer: Bad Boys.</td><td></td><td>More than 2000 protesters involved in Women's Pentagon Action protest violence by weaving a human chain around the Pentagon.</td></tr>
<tr><td></td><td>Michelle Cliff: Claiming an Identity They Taught Me to Despise, poetry.</td><td></td><td></td></tr>
<tr><td></td><td>Ann Cornelisen: Strangers and Pilgrims: The Last Italian Migration, nonfiction.</td><td></td><td>The first National Women's History Week is celebrated during the first week of March. In 1987 it is expanded into a month.</td></tr>
<tr><td></td><td>Lucha Corpi, Chicana poet and novelist: Palabras de mediodia/Noon Words.</td><td></td><td></td></tr>
<tr><td></td><td>Janet Dailey, best-selling romance author: Ride the Thunder.</td><td></td><td>Jean Harris is convicted of killing her lover, the inventor of the Scarsdale diet Herman Tarnower.</td></tr>
<tr><td></td><td>Kiana Davenport: The Power Eaters, a novel.</td><td></td><td>In El Salvador, three U.S. nuns and a lay worker are murdered.</td></tr>
</table>

TEXTS	CONTEXTS
1980 Jude Devereaux, popular romance novelist who creates strong heroines: *The Black Lyon*.	**1980** The first National Hispanic Feminist Conference held in California.
Rita Dove, African American poet: *The Yellow House on the Corner*.	Judy Chicago begins work on *The Birth Project*, employing needlework and ceramics to depict childbirth. Hundreds of women are employed to help with the multimedia project.
Sandra Maria Esteves, Puerto Rican poet: *Yerbabuena*.	
Louise Glück: *Descending Figure*, poetry.	Meryl Streep, actress acclaimed for her work on stage, in film, and in television, receives her first Oscar for her supporting actress role in *Kramer vs. Kramer*. She is subsequently honored as Best Actress in 1982 for *Sophie's Choice*.
Jorie Graham, poet: *Hybrids of Plants and Ghosts*.	
Judy Grahn, poet and novelist: *The Work of a Common Woman*.	
Karen Horney: *The Adolescent Diaries of Karen Horney*.	The Bay Area Women's Philharmonic is formed, the only professional female orchestra in the U.S. Its goal is to discover, preserve, and perform works of women composers.
Velina Hasu Houston, African American/Japanese American dramatist: *Asa Ga Kimashita (Morning Has Broken)*.	
	An ecofeminist conference is held in Massachusetts.
Maxine Hong Kingston: *China Men*, winner of the American Book Award.	For the first time, the Democratic party includes gay rights in its convention platform.
Judith Krantz: *Princess Daisy*, a novel.	
Shirley Lim, Chinese American poet: *Crossing*	Ronald Reagan is elected President. In this election, 5.5 million more women

TEXTS		CONTEXTS
1980	*the Peninsula and Other Poems.*	1980	vote than men; however, 8 to 10% fewer women than men vote for Reagan, resulting in the coinage of the term "gender gap."

TEXTS

1980   *the Peninsula and Other Poems.*

Ruth Limmer, working from journals, notebooks, stories, and letters, puts together *Journey around My Room: The Autobiography of Louise Bogan.*

Hazel Ai Chun Lin: *Weeping May Tarry, My Long Night With Cancer*, autobiography.

Audre Lorde: *The Cancer Journals*, about her experience with breast cancer. She dies of the disease in 1992.

Margarita Melville: *Twice a Minority: Mexican American Women.*

Bette Midler, comedienne, actress, and singer: *A View from a Broad*, a comic memoir.

Joyce Carol Oates: *Bellefleur*, a novel.

Jane O'Reilly, journalist and memoirist: *The Girl I Left Behind: The Housewife's Moment of Truth, and Other Feminist Ravings.*

Marge Piercy: *The Moon Is Always Female*, poetry.

CONTEXTS

1980   vote than men; however, 8 to 10% fewer women than men vote for Reagan, resulting in the coinage of the term "gender gap."

Nancy Reagan spends $46,000 on her inaugural wardrobe; the average family on welfare this year receives $4600.

TEXTS   CONTEXTS

1980   Patricia Preciado Martin,   1980
        Chicana folklorist and fic-
        tion writer: *The Legend of
        the Bellringer of San
        Agustín*, a bilingual chil-
        dren's story.

        Rina Rocha, Chicana
        poet: *Eluder*.

        Mary Lee Settle: *The
        Scapegoat*.

        Han Suyin: *My House
        Has Two Doors*, autobiog-
        raphy.

        Rowena Tiempo-
        Torrevillas, Filipina Amer-
        ican fiction writer: *"Upon
        the Willows" and Other
        Stories*.

        Eudora Welty: *The Col-
        lected Stories of Eudora
        Welty*.

        Merle Woo, Chinese
        American dramatist: *Bal-
        ancing*.

        Wakako Yamauchi: *The
        Music Lessons*, a play.

1980–1987   1980–1987   Sales of women's suits rise
                                                      by 6 million units; sales of
                                                      dresses decline by 29
                                                      million.

*   *   *

TEXTS	CONTEXTS
1981 Lisa Alther: *Original Sins,* a novel.	1981 Fifty-two hostages are released in Iran.
Doris Betts: *Heading West.*	Scientists identify Acquired Immune Deficiency Syndrome (AIDS); in this year, 225 people die of AIDS and the Gay Men's Health Crisis is formed in New York City.
Lorna Dee Cervantes, poet: *Emplumada: Poems.*	
C. J. Cherryh: *The Pride of Chanur*, a science-fiction novel.	
Diana Chow, Chinese American poet: *An Asian Man of a Different Color.*	Sandra Day O'Connor becomes the first female Supreme Court justice.
Janet Dailey: *Nightways* and *This Calder Sky*, romance novels.	Fourteen percent of all judges and lawyers are women.
Angela Davis, African American author, scholar, and activist: *Women, Race, and Class.*	A Human Life Amendment, declaring a fetus a person, is first introduced in Congress.
H.D. (Hilda Doolittle): *HERmione*, published posthumously.	Cosmetic surgery becomes the fastest growing medical specialty.
Andrea Dworkin: *Pornography: Men Possessing Women.*	Studies estimate up to three-quarters of all women suffer from Premenstrual Syndrome (PMS), an estimate that throws its definition as an "abnormal" hormonal cycle into question.
Mari Evans: *Nightstar,* poetry.	
Lillian Faderman: *Surpassing the Love of Men: Friendship and Love between Women from the Renaissance to the Present.*	The Congressional Caucus for Women's Issues introduces the Women's Economic Equity Act, a

TEXTS		CONTEXTS
1981	Caroline Gordon: *The Collected Stories*.	1981	comprehensive package of bills concerning issues such as child care, insurance, and pensions.

TEXTS

1981

Caroline Gordon: *The Collected Stories*.

Patricia Hampl: *A Romantic Education*, a memoir.

bell hooks: *Ain't I A Woman?*

Clara Mitsuko Jelsma, Japanese American autobiographer: *Teapot Tales*.

Akemi Kikumura, Japanese American autobiographer: *Through Harsh Winters: The Life of a Japanese Immigrant Woman*.

Alice Koller: *An Unknown Woman*, described by one reviewer as "a woman's Walden."

Elisabeth Kübler-Ross: *Living with Death and Dying*.

Helena Kuo: *Dong Kingman's Watercolors*.

Bette Bao Lord: *Spring Moon: A Novel of China*.

Beverly Lowry: *Daddy's Girl*.

Alison Lurie: *The Language of Clothes*.

CONTEXTS

1981

comprehensive package of bills concerning issues such as child care, insurance, and pensions.

A domestic violence bill passes in the House but is defeated in the Senate, largely due to a vigorous campaign by conservative Christian groups.

The Bureau of Labor Statistics reports that almost twice as many women who are heads of households are unemployed than are male heads of household (10.6 percent for women compared with 5.8 percent for men).

National Institute for Women of Color is founded.

Centennial anniversary of the American Association of University Women.

The West Coast Ecofeminist Conference is held in California.

The world watches as Lady Diana Spencer marries Prince Charles of England.

A *Cosmopolitan* survey finds 41 percent of women engage in extra-

TEXTS		CONTEXTS
1981	Ruthanne Lum McCunn: *Thousand Pieces of Gold*, a fictionalized biography of Lalu Nathoy (Polly Bemis), who was sold in 1872 on the block in San Francisco, but was at the end of her life a respected homesteader on the Salmon River in Idaho.	1981

marital affairs, up from 8 percent in 1948.

The Hearst Corporation purchases William Morrow & Co., adding it and its subsidiaries to Hearst's other imprints, including Avon and Arbor House.

Maria Martinez, Chicana poet: *Sterling Silver Roses.*

Lena Horne wins a Tony Award for her one-woman Broadway show, *Lena Horne: The Lady and Her Music.*

Joyce Maynard: *Baby Love*, a novel about the experiences of several teenage mothers.

The Marciano brothers introduce "Guess" jeans to American customers.

Mary Mebane, African American autobiographer: *Mary.*

Kitchen Table: Women of Color Press is established.

Toni Morrison: *Tar Baby*, a novel.

A cover story of an issue of the *New York Times Magazine* begins, "The women's movement is over. . . ."

Sylvia Plath: *The Collected Poems of Sylvia Plath*, published posthumously, winner of Pulitzer Prize for poetry in 1982.

Minnie Bruce Pratt, poet and critic: *The Sound of One Fork*, poetry.

Adrienne Rich: *A Wild Patience Has Taken Me This Far: Poems, 1978–1981.*

TEXTS	CONTEXTS
1981 Jane Rule: *Outlander*, collection of short stories with lesbian themes.	1981

Anne Sexton: *The Complete Poems*, posthumously published.

Marjorie Shostak, American anthropologist, interviews Nisa, a member of one of the few remaining pre-agricultural tribes, and together they produce *Nisa: The Life and Words of a !Kung Woman*.

Alix Kates Shulman: *On the Stroll*.

Leslie Marmon Silko: *Storyteller*, collection of stories, poems, and photographs. Silko receives a MacArthur Foundation award this same year.

Elizabeth Spencer: *The Collected Stories of Elizabeth Spencer*.

Danielle Steel, popular romance novelist: *Remembrance*.

Gina Valdez, Chicana novelist: *There Are No Madmen Here*.

Alice Walker: *You Can't Keep a Good Woman Down*, short stories.

	TEXTS		CONTEXTS
1981	Wendy Wasserstein: *Isn't It Romantic?*, a play.	1981	
1981–1989		1981–1989	Sexual harassment charges filed with the Equal Employment Opportunity Commission rise 70 percent.
1982	*All the Women Are White, All the Blacks Are Men, But Some of Us Are Brave*, Gloria T. Hull, Patricia Bell-Scott, and Barbara Smith, eds. *Breaking the Silences: 20th Century Poetry by Cuban Women*, Margaret Randall, ed. Two highly successful and continuing series of mystery novels featuring female detectives are launched: Sara Paretsky's *Indemnity Only*, with V. I. Warshawski, and Sue Grafton's *"A" Is for Alibi*, with Kinsey Millhone. Paula Gunn Allen, Laguna Pueblo novelist, poet, and critic: *Shadow Country*, a collection of verse. Marion Zimmer Bradley: *The Mists of Avalon*, best-selling rewriting of the Arthurian legend from the	1982	The Equal Rights Amendment is defeated when it fails to be ratified by the required 38 states; Phyllis Macalpin (Stewart) Schlafly, founder and chair of STOP ERA and the Eagle Forum, hosts an end-of-ERA party. The first state lesbian and gay rights bill is passed, in Wisconsin. The first national convention of the Older Women's League is held in Louisville, Kentucky. In Wisconsin, a judge hearing the case of a 24-year-old man who sexually assaulted a five-year-old declares the child the "aggressor" in the case and describes her as "an unusually sexually permissive young lady"; he is subsequently recalled from the bench. With 27 percent of all Filipina women holding col-

TEXTS	CONTEXTS
1982 perspective of the female characters.	1982 lege degrees, they are better educated than any other population group, male or female, in the country.

TEXTS

1982

perspective of the female characters.

Rita Mae Brown: *Southern Discomfort*, a novel.

Irma Cervantes, Chicana poet: *Sparks, Flames, and Cinders*.

Theresa Hak Kyung Cha, Korean American poet and short-story writer: *Dictee*, prose and poetry.

Diana Chang: *The Horizon Is Definitely Speaking*, poetry.

Annie Dillard: *Teaching a Stone to Talk: Expeditions and Encounters*, nature writing, and *Living by Fiction*, literary criticism.

Carolyn Forché: *The Country Between Us*, poetry written in reaction to Forché's experiences in El Salvador, it reignites debates over the "appropriateness" of political subjects for poetry.

Betty Friedan: *The Second Stage*.

Carol Gilligan: *In a Different Voice: Psychological Theory and Women's Development*.

CONTEXTS

1982

lege degrees, they are better educated than any other population group, male or female, in the country.

The Vietnam Veterans Memorial is dedicated. The V-shaped memorial, with walls of black granite inscribed with the names of U.S. men and women killed or missing in the Vietnam War, was designed by Maya Ying Lin, a Yale architecture student whose plan was chosen in a public competition.

Maggie Brewer becomes the first woman Marine general.

Barnard College hosts a conference that launches what come to be known as "the sex debates" about pornography, sexual politics, and pleasure.

"Victoria's Secret" becomes a national chain of lingerie stores.

Millions go on the "Beverly Hills Diet."

USA Today is founded.

TEXTS	CONTEXTS
1982	Judy Grahn: *The Queen of Wands*, poetry.	1982

Maureen Howard: *Grace Abounding*, a novel.

Jeanne Joe, Chinese American essayist: *Pieces of a Childhood*, about being raised by a single parent in Chicago's Chinatown.

Chungmi Kim, Korean American poet: *Chumgmi, Selected Poems*.

Judith Krantz: *Mistral's Daughter*, a novel

Carol Lem: *Don't Ask Why*.

Genny Lim, Chinese American dramatist: *Paper Angels*.

Susan Lloyd completes a revision of *Roget's Thesaurus* that results in a non-sexist edition.

Audre Lorde: *Zami: A New Spelling of My Name*, biomythography.

Mina Loy: *The Last Lunar Baedecker*, collection of poetry.

Alice McDermott: *A Bigamist's Daughter, a Novel*.

	TEXTS	CONTEXTS

1982	Laureen Mar, Chinese American poet: *Living Furniture*.	1982

Bobbie Ann Mason: *Shiloh and Other Stories*.

Gloria Naylor, African American novelist: *The Women of Brewster Place*, winner of American Book Award and National Book Award.

Naomi Shihab Nye, poet: *Hugging the Jukebox*, winner of the National Poetry Series Award.

Joyce Carol Oates: *A Bloodsmoor Romance*, a novel, and *Invisible Woman: New and Selected Poems*.

Alicia Ostriker: *A Woman under the Surface: Poems and Prose Poems*.

Marge Piercy: *Circles on the Water*, poetry.

Sylvia Plath: *The Journals of Sylvia Plath*, published posthumously.

Katherine Quintana Ranck, Chicana novelist: *Portrait of Dona Elena*.

Susan Sheehan: *Is There No Place on Earth for*

TEXTS	CONTEXTS

1982   *Me?*, winner of the Pulitzer Prize for general nonfiction in 1983.   1982

Kate Simon: *Bronx Primitive: Portraits in a Childhood*, autobiography.

Lee Smith: *Cakewalk*, a novel.

Cathy Song, Korean American poet: *Picture Bride*, which wins the Yale Series of Younger Poets competition.

Meredith Tax, Jewish American novelist: *Rivington Street*.

Sheila Ortiz Taylor, Chicana novelist: *Faultline*.

Anne Truitt, minimalist sculptor and memoirist: *Daybook: The Journal of an Artist*.

Anne Tyler, novelist and short-story writer: *Dinner at the Homesick Restaurant*.

Yoshiko Uchida, Japanese American autobiographer: *Desert Exile: The Uprooting of a Japanese American Family*.

Mona Van Duyn, poet: *Letters from a Father*.

	TEXTS		CONTEXTS
1982	Evangelina Vigil, Chicana poet: *Thirty an' Seen a Lot.*	1982	
	Alice Walker: *The Color Purple*, wins American Book Award and a Pulitzer Prize.		
	Alice Waters, chef and author: *The Chez Panisse Menu Cookbook*, an influential work based on her restaurant's emphasis on classical meals based on fresh, seasonal ingredients.		
	Sylvia Wilkinson: *Bone of My Bones.*		
1983	*Black Women Writers 1950–1980*, Mari Evans, ed.	1983	U.S. troops invade Grenada.
	Home Girls: A Black Feminist Anthology, Barbara Smith, ed.		Some 444 Women's Studies programs offer courses in colleges and universities nationwide.
	Shirley Abbott: *Womenfolks: Growing Up Down South.*		Hardcover books represent 46 percent of books sold, down from 54 percent five years earlier.
	Kathy Acker: *Great Expectations*, a novel.		
	Paula Gunn Allen: *The Woman Who Owned the Shadows*, a novel.		Minneapolis passes an anti-pornography ordinance but it is vetoed by the city's mayor; Indianapolis's anti-pornography ordinance, passed in 1984, is struck down in federal court.
	Lynne Alvarez, Chicana poet and playwright: *The*		

TEXTS		CONTEXTS	
1983	*Guitarron* and *Hidden Parts*, winner of Kesselring Award.	1983	Elizabeth Dole, the first female Secretary of Transportation, is sworn in by Sandra Day O'Connor, the first female Supreme Court Justice.
	Gloria Anzaldua and Cherríe Moraga, eds.: *This Bridge Called My Back: Writings by Radical Women of Color.*		Asian Immigrant Women Advocates is formed to fight for economic justice in Oakland, California.
	Mei-Mei Berssenbrugge: *The Heat Bird* and *Packrat Sieve.*		The first national meeting of incest survivors is hosted by VOICE, Inc., in Kansas City.
	Becky Birtha, African American lesbian short-story writer and poet: *For Nights like This One: Stories of Loving Women.*		A woman is gang-raped on a pool table in a bar in New Bedford, Massachusetts; her story and case against her rapists and those who cheered them on captures public attention and becomes the subject of the film *The Accused*, for which actress Jodie Foster wins an Oscar in the starring role in 1988.
	Elizabeth Bishop: *The Complete Poems, 1927–1979.*		
	Judy Blume: *Smart Women*, a novel		
	Erma Bombeck: *Motherhood: The Second Oldest Profession.*		
	Ignatia Broker, an Ojibway elder, storyteller, and educator: *Night Flying Woman: An Ojibwa Narrative*, a telling of the life of Ni-bo-wi-se-gwe, Broker's great-great-grandmother.		Sally Ride becomes the first American female astronaut in space.
			Twenty percent, or one in five, babies in the U.S. are delivered through Cesarean section, up 7 percent since 1977.

	TEXTS		CONTEXTS
1983	Amy Clampitt (1920–1995), whose poems have been appearing in *The New Yorker* since 1978, publishes her first collection: *The Kingfisher*. She describes her design as that of an "illuminated manuscript" with "verbal handwork."	1983	The Dalkon Shield, an intrauterine contraceptive device, proves unsafe in many cases, leading to its withdrawal from the market.
	Ann Cornelisen: *Any Four Women Could Rob the Bank of Italy*, a novel.		Popular singer Karen Carpenter dies from complications of her long struggle with anorexia.
	Janet Dailey: *Calder Born, Calder Bred*, popular romance novel.		Dr. Barbara McClintock, the geneticist who discovered "jumping genes," becomes the first woman to win an unshared Nobel Prize for medicine.
	Toi Derricotte: *Natural Birth*, poetry.		Singer and actress Madonna releases her first album, *Madonna*.
	Barbara Ehrenreich: *The Hearts of Men: The American Dream and the Flight from Commitment*.		Barbara Kruger, a feminist artist who often puts her photographs on billboards, forming subversive collages, opens her exhibit *We Won't Play Nature to Your Culture*.
	Patricia Enrado, Filipina fiction writer: *House of Images*.		
	Nikki Giovanni: *Those Who Ride the Night Winds*, poetry.		Performance artist Laurie Anderson opens her magnum opus, "United States, Parts I–V."
	Marita Golden, African American novelist: *Migrations of the Heart*, autobiography.		Audrey Flack, who has done expressionist self-portraits and now works with sculpture, produces many Photorealist can-

TEXTS	CONTEXTS
1983	1983

TEXTS

1983

Rosa Guy, African American novelist: *A Measure of Time*.

Joy Harjo: *She Had Some Horses*, poetry.

Momoko Iko: *The Gold Watch*.

Joyce Johnson: *Minor Characters*, an account of her affair with Jack Kerouac and experiences with the Beat Generation; winner of the National Book Critics' Circle Award for biography and autobiography.

Gayl Jones: *White Rat*, short stories.

Elaine H. Kim with Janice Otani: *With Silk Wings: Asian American Women at Work*, pictorial history.

Wendy Law-Yone, Burmese American novelist: *The Coffin Tree*.

Shirley MacLaine, actress, entertainer, and New Age explorer: *Out on a Limb*.

Paule Marshall: *Reena and Other Short Stories*, reissue of short fiction, critical es-

CONTEXTS

1983

vases, such as *Fruits of the Earth*, in this year.

Underwear manufacturer Jockey introduces its "Jockey for Her" line, featuring comfortable cotton undergarments.

TEXTS	CONTEXTS
1983 say, and a new novella, "Merle," and *Praisesong for the Widow*, a novel.	1983

Mary Mebane: *Mary Way-farer*, autobiographical novel.

Cherríe Moraga, Chicana short-story writer: *Loving in the War Years: Lo que nunca paso por sus labios.*

Marsha Norman: *'night Mother*, winner of the Pulitzer Prize for drama.

Estela Portillo Trambley: *Sor Juana and Other Plays.*

Patricia Preciado Martin: *Images and Conversations: Mexican-Americans Recall a Southwestern Past.*

Francine Prose: *Hungry Hearts*, a novel.

Ninotchka Rosca: *The Monsoon Collection*, stories.

Joanna Russ: *How to Suppress Women's Writing*, a humorous and insightful exploration of the social forces that led to the neglect and disparagement of women's writing.

TEXTS	CONTEXTS
1983 Susan Fromberg Schaeffer: *The Madness of a Seduced Woman*.	1983
Lee Smith: *Oral History*, a novel.	
Danielle Steel: *Changes* and *Crossings*, novels.	
Gloria Steinem: *Outrageous Acts and Everyday Rebellions*.	
Carmen Tafolla, Chicana poet: *Curandera*.	
Joyce Carol Thomas, educator and young-adult novelist: *Bright Shadow*.	
Bessie Toishigawa-Inouye, Japanese American dramatist: *Reunion*.	
Kitty Tsui, Chinese American poet: *The Words of a Woman Who Breathes Fire*.	
Alice Walker: *In Search of Our Mother's Gardens*, collection of essays.	
Eudora Welty: *One Writer's Beginnings*.	
1983–1987	1983–1987 This four-year period shows a 100 percent increase in the number of women entering domestic shelters.

*   *   *

TEXTS	CONTEXTS
1984	1984

TEXTS

1984   *Filipina I*, anthology of fiction and poetry by Filipina writers, Marra Lanot and Mila Garcia, eds., *Filipina II*, essays and journalism, published 1985.

The New Our Bodies, Ourselves.

That's What She Said, an anthology of poetry and fiction by Native American women, Rayna Green, ed.

Kathy Acker: *Blood and Guts in High School.*

Alice Adams: *Superior Women*, a novel.

Lynne Alvarez: *The Dreaming Man.*

Mary Catherine Bateson: *With a Daughter's Eye: A Memoir of Margaret Mead and Gregory Bateson.*

Barbara Brinson-Pineda: *Vocabulary of the Dead*, poetry.

Linda Brown, African American novelist: *Rainbow Roun' Mah Shoulder.*

Rosellen Brown: *Civil Wars.*

CONTEXTS

1984   The Family Violence Prevention and Services Act helps finance battered women shelters.

Some 53 percent of women polled believe there will be a woman President by the turn of the century; three years later, only 40 percent express this belief.

President Reagan institutes an international gag rule on family planning clinics abroad receiving U.S. funds.

Twenty-nine American abortion and family planning clinics undergo bombing and arson attacks.

The Supreme Court guts educational bias protection under Title IX.

The Supreme Court rules that the Jaycees cannot bar women from membership.

Two parts of the Economic Equity Act are passed; the first helps women collect on private pensions; the second enforces child support by allowing for interstate col-

TEXTS	CONTEXTS
1984	1984

TEXTS

1984

Rosemary Catacalos, Chicana poet: *Again for the First Time*.

Sandra Cisneros: *The House on Mango Street*, a lyrical novel that wins the Before Columbus Award.

J. California Cooper, African American short-story writer and novelist: *A Piece of Mine*, short stories.

Jane Cooper, poet: *Scaffolding: New and Selected Poems*.

Kiana Davenport: *Wild Spenders*, a novel.

Suzette Hayden Elgin, science-fiction writer and communications scholar: *Native Tongue*, a novel.

Louise Erdrich, Native American novelist and poet: *Love Medicine*, novel, and winner of the National Book Critics Circle Award, and *Jacklight*, poetry.

Sandra Maria Esteves, Puerto Rican poet: *Tropical Rains: A Bilingual Downpour*.

Linda Kalayaan Faigao, Filipina dramatist: *State without Grace*.

CONTEXTS

1984

lection and withholding of wages.

Astronaut Kathryn Sullivan walks in space, the first U.S. woman to do so.

The Reverend Jesse Jackson runs for President.

The Democratic Party names Congresswoman Geraldine Ferraro as its vice presidential nominee, making her the first woman to run as the vice presidential candidate for a major political party.

Ronald Reagan is re-elected President.

One-third of all law school graduates are women.

Seventy-five percent of American women aged 18 to 35 regard themselves as fat, while only 25 percent are actually overweight; the same year, a survey for *Glamour* magazine finds that more women would choose weight loss over success in work or in interpersonal relations as a potential source of happiness.

The first black Miss America, Vanessa Williams, relinquishes her ti-

TEXTS	CONTEXTS
1984 Ellen Gilchrist, novelist, short-story writer, poet: *The Annunciation*, a novel, and *Victory over Japan*, collection of short stories and winner of National Book Award.	**1984** tle after nude photographs taken when she was younger appear in *Penthouse* magazine.

Beatriz Gonzalez, Chicana poet: *The Chosen Few*.

Judy Grahn: *Another Mother Tongue: Gay Words, Gay Worlds*, essays.

Former news anchor Christine Craft wins a monetary award against a Kansas City television station for demoting her based on her looks and her failure to be "deferential" to men; even though two juries find in her favor, a judge later overturns their ruling.

Doris Kawano, Japanese American autobiographer: *Harue, Child of Hawaii*.

In the Los Angeles Olympics, Joan Benoit wins the first women's marathon.

Susan Kenney: *In Another Country*, a novel.

Some 1.6 million office visits are made to physicians for infertility services, up from 600,000 in 1968.

The Kensington Ladies' Erotica Society: *Ladies' Own Erotica*.

Carolyn Kizer: *Mermaids in the Basement: Poems for Woman* and *Yin: New Poems*. The latter wins the Pulitzer Prize for poetry in 1985.

Andrea Lee: *Sarah Phillips*, an autobiographical novel about her experiences growing up as an economically privileged African American girl.

	TEXTS		CONTEXTS
1984	Amy Ling, Chinese American poet: *Chinamerican Reflections: Poems and Paintings*.	1984	

Audre Lorde: *Sister Outsider*, essays.

Alison Lurie: *Foreign Affairs*, Pulitzer Prize-winning novel.

Jill McCorkle: *July 7th: A Novel*.

Pat Mora, Chicana poet: *Chants*.

Joyce Carol Oates: *Mysteries of Winterthurn*, a novel.

Sharon Olds, poet: *The Dead and the Living*.

Jayne Anne Phillips: *Machine Dreams*, a novel.

Janice Radway, feminist scholar: *Reading the Romance: Women, Patriarchy, and Popular Literature*, a study combining interviews, reader response criticism, sociological analysis, and feminist psychology to examine women's relationship to romance fiction.

Myrna Pena Reyes, Filipina poet: *The River Sing-*

TEXTS	CONTEXTS
1984 *ing Stone*, collection of poetry.	**1984**
Joanna Russ: *Extra(ordinary) People*, a science fiction novel.	
Sonia Sanchez: *Homegirls and Handgrenades*, winner of the American Book Award.	
Sarah Schulman, lesbian novelist and social critic: *The Sophie Horowitz Story*, a novel.	
Barbara Tuchman: *The March of Folly: From Troy to Vietnam*, history.	
Katherine Wei and Terry Quinn: *Second Daughter, Growing Up in China 1930–1949*, a memoir.	
Roberta Hill Whiteman, Native American woman of the Oneida tribe: *Star Quilt*.	
Nellie Wong: *The Death of a Long Steam Lady*, poetry.	
1985 Landmark studies and anthologies in the recovery of literature by women and the study of the role of gender and race in literature and literary history appear: Barbara Chris-	**1985** Fifteen thousand people die of AIDS. United Nations World Women's Conference is held in Nairobi.

TEXTS	CONTEXTS
1985 tian's *Black Feminist Criticism: Perspectives on Black Women Writers*, Lucy M. Freibert and Barbara A. White's *Hidden Hands: An Anthology of American Women Writers, 1790–1870*, Annette Kolodny's *The Land Before Her: Fantasy and Experience of the American Frontiers, 1630–1860*, Marjorie Pryse and Hortense J. Spillers's *Conjuring: Black Women, Fiction, and Literary Tradition*, and Jane Tompkins's *Sensational Designs: The Cultural Work of American Fiction, 1790–1860*, followed by Cathy N. Davidson's *Revolution and the Word: The Rise of the Novel in America* in 1986. *Lesbian Nuns: Breaking Silence*, Rosemary Curb and Nancy Manahan, eds. Gemma Bergonio, Filipina poet: *Mirror at Dawn and Other Poems*. Beth Brant, Native American fiction writer, poet, essayist, and activist: *Mohawk Trail*, a collection of prose and poetry. Olga Broumas and Jane Miller: *Black Holes, Black Stockings*, collaborative poetry.	1985 The median age of marriage for women is 23.2 years; for men, 25.5 years. EMILY's (Early Money Is Like Yeast) List, a pro-choice, pro-women's-rights Democratic group, begins its fund-raising for and sponsorship of Democratic women candidates. Montana becomes the first state to ban insurance rates based on marital status and sex. Tracy Thurman becomes the first woman to win a civil suit against her husband for battery. Portland, Oregon's, Penny Harrington becomes the first female chief of a major U.S. police department. The Meese Commission on pornography is established. The first meeting of the Indigenous Women's Network, a coalition for the rights of Native American women, is held in Washington state. Amy Eilberg is ordained as Conservative Judaism's first woman rabbi.

TEXTS	CONTEXTS

1985 Evelina Chao, Chinese American novelist: *Gates of Grace.*

Judy Chicago: *The Birth Project*, about her multimedia art exhibit.

Carolyn Chute: *The Beans of Egypt, Maine*, a novel.

Margarita Cota-Cardenas, Chicana novelist: *Puppet*, an experimental novel.

The Diary of Alice Dunbar-Nelson, Gloria T. Hull ed. and publisher.

Gretel Ehrlich, Wyoming novelist and essayist, writing about life in the West: *The Solace of Open Spaces.*

Sheila Finch, fantasist: *Infinity's Web.*

Elizabeth Frank: *Louise Bogan: A Portrait*, winner of Pulitzer Prize for biography in 1986.

Jeanne Wakatsuki Houston: *Beyond Manzanar: A View of Asian American Womanhood.*

Susan Howe: *My Emily Dickinson*, a work of creative scholarship.

1985 Gwendolyn Brooks becomes the first African American woman to serve as Poetry Consultant to the Library of Congress.

Lily Tomlin takes her one-woman comedy show with its strong social messages, *The Search for Signs of Intelligent Life in the Universe*, around the country. It is co-written by Tomlin and Jane Wagner.

Tania Aebi, 19, sets sail alone on a voyage around the world, which she completes in 1987, becoming the first American woman and the youngest person to sail around the world solo.

Libby Riddles becomes the first woman to win the Iditarod Trail Sled Dog Race, a 1135-mile race from Anchorage to Nome, Alaska.

Folk music becomes popular again with the advent of singers such as Suzanne Vega, who releases her first album this year.

The *Jane Fonda Workout Video* becomes the top-grossing video of all time. Fonda is voted "The Number One Heroine of Young Americans" in a U.S News Roper poll.

TEXTS	CONTEXTS
1985 Angela de Hoyos: *Woman, Woman.*	1985 Americans spend more than $5 billion on efforts to lose weight.

Josephine Humphreys, southern novelist: *Dreams of Sleep.*

Ada Louise Huxtable: *The Tall Building Artistically Reconsidered.*

June Jordan: *Living Room: New Poems, 1980–84.*

Jamaica Kincaid, Antiguan-born fiction writer: *Annie John.*

Ruthanne Lum McCunn: *Sole Survivor*, biography.

Shirley MacLaine: *Dancing in the Light.*

Diane Mei Lin Mark and Ginger Chih: *A Place Called Chinese America*, pictorial history.

Bobbie Ann Mason: *In Country*, a novel.

Pat Matsueda, Japanese American poet: *The Fishcatcher.*

Nicholasa Mohr: *Rituals of Survival: A Woman's Portfolio*, six vignettes about adult Puerto Rican women, each representing

TEXTS	CONTEXTS
1985 different lifestyles, ages, and circumstances.	1985

Mary Monroe, African American novelist: *The Upper Room*.

Bharati Mukherjee: *Darkness*, short stories.

Gloria Naylor: *Linden Hills*, a novel.

Grace Paley: *Later the Same Day*, collection of stories.

Linda Pastan: *A Fraction of Darkness*, poetry.

Cecile Pineda, Chicana novelist: *Face*.

Anne Rice: *The Vampire Lestat*, a novel.

May Sarton: *The Magnificent Spinster*.

Anne Sexton: *No Evil Star: Selected Essays, Interviews, and Prose*, Steven E. Colburn, ed., posthumously published.

Ntozake Shange: *Betsey Brown*, a novel.

Carroll Smith-Rosenberg, feminist social historian: *Disorderly Conduct: Visions of Gender in Victorian*

TEXTS	CONTEXTS
1985	1985

America, an influential
investigation into the
gendered nature of
intimate relationships
in 19th-century
America.

Danielle Steel: *Secrets*, a
novel.

Han Suyin: *The Enchant-
ress*, a novel.

Meredith Tax: *Union
Square*.

Luisah Teish, African
American author: *Jamba-
laya: The Natural Woman's
Book of Personal Charms
and Practical Rituals*, described as a collection of
ceremonies for the Afri-
can and African American
extended family.

Minh Duc Hoai Trinh,
Vietnamese American
novelist: *This Side, the
Other Side*.

Linda Ty-Casper:
Fortress in the Plaza and
Awaiting Trespass, no-
vellas.

Anne Tyler: *The Acciden-
tal Tourist*, a novel.

Luz Maria Umpierre: *En
el pais de la maravillas*

TEXTS	CONTEXTS
1985 and *Y otras desgracias/And Other Misfortunes.*	**1985**
Helena Maria Viramontes, Chicana short-story writer: *The Moths and Other Stories.*	
Anna Lee Walters, Native American author: *The Sun Is Not Merciful,* short stories.	
Yoko Kawashima Watkins, Japanese American novelist: *So Far from the Bamboo Grove.*	
mid-1980s	**mid-1980s** Poet Robert Bly conducts all-male workshops, launching the "Men's Movement."
1986 At a breakfast meeting at the Bouchercon Conference, an annual mystery writers' meeting, a group of women led by Sara Paretsky founds Sisters in Crime, an organization whose goal is to promote mysteries written by women.	**1986** In the Iran-Contra deal, arms are traded for hostages.
	U.S. planes bomb Libya.
Ai: *Sin: Poems.*	The Parental and Medical Leave Act is introduced in Congress.
Kathy Acker: *Don Quixote,* a novel.	Full-time working women make only about 64 cents to a man's dollar.
Paula Gunn Allen: *The Sacred Hoop: Recovering the*	Unanimous decision by the Supreme Court finds that sexual harassment is illegal job discrimination.

TEXTS		CONTEXTS
1986	*Feminine in American Indian Tradition.*	1986	Seventy-two percent of childhood sexual abuse is perpetrated by fathers and stepfathers.

1986

TEXTS

Feminine in American Indian Tradition.

Maya Angelou: *All God's Children Need Traveling Shoes*, autobiography.

Ann Beattie: *Where You'll Find Me*, short stories.

Rita Mae Brown: *High Hearts*, a novel.

Olivia Castellano: *Spaces That Time Missed*, poetry.

Ana Castillo: *The Mixquihuala Letters*, poetry.

Suzy McKee Charnas: *Dorothea Dreams*, science fiction/fantasy novel.

Denise Chavez, Chicana novelist: *The Last of the Menu Girls*, winner of the Puerto del Sol fiction award.

Nien Cheng: *Life and Death in Shanghai*, autobiography by Chinese American woman.

Alice Childress: *Like One of the Family: Conversations from a Domestic's Life.*

Cheryl Clarke: *Living as a Lesbian*, poetry.

1986

CONTEXTS

Seventy-two percent of childhood sexual abuse is perpetrated by fathers and stepfathers.

The space shuttle *Challenger* explodes, killing all seven crew members, including schoolteacher Christa McAuliffe and astronaut Judith Resnik.

Randall Terry forms "Operation Rescue," an anti-abortion movement determined to close family planning clinics nationwide.

Sears wins in a lawsuit charging the company with sex discrimination in hiring policies and practices.

In the much-publicized "Preppy Murder" case, Robert Chambers is accused of murdering Jennifer Levin.

Media and trend analyst Faith Popcorn coins the word "cocooning" to describe what she sees as an increasing American trend to stay home and "nest."

Women's AIDS Project, the first of its kind, is formed in Los Angeles.

TEXTS	CONTEXTS
1986 Rita Dove: *Thomas and Beulah*, Pulitzer Prize-winning volume of poetry.	**1986** A Gallup poll for *Newsweek* finds that a majority of women (56 percent) consider themselves feminists while 4 percent consider themselves "anti-feminists."
Louise Erdrich: *The Beet Queen*, a novel.	
Cynthia Felice: *Double Nocturne*, a science-fiction novel.	One hundred thousand women march for pro-choice in Washington, D.C.
Ellen Gilchrist: *Drunk with Love*, short stories.	Ann Bancroft becomes the first woman ever to walk to the North Pole.
Marianne Gingher: *Bobby Rex's Greatest Hits*.	
Tama Janowitz: *Slaves of New York*, short stories.	Canadian-born k.d. lang becomes country music's first openly lesbian hit singer.
Ronyoung Kim (1926–1987), Korean American novelist: *Clay Walls*.	
Audre Lorde: *Our Dead behind Us*, a collection of essays.	Dorothy I. Height, African American human rights activist, member of President's Commission on the "Status of Women," delegate for the United Nations Mid-Decade Conference on Women, and president of the National Council of Negro Women, organizes the Black Family Reunion Celebration to emphasize the strengths of African American families.
Nancy Mairs: *Plaintext: Deciphering a Woman's Life*.	
Carole Maso: *Ghost Dance*, a novel.	
Sue Miller, novelist and short-story writer: *The Good Mother*.	
Nicholasa Mohr: *Going Home*, a juvenile novel and sequel to *Felita*.	An estimated 5 to 10 percent of all adolescent girls and young women are anorexic; 90 to 95 percent

TEXTS	CONTEXTS
1986 Pat Mora, Chicana poet: *Borders*.	1986 of anorexics are young and female; a disproportionate number are white and upper- or middle-class; as many as 19 percent die from this disease.

TEXTS

1986   Pat Mora, Chicana poet: *Borders*.

Cherríe Moraga: *Giving Up the Ghost: Teatro in Two Acts*.

Aurora Levins Morales: *Getting Home Alive*, short stories, essays, prose poems, and poetry by Puerto Rican American author, in collaboration with her mother, Rosario Morales.

Tran Thi Nga and Wendy Larson: *Shallow Graves: Two Women and Vietnam*, poetry.

Joyce Carol Oates: *Marya, a Life*, a novel.

Francine Prose: *Bigfoot Dreams*, a novel.

Adrienne Rich: *Blood, Bread, and Poetry*, essays, and *Your Native Land, Your Life*, poetry.

Beverly Silva, Chicana short-story writer: *The Cat and Other Stories*.

Kate Simon: *A Wider World*, memoir.

Mona Simpson, novelist: *Anywhere but Here*.

CONTEXTS

1986   of anorexics are young and female; a disproportionate number are white and upper- or middle-class; as many as 19 percent die from this disease.

TEXTS	CONTEXTS
1986 Joan Slonczewski: *A Door into the Ocean*, a utopian novel.	**1986**
Estela Portillo Trambley: *Trini*, a novel.	
Sherley Ann Williams, African American novelist: *Dessa Rose*.	

1987 *Rivers Running Free*, Judith Niemi, ed., is an anthology of canoeing women.	**1987** Women make up 15.2 percent of physicians in the U.S.
Gloria Anzaldúa: *Borderlands/La Frontera: The New Mestiza*.	Forty-thousand people die of AIDS.
Doris Jean Austin, African American novelist: *After the Garden*.	The National March on Washington for Lesbian and Gay Rights draws some 500,000 people.
Marita Bonner (1899–1971), African American author: *Frye Street and Its Environs: Collected Works of Marita Bonner*, reprinted posthumously.	Of women surveyed, 87 percent say there is nothing wrong with a single woman bearing and raising a child by herself.
Octavia Butler begins her *Xenogenesis* series.	Women own 30 percent of all U.S. businesses.
Xam Wilson Cartier, African American novelist: *Be-bop, Re-bop*.	No abortion services are offered by 85 percent of U.S. counties.
Marilyn Chin, Chinese American poet: *Dwarf Bamboo*.	The National Clearinghouse for the Defense of Battered Women is founded and based in Philadelphia.

TEXTS		CONTEXTS	
1987	Sandra Cisneros: *My Wicked Wicked Ways*, poetry.	1987	The Fund for the Feminist Majority is founded.
	Michelle Cliff: *No Telephone to Heaven*, a novel.		Elizabeth Morgan chooses jail in lieu of letting her daughter spend time alone with her ex-husband, whom Morgan accuses of molesting the girl; she is released two years later through a congressional act and wins custody of her child.
	Lucille Clifton: *Good Woman: Poems and a Memoir: 1969–1980.*		
	J. California Cooper: *Some Soul to Keep*, short stories.		
	Janet Dailey: *Heiress*, romance novel		The Supreme Court denies that men are discriminated against through disability leaves for pregnancy and childbirth.
	Annie Dillard: *An American Childhood*, a memoir.		Confirmation of conservative judge Robert H. Bork's appointment to the Supreme Court is denied.
	Carrie Fisher, actress and novelist: *Postcards from the Edge*, later filmed.		
	Fannie Flagg: *Fried Green Tomatoes at the Whistle Stop Cafe*, filmed in 1992.		English Professor Julia Prewitt Brown wins a nine-year job-bias case against Boston University and becomes the first woman professor reinstated with tenure after losing her tenure decision.
	Kaye Gibbons: *Ellen Foster*, a novel.		
	Gail Godwin: *A Southern Family*, a novel.		
	Vivian Gornick: *Fierce Attachments*, a memoir.		Beulah Mae Donald wins her suit against the United Klans of America for the lynching of her son. Her award of $7 million shuts down that unit of the KKK.
	Judy Grahn: *The Queen of Swords*, poetry.		

TEXTS	CONTEXTS
1987 Molly Hite, feminist literary critic and novelist: *Class Porn*, a novel.	1987 The Supreme Court requires Rotary International to admit women members.

1987   Molly Hite, feminist literary critic and novelist: *Class Porn*, a novel.

Josephine Humphreys: *Rich in Love*, a novel.

Diane Johnson: *Persian Nights*, a novel.

Susanna Kaysen, novelist and memoirist: *Asa, As I Knew Him*, a novel.

Denise Levertov: *Breathing the Water*, poetry.

Beverly Lowry: *The Perfect Sonya*.

Jill McCorkle: *Tending to Virginia*, a novel.

Colleen McElroy: *Jesus and Fat Tuesday, and Other Short Stories*.

Shirley MacLaine: *It's All in the Playing*.

Terry McMillan, African American novelist: *Mama*, a novel.

Sue Miller: *Inventing the Abbotts and Other Stories*.

Toni Morrison: *Beloved*, wins Pulitzer Prize and Robert F. Kennedy Book Award.

1987   The Supreme Court requires Rotary International to admit women members.

Fawn Hall, Pentagon secretary, testifies before Congress about Oliver North's shredding of "Contragate" documents.

Congresswoman Patricia Schroeder announces that a shortage of funds will prevent her from seeking the Democratic presidential nomination in 1988.

Jill Wine-Banks becomes the first female executive director of the American Bar Association.

Wilma Mankiller becomes the first woman elected chief of the Cherokee Nation of Oklahoma.

Verna Williamson becomes the first woman governor of the largest pueblo (Isleta) in New Mexico.

After her own son is murdered, Clementine Barfield of Detroit founds So-Sad, an organization helping families of children killed in urban violence.

TEXTS	CONTEXTS
1987 Faye Moskowitz, Jewish American author: *A Leak in the Heart.*	1987 Louise Chia Chang and Elizabeth Lee Wilmer, high school students, place first and second, respectively, in the prestigious Westinghouse Science Talent Search.
Bharati Mukherjee: *The Sorrow and the Terror: The Haunting Legacy of Air India 182.*	Hearing-impaired actress Marlee Matlin wins an Academy Award for Best Actress for *Children of a Lesser God.*
Eleanor Munro: *On Glory Roads: A Pilgrim's Book about Pilgrimage.*	
Joyce Carol Oates: *You Must Remember This*, a novel.	The popular television show *Cagney and Lacey* is canceled; it had been widely credited for being one of the few shows to portray women's lives realistically and sympathetically.
Sharon Olds: *The Matter of This World: New and Selected Poems.*	
Cynthia Ozick: *The Messiah of Stockholm*, a novel.	
Marge Piercy: *Gone to Soldiers*, a novel.	The film *Fatal Attraction* opens and the Glenn Close character soon becomes "the most hated woman in America."
Mary Helen Ponce, Chicana novelist and short-story writer: *Taking Control*, stories.	The National Museum of Women in the Arts opens.
Juanita Ramos: *Companeros: Latina Lesbians.*	
Joanna Russ: *The Hidden Side of the Moon*, short stories.	
Jessica Saiki, Japanese American novelist: *"Once, a Lotus Garden," and Other Stories.*	

TEXTS   CONTEXTS
──────────   ──────────

1987   Sonia Sanchez: *Under a So-*   1987
        prano Sky, poetry.

        Melissa Scott, science-
        fiction writer: *The Kindly*
        Ones, a novel in which the
        gender of the first-person
        narrator is never iden-
        tified.

        Alix Kates Shulman: *In Ev-*
        ery Woman's Life . . . A
        Time Must Come to
        Think About Marriage, a
        novel.

        Eileen Simpson: *Orphans,*
        Real and Imaginary, a
        memoir of life with her
        first husband, John Ber-
        ryman, and his circle of
        fellow writers, including
        Randall Jarrell, Delmore
        Schwartz, Robert Lowell,
        Jean Stafford, Allen
        Tate, and Caroline
        Gordon.

        Rosamond Smith, a
        pseudonym for Joyce
        Carol Oates: *Lives of the*
        Twins, a suspense
        novel.

        Ruth Stone: *Second-Hand*
        Coat, poetry.

        Yoshiko Uchida: *Picture*
        Bride: A Novel.

        Evangelina Vigil: *The*
        Computer Is Down,
        poetry.

TEXTS	CONTEXTS
1987 Marta Weigle edits *Two Guadalupes: Hispanic Legends and Magic Tales from Northern New Mexico.*	1987

TEXTS	CONTEXTS
1988 The publication of the Schomburg Library of Nineteenth-Century Black Women Writers, under the general editorship of Henry Louis Gates, Jr., makes accessible thirty volumes of writing by nineteenth-century black women, much of it long unavailable. *Las Mujeres Hablan: An Anthology of Nuevo Mexicana Writers*, Diana Tey-Rebolledo, Erlinda Gonzales-Berry, and Teresa Marquez, eds. *Without Ceremony*, special issue of *Ikon 9*, edited by Asian Women United of New York. *You Can't Drown the Fire: Latin American Women Writing in Exile*, Alicia Partnoy, ed. Kathy Acker: *Empire of the Senseless*, a novel. Paula Gunn Allen: *Skins and Bones: Poems 1979–87.* Rita Mae Brown: *Bingo*, a novel.	1988 Ninety percent of federal AFDC recipients are women; 66 percent of those dependent on federally subsidized housing and legal services are women; 60 percent of those drawing on Medicaid and receiving food stamps are women. Congress passes the Civil Rights Restoration Act, restoring many of the rights (including protection against educational bias) stripped away by the Supreme Court in recent years. The Family Support Act passed by Congress puts steps in place for automatic withholding from the parent's paycheck in child support cases. More first children are born than in any other year on record. A study calculates that on any given night in the U.S., there are about 735,000 people homeless.

TEXTS	CONTEXTS
1988 Carolyn Chute: *Letourneau's Used Auto Parts*, a novel.	1988 Thirty-five states pass parental consent requirements for abortion; 30 states and Washington, D.C., ban state Medicaid-funded abortions.

TEXTS

1988   Carolyn Chute: *Letourneau's Used Auto Parts*, a novel.

Mary Higgins Clark: *Weep No More, My Lady*, a suspense novel.

Ella Deloria: *Waterlily*, a novel written in the 1940s but published posthumously. Put together from ethnographic materials and interviews, it depicts a Sioux woman's life in the nineteenth century.

Beverly Donofrio: *Riding in Cars with Boys: Confessions of a Bad Girl Who Makes Good*, memoirs of a teenage mother.

Grace Edwards-Yearwood, African American novelist: *In the Shadow of the Peacock*.

Gretel Ehrlich: *Heart Mountain*, a novel.

Phyllis Eisenstein: *The Crystal Palace*.

Louise Erdrich: *Tracks*, a novel.

Martha Gellhorn: *The Face of War*, a collection of journalistic essays.

CONTEXTS

1988   Thirty-five states pass parental consent requirements for abortion; 30 states and Washington, D.C., ban state Medicaid-funded abortions.

The "Baby M" case: the Supreme Court rules that surrogate contracts, like the one between William and Elizabeth Stern and surrogate mother Mary Beth Whitehead (artificially inseminated with Stern's sperm), cannot be enforced and custody goes to the sperm donor (the father) instead of the egg donor (the surrogate mother).

Grieving mother Cynthia Harris forms Stop! the Madness Foundation in Washington, D.C., to fight drug-related crimes there.

More than 2 million women have had breast implants; 100,000 have had liposuction.

Jane Rideout, chemist, leads a team of researchers to win the patent for AZT, an AIDS drug.

Lansing, Michigan's, Playboy Club, the last in the nation, closes.

TEXTS	CONTEXTS
1988	**1988**
Nikki Giovanni: *Sacred Cows and Other Edibles*.	The *Columbia Literary History of the United States* is published.
Judy Grahn: *Mundane's World*, a novel.	Only 43 communities produce competing daily newspapers, down from some 500 sixty-five years before.
Alice Hoffman: *At Risk*, a novel about AIDS.	
Velina Hasu Houston: *My Life a Loaded Gun*, a play.	*Sassy* magazine, modeled upon the Australian teen magazine *Dolly*, appears on the newsstands, providing girls with explicit information on sexuality; *Sassy*'s frankness is eventually watered down after conservative groups pressure its advertisers.
Janet Kagan, science-fiction writer: *Hellspark*.	
Barbara Kingsolver: *The Bean Trees*, a novel.	
Alice P. Lin, Chinese American memoirist: *Grandmother Had No Name*.	Florence Griffith Joyner and Jackie Joyner-Kersee, sisters-in-law, win five gold medals between them at the Olympics.
Ruthanne Lum McCunn: *Chinese American Portraits: Personal Histories 1828– 1988*.	
	Soviet troops begin withdrawal from Afghanistan.
Bobbie Ann Mason: *Spence + Lila*, a novel.	New Alliance Party candidate Lenora Fulani becomes the first woman and first black whose name appears on all 50 states' ballots as a presidential candidate.
Eleanor Munro: *Memoir of a Modernist's Daughter*.	
Gloria Naylor: *Mama Day*, a novel.	
Marge Piercy: *Available Light*, poetry.	Only two women run for Senate, the smallest number in a decade and down from ten in 1984.

TEXTS		CONTEXTS	
1988	Patricia Preciado Martin: *Days of Plenty, Days of Want*, stories.	1988	Gertrude Elion, research scientist and the first woman elected to the National Inventors Hall of Fame, receives the Nobel Prize in Medicine along with her longtime research partner, George Hitchings.
	Anne Rice: *The Queen of the Damned*, third in the Vampire Chronicles.		
	Jane Smiley, novelist, essayist, and short-story writer: *The Greenlanders*, a historical saga.		Women cast 10 million more ballots than men in the presidential election; George Bush wins.
	Lee Smith: *Fair and Tender Ladies*, a novel.		
	Sherri S. Tepper, science-fiction and fantasy writer: *The Gate to Women's Country*.		
	Anne Tyler: *Breathing Lessons*, Pulitzer Prize-winning novel.		
	Diana Velez: *Reclaiming Medusa: Short Stories by Contemporary Puerto Rican Women*.		
	Alma Luz Villanueva: *The Ultraviolet Sky*.		
	Diane Wakoski: *Emerald Ice: Selected Poems 1962–87*.		
	Wendy Wasserstein: *The Heidi Chronicles*, first female author to win a Tony Award for Best		

	TEXTS		CONTEXTS
1988	Play, she also receives a Pulitzer Prize for drama.	1988	
	Phyllis A. Whitney, author of many gothic and romantic suspense novels, is named a Grand Master by the Mystery Writers of America.		
	Mitsuye Yamada: *Desert Run: Poems and Stories*.		
	Hisaye Yamamoto: *Seventeen Syllables and Other Stories*.		
	Wakako Yamauchi: *The Trip*, a play.		
1989	Paula Gunn Allen: *Spider Woman's Granddaughters: Traditional Tales and Contemporary Writing by Native American Women*.	1989	The Berlin Wall begins to come down.
			Fourteen women university students are killed at the University of Montreal by a man shouting "You're all f---ing feminists!"
	Dorothy Allison: *Trash*, stories.		
	Mary Catherine Bateson: *Composing a Life*, biography.		A pro-choice march in Washington, D.C., draws some 300,000 to 500,000 people.
	Bebe Moore Campbell: *Sweet Summer: Growing Up with and without My Dad*, a memoir.		Only one-third of women consider themselves feminists.
	Jill Churchill: *Crime and Punishment*, winner of an Agatha Award.		*Webster v. Reproductive Health Services* returns to states the authority to

TEXTS		CONTEXTS	
1989	Cheryl Clarke: *Humid Pitch: Narrative Poetry*.	1989	limit a woman's right to a legal abortion.
	Jill Ker Conway, Australian-born emigrée to the U.S., historian and memoirist: *The Road from Coorain*, describing her childhood in the Australian outback.		A *New York Times* poll of women finds job discrimination "the most important problem facing women today."
	J. California Cooper: *Homemade Love*, winner of the American Book Award.		A Gallup poll finds that 55 percent of women versus 31 percent of men say that they are the ones who wanted a divorce; 20 percent say both wanted it.
	Lucha Corpi: *Delia's Song*, a novel.		*Stowe v. Davis* rules that life begins at conception and awards frozen embryos of a divorcing couple to the wife, Mary Sue
	Annie Dillard: *The Writing Life*, memoir.		Stowe; an appeals court reverses this decision and awards joint custody.
	Rita Dove: *The Yellow House on the Corner*, poetry.		
	Katherine Dunn: *Geek Love*, a novel.		A Florida woman addicted to cocaine, though she had sought (and been denied) treatment for her addiction, is found guilty of "transmitting prohibited drugs to a minor"—her fetus.
	Alicia Gaspar de Alba, Chicana poet and short-story writer: *Beggar on the Cordoba Bridge*, poetry.		
	Kaye Gibbons: *A Virtuous Woman*, a novel.		African American Barbara Harris becomes the first woman bishop of the U.S. Episcopal Church.
	Ellen Gilchrist: *Light Can Be Both Wave and Particle*, stories, and *The Anna Papers*, a novel.		That a "Yuppie" female jogger is raped and beaten

TEXTS		CONTEXTS	
1989	Kimiko Hahn, Japanese American poet: *Air Pocket*.	1989	in Central Park by a group of "wilding" black youths becomes a major national news story.
	Irene Beltran Hernandez, Chicana novelist: *Across the Great River*.		Total daily circulation of the country's 1687 newspapers is 63,263,000.
	Joyce Johnson: *In the Night Café*, a novel.		Deborah Norville replaces Jane Pauley as co-host of the "Today Show."
	Cynthia Kadohata, Japanese American novelist: *The Floating World*.		Only eight out of 100 of the most frequently seen television correspondents are women, down from
	Barbara Kingsolver: *Holding the Line: Women in the Great Arizona Mine Strike of 1983*.		15 the previous year.
	Maxine Hong Kingston: *The Tripmaster Monkey*, a novel.		Jazz pianist and saxophonist Billy Tipton dies at 75, leaving behind a wife and three adopted sons. It was only at "his" death that it was revealed that "Billy" was actually a "she."
	Natalie Kusz: *Road Song*, memoir.		
	Onnie Lee Logan with Katherine Clark: *Motherwit: An Alabama Midwife's Story*, a memoir of Logan's experiences as a domestic servant and midwife in Alabama from 1931 to 1984.		A congressional committee reports only a 9 percent "take-home baby" success rate for *in vitro* fertilization clinics.
			The Food and Drug Administration bans importation of RU 486 — "the abortion pill" — for private use.
	Shirley Lim: *Modern Secrets*, poetry.		
	Terry McMillan: *Disappearing Acts*, a novel.		U.S. troops invade Panama.

TEXTS	CONTEXTS
1989 Nancy Mairs: *Remembering the Bone House: An Erotics of Place and Space*, essays.	1989 Whoopi Goldberg becomes the second African American woman to win an Oscar when she wins as Best Supporting Actress for *Ghost*.

TEXTS

Nancy Mairs: *Remembering the Bone House: An Erotics of Place and Space*, essays.

Making Waves, an Anthology of Writings by and About Asian American Women, edited by Asian Women United of California.

Susan Minot, novelist and short-story writer: *Lust and Other Stories*.

Bharati Mukherjee: *Jasmine*, a novel.

Judith Ortiz Cofer, Puerto Rican-born poet, novelist, and memoirist: *The Line of the Sun*, a novel.

Marge Piercy: *Summer People*, a novel.

Mary Helen Ponce: *The Wedding*, a novel.

Gilda Radner (1946–1989), comedienne and autobiographer: *It's Always Something*, about her battle with cancer.

Susan Fromberg Schaeffer: *Buffalo Afternoon*, a novel.

CONTEXTS

Whoopi Goldberg becomes the second African American woman to win an Oscar when she wins as Best Supporting Actress for *Ghost*.

Singer Tina Turner receives three Grammy awards for her album *Private Dancer*.

TEXTS		CONTEXTS
1989	Sarah Schulman: *After Delores*, a novel.	1989
	Mary Lee Settle: *Charley Bland*, a novel.	
	Lee Smith: *Me and My Baby View the Eclipse*, short stories.	
	Susan Sontag: *AIDS and Its Metaphors*.	
	LaVyrle Spencer, popular romance novelist: *The Fulfillment* and *Morning Glory*.	
	Suleri, Indian American novelist: *Meatless Days*, a novel.	
	Amy Tan, Chinese American novelist: *The Joy Luck Club*, a novel.	
	Paula Vogel: *And Baby Makes Seven*, a play about lesbian parenting.	
	Alice Walker: *The Temple of My Familiar*, a novel.	
	Celeste West: *The Lesbian Love Advisor*.	
1990s		1990s	An estimated one out of two marriages end in divorce; studies show that women's standard of living declines 73 percent and men's rises 42 per-

TEXTS	CONTEXTS
1990s	**1990s** cent on average after divorce.
	Twenty-one percent of women report physical abuse by male partners; over 3 million women are assaulted by a partner every year.
	Estimates suggest as many as one in three women are raped.
	The cosmetic industry does $17.5 billion worth of business in the U.S. annually.
1990 Susie Bright: *Susie Sexpert's Lesbian Sex World*.	**1990** African American dancer and choreographer Judith Jamison becomes director of the Alvin Ailey Dance Company.
Rita Mae Brown, popular novelist, with *Wish You Were Here* begins a series of mysteries co-written with her cat, Sneaky Pie Brown.	Women direct 20 out of 406 feature films; between the years 1940 and 1980, women directed only 14 feature films total.
Elena Castedo, Spanish-born novelist: *Paradise*.	Dr. Antonia Coella Novello becomes the first woman and first Hispanic in the position of Surgeon General of the U.S.
Amy Clampitt, poet: *Westward*.	
Michelle Cliff: *Bodies of Water*.	Outspoken Democrat Ann Richards wins election as governor of Texas.
Wanda Coleman: *African Sleeping Sickness: Stories and Poems*.	

TEXTS	CONTEXTS
1990	1990

Patricia Cornwell introduces her Dr. Kay Scarpetta, M.E., mystery series with *Postmortem*. Praised for the attention to details of forensic evidence (Cornwell worked for several years as a computer analyst in the office of the chief medical examiner of Virginia), *Postmortem* wins several awards for best first novel of the year, including the Edgar, the Macavity, the Creasey, and the Anthony.

Lucha Corpi: *Variaciones sobre una tempestad/ Variations on the Storm*, poetry.

Mary Crow Dog: *Lakota Woman*, autobiography.

Carol Emshwiller, science-fiction writer: *Carmen Dog*.

Louise Glück: *Ararat*, poetry.

Marilyn Hacker: *Going Back to the River*, a collection of poetry.

Jessica Hagedorn: *The Dog Eaters*, a novel.

Joy Harjo: *In Mad Love and War*, poetry.

Sharon Pratt Dixon becomes the first black woman to be elected mayor of a major U.S. city (Washington, D.C.).

Women hold 25 seats (4.7 percent) in the U.S Congress; 23 are in the House of Representatives and 2 in the Senate.

Only 18 percent of the 13 million government-handled child support payments are collected.

The Act for Better Child Care (ABC) becomes law, enacting comprehensive child care legislation.

Twenty-six women imprisoned for killing or assaulting their batterers are pardoned by Governor Richard Celeste in Ohio.

Surrogate mother Anna Johnson loses her court plea for custody of the child she carried for Mark (who donated the sperm) and Christina Calvert (who donated the egg). The court's decision affirms genetics as the main criterion for parenthood.

With the appointment of Justice Sandra

TEXTS	CONTEXTS
1990 *A Brighter Coming Day: A Frances Ellen Watkins Harper Reader*, Frances Smith Foster, ed.	1990 Gardebring, the Minnesota Supreme Court becomes the first to seat a majority of women.
Alice Hoffman: *Seventh Heaven*, a novel.	In Houston, Mayor Kathy Whitmire appoints Elizabeth M. Watson chief of police. She is the first to so serve in one of the nation's 20 largest cities.
Linda Hogan, Chickasaw author: *Mean Spirit*, a novel about the displacement of the Osage people when oil was discovered on their lands in the 1920s.	
	Lorna Simpson, known for works that juxtapose photographs and text, becomes the first African American woman granted a solo exhibition at the Museum of Modern Art.
Jamaica Kincaid: *Lucy*, a novel.	
Barbara Kingsolver: *Animal Dreams*, a novel.	A record 3.1 million women hold two jobs at once.
Alice Koller: *The Stations of Solitude*, philosophical memoir.	After ceasing circulation for over a year, *Ms.* magazine is reissued with no advertisements.
Ursula K. Le Guin: *Tehanu*, which revisits the world created in her earlier Earthsea creations.	
Nancy Mairs: *Carnal Acts*, personal essays.	A bomb planted under Earth First! activist Judi Barri's car explodes, crippling her and injuring her passenger and fellow activist, Darryl Cherney.
Lee Maracle, Native American (Métis people) author, poet, scholar, and activist: *Bobbie Lee: Indian Rebel*.	The U.S. Post Office issues a stamp commemorating poet Marianne Moore.
Colleen McElroy: *What Madness Brought Me Here:*	

TEXTS	CONTEXTS
1990	1990

New and Selected Poems, 1968–1988.

Tina McElroy Ansa, African American novelist: *Baby of the Family.*

Sue Miller: *Family Pictures*, a novel.

Kate Millett: *The Loony-Bin Trip*, autobiography.

Joyce Carol Oates: *Because It Is Bitter and Because It Is My Heart* and *I Lock My Door upon Myself*, novels.

Judith Ortiz Cofer: *Silent Dancing: A Partial Remembrance of a Puerto Rican Childhood*, personal essays.

Minnie Bruce Pratt: *Crime against Nature*, a poetry cycle about losing custody of her child after coming out as a lesbian.

Anne Rice: *The Witching Hour*, the first in the Mayfair Witches series.

Dori Sanders, African American novelist: *Clover: A Novel.*

Kate Simon: *Etchings in an Hourglass*, memoir.

TEXTS	CONTEXTS
1990 Linda Ching Sledge, Chinese American novelist: *Empire of Heaven*. Laurel Thatcher Ulrich: *A Midwife's Tale: The Life of Martha Ballard, Based on Her Diary, 1785–1812*, winner of the Pultizer Prize for history. Mona Van Duyn: *Near Changes*, Pulitzer Prize-winning volume of poetry. Michele Wallace: *Invisibility Blues*.	1990
1990–1991	1990–1991 Communist governments collapse throughout Eastern Europe and Russia.
1991 Ai: *Fate*, poetry. Meena Alexander: *Nampally Road*, a novel. Julia Alvarez: *How the Garcia Girls Lost Their Accents*, a novel. Gloria Anzaldúa: *Making Faces, Making Soul/Haciendo caras: Creative and Critical Perspectives by Feminists of Color*. Kay Boyle: *The Collected Poems*.	1991 Women earn 70 cents for every dollar a man makes; 1.5 times more women begin businesses than men. Some 41.7 percent of the adult population is single. Although 80 to 85 percent of custodial parents are mothers, when fathers fight for custody they win 70 percent of the time. The first class-action sexual harassment suit is filed before a Minnesota court on behalf of a group of

TEXTS		CONTEXTS

1991   Lorene Cary: *Black Ice*, a memoir.

Lorna Dee Cervantes: *From the Cables of Genocide: Poems on Love and Hunger.*

Sandra Cisneros: *Woman Hollering Creek and Other Stories.*

Lucille Clifton: *Quilting: Poems 1987–1990.*

Elizabeth Cox, southern novelist: *The Ragged Way People Fall Out of Love.*

Lillian Faderman: *Odd Girls and Twilight Lovers: A History of Lesbian Life in Twentieth-Century America.*

Susan Faludi: *Backlash: The Undeclared War against American Women.*

Zelda Fitzgerald (1899–1948): *The Collected Writings of Zelda Fitzgerald*, published posthumously.

Mary Gaitskill: *Two Girls, Fat and Thin*, a novel.

Gail Godwin: *Father Melancholy's Daughter*, a novel.

1991   female miners at the Eveleth Taconite Company.

Clarence Thomas is appointed to the Supreme Court despite allegations of sexual harassment by law professor and former EEOC colleague Anita Hill.

The Supreme Court rules in Rust v. Sullivan that the government can prevent federally funded clinics from even mentioning abortion when counseling pregnant women; the decision is soon referred to as "the gag rule."

Norplant, a contraceptive device consisting of rods implanted under the skin for up to 3 to 5 years, is approved for use in the U.S.

Bernadette Healy becomes the first woman director of the National Institutes of Health. She promises to end the "Ice Age" of medical response to women's health needs and launches the Women's Health Initiative, a 15-year, $600 million study, emphasizing research on osteoporosis, cancer, and heart disease.

TEXTS	CONTEXTS
1991 Jewelle Gomez: *The Gilda Stories*, a lesbian vampire tale.	1991 In *International Union v. Johnson Controls*, the Supreme Court decision finds a fetal-protection plan at the Johnson Controls plant violates the 1978 Pregnancy Discrimination Act; the victory is double-edged since it allows fertile women to work in the plant's high-risk, high-paying jobs.
Jorie Graham: *Region of Unlikeness*, poetry.	
Katharine Hepburn, actress, feminist: *Me: Stories of My Life*.	
Molly Ivins, political satirist: *Molly Ivins Can't Say That, Can She?*, best-selling humor.	A California judge sentences a woman convicted of child abuse to have contraceptive rods—Norplant—inserted.
Gish Jen, Chinese American novelist: *Typical American.*	
Gloria Kaufman edits *In Stitches: A Patchwork of Feminist Humor and Satire.*	A judge rules that the Virginia Military Institute can remain an all-male institution, claiming that all-male schools insure educational diversity and citing the importance of bonding rituals.
Paule Marshall: *Daughters*, a novel.	
Linda Pastan: *Heroes in Disguise*, poetry.	
Marge Piercy: *He, She, and It*, a novel.	Women receive almost as many law degrees as do men; however, women lawyers earn only 75 cents for every dollar made by their male counterparts, down from 89 cents for every dollar in 1983.
Letty Cottin Pogrebin, Jewish American autobiographer, feminist, and long-time contributor to *Ms.*: *Deborah, Golda, and Me.*	
Yvonne Sapia, Puerto Rican fiction writer: *Valentino's Hair.*	The National Women of Color Association is formed.

TEXTS	CONTEXTS
1991	1991

Gail Sheehy: *The Silent Passage: Menopause.*

Bapsi Sidwa, South Asian American writer: *Cracking India.*

Leslie Marmon Silko: *The Almanac of the Dead*, a novel.

Jane Smiley: *A Thousand Acres*, winner of the Pulitzer Prize for fiction and the National Book Critics' Circle Award.

May Swenson: *The Love Poems of May Swenson*, published posthumously.

Amy Tan: *The Kitchen God's Wife*, a novel.

Anne Tyler: *Saint Maybe*, a novel.

Patricia J. Williams: *The Alchemy of Race and Rights: Diary of a Law Professor.*

Naomi Wolf: *The Beauty Myth: How Images of Beauty Are Used Against Women.*

Eleven percent of all university presidents are women.

Three of the 1000 Chief Executive Officers of Fortune 1000 companies are women.

A *Ms.* magazine survey finds that 73 percent of women limit the places they go alone due to fear of attack.

World Women's Conference for a Healthy Planet is held in Miami.

Pearl E. Primus, dancer, choreographer, anthropologist, and authority on African dance, is awarded the National Medal of Arts, the highest honor given by the NEA.

Performance artist Anna Deavere Smith receives acclaim for her *Fires in the Mirror: Crown Heights, Brooklyn.*

Martha Mayer Erlebacher, a painter influenced by the Old Masters, exhibits *Fate Comes.*

Barbara Brandon's *Where I'm Coming From* becomes the first syndicated comic

TEXTS	CONTEXTS
1991	1991 strip by an African American woman cartoonist.

Jodie Foster wins her second Academy Award for Best Actress, for her portrayal of FBI cadet Clarice Starling in *Silence of the Lambs.*

Flight attendants at American Airlines win a lawsuit forcing the company to drop strict weight rules; that same year, a Continental Airlines employee is rehired after filing a lawsuit against the company that fired her for not wearing make up.

Arlette Rafferty Schweitzer becomes the first woman to give birth to her own grandchildren; she carries the twins for her daughter.

Sarah Eileen Williamson becomes the first girl ever elected mayor of the Reverend Edward J. Flanagan's Boys Town.

On the eve of the Persian Gulf war, a 25 percent gender gap reflects that more men than women support military intervention.

A survey for *McCall's* shows 84 percent of re-

TEXTS	CONTEXTS
1991	**1991** spondents approve of combat duty for women.
1991–1992	**1991–1992** By the end of the Persian Gulf war, 13 U.S. women soldiers have been killed and two taken prisoner.
1992 Dorothy Allison: *Bastard Out of Carolina*, a novel. Rosellen Brown: *Before and After*, suspense novel. Bebe Moore Campbell: *Your Blues Ain't Like Mine*, a novel. Blanche Wiesen Cook: *Eleanor Roosevelt*, a biography. Mary Daly: *Outercourse: The Be-Dazzling Voyage: Containing Recollections from My Logbook of a Radical Feminist Philosopher*. Annie Dillard: *The Living*, a novel. Rita Dove: *Through the Ivory Gate*, a novel. Marian Wright Edelman, African American activist and founder of the Children's Defense Fund: *The Measure of Our Success: A Letter to My Children and Yours*.	**1992** Women represent two-thirds of all poor American adults; more than 80 percent of all full-time working women earn less than $20,000 a year, and the gender-based pay gap is worse in America than in any other country in the developed world. Seventy percent of all wives outlive their husbands. An estimated 2.9 million children are reported to child protective service agencies for suspected abuse, up about 213,000 since 1991; confirmed deaths from child abuse total an estimated 1,261, with 84 percent of fatalities occurring among children under age five and 43 percent under age one. Women hold only 4.5 percent of all seats on the boards of Fortune 500 companies.

TEXTS	CONTEXTS
1992	1992

TEXTS

1992 M.F.K. Fisher: *To Begin Again: Stories and Memoirs, 1908–1929.*

Cristina Garcia, Cuban-born novelist: *Dreaming in Cuban.*

Pam Houston: *Cowboys Are My Weakness*, short stories about women living in the traditionally male-oriented West.

Cynthia Kadohata: *In the Heart of the Valley of Love.*

Denise Levertov: *Evening Train*, her 21st collection of poems.

Mary McCarthy: *Intellectual Memories*, posthumously published autobiography.

Jill McCorkle: *Crash Diet*, short stories.

Terry McMillan: *Waiting to Exhale*, a novel.

Toni McNaron: *I Dwell in Possibility*, a memoir.

Margaret Maron, mystery author, publishes *Bootlegger's Daughter*, the first in a series focusing on Deborah Knott, judge and sleuth. The novel virtually

CONTEXTS

1992 Over 500,000 women "March for Women's Lives" in Washington, D.C.

In *Planned Parenthood v. Casey*, the Supreme Court affirms the constitutionality of abortion but allows individual states to place restrictions that do not unduly burden the woman.

Cesarean sections and hysterectomies are the third and sixth, respectively, most common surgical procedures in the U.S.

Dow Corning withdraws its silicone breast implants from the market after the FDA and the media question their safety.

An estimated 1.4 million women have had breast cancer, with an estimated 175,000 diagnosed each year.

Of the approximately 1 million Americans infected with the HIV virus, 10 percent are women. Among teens, the figure is 25 percent. AIDS is the fifth leading killer of women 25 to 44 years of age.

TEXTS	CONTEXTS

1992   sweeps the mystery awards for 1993, winning an Edgar, an Anthony, an Agatha, and a MacAvity.

1992   After a long guardianship battle, the Minnesota Court of Appeals rules that Sharon Kowalski, brain-damaged in a 1983 car crash, can go home with her lover, Karen Thompson.

Toni Morrison: *Jazz*, a novel; *Playing in the Dark: Whiteness and the Literary Imagination*, an analysis of the presence of African Americans in the American literary imagination; and, as editor, *Race-ing Justice, En-gendering Power: Essays on Anita Hill, Clarence Thomas, and the Construction of Social Reality*.

William Kennedy Smith, nephew of Senator Ted Kennedy, is acquitted of rape charges stemming from an incident at the Kennedys' Palm Beach estate; the trial is televised and watched by millions of viewers.

Gloria Naylor: *Bailey's Cafe*, a novel.

Boxer Mike Tyson is convicted of raping a beauty pageant contestant and sentenced to up to ten years in jail.

Barbara Neely: *Blanche on the Lam* begins a mystery series with African American cleaning woman Blanche White as sleuth.

The U.S. Navy investigates allegations that, at its annual Tailhook Association conference, 26 women were sexually harassed. In 1994 former Navy Lieutenant Paula Coughlin is awarded $6.7 million in damages.

The New Our Bodies, Our Selves, revised and updated for the 1990s.

Joyce Carol Oates: *Black Water*, a novel.

A jury acquits Los Angeles police officers of beating Rodney King; the verdict sparks riots throughout the city.

Sharon Olds: *The Father*, poetry.

Grace Paley: *New and Collected Poems*.

TEXTS	CONTEXTS
1992 Severna Park: *Speaking Dreams*, a lesbian science-fiction novel.	1992 Five female Stroh's Brewery employees sue the company for sexual harassment stemming from Stroh's advertisements featuring a "Swedish Bikini Team."
Marge Piercy: *Mars and Her Children*, poetry.	
Patricia Preciado Martin: *Songs My Mother Sang to Me: An Oral History of Mexican American Women*.	The diet industry earns $30.2 billion annually.
Anna Quindlen, Pulitzer Prize-winning newspaper columnist and novelist: *Object Lessons*, a novel.	Leona Bentsen unsuccessfully challenges the Supreme Court decision forbidding the importation of RU 486 ("abortion") pills into the U.S.
Lee Smith: *The Devil's Dream*, a novel.	Vice President Dan Quayle links the L.A. riots and television character Murphy Brown's single motherhood, claiming both to be signs of the nation's lack of "family values."
Susan Sontag: *The Volcano Lover*, a novel.	
Gloria Steinem: *Revolution from Within: A Book of Self-Esteem*.	
Susan Straight: *I Been in Sorrow's Kitchen and Licked Out All the Pots*, a novel.	Bill Clinton defeats George Bush in the presidential election; his wife Hillary Rodham Clinton becomes the first presidential spouse to hold a professional degree.
Donna Tartt: *The Secret History*, a best-selling novel.	
Carol Tavris, social psychologist, lecturer, and writer: *The Mismeasure of Woman: Why Women Are Not the Better Sex, the Infe-*	Of 106 women who run for the House of Representatives, 47 win seats; 5 of the 11 female Senate candidates win seats.

TEXTS	CONTEXTS
1992 *rior Sex, or the Opposite Sex.*	1992 Carol Moseley Braun wins Senate election in Illinois and becomes the country's first African American woman senator.
Alma Luz Villanueva: *Naked Ladies.*	
Alice Walker: *Possessing the Secret of Joy*, a novel about female genital mutilation, sparks debate and controversy over the practice.	California becomes the first state to elect two women, Barbara Boxer and Dianne Feinstein, to fill its two Senate seats.
Anna Lee Walters: *Talking Indian: Reflections on Survival and Writing.*	North Carolina elects Eva Clayton to Congress, making her the first African American representative elected in the state since 1901 and its first woman of color; Clayton is elected president of the freshman congressional class.
Marianne Williamson, lecturer and writer in spiritual psychotherapy: *A Return to Love: Reflections on the Principles of a Course in Miracles.*	
Carol Wrightman: *Writing Dangerously: Mary McCarthy and Her World*, a National Book Award-winning biography.	Mae Jemison, who became the first African American woman astronaut in 1987, participates in a NASA shuttle mission on the space shuttle *Endeavor*, where she serves as a mission specialist, responsible for conducting various experiments during the flights.
	Take Our Daughters to Work Day is inaugurated. By 1994, approximately 25 to 30 million adults have participated.
	Colonel Margarethe Cammermeyer is discharged

TEXTS	CONTEXTS
1992	1992 from the Washington state National Guard after acknowledging that she is a lesbian. In 1994, a U.S. district court judge orders her reinstatement.

The Independent Women's Forum is founded by and for hardcore conservative professional women.

Colorado passes Amendment 2, which prohibits local governments from protecting gays and lesbians from discrimination. It is declared unconstitutional in 1994 by the Colorado State Supreme Court.

Holly Hughes, lesbian performance artist, receives an NEA grant, denied two years earlier.

Callie Khouri receives an Oscar for Best Original Screenplay for *Thelma and Louise*, a female buddy movie starring Susan Sarandon and Geena Davis, who were both nominated for Best Actress awards.

Julie Dash is the first black woman writer and director to make a nation-

TEXTS	CONTEXTS
1992	1992 ally distributed feature film, *Daughters of the Dust.*

| 1993 *The Sleeper Wakes: Harlem Renaissance Stories by Women*, Marcy Knopf, ed. | 1993 The Vietnam Women's Memorial Project opens in Washington, D.C. The seven-foot tall sculpture, done by Glenna Good- |

On January 20, Maya An-
gelou reads "On the Pulse
of the Morning" at the
presidential inauguration
of Bill Clinton. Angelou
is the first woman and the
first African American to
do so.

Marilou Awiakta: *Selu:
Seeking the Corn Mother's
Wisdom*, described by Awi-
aktu as "seedthoughts for
the twenty-first century."

E. M. Broner: *The Telling:
The Story of a Group of
Jewish Women Who Jour-
ney to Spirituality through
Community and Ceremony.*

Rita Mae Brown: *Venus
Envy*, a novel.

Ana Castillo: *So Far from
God*, a novel.

Mary Crow Dog: *Ohitka
Woman*, a sequel to the au-
tobiographical bestseller
Lakota Woman.

Sarah L. Delaney and A.
Elizabeth Delaney (1891–

acre, honors the American
women who served in the
war.

Lyn St. James becomes
the second woman to qual-
ify to race in the Indianapolis 500.

President Clinton ap-
points Ruth Bader Gins-
burg to the Supreme
Court, making her the second woman ever to sit on
the bench and making
this the first time in history when two women so
serve.

President Clinton ap-
points Miami district at-
torney Janet Reno as the
first woman U.S. Attorney
General; previous nomin-
ees Zoe Baird and Kimba
Wood had stumbled over
"Nannygate," a failure to
pay social security taxes
for domestic employees
that did not prevent the
appointment of male nom-
inees to cabinet posts who
also failed to pay.

TEXTS	CONTEXTS
1993	1993

TEXTS

1993

1995), with Amy Hill Hearth: *Having Our Say: The Delaney Sisters' First 100 Years*, based on the stories of two African American sisters who were born in the post-Reconstruction South and lived in Harlem during its renaissance.

Rita Dove is named Poet Laureate.

The Selected Letters of Mary Moody Emerson, Nancy Craig Simmons, ed., demonstrates the strong intellectual influence of Ralph Waldo Emerson's aunt on her nephew.

M.F.K. Fisher: *Stay Me, Oh Comfort Me: Journals and Stories, 1933–1941*.

Jan Freeman, poet: *Hyena*.

Betty Friedan: *The Fountain of Age*, a nonfictional work on menopause.

Kaye Gibbons: *Charms for the Easy Life*, a novel.

Brett Harvey: *The Fifties: A Women's Oral History*.

Susanna Kaysen: *Girl, Interrupted*, an autobiographical memoir about being

CONTEXTS

1993

Acknowledging that women can react differently to drugs than do men and thus that some recommended dosages may have been in error, the FDA ends a 16–year ban on including women in drug safety tests.

Ellen V. Futter, president of Barnard College at age 31, becomes president of the American Museum of Natural History and the first woman to head a major New York City museum.

Judith Rodin becomes the first female president of an Ivy League school when she is appointed president of the University of Pennsylvania.

By this date, two-thirds of all books sold are paperbacks.

TEXTS	CONTEXTS
1993	committed to a psychiatric ward as a teenager. Barbara Kingsolver: *Pigs in Heaven*, a novel. Audre Lorde: *The Marvelous Arithmetics of Distance, Poems 1987–1992*, posthumously published. Wilma Mankiller: *Mankiller: A Chief and Her People*, an autobiography written with Michael Wallis. Bobbie Ann Mason: *Feather Crowns*, a novel. Sue Miller: *For Love*, a novel. Cherríe Moraga: *The Last Generation*. Toni Morrison is awarded the Nobel Prize for literature. Bharati Mukherjee: *The Holder of the World*, a novel. Fae Myenne Ng: *Bone*, a novel. Kathleen Norris: *Dakota: A Spiritual Geography*. Joyce Carol Oates: *Foxfire: Confessions of a Girl Gang*, a novel.	1993

TEXTS	CONTEXTS
1993	1993

E. Annie Proulx: *The Shipping News*, Pulitzer Prize-winning novel.

Jewell Parker Rhodes: *Voodoo Dreams: A Novel of Marie Laveau*.

Adrienne Rich: *What Is Found There: Notebooks on Poetry and Politics*.

Kate Roiphe: *The Morning After: Sex, Fear, and Feminism on Campus*.

Dori Sanders: *Her Own Place*, a novel.

The Power of Her Sympathy: The Autobiography and Journal of Catharine Maria Sedgwick, Mary Kelley, ed.

Elizabeth Marshall Thomas: *The Hidden Life of Dogs*.

Helena María Viramontes: *Paris Rats in E.L.A.*, short stories.

Bailey White: *Mama Makes Up Her Mind, and Other Dangers of Southern Living*, humorous essays.

Naomi Wolf: *Fire with Fire: The New Female Power and How It Will Change the 21st Century*.

*   *   *

TEXTS	CONTEXTS
1994 Dorothy Allison: *Skin: Talking About Sex, Class, and Literature*, essays.	1994 Barbra Streisand goes on concert tour for the first time in 27 years; a record number of fans pay unprecedented prices to see the show.
Julia Alvarez: *In the Time of the Butterflies*, a novel.	
Maya Angelou: *Wouldn't Take Nothing for My Journey Now*, autobiography.	Actress Roseanne sparks debate when she kisses another woman, Mariel Hemingway, on her television show.
Doris Betts: *Souls Raised from the Dead*, a novel.	
Ruthie Bolton: *Gal, a True Life*.	Paula Jones files suit against President Bill Clinton, accusing him of sexual harassment.
J. California Cooper: *In Search of Satisfaction*, a novel.	After football and media star O. J. Simpson is accused of the stabbing death of his wife, Nicole Brown Simpson, and her friend, Ronald Goldman, calls to domestic violence hotlines reportedly increase greatly. The pretrial hearing is one of the most-watched television events of the century.
Susan J. Douglas: *Where the Girls Are: Growing Up Female with the Mass Media*.	
Louise Erdrich: *The Bingo Palace*, the concluding novel in Erdrich's four-volume series tracing the interconnecting lives of several Native American families.	
Carolyn Forché: *The Angel of History*, poetry.	Jacqueline Kennedy Onassis dies from cancer at age 64.
Nikki Giovanni: *Racism 101*, essays.	Czech-born and openly lesbian U.S. tennis player Martina Navratilova retires from singles play after one of the most successful sports careers on record: she has played for
Gail Godwin: *The Good Husband*, a novel.	

TEXTS	CONTEXTS
1994 Doris Kearns Goodwin: *No Ordinary Time: Franklin and Eleanor Roosevelt: The Home Front in World War II*, Pulitzer Prize-winning history.	1994 20 years, garnered 167 titles, and earned over $20 million. She continues to play doubles and mixed doubles and in 1995 wins a Wimbledon mixed doubles title, giving her 19 Wimbledon titles, just one short of the record held by Billie Jean King.
Shirlee Taylor Haizlip: *The Sweeter the Juice: A Family Memoir in Black and White*, detailing the author's experiences tracing the black and the white branches of her family.	Speed skater Bonnie Blair becomes the first woman in history to win five Olympic gold medals.
Jane Hamilton, novelist: *A Map of the World*.	Surgeon General Joycelyn Elders is asked to resign after stating publicly that she believes school children should be taught about masturbation as part of general sex education.
Joan Hedrick: *Harriet Beecher Stowe: A Life*, winner of Pulitzer Prize for biography.	
Alice Hoffman: *Second Nature*, a novel.	A joint *Working Mother/Gallup* poll reveals that roughly 75 percent of mothers employed outside the home are greatly satisfied with both work and family.
Helen Lefkowitz Horowitz: *The Power and Passion of M. Carey Thomas*, a biography of a founding dean and second president of Bryn Mawr and a leading figure in higher education for women in the early 20th century.	Of the 20 MacArthur Fellowships awarded this year, seven go to women.
Virginia Kelley, mother of President Bill Clinton: *Leading with My Heart: My Life*, with James Mor-	New York becomes the second state after Florida to rule against defendants' claiming that the way a

TEXTS	CONTEXTS
1994	1994

gan. She passes away later in the year.

Norma McCorvey, with Andy Meisler, publishes an account of her life and her struggles at the forefront of the abortion debate: *I Am Roe*.

Sharyn McCrumb: *She Walks These Hills*, a novel about Appalachia.

Nancy Mairs: *Voice Lessons: On Becoming a (Woman) Writer*, essays.

Anchee Min: *Red Azalea*, an autobiography about growing up in China during Mao's Cultural Revolution.

Marlo Morgan: *Mutant Message Down Under*, a fictional account of a woman traveling the outback with Aborigines in Australia.

Joyce Carol Oates: *What I Lived For*, a novel.

Susan Power, Native American novelist: *The Grass Dancer*.

Anna Quindlen: *One True Thing*, a novel.

woman dresses is a defense for sexually assaulting her.

An *Esquire* poll reports that of 1000 women between the ages of 18 and 25, 65 percent would prefer winning a Pulitzer Prize to a Miss America crown, 57 percent would rather be Hillary Rodham Clinton than Princess Di, and, if only having one child, 54 percent would prefer a daughter to a son.

The largest settlement in a sexual harassment case—$7.1 million—is awarded to Rena Weeks, a former secretary at the world's largest law firm. The amount is later reduced.

The Academy Award for Best Short Documentary is awarded to *Defending Our Lives*, a film focusing on women imprisoned for killing their batterers. Since the film's release, several of the women featured have had their sentences commuted or have been granted early parole.

Roberta Cooper Ramo becomes the first woman

	TEXTS		CONTEXTS
1994	With the publication of the third in the May-flower Series, *Taltos*, and the release of the movie version of *Interview with the Vampire* and tie-in re-prints of the novels in the Vampire Chronicles se-ries, Anne Rice has four novels on the bestseller lists.	1994	elected president of the American Bar Association, which has been in exis-tence since 1878.

With the publication of the third in the May-flower Series, *Taltos*, and the release of the movie version of *Interview with the Vampire* and tie-in re-prints of the novels in the Vampire Chronicles se-ries, Anne Rice has four novels on the bestseller lists.

May Sarton: *Encore: A Journal of the Eightieth Year.*

Sarah Schulman: *My American History: Lesbian and Gay Life During the Reagan/Bush Years.*

Mab Segrest, lesbian es-sayist and civil rights activ-ist: *Memoir of a Race Traitor.*

Linda Gray Sexton: *Searching for Mercy Street: My Journey Back to My Mother, Anne Sexton.*

Ntozake Shange: *Liliane: Resurrection of the Daugh-ter*, a novel.

Carol Shields, novelist: *The Stone Diaries*, winner of the Pulitzer Prize for best novel in 1995; in 1993, when it was first published in London, it

elected president of the American Bar Association, which has been in exis-tence since 1878.

Women own more than 6.5 million businesses in the United States.

Twelve-year-old Vicki Van Meter, who in 1993 became the youngest fe-male to fly a plane across the U.S., becomes the youngest female to fly a plane across the Atlantic Ocean.

TEXTS	CONTEXTS
1994 was shortlisted for the Booker Prize.	1994
Anna Deavere Smith: *Twilight: Los Angeles 1992*, based on her one-woman show about the L.A. riots.	
LaVyrle Spencer: *Family Blessings*, romance novel.	
Gloria Steinem: *Moving Beyond Words: Age, Rage, Sex, Power, Money, Muscles: Breaking the Boundaries of Gender*.	
Dorothy West, the last surviving member of the Harlem Renaissance, publishes her first novel in several decades: *The Wedding*.	
Marguerite Young: *Inviting the Muses: Collected Stories and Essays*.	
The Oxford Companion to Women's Writing in the United States, Cathy N. Davidson and Linda Wagner-Martin, eds.	
2000	2000 The world's population is projected to reach an estimated 6.3 billion.

WORKS CONSULTED

Allen, Paula Gunn. *The Sacred Hoop: Recovering the Feminine in American Indian Traditions*. Boston: Beacon, 1986.

"Almanac." *Life*. May 1994, pp. 37–44.

Alter, Judy, and A. T. Row, eds. *Unbridled Spirits: Short Fiction about Women in the Old West*. Fort Worth: Texas Christian Univ. Press, 1994.

Augenbraum, Harold, and Ilan Stavans. *Growing Up Latino: Memoirs and Stories*. Boston: Houghton Mifflin, 1993.

Ballantine, Betty, and Ian Ballantine. *The Native Americans: An Illustrated History*. Atlanta: Turner Publishing, 1993.

Barclay, Donald A., James H. Maguire, and Peter Wild. *Into the Wilderness Dream: Exploration Narratives of the American West, 1500–1805*. Salt Lake City: Univ. of Utah Press, 1994.

Bardes, Barbara, and Suzanne Gossett. *Declarations of Independence: Women and Political Power in Nineteenth-Century American Fiction*. New Brunswick: Rutgers Univ. Press, 1990.

Barlow, Judith E., ed. *Plays by American Women, 1930–1960*. New York: Applause, 1994.

Bataille, Gretchen, ed. *Native American Women: A Biographical Dictionary*. New York: Garland, 1993.

——, and Kathleen Mullen Sands. *American Indian Women: Telling Their Lives*. Lincoln: Univ. of Nebraska Press, 1984.

Baym, Nina. *Woman's Fiction: A Guide to Novels by and about Women in America, 1820–1870*. Ithaca: Cornell Univ. Press, 1978.

Blain, Virginia, Isobel Grundy, and Patricia Clements, eds. *The Feminist Companion to Literature in English: Women Writers from the Middle Ages to the Present*. New Haven: Yale Univ. Press, 1990.

Blair, Walter. *Native American Humor*. New York: Harper & Row, 1960.

Braude, Ann. *Radical Spirits: Spiritualism and Women's Rights in Nineteenth-Century America*. Boston: Beacon, 1989.

Brown, Dorothy H., and Barbara C. Ewell. *Louisiana Women Writers: New Essays and a Comprehensive Bibliography*. Baton Rouge: Louisiana State Univ. Press, 1992.

Bufwack, Mary A., and Robert K. Oermann. *Finding Her Voice: The Saga of Women in Country Music*. New York: Crown, 1993.

Buhle, Mary Jo, and Paul Buhle, eds. *The Concise History of Woman Suffrage: Selections from the Classic Work of Stanton, Anthony, Gage, and Harper*. Urbana: Univ. of Illinois Press, 1979.

Bynum, Victoria E. *Unruly Women: The Politics of Social and Sexual Control in the Old South*. Chapel Hill: Univ. of North Carolina Press, 1992.

Cahill, Susan, ed. *Growing Up Female: Stories by Women Writers from the American Mosaic*. New York: Mentor, 1993.

———, ed. *Writing Women's Lives: An Anthology of Autobiographical Narratives by Twentieth-Century American Women Writers*. New York: HarperPerennial, 1994.

Carby, Hazel V. *Reconstructing Womanhood: The Emergence of the Afro-American Woman Novelist*. New York: Oxford Univ. Press, 1987.

Chase's Annual Events: The Day-by-Day Directory to 1994. Chicago: Contemporary Books, 1994.

Chin, Frank, Jeffrey Paul Chan, Lawson Fusao Inada, and Shawn Wong. *Aiiieeeee!: An Anthology of Asian American Writers*. 2nd ed. New York: Mentor, 1983.

Cole, Bruce, and Adelheid Gealt. *Art of the Western World: From Ancient Greece to Post-Modernism*. New York: Summit Books, 1989.

Cole, Johnnetta B., ed. *All American Women: Lines That Divide, Ties That Bind*. New York: Free Press, 1986.

Conway, Jill Ker, ed. *Written by Herself. Autobiographies of American Women: An Anthology*. New York: Vintage, 1992.

Cott, Nancy F. *The Grounding of Modern Feminism*. New Haven: Yale Univ. Press, 1987.

———, ed. *Root of Bitterness: Documents of Social History of American Women*. New York: Dutton, 1972.

Cott, Nancy F., and Elizabeth H. Pleck. *A Heritage of Her Own: Toward a New Social History of American Women*. New York: Simon and Schuster, 1979.

Coultrap-McQuin, Susan. *Doing Literary Business: American Women Writers in the Nineteenth Century*. Chapel Hill: Univ. of North Carolina Press, 1990.

Cowan, Ruth Schwartz. *More Work for Mother: The Ironies of Household Technology from the Open Hearth to the Microwave*. New York: Basic Books, 1983.

Cowan, Tom, and Jack Maguire. *Timelines of African-American History: 500 Years of Black Achievement*. New York: Roundtable Press, 1994.

Davidson, Cathy N. *Revolution and the Word: The Rise of the Novel in America*. New York: Oxford Univ. Press, 1986.

Davidson, Cathy N. and Linda Wagner-Martin, eds. *The Oxford Companion to Women's Writing in the United States*. New York: Oxford Univ. Press, 1994.

Davis, Thadious M. "Women's Art and Authorship in the Southern Region: Connections." In *The Female Tradition in Southern Literature*, ed. Carol S. Manning. Urbana: Univ. of Illinois Press, 1993.

Delaney, Janice, Mary Jane Lupton, and Emily Toth. *The Curse: A Cultural History of Menstruation*. Rev. ed. Urbana: Univ. of Illinois Press, 1988.

D'Emilio, John, and Estelle B. Freedman. *Intimate Matters: A History of Sexuality in America*. New York: Harper & Row, 1988.

Donovan, Josephine. *New England Local Color Literature: A Women's Tradition*. New York: Continuum, 1983.

DuBois, Ellen Carol, and Vicki L. Ruiz, eds. *Unequal Sisters: A Multicultural Reader in U.S. Women's History*. New York: Routledge, 1990.

Dworkin, Andrea. *Right-Wing Women*. New York: Putnam, 1983.

Echols, Alice. *Daring to Be Bad: Radical Feminism in America, 1967–1975*. Minneapolis: Univ. of Minnesota Press, 1989.

Ehrenreich, Barbara, and Deirdre English. *For Her Own Good: 150 Years of the Experts' Advice to Women*. New York: Anchor, 1978.

Eisler, Benita, ed. *The Lowell Offering: Writings by New England Mill Women, 1840–1845*. New York: Harper & Row, 1977.

Elliott, Emory, gen. ed. *Columbia Literary History of the United States*. New York: Columbia Univ. Press, 1988.

Encyclopedia Brittanica. Vol. 26. Chicago, 1994.

Evans, Sara M. *Born for Liberty: A History of Women in America*. New York: Macmillan, 1989.

Faderman, Lillian. *Surpassing the Love of Men: Romantic Friendship and Love Between Women from the Renaissance to the Present*. New York: William Morrow, 1981.

Faludi, Susan. *Backlash: The Undeclared War against American Women*. New York: Crown, 1991.

Fargis, Paul, and Sheree Bykofsky, eds. *The New York Public Library Desk Reference*. 2nd ed. New York: Prentice-Hall, 1993.

Fee, Elizabeth, and Nancy Krieger. "Health, Politics, and Power." *Women's Review of Books* 11 (July 1994): 4–5.

Fetterley, Judith, ed. *Provisions: A Reader from 19th-Century American Women*. Bloomington: Indiana Univ. Press, 1985.

Fetterley, Judith, and Marjorie Pryse, eds. *American Women Regionalists: 1850–1910. A Norton Anthology*. New York: Norton, 1992.

Flexner, Eleanor. *Century of Struggle: The Women's Rights Movement in the United States*. Rev. ed. Cambridge: Belknap Press of Harvard Univ. Press, 1975.

Flora, Joseph M., and Robert Bain, eds. *Contemporary Fiction Writers of the South*. Westport, Conn.: Greenwood, 1993.

Foner, Eric, and John A. Garraty, eds. *The Reader's Companion to American History*. Boston: Houghton Mifflin, 1991.

Freeman, Jo, ed. *Women: A Feminist Perspective*. 4th ed. Mountain View, Calif.: Mayfield Publishing, 1989.

Freibert, Lucy M., and Barbara A. White, eds. *Hidden Hands: An Anthology of Women Writers, 1790–1870*. New Brunswick: Rutgers Univ. Press, 1985.

Friedman, Lawrence M. *A History of American Law*. 2nd ed. New York: Simon & Schuster, 1985.

Frost, Elizabeth, and Kathryn Cullen-DuPont, eds. *Women's Suffrage in America: An Eyewitness History*. New York: Facts on File, 1992.

Gates, Henry Louis, Jr., ed. *Reading Black, Reading Feminist: A Critical Anthology*. New York: Meridian, 1990.

Gaymon, Gloria Leaks. "African American Women's Firsts." *Ms*. Dec. 1992, p. 93.

Gorman, Ed, Martin H. Greenberg, Larry Segriff, and Jon L. Breen. *The Fine Art of Murder*. New York: Carroll & Graf, 1993.

Griffin, Lynne, and Kelly McCann. *The Book of Women: 300 Notable Women History Passed By*. Holbrook, Mass.: Bob Adams, 1992.

Grun, Bernard, ed. *The Timetables of History: A Horizontal Linkage of People and Events*. New York: Simon and Schuster, 1982.

Haight, Anne L. *Banned Books: 387 B.C. to 1978 A.D.* 4th ed., updated and enlarged by Chandler B. Grannis. New York: R.R. Bowker, 1978.

Harris, Ann Sutherland, and Linda Nochlin. *Women Artists, 1550–1950.* New York: Knopf, 1984.

Harris, Barbara J. *Beyond Her Sphere: Women and the Professions in American History.* Westport, Conn.: Greenwood, 1978.

Hart, Jamie, and Elsa Barkley Brown, comps., with assistance from N. H. Goodall. *Black Women in the United States: A Chronology.* In *Black Women in America: An Historical Encyclopedia*, ed. Darlene Clark Hine. Brooklyn, N.Y.: Carlson, 1993. Pp. 1309–18.

Harvey, Brett. *The Fifties: A Women's Oral History.* New York: HarperPerennial, 1993.

Hatch, Jane M., ed. *The American Book of Days.* 3d ed. New York: H. W. Wilson, 1978.

Hong, Maria, ed. *Growing Up Asian American: An Anthology.* New York: William Morrow, 1993.

Howe, Florence. *No More Masks!: An Anthology of Twentieth-Century American Women Poets.* New York: HarperPerennial, 1993.

Jensen, Malcolm C. *America in Time: America's History Year by Year through Texts and Pictures.* Boston: Houghton Mifflin, 1977.

Johnson, David E. *From Day to Day: A Calendar of Notable Birthdays and Events.* Metuchen, N.J.: Scarecrow, 1990.

Johnson, Deidre. *Edward Stratemeyer and the Stratemeyer Syndicate.* New York: Twayne, 1993.

Jones, Jacqueline. *Labor of Love, Labor of Sorrow: Black Women, Work and the Family, from Slavery to the Present.* New York: Vintage, 1985.

Kelley, Mary, ed. *The Power of Her Sympathy: The Autobiography and Journal of Catharine Maria Sedgwick.* Boston: Massachusetts Historical Society, 1993.

Kim, Elaine H. *Asian American Literature: An Introduction to the Writings and Their Social Context.* Philadelphia: Temple Univ. Press, 1982.

Knopf, Marcy. *The Sleeper Wakes: Harlem Renaissance Stories by Women.* New Brunswick: Rutgers Univ. Press, 1993.

Kolodny, Annette. *The Land Before Her: Fantasy and Experience of the American Frontiers, 1630–1860.* Chapel Hill: Univ. of North Carolina Press, 1984.

———. *The Lay of the Land: Metaphor as Experience and History in American Life and Letters.* Chapel Hill: Univ. of North Carolina Press, 1975.

Kroeger, Brooke. *Nellie Bly: Daredevil, Reporter, Feminist.* New York: New York Times, 1994.

Lauter, Paul, ed. *Reconstructing American Literature: Courses, Syllabi, Issues.* New York: Feminist Press, 1983.

———, gen. ed. *The Heath Anthology of American Literature*, vols. 1 and 2. 2nd ed. Lexington, Mass.: D. C. Heath, 1994.

Lim, Shirley Geok-lin, and Amy Ling. *Reading the Literatures of Asian America.* Philadelphia: Temple Univ. Press, 1992.

Ling, Amy. *Between Worlds: Women Writers of Chinese Ancestry.* New York: Pergamon Press, 1990.

López, Tiffany Ana, ed. *Growing Up Chicana/o: An Anthology.* New York: William Morrow, 1993.

Lucie-Smith, Edward. *American Realism*. New York: Harry N. Abrams, 1994.

Macdonald, Anne L. *Feminine Ingenuity: How Women Inventors Changed America*. New York: Ballantine Books, 1992.

———. *No Idle Hands: The Social History of American Knitting*. New York: Ballantine, 1988.

Malloy, William. *The Mystery Book of Days*. New York: Mysterious Press, 1990.

Manning, Carol S. "The Real Beginning of the Southern Renaissance." In *The Female Tradition in Southern Literature*, ed. Carol S. Manning. Urbana: Univ. of Illinois Press, 1993.

Matthews, Glenna. *The Rise of Public Woman: Woman's Power and Woman's Place in the United States, 1630–1970*. New York: Oxford Univ. Press, 1992.

Moers, Ellen. *Literary Women: The Great Writers*. New York: Oxford Univ. Press, 1976.

Moraga, Cherríe, and Gloria Anzaldúa. *This Bridge Called My Back: Writings by Radical Women of Color*. 2nd ed. New York: Kitchen Table, 1983.

Morantz-Sanchez, Regina Markell. *Sympathy and Science: Women Physicians in American Medicine*. New York: Oxford Univ. Press, 1985.

Morgan, Robin, ed. *Sisterhood Is Powerful: An Anthology of Writings from the Women's Liberation Movement*. New York: Vintage, 1970.

Moynihan, Ruth Barnes, Cynthia Russett, and Laurie Crumpacker, eds. *Second to None: A Documentary History of American Women. Vol. 1: From the 16th Century to 1865. Vol. 2: From 1865 to the Present*. Lincoln: Univ. of Nebraska Press, 1993.

Munro, Eleanor. *Originals: American Women Artists*. New York: Simon and Schuster, 1979.

The News and Observer (Raleigh, N.C.) 1992–1994.

Newton, Sarah E. *Learning to Behave: A Guide to American Conduct Books Before 1900*. Westport, Conn.: Greenwood, 1994.

Nichols, Victoria, and Susan Thompson. *Silk Stalkings: When Women Write of Murder*. Berkeley: Black Lizard Books, 1988.

"1994 in Review." *Ms.* 5, no. 4 (Jan./Feb. 1995): 46–53.

Norton, Mary Beth. *Liberty's Daughters: The Revolutionary Experience of American Women, 1750–1800*. Boston: Little, Brown, 1980.

"100 American Women Who Made a Difference." *Women's History: Celebrating Women's History Month* 1,1 (1995, special collector's issue).

Ousby, Ian, ed. *The Cambridge Guide to Literature in English*. Cambridge, Eng.: Cambridge Univ. Press, 1993.

Padilla, Genaro M. *My History, Not Yours: The Formation of Mexican American Autobiography*. Madison: Univ. of Wisconsin Press, 1993.

Parini, Jay, ed. *The Columbia History of American Poetry*. New York: Columbia Univ. Press, 1993.

Pattee, Fred Lewis. *The Feminine Fifties*. New York: Appleton-Century, 1940.

Patterson, James, and Peter Kim. *The Day America Told the Truth*. New York: Prentice-Hall, 1991.

Pearlman, Mickey, and Katherine Usher Henderson. *A Voice of One's Own: Conversations with America's Writing Women*. Boston: Houghton Mifflin, 1990.

Perkins, George, Barbara Perkins, and Phillip Leininger, eds. *Benét's Reader's Encyclopedia of American Literature*. New York: HarperCollins, 1991.

Poey, Delia, and Virgil Suarez. *Iguana Dreams: New Latino Fiction.* New York: Harp-erPerennial, 1992.

Read, Phyllis J., and Bernard L. Witlieb. *The Book of Women's Firsts: Breakthrough Achievements of Almost 1,000 American Women.* New York: Random House, 1992.

Rennolds, Margaret B., ed. *National Museum of Women in the Arts.* New York: Harry N. Abrams, 1987.

Riley, Glenda. *Inventing the American Woman: A Perspective on Woman's History, 1865 to the Present.* Arlington Heights, Ill. Harlan Davidson, 1986.

Riley, Patricia. *Growing Up Native American: An Anthology.* New York: William Morrow, 1993.

Robbins, Trina. *A Century of Women Cartoonists.* Northampton, Mass.: Kitchen Sink Press, 1993.

Robertson, Patrick. *The Book of Firsts.* New York: Clarkson N. Potter, 1974.

Root, Waverley, and Richard de Rochement. *Eating in America: A History.* New York: William Morrow, 1976.

Rose, Phyllis. *The Norton Book of Women's Lives.* New York: Norton, 1993.

Rosenberg, Rosalind. *Beyond Separate Spheres: Intellectual Roots of Modern Feminism.* New Haven: Yale Univ. Press, 1982.

Rossi, Alice S., ed. *The Feminist Papers: From Adams to de Beauvoir.* New York: Bantam, 1973.

Rossiter, Margaret W. *Women Scientists in America: Struggles and Strategies to 1940.* Baltimore: The Johns Hopkins Univ. Press, 1982.

Rothblum, Esther D., and Kathleen A. Brehony. *Boston Marriages: Romantic but Asexual Relationships among Contemporary Lesbians.* Amherst: Univ. of Massachusetts Press, 1993.

Rubin, Louis D., Jr., Blyden Jackson, Rayburn S. Moore, Lewis P. Simpson, and Thomas Daniel Young. *The History of Southern Literature.* Baton Rouge: Louisiana State Univ. Press, 1985.

Russ, Joanna. *How to Suppress Women's Writing.* Austin: Univ. of Texas Press, 1983.

Russell, Sandi. *Render Me My Song: African-American Women Writers from Slavery to the Present.* New York: St. Martin's Press, 1990.

Ryan, Mary P. *Women in Public: Between Banners and Ballots, 1825–1880.* Baltimore: The Johns Hopkins Univ. Press, 1990.

Schlissel, Lillian. *Women's Diaries of the Westward Journey.* New York: Schocken Books, 1982.

Schneir, Miriam, ed. *Feminism: The Essential Historical Writings.* 1972. Reprint. New York: Vintage, 1994.

———, ed. *Feminism in Our Time: The Essential Writings, World War II to the Present.* New York: Vintage, 1994.

Scott, Bonnie Kime. *The Gender of Modernism: A Critical Anthology.* Bloomington: Indiana Univ. Press, 1990.

Sgrignoli, Tonice. *365 Days of Women Calendar.* Workman Publishing, 1994.

Shockley, Ann Allen. *Afro-American Women Writers, 1746–1933: An Anthology and Critical Guide.* New York: New American Library, 1989.

Showalter, Elaine, Lea Baechler, and A. Walton Litz, eds. *Modern American Women*

Writers: Profiles from Their Lives and Works—From the 1870s to the Present. New York: Collier Books, 1991.

Sicherman, Barbara, and Carol Hurd Green. *Notable American Women: The Modern Period. A Biographical Dictionary.* Cambridge: Harvard Univ. Press, 1980.

Slung, Michele B., ed. *Crime on Her Mind: Fifteen Stories of Female Sleuths from the Victorian Era to the Forties.* New York: Pantheon, 1975.

Smith, Jessie Carney. *Black Firsts: 2,000 Years of Extraordinary Achievement.* Detroit: Visible Ink, 1994.

Smith, Valerie, Lea Baechler, and A. Walton Litz, eds. *African American Writers: Profiles from Their Lives and Works—From the 1700s to the Present.* New York: Collier Books, 1991.

Smith-Rosenberg, Carroll. *Disorderly Conduct: Visions of Gender in Victorian America.* New York: Oxford Univ. Press, 1986.

Solomon, Barbara H., ed. *Rediscoveries: American Short Stories by Women, 1832–1916.* New York: Mentor, 1994.

Stephens, Autumn. *Wild Women: Crusaders, Curmudgeons, and Completely Corsetless Ladies in the Otherwise Virtuous Victorian Era.* Berkeley: Conari Press, 1992.

Stern, Madeleine B. *We the Women: Career Firsts of Nineteenth-Century America.* Lincoln: Univ. of Nebraska Press, 1962.

Strasser, Susan. *Never Done: A History of American Housework.* New York: Pantheon, 1982.

Streitmatter, Rodger. *Raising Her Voice: African American Women Journalists Who Changed History.* Lexington: Univ. Press of Kentucky, 1994.

Swanson, Jean, and Dean James. *By a Woman's Hand: A Guide to Mystery Fiction by Women.* New York: Berkley Books, 1994.

Tanenbaum, Leora. "Five (Nearly) Forgotten Feminists." *Boston Phoenix*, June 30, 1995: 6–8.

Tate, Claudia. *Black Women Writers at Work.* Harpenden, Eng.: Oldcastle Books, 1983.

Tebbel, John. *Between Covers: The Rise and Transformation of Book Publishing in America.* New York: Oxford Univ. Press, 1987.

Todd, Janet, ed. *A Dictionary of British and American Women Writers, 1660–1800.* Totowa, N.J.: Rowman and Littlefield, 1987.

Tompkins, Jane. *Sensational Designs: The Cultural Work of American Fiction, 1790–1860.* New York: Oxford Univ. Press, 1985.

Trager, James. *The People's Chronology: A Year-by-Year Record of Human Events from Prehistory to the Present.* New York: Henry Holt, 1992.

Tufts, Eleanor. *American Women Artists: 1830–1930.* Washington, D.C.: The National Museum of Women in the Arts, 1987.

———. *Our Hidden Heritage: Five Centuries of Women Artists.* New York: Paddington Press, 1974.

"20 Years of the U.S. Women's Movement." *Ms.* July/August 1992, color insert.

Unterbrink, Mary. *Funny Women: American Comediennes, 1860–1985.* Jefferson, N.C.: McFarland, 1987.

Vare, Ethlie Ann, and Greg Ptacek. *Mothers of Invention: From the Bra to the Bomb, Forgotten Women and Their Unforgettable Ideas.* New York: William Morrow, 1986.

Walker, Roger W. "The A.F.L. and Child-Labor Legislation: An Exercise in Frustration." *Labor History Journal* 11: 323–40.

Weekly Reader: 60 Years of News for Kids, 1928–1988. Intro. Hugh Downs. New York: World Almanac, 1988.

Weiss, Andrea. *Vampires and Violets: Lesbians in Film*. New York: Penguin, 1992.

Winn, Dilys. *Murderess Ink: The Better Half of the Mystery*. New York: Workman Publishing, 1979.

Wolf, Naomi. *The Beauty Myth: How Images of Beauty Are Used Against Women*. New York: Anchor/Doubleday, 1991.

"Womanews." *Chicago Tribune*, Dec. 20 and 27, 1992, sec. 6.

Women's Review of Books, 11, no. 12 (Sept. 1994): 35–40.

The World Book Encyclopedia. Vol. 2. Chicago: World Book, 1993.

Young, Serinity, ed. *An Anthology of Sacred Texts by and about Women*. New York: Crossroad, 1993.

Zophy, Angela Howard, ed., with Frances M. Kavenik. *Handbook of American Women's History*. New York: Garland, 1990.

INDEX